COMFORT SOUP FOR THE MIND

A True Story

By: Suzanna Marie Terrell

1/ Suzanna Terrell is also Author of :
"MIRACULUM"
When A Demon Named Miraculum Decides To Seek Therapy From A Good-Hearted Psychiatrist**…**
Fiction. (This book is now available in Kindle.)
Which can be found at: www.createspace.com/3679270   &   www.amazon.com

2/ Suzanna Terrell is also Author of: **"SCIENTIFIC PROOF THAT DEATH DOES NOT EXIST.** *SIMPLE* **PHYSICS. 'MY LITTLE BLUE BOOK'** "
(FREE! On You-Tube!)—My gift to you.

3/ Suzanna Terrell is Author of: **"PLAN 'B' "**
Which can be found at: www.amazon.com

4/ Suzanna Terrell is Author of: **"Handbook For The Dead, The Living Dead, And Those Who Occasionally Wished They Were Dead"** Nonfiction.
(This book is now available in Kindle.) Find it at:
https://www.createspace.com/3393541 And at: www.amazon.com Link:
http://www.amazon.com/gp/product/0615310656
This book by Suzanna Terrell is also available under the title:
"Comfort Soup For The Mind"

5/ Suzanna Terrell is Author of: **Healing From : Trauma [CD #1] and [CD # 2] --**
Includes Healing From Severe Post Traumatic Stress
The Most POWERFUL Healing TECHNIQUES For:
Divorce, Severe Post Traumatic Stress Disorder, Kidnapping, Rape, Abuse, Injustice, Loss of a Loved-One, Harm or Loss of a Child, and other traumatic events.
     These CD's can be found at: [CD #1] www.createspace.com/2018745
[CD #2] createspace.com/2023259   And also at: www.amazon.com

6/ Suzanna Terrell is Author of: **"RESTLESS IN PURGATORY"**
–A COLLECTION OF POEMS AND SHORT STORIES

COMFORT SOUP FOR THE MIND --- S. TERRELL

TABLE OF CONTENTS /CHAPTERS :

COMFORT SOUP FOR THE MIND --- S. TERRELL

<u>TABLE OF CONTENTS</u>　　CONTINUED

ONE

SOMEONE ELSE IS IN THE ROOM

"**A** *long long* time ago the Indians would make themselves brothers and sisters to their best friends by mixing their blood together." ---Suzanna.

"How do they mix their blood together?" ---Holli.

I, Suzanna, answered with a tingling joy in the words. "They cut their fingers open. Then press their fingers together at the wound until their heart pumps each others blood into the other person."

How was I to know that tonight my world would change forever? That I'd become like a person haunted.

Holli leaned her head against the side of the open window. Far out in the flowing galaxy stars beamed their light down into her already twinkling eyes. Tonight as every night the alluring and mysteriously provocative howls of coyotes echoed from the deep countryside. Sizzling, the air was like the sweet dreamy songs of bewitching sirens. Each howl teased with the ravishment of strange shivers washing from the toes to the elbows and down the arms. What other creature of the night can wail and moan so hauntingly?

The fresh clean scent of rain enticingly began to engorge the air. Moisture deepened on the windchimes down below on the outside porch. Celestial music blissfully jingled from the long gold cylinders as the wind brushed against the chimes. Lunar light sparkled glamorously upon the metallic musical chimes as if they were jewels. Amulets of sound sparkled below. Gently your mind is guided into a deep tranquil state with such alluring sounds. Holli smiled with enchanting happiness. Joy is an alluring conjury of a cure, dispersing all but the euphoric soundness of mind and wellbeing so vital to the soul. You can feel it now with such a smile. Mesmerized into the magnetic deep state of relaxation. My own toes began to tingle. Leaning my face into the pleasing caress of the gentle wind flowing from the window, I, Suzanna, whisper: —Do you think everyone else in the house are asleep already Holli?"

Holli knew we wouldn't be disturbed as we fell gently into the enchantment of the night. The lights were dim in the house. "Oh yes", whispered Holli with thrilling excitement. A decadent concentration full of deep relaxation fills your mind with such a delightful moment as this. Crickets chirp in soothing sirenic charms from the pleasing night magicking profound relaxation from the tips of your toes to the top of your head with its sound. "We're free", said Holli and then she giggled.

Squeezing my hand Holli laughed irresistibly. So I, Suzanna, felt pleasant warmth radiating from my toes and throughout every inch of my feet also. Dancing on my toes I whispered, "Isn't it exciting that we get to spend the night?" Penetrating the air were the shivering spine-tingling howls of the coyotes yet again. The wind rumbled the chimes for a more impassioned twinkling of music. The healing scent of rain swelled heavier abreast the air.

Being five years old was not a children's game for me, Suzanna, or my best friend: Holli. We took being young little people very seriously. And playing together was as necessary as air. Somewhere I'd heard that you could become blood-sister (or blood-brothers). That somehow it was a ritual passed on from the American Indians. We stood at the upstairs window looking out upon the moon drenched front yard.

Wind from the open window wisped soft blue curtains of a flower-lace pattern against Holli's long dark almost black hair. The moon glistening silver against the ebony strands. Her skin was like a permanent summer of coconut butter and beaches with its golden-olive color.

The chimes swayed in a gust of wet wind sending forth a charming vibration. Like a spell. A healing medicine that seemed to woo softly to the soul. Scratching my chin I watched the breeze fluff the long silky strands of Holli's hair and I found myself thinking about her favorite color. Holli's favorite color was blue. Her mother was a homemaker as far as I knew. Her father was in the armed forces. She had an older brother whose age was far enough away from her own that it made them practically strangers. I understood this and felt a kinship with Holli because of the distance between herself and her brother. I personally have a brother and a sister of my own and we would often somehow seem to be worlds apart during this year around 1969. It was a common event for siblings to be closer to one another in their younger years. As the older siblings get closer to their teens they drift away from play and family for a while. Sometimes they seeped away for a very long while. Kind-hearted Holli was in love with drawing and coloring. Art was another bond we shared. When you're just around five years old you feel that any commonality with another child is some wild and fabulous gift you were especially put on the earth to share! However, when you're young into the world you're also under the delusion that everyone else in the world is just like you. It becomes an actual shock to discover differences. Placing my tiny snow-white fingers around an edge of the light blue flower-lace curtains I saw them flitting up and down from the flowing breeze. I thought to myself how wonderful that the only differences between Holli and I were her golden skin to my paper white skin. Her long illustrious dark hair flowed in contrast to my short fluffy blonde curls.

Sweet Holli with the coconut butter and beaches skin. Her long ebony hair was glistening from the moonlight and flowing in the wind from the open window. Holli deeply loves horses. Who could blame her? We shared a mutual awe of a horse's large muscular body covered in a fine satiny fur. She had plastic horses to play with; brown ones and white ones. Cream colored ones. Black horses with thick plastic manes. Tiny glass horses sat on Holli's bureau. You could see an actual rainbow if you held one of those glass horses to your eye and looked up into a light bulb. She had soft plush stuffed toy-horses that made a good pillow beneath your head.

Placing my elbow on the windowsill and resting my cheek in the palm of my hand. I drank in Holli's beauty. My own features are a ghostly contrast to Holli. My hair was curly blonde. My translucent skin was as white as the moon. I loved my sister moon. For in the moonlight you don't get burned. You can stare up at the moon and not go blind. Holli lifted her hand and petted my hair. "You're hair is soft like an angel's hair", she said. Leaning my forehead down I let it fall into Holli's small fingers.

The breeze puffed from the window. The light blue flower-lace curtain brushed in the wind against my cheek. Everyone else in the house had already fallen asleep. We were free to dream of our next game to play.

Holli's two-story country house of peeling white paint positioned itself in mile after circling mile from any other. Her family lived in this house out in the country on borrowed time from the U.S. armed forces. This particular night was warm. It was a full moon night. The darkness was thick with the heated fragrance of blue bonnets and sunflowers. Flower smells both sweet and pungent floating on the wind. The wind smelled alluringly of moisture. The stimulating invocation of delectable scents mixing to entrance the flow of blood in your heart. You can feel it circulating with an attractive growing sense of awareness. Captivating, for at this age it felt like the sense of your own blood pulsing and flowing in every capillary and vein was a miracle. The smells of the sunflowers and blue bonnets swirled in my nostrils now with a faint scent of lilac. The air wafting with such a fragrant bouquet sent a tingling excitement stirring in waves up my calves and through my knees and down my back. Gentle waves of relaxation and happiness. I took a deep breath. It was a sweet inhalation. Outside treasures awaited us. Feeling warmth in my heart I smiled at the beautiful silver moon glowing with its magnificent light.

"A long, *long* time ago", I repeated, "The Indians would make themselves brothers and sisters to their best friends by mixing their blood together." I felt a joy in speaking the words, as if the words themselves were full of mystical wonder.

The breeze from the open window caused an edge of the blue flower-pattern lace curtain to hit Holli in the eye and a long strand of her ebony hair to lie across her face and curl under her nose. She wiped the strand of dark hair away and rubbed her eye. "I want to be blood-sisters", exclaimed Holli. "So we'll be friends forever!"

"Friends forever!"

"But will we have to cut our fingers open?"

"Yes!"

"Really?" Holli's face tightened in an expression of fear.

"Well, yes. But not open too much I wouldn't think. We don't want it to hurt. But our blood will be mingled from then on. And we'll be real true blood-sisters *forever*!"

"Will our hearts really pump each others blood?"

"Yes. That's how the legend goes!" I was feeling happy beyond measure. And it warmed me like firelight to see Holli smile now.

"Who told you the legend?"

"I think I saw it on TV."

"Oh."

"Or at least I think I saw it on TV"--I paused and thought about it. "I don't remember now if it was on TV or not."

"Oh." Holli gave it a little thought and sweetly smiled again. "So we'll be sisters for all our lives?"

"Oh yes. We'll be at each other's weddings. And our husbands will be friends too. And we'll have children at the same time. They'll play together like we do. We'll grow old together. Yeah!!" I hopped up and down.

"Very old?" Holli laughed.

"So old it'll be *silly*!" Now we were *both* laughing!

"Come on", said Holli. "Let's go find something. So we can be blood-sisters." Holli took my hand in hers. "Something sharp."

"Yes."

Holding hands we scampered down the hallway and into her bedroom. It was a huge bedroom really. All of Holli's toys (mostly stuffed animals) were neatly placed. Her bed was a queen size and looked like it could hold a whole gaggle of five-year olds! I ran to her bedroom window to look out again at the mesmerizing moon. A shiny giant silver disk, that glowed and glimmered. The moisture collecting in the air made the moon look like it had a magenta colored ring around it. Holli was busy looking through her treasure chest for something sharp. If the sharp object looked mystical and magical, then all for the better! She came up with an old silver baby spoon.

"Holli, how come your bedroom is upstairs but your parents sleep downstairs?" My own home didn't have an upstairs so somehow the idea of a long stairway seemed irresistibly attractive.

"I don't know." Holli showed me the baby spoon. "This is all I've got." We both giggled ridiculously.

I turned and fumbled with the knobs on her little ocean-blue radio that sat on her white windowsill. Suddenly the radio kicked on and a startlingly loud clambering of two male voices boomed forth. "Oh!"— I cried. Holli turned down the volume reflexively. We both hunched our shoulders to our ears and grinned. Then Holli and I bubbled in laughter again. Spouting from the radio at a more acceptable volume was a song by The Archie's called "Sugar, Sugar". "Ah sugar, sugar", I sang along, "ahhh honey, honey." Holli shook her shoulders in a little dance to the song. I was forever singing. I'd go to Ms. Gold's house to play with the other kids she was baby-sitting. And we'd whiz down the slide, my voice the loudest it seemed, singing "Raindrops Keep Falling on My Head" by B.J. Thomas. Or one of my other favorite songs so popular that year! I was absolutely certain the song "Aquarius" by the Fifth Dimension was a special song because Aquarius was my 'sign'.

"Ahhh sugar, sugar!" I continued to sing.

"Let's play!" Holli took my hand. She turned off the radio and then tugged me along.

"Okay!"

The time around 1969 had such an array of events! Golda Meir was sworn in as premier of Israel. In Canada the House of Commons approved a bill making French the official second language. And in *France* Charles de Gaulle resigned after voters rejected his proposed constitutional reforms. What could be more enticing? Certainly more enticing was that at last introduced to the world was the scanning electron microscope! How about the National Accelerator Lab in Illinois which began to give scientists more information about subatomic particles? Even more impressive would be the Atomic Energy Commission announcing the worlds largest super-conducting magnet! But did Holli and I care about these things at that time in our lives? Of course not! We were five years old for peat's sake! We're talking about a mild inability to find much significance in anything beyond the happiness of food, good sleep, and entertainment. We were far more entertained at the time by the movie "The Love Bug" starring Buddy Hackett. Saddened by the movie "Goodbye Mr. Chips" with Peter O'Toole. Shocked by Newman and Redford in "Butch Cassidy and the Sundance Kid." And music! Ohhhh music! How we could giggle when Cash sang "A Boy Named Sue." Cry when Peter, Paul, and Mary crooned "Leaving on a Jet Plane." Mmmmmm, music is the most mouth-watering treat of all! "Ahhhhh honey, honey. Doot-da-doot-doo. Sugar, sugar", I continued to sing while Holli and I skipped holding hands down the hallway.

We stopped at the upstairs window off of the hallway where we had been earlier. Oh yes, many things were taking place in 1969. Vladimir Nabokov published his new novel, "Aida" that year. A book I would read and deliciously enjoy some eleven years later up in the rafters and attic above the high school theater/stage. One day sharing the sensually tasty book by taking turns reading it from the dusty stage rafters with a friend of mine.

Holli leaned forward and kissed my cheek then smiled at me. Enthralling to hear sifted in the wind the languid siren song of the coyotes. Again the alchemistical allure of the delightful tinkling chimes. Various tones of magical music flowed while the wind caressed those chimes. Droplets of dew shimmered upon the lawn outside in soft pastel colors from the moonlight, like a million dollars worth of precious jewels. A soothing glow deep in my stomach began radiating slowly into my chest. Relaxation and happiness tingled in my fingers and throughout my neck. Taking in and releasing a deep breath. The warm wind from the open windows kissed my hair. Happiness.

Holli placed her hands flat on the screen-less windowsill. Straightening both arms and leaning forward she could see down from the second story. Holli closed her eyes and drank in the warm Mid-western night breeze. She sprang back with excitement. Tugging on her blue flannel pajamas with the little sheep's and cloud's on it. My spending the night was a last minute decision. I still wore my yellow and white checked dress. I spun around in my favorite dress just to watch the edges fly up! I had already reached that fun magical moment where a child forgets there are any adults in the house---perhaps in the world? Eerily quiet, the home's parents lay sleeping unawares.

"Let's go get a knife Suzanna. I want us to be blood-sisters forever. I love you."

"I love you too; best friends forever."

"For all our lives!"

"Right!"

My tiny hand gave Holli's little hand a squeeze and we shared a little peck of a kiss.

"Let's go downstairs to the kitchen and get a knife." Holli said this while leading the way as we held hands.

We were both so small in stature that we'd go to the bathroom together. We'd both share the toilet seat at the same time. ABC gum, "Already Been Chewed", was another thing we shared. Usually the pink cotton candy flavored bubble-gum kind. Pea's in a pod. And soon, sister's in blood.

We hopped and skipped down the stairs into the kitchen. Rummaging through drawers we searched for the perfect blade. Our bare feet pattered on the new 1969 brown and green vinyl floor. Holli's home fairly empty of objects and clutter since they moved so much. Her father in the armed forces seemed a lot to me like my own father whom was a preacher. We moved around a lot too. My mother, on the other hand, was a teacher. And my father the minister was a pack rat. We had all sorts of clutter at my own house. Of course I hated this. I literally dreamed of having my own home that had zero clutter and tons of open space.

"How about this one? It's real sharp!" Holli held up a razor-whetted knife with a black wood handle.

I came over and inspected the blade. Turning it over in my hand we saw it shine. We both inspected it carefully. Then the air caught and stuck like hot steam in our lungs in a moment of reticence when the blade glinted. A flash image of blood pouring thickly like a river down our arms darted through my mind. I could tell by the shaky wet gleam in Holli's eyes that she had envisioned it also.

"You know Holli?" I let go of the knife to let it plop in her palm. "When I went to the doctor they used a pin, like a needle, to get blood from my finger."

"Maybe we should use that."

"Definitely." --Which came out sounding like 'deafently.'

"I know where a needle is." Holli threw the knife back in the drawer. She did a quick spin around and began skipping out of the kitchen. I followed, skipping along behind her.

Our feet padded and popped with a soft noise on the hardwood floor in the hallway. Tromping through the hallway we marched into the living room. A single drawer in the old oak dressing table felt warm to the touch from the wood-burning fireplace next to it. Inside were some light-blue yarn balls. Yellow yarn also peeked up among the articles. Thread of various colors in black, gray, and red were there. Scissors. Needles. Holli slid the drawer out as if opening a secret. Quietly she produced a thick keen-looking needle.

"Let's go to the mountain!" I whispered with an out-of-breath excitement. Holli's eyes sparkled. She bit her lip in a sly smile. We darted as though running towards our destiny. Out of the house. Into the black velvets and grays and silver draped colors of the full moon outside.

Pausing only a moment to catch our breath and feel the damp grass beneath our feet. Then we ran holding hands with Holli in the lead. Toward the mountain! Our bare feet would have made us think otherwise. We were lucky to be in the front yard since her back yard has so many stickers. The mountain was actually a large moss and clover coated hill. If ever there is a moment where angels force humans to choose a certain path then perhaps this was one such moment. We sat shoulder to shoulder and cross-legged upon the soft moist clover. Our nostrils filled with the sweet green scent. One lone pine tree shaking its needles in a gust of wind added a waft of its pungent smell. I thought Holli looked like some magical native child. Her hair was flying in wispy strands against the breezes invisible touch. She handed me the needle.

Summoning bravery. Calling down determination from the stars. Placing the sharp point of the needle against the fleshy tip of my left-hands middle finger. Letting out a long breath. I turned my gaze to the full moon and pressed the needle past the pop of the skin and into flesh itself. I realized I was holding my breath. Consciously forcing myself to breathe in and out once more before yanking the needle out. Simultaneously handing Holli the needle, I looked down at my finger. The blood spot on my finger pooled upward into a shimmering glistening red droplet that expanded and grew larger. Turning my head upward and to the right I was just in time to see Holli hunched over her hand and pressing the needle down into her fingertip.

Wince of pain and it was done. Holli stood up and glided slowly toward the pine tree. Leaning inward Holli pressed the needle into its trunk. Who knows, maybe that needle is still lodged in that tree to this day. Holli sat back down next to me. We pressed our wounded fingers hard and deep together. Small single thin streams of blood did not run from our fingers, down our arms, and drip off our elbows like I had expected it too. Staring into each other's eyes intensely we felt the longing and hope and love of the innocents. And fear too. We felt the fear of being alone without a best friend; of not having each other.

"I can feel my heart pounding." My blood sent a flood of adrenaline sliding through my heart.

"So can I." --Replied Holli. "Is your heart pounding your blood into my body now?"

"Yes. And your heart pounds your blood into my body. We're blood-sisters now Holli. Friends forever."

"For ever. And ever."

We jumped to our feet in a synchronized squeal of a child's excitement and happiness. Hugging each other and jumping up and down. Holli's straight black hair floated around her smiling face. I wished my blonde curly hair was long and dark and straight like hers. I was smiling too. It was such a sweet magical moment. Such an enchanted moment indeed, as if the world had no room for worry or loneliness. It was as if some dream-catcher wished upon long ago had finally caught us in its mystical web. Laughing out loud we jumped up and down again. We were filled up with a fabulous thrill that felt like a thousand tiny

prickles of electricity. Bending onto our knees we wiped the blood away from our skin by rubbing our palms and fingers into the pleasing fuzzy moss. A streak of wide lightening flashed incandescent at the horizon. Dark clouds folded in on themselves and expanded. Thunder ripped against the quiet like a warning of things to come.

"Let's go ride my horse!" Holli thrilled.

"Yeah! Let's go ride your horse!"

"Come on!" She grabbed my hand and we began running through the dark by the light of the swollen moon. We ran down the clover and moss mountain. Running and crossing the left side of the front yard. Yelping out loud I stopped near the corner of the homes front door. Something had stabbed me! Hopping on my left foot I yelped again at the violent sting in the bottom of my left foot. At first I thought some insect had bit the flesh and injected me with its venom. What was that throbbing pain in my foot? Cradling my foot in my arms I plopped down onto my bottom in the grass. Hollering: "Ouch! Owe-owe!"

Examining carefully I looked at the soft flesh on the underneath of my right foot. Rubbing my foot I felt a biting sting against the finger I was rubbing with. As my eyes adjusted to the nightly shadows I became aware of the source of hurt.

Holli was bent down in front of me. Her long dark hair fell across her face as she leaned forward to scrutinize the bottom of my foot. "Ooo" stated Holli with a gentle hush. "You stepped on a sticker?"

"Yes."

Holli picked at the sticker but succeeded only in pricking her finger. "Owe! It bit me!" Holli shook her finger rapidly and then stuck it in her mouth.

"I can get it." I had the long-growing healthy fingernails of my Grandaddy Barns. Placing the tips of the long fingernails of my right hand's thumb and forefinger over one of the sticker's prickles I was able to fairly painlessly extract the source of my hurt and toss it away. The bottom of my foot felt sore, but I knew the soreness would soon go away. "Let's go put some shoes on. Okay?"

Holli nodded her head in agreement. "Okay."

The sidewalk which led to the front door was only about twelve steps away. Rising to my feet I silently prayed there would be no more stickers between the sidewalk and where Holli and I stood. Tiptoeing carefully I made my way over to the sidewalk. Holli also tiptoed. She swung her arms when she reached the sidewalk and bounded onto the smooth concrete in a large single hop. I sidestepped onto it. Arms stretched out we placed our hands on each other's shoulders and bounced around in a full circle. Exclaiming together happily we hooted--"Yea! We made it!" "We're safe from the vicious sticker-crocodile"—I added for fun. Ending our bouncing circle we tightly hugged. Happily we grasped our hands. Swinging our clasped hands back and forth, we walked to the front door. Holli opened the door and then gave it a little push so that it swung open. We stepped into the foyer. As I watched Holli bend down to slip on her sneakers that had been sitting on the linoleum floor of the foyer it occurred to me that I had no idea where my own shoes were. Had I left them upstairs in Holli's bedroom? A pair of large black leather shoes that belonged to either Holli's brother or her father sat neatly next to each other in front of the foyer closet. Eyeing the leather shoes I placed a finger to my lips in consideration of the situation. After a few seconds I had made up my mind. I stepped into the large shoes. "Holli is it okay if I wear these? I don't know where my shoes are."

Holli looked up from where she was sitting putting her sneakers on. Shaking her head 'no' she finished slipping her shoes on and stood up. "I've got some shoes in the closet. You can wear my shoes." This was a far better solution since the leather shoes were far too big for me to be able to walk properly. I stepped backwards and out of the way for Holli to open the closet door. She bent down and extracted a pair of purple flip-flops. Closing the closet door she bent once again to set the flip-flops in front of my leather clad feet. The men's shoes had swallowed up my feet and ankles like big clumsy boats.

"Thanks!"—I told Holli feeling deeply grateful for the small sized flip-flops to wear. Slipping my toes into the better fitting little purple flops I looked to Holli with relief. I smiled at my blood-sister and she petted my fluffy blonde hair and smiled back. "Guess what Holli. I already know who I'm gonna marry! It's either going to be Juan. He's my boyfriend in New Mexico. Or I might marry Michael Al . We look alike you know. We both have blonde hair and his skin is real white."

Holli smiled warmly. "Which one do you think it will be?"

"I don't know. Juan and I could have kids with suntan skin and that would be neat."

"Can I be in your wedding?"

"Of course! You'll have to be. We're blood-sisters now."

"Can I wear a pretty dress?"

"Yes! Very pretty! Made of burgundy and gold colors. The prettiest dress in the whole world."

"What's "burr-gone-dee?""

"It's a color. Like the color of a dark purple-red rose. Like the color of wine."

"My mother drinks wine."

My expression fell into dismay. "Holli, can I be in your wedding too?"

"You'd better be!" Holli shuffled her feet. "I don't have a boyfriend yet though."

I shrugged. "Shall we go horse back riding now?"

"Alright!" Holli tugged me back outdoors. "Let's go ride my horse!" The two of us began running swiftly through the warm sweet night. The smells of lilacs, bluebonnets, and sunflowers perfumed the air heavily. A mixture of flower smells like sugar and soap. Hanging in the weighty humidity amidst the other smells was the thin honey scent of honeysuckle rising from nearby bushes.

"Horses are so cool!" I purposely breathed in the fragrances with deep pleasurable inhalations through my nostrils. It was lovely! "I love horses!"

"So do I! Did you know my horse loves me? She does. She really does. She listens to me. And I can make her go, or stop, or turn a circle. Did you know she can jump barrels?" Holli was breathing hard from the run.

Feeling a stitch burning my ribs I stopped to catch my breath and massage my side with my fingers. We'd made it to the stable. It was large and cow-boyish' and fantastic! Every part of it was made of rustic lumber for as far as I could see. There was no floor to speak of as the ground was left to be a sneezy wheezy mixture of loose dirt and sod. Breathing and swallowing as my eyes took in the stable. I watched Holli open the wooden fence. She skipped from foot to foot with her knees raised high until she stood in the middle of the riding ring. Turning to face me Holli stretched out her arm and ghostly beckoned to me with a languid flowing motion of her hand.

Looking up I searched the night sky for the moon. Hoping, I wanted to see the maroon ring again. Mother moon was shining bright and bulbous. Yet the ring around the moon had changed in color to a blood red. It was a sign of changing weather. It was a divine prophecy of rain.

The treasure of diamonds shining in the sky now had their starlight covered by dark rolling clouds. The clouds seem to billow and then fold back in on themselves. Turning my gaze back to Holli I saw her ghostly beckoning again. Wind whipped harder. Gathering Holli's straight ebony hair the blustery winds tossed the long strands in the air and over her forehead. My fluffy blonde curls framed a halo about my head from the moonlight gleaming through it. Holli looked like the moon's shine had woven long glowing spider webs of silver metal into her hair.

Wind pushed and curled around our bodies even harder. Smiling with happiness and excitement I sprinted into a soft jog. Running into the riding ring I didn't stop until I stood by Holli's side. Low-pitched gargles of deep thunder burst rolled from the billowing sky. Completely thrilled I pranced back and forth on my feet and glanced from the sky to Holli. "Oh Holli! I think it's going to rain! Oh, I hope it rains!"

"I don't like the rain. You really like the rain?"

"How come you don't like it?"

"Because it means you can't play outside."

"Even if it's a warm rain?"

"Yep. Your mother let you play in the rain?"

"No. She doesn't like me too." Hard caresses of flourishing wind blossomed in fluxing waves against our arms and faces. The thriving progression of storm boomed a thunderous percussion like a thousand deer-skin drums pounding in rolling unison. Hopping up and down we felt a joyously electrified emotion. I clapped my hands. "Yippee! I looove thunder! I like it when it's so loud you can *feel* it!" Barely beginning to fall, slow drops of rain tickled our faces. Sparse raindrops left tiny dark spots in the parched dirt.

Holli and I raised our palms up into the few scattered droplets of rain. Feeling the wet drops that tickled on our chins and noses and hands. We both giggled gleefully. Holli looked at me and laughed. Then she waved a hand in my direction as if giving a dismissal wag and said, "I'll go get her." She was referring to the horse of course. The moment was all so frightfully exciting! Holli called back to me: "She's a really big horse. Do you think you can get on her?"

"I'll try! I think I can." A reverberating pound of thunder roared with jolting volume. It was followed by soft waves of pattering thumping thunder. Crackling electric shards of lightening broke into bright splinters across the sky. The natural light show that was slowly taking place in the heavens filled me with vibrant enthusiasm. It dawned on me that it had fallen quiet for a moment after the thunder and lightening. For now I was keenly aware of the distinct return of night songs. Crickets chirped. Night bird's singing. The clear word 'who' sounding ghostly from an owl.

Holli brought forth the large beautiful animal. Pulling the equine along with the pressure of her hand, she pressed behind the flank of its muscular leg. The beauty of the horse was indescribable. Its mane was a healthy thick sheen of cinnamon and chestnut. The horse's lean muscles were coated in slick shining fur the color of rich amber honey. Its sleek equine back and neck were nakedly free from any bit or reigns or saddle.

Moonlight shone precariously upon the stable. Odd shadows formed. Weird and spooky shadow-specters appeared. Foregoing any attempts to put on a saddle Holli motioned for me to walk with her. "Come on Suzanna, I need you to help me get the ladder."

"We're not going to put on a saddle? Isn't there supposed to be a saddle?"

"No. We can ride bare back."

"Won't we fall off?"

Leaning against the corner of the gray wood barn was the ladder glimmering silver in the moonlight. I helped Holli grasp hold of the ladder. We scooted the tall metal ladder next to the grown horse. Holli said, "Don't worry. We won't fall off. I always ride bare back. I've done it lots of times."

"We won't just slide off?"

"No!" Holli laughed. "You just hold onto the mane."

"Can I just hold on to you?"

"Yea, you'll do that too. Are you scared?"

"No! It's too exciting!" Honestly I was not even scared in the least. Well, perhaps it was fear hidden inside excitement. In fact my entire body tingled along with relaxation at the same time. You can feel your body melt into the ground like butter in the sun with such deep warm relaxation! It gave me a sudden pleasant hunger. I could practically smell buttered toast with just the thought of it. "Mmmm, comfort food", I thought to myself. Buttery browned grill cheese sandwiches. Hot thick spicy tomato soup. The spicy chocolate meats my baby-sitter in New Mexico used to create.

Holli climbed the ladder. She grabbed a fistful of the equines wind-whipped cinnamon and chestnut mane. Holli pulled herself onto the musty-scented, gorgeous, amber/honey colored animal. Then offering her help she reached for me. I climbed the ladder then took her out-stretched hand into my right hands grasp while holding the thick horses mane with my left hand. It was so much easier to heave myself onto the magnificent creature then I had expected it to be. The horse remained oddly still. Then the lovely beast snorted out a warm blustery if uncertain grumble. The sky shuddered with another rolling drum-thunder. Thunder boomed then echoed away like ghosts groaning.

Streaking fingers of lightening flickered through the dark clouds above. Wind whirred around us. Encircling air gusting. The whipping wind carried the soothing scent of the honeysuckle. Holli gently kicked the heels of her feet into the horse. She made a clicking clucking noise with her tongue and cheek. Magnificent amber fur-covered muscles moved in a calm motion. At Holli's direction the horse led us away from the wood barn and into the center of the fenced riding ring. I wrapped my arms tightly around Holli's waist. Our bodies moving along to the rhythm of the horses walk which was both smooth and jaunty at the same time. Breathing in long and slow I could smell the clean refreshing scent of ozone. Smacking my lips, my mouth was full of an earthy and delightful flavor like distilled water. The air swirling over my tongue left the comforting metallic taste of ozone.

For several minutes the soft large creature walked in big circles around the ring bringing great enjoyment to its two small passengers. Such deep profound pleasure filled our young hearts on this cabalistic night ride.

The warmth of the night made what happened next all the more cryptic. Frightening. As if up from the bowels of some ancient frozen wasteland a cold wind blew upon us and then hovered over us. In a sudden and most unwelcome change a most foul stench wafted in and out of our nostrils. Stung our eyes.

"Is that a skunk's smell?" I asked Holli.

"No. We get lots of skunks here, and that's not a skunk smell. It smells like something..."

Then speaking on top of each other Holli said "Dead" and I said: "rotting." I felt frightened as I saw that the horse's eyes rolled and lolled in its sockets while it puffed grunts from its nose. Stamping its feet it sounded out a whinny. It seemed to me as if the horse had a fear of the smell. There was a branch-cracking sound from somewhere out in the darkness.

"Who's there?" I called.

"You heard it too?"

"Like there's someone out there."

"That's what I felt! I thought that too."

"You did?"

"Yes."

"Like someone's here."

"Like something bad Suzanna?"

"Does it feel like some kind of danger to you Holli?" I wrapped my arms even tighter around Holli's waist. We were inadvertently scaring each other now.

"Like something bad."

"Maybe we should go back inside."

"Yeah, that's what I was thinking."

"We're being silly." I gave the moment a little thought. "I'm sure it's nothing Holli. The wind is getting stronger. It's just the wind breaking through the trees!" I realized the wind had grown so harsh and wild that I needed to yell just to be heard. Yet as inexplicable as it may have been I had the distinct sensation of fear. Tiny hairs rose upwards on my arms amidst goose bumps. I felt a sharp intense sensation that warned of danger. Holli felt it also. I wanted to be bravely practical. And I didn't want to admit I was scared. "Still", I added, "I think we should go back inside the house!"

"Me too!"

We looked around and could not see anyone. Yet we felt some inexplicable feeling as if we had the distinct knowledge that indeed someone was there. Someone was watching us. They were nearly upon us. They had ill intentions. Ripples of even more goose bumps and raised hair flowed down our arms. Cold air formed into a solid pressure that pushed down on us with an unmistakably heavy sensation. Stamping its feet the horse whinnied again. A guttural growl sounded out and thrust itself across us. Like from the larynx of a man's throat yet not entirely human either.

"What's that!" I felt electrified with fear.

"I know that sound!" Holli pulled back on the beast's mane to still the horse. "That's the sound of a wild cat!"

Holli was afraid yet remained remarkably controlled. "Come on Suzanna, we better get inside."

"A wild cat?" Terror pressed into me. It was the strangest sound I'd ever heard. Was it the cat that made that wretched smell? "What do you mean by a wild cat? Do you mean like a leopard or something?"

"No." Holli struggled with the honey-amber horse. It kept kicking its hooves in the dirt making it difficult to stay on board of its back. "Not a leopard."

"What then?" I demanded. "Like a panther?!"

"No, no! Not a panther or a leopard!" Struggling with the horse again as it stomped its hooves. The horse was pulling and twitching and whinnying. The thrashing made it very difficult for Holli to maintain control of the animal. "Just a wild cat. Not a house cat though. They're big! A bunch of them live up in the hills. The wild cat's and the coyote's eat Daddy's chickens."

Like someone brushing up against us the wind pushed on our bodies in a bold gust. Losing its temper the horse fretfully screamed. Grossly powerful the wind kicked up again sending our hair to flap against our faces and dirt to whelp our eyes. Once again the wild animal growl sounding both human and inhuman scraped our ears and raised our alarm. The wind pricked up Holli's dark hair and my blonde hair and pounded the back of our heads. The horse whinnied out another piercing scream. With a shocking jolt the horse raised itself high onto its back legs. Whinnying horribly, the horse balked.

Sliding backward I squeezed Holli's waist hard and for dear life. Raised high the horse's front hooves began thrashing wildly into the air. Instinctively we both clamped our legs onto the horse. Holli held onto the horses mane. I was holding Holli. Slamming its front hooves down the horse fell onto the earth with a mountainous and jolting thud. Lifting its hooves into the air, the horse brought them back down in another pounding stomping crush of the ground. The horse whinnied in a screeching reverberation that sounded like sheer terror. The sound sent chills down my spine. The storm was getting worse and sent out another thunder-clap to loudly billow through the air. Droplets of rain fell harder. Bellowing another whinny the shiny amber horse raised itself onto its back legs again with its front hooves clawing once more at the air. Sliding down-wards and back-wards Holli and I screamed. Without warning the huge equine burst into a complete galloping run!

Volumes of wrenched screams wailed uncontrollably from our tonsils. High, shrill, horrified sounds wouldn't stop boiling up from our vocal cords. Was one or both of us about to die? Soon to be thrown from the horse and trampled to death? There was little doubt we'd fall and be trampled to death. Or a solid hit to the head from a hoof or the hard ground. The moment was licentiously clear. Death or permanent injury was about to suck us into its gravitational pull as ruthlessly as a celestial body drawn into a black hole.

Suddenly I heard a man's shout. Was it the voice of Holli's father? Opening up my eyes from my tightly clenched and squinting vision, I peeked. Holli's father was running toward the riding ring at high speed. We had awakened him with our screams. His eyes were wide with fear. His arms were reaching outward as if that would help him run faster. His short brown hair, white undershirt, and boxer shorts were sticking flat against him in his obvious sweat. Precautions thrown to the wind Holli's father slammed straight toward the wildly running horse. In a massive lunge forward he clenched both of his fists upon great hunks of the mane. His feet could barely keep up and Holli's father came unfathomably close to being dragged by the horse. His feet were scrambling and his arm muscles shaking. He yanked downward on the cinnamon mane and commanded, "Whoooa!"

Brown fur was mussed and frothy moist. The horse came instantly to a skidding stop with its hooves digging into the sod. Holli's father petted the equine's nose and forehead and spoke comfortingly to it. Its eyes no longer lolled about in fear. The presence of Holli's dad seemed to miraculously calm the beast. Holli and I felt better now too! No longer did we feel a cold air pressing down upon us. Simply the wild wet winds comfortable summer's night warmth. Nor did any malodorous bizarre stench surround us. Instead the natural light scent of mesquite trees and tall grass blended with blooming flowers had come back. It was a full rain now and we were all getting soaked. The relief was so complete for Holli and I that our moods were delightedly tickled. Holli's father felt a relief that was stricken with a mixture of horror and anger.

One at a time he eased us both down off the horse and onto solid ground. We children looked at each other with wildly thrilled smiles. We plopped down onto our backs in the stirred up dirt and rain and began laughing.

"It's not funny!"---Her father chortled with utter consternation. Shaking his head at us with frustration he turned and guided the horse back into its home in the barn

"That was so ridiculous!" I hollered between laughs. Raindrops fell into our eyes.

Holli guffawed, snorted, and shook with rolling laughter as she exclaimed: "Yea, how stupid!"

"There wasn't anybody out there now was there! And that was either a skunk we smelled or that wild cat had gas!" As I lay on my back I held my ribs in relief and laughter. The idea of a cat with stinky gas made us both laugh harder. It also seemed extremely funny to me that Holli's dad was outside in his underwear! Laying down looking up at the sky I felt myself involuntarily jump as a boom of thunder like a million bass drums crashed through the air. Lightening blasted electrical in spreading streaks like tree roots. It was enthralling.

Holli laughed. Then she fell into a putt-putt stop/start of giggles while trying to catch her breath. She breathed in deeply then sighed. "I've never seen my horse scared like that before. She's never even done anything like that before! She's real gentle that's why she's mine and I can ride her. Even bare back!"

"Stop laughing, it's not funny. And who was *here*? What were you talking about?" The father demanded with uncertainty. He had finished putting the horse back in it's stall and was walking with long steps toward us.

"Ohhh"--I replied sitting up. "It was weird. Just a wild cat and nothing more." Nothing more? I might have been severely wrong about that!

"So it was a wild cat that frightened the horse?" Holli's father inquired.

Holli sat up and shouted: "Yep! I heard it. Sounded just like a wild cat!"

Standing up I scanned the riding ring for the flip-flops I'd been wearing but which had fallen off when the horse reared. Locating them a few feet from each other in the dirt I gathered the flip-flops into my arms.

Thunder clapped outrageously against our eardrums. Lightening rooted across the sky with blinding flashes. Rain pitter patted over us all. "Get inside!" Holli's dad's voice struggled in volume against the air as the wind began to kick up again. "Inside the house! Now!" We obeyed. Following, we walked behind her father's long quick strides. I stopped at the edge of the riding ring's gate to slip the purple flops back on my feet. Out of the fenced corral and through the yard we sprinted. Her father practically leapt onto the sidewalk and up to the home's front door. He was opening the door already as Holli and I stepped onto the sidewalk.

All at once I became aware of an unusual and interesting sound. "Wait!" I tapped Holli on the shoulder to make her stop walking. She turned and looked at me. "What is that honking snorty sound?"

Holli's face twisted in momentary confusion. Then she had the expression of recognition and smiled. "Oh! That's the frogs. The bullfrogs are the really big croaky ones."

"Those are frogs?" I was surprised by the sheer number of the amphibious songs. "There are so many of them!"

"They come out in the rain."

"Come on!" Holli's father gestured for us to hurry. "You're getting wet! There's a storm blowing in! Come on! Get inside!"

We ran the rest of the sidewalk and stepped inside the house. The rescuing dad closed the door behind us but didn't lock it. He shook his head at us again. "Up to bed! Now! You girls could have been killed!" Holli's father bent down, enwrapping his daughter in his arms. Eyes closed momentarily he squeezed her in gratitude for her safety. To my complete and utter shock he pulled me up into the warmth of Holli's body and his arms. The softness of his hair brushed against my forehead as he bowed his head in an extended hug. He seemed honestly full of love and concern. Standing up he patted us both on the back. Hoarsely he uttered, "Get on up to bed. And don't ride any horses again by yourselves." Then with a pointed finger and an extraordinarily slow blink he added: "Ever!"

Grasping hands Holli and I ran happy and unworried through the house. Together we shouted a perfectly sincere "Okay" back to her father.

"We're sisters!" Holli sang her words with exhilaration as we skipped onto the stairs.

"We're sisters!" I spoke this with the intoxication that comes with the hope and faith of a child's belief that the world could be made a perfect place. Not even out of breath we hopped the stairs. We both halted at the last step of the staircase. Without the need to consult each other and synchronize our actions we simply leapt off of the last step hand in hand. We jumped and skipped around the hallway and then burst into Holli's darkened bedroom. One small nightlight on the other side of the large room was the only illumination.

Her father hustled up the stairs behind us in long lanky exhausted swings of his arms and legs. Heavier thuds from the father's feet followed behind us as we jumped onto the queen-sized bed. It had grayish white linens and a thin dark-blue flowered blanket. Pouncing on Holli I tickled her and we both felt giggles come bubbling up. I heard a deep male voice. Looking over I saw him in silhouette. Light was shining from the hallway behind him. He stood in the hallway just a few feet from the bedroom door. "You two go to sleep now. No playing around." Holli's father confoundedly breathed with exhaustion. Leaning forward he grabbed the round handle and closed Holli's bedroom door. Then he turned away and disappeared down the hall on his trek back to bed and slumber.

"Okay!" --Synonymously mumbled Holli whilst I whooped the word.

Light faded with the execution of the door. Moonlight waned. Adjustment of the eyes and the moonlight blossomed into greater luminosity. Holli produced two dry nightgowns from her dresser and we quickly changed our clothes. "I'm tired" groaned Holli through a yawn. She crawled onto the bed. Holli moaned and sighed in one quick breath. She rolled onto her right side towards the window then covered her head with the sheet. Only a wisp of dark hair and her small golden-tan nose stuck out from the sheet. Sleep beckoned Holli and she fell into it quickly.

Sitting up in the bed and looking at Holli I wondered why she had tugged the covers over her head. I liked my covers up over my ears but not over my entire head. Thinking now that since we were 'sisters', I might do the same and pull the covers higher up. Listening to the rain outside sway and dissipate, I glanced at the moons shine upon the bed. I noticed a large indentation in the bed in front of me. It was a hollowed indentation in bedding and mattress as if someone had just been sitting there. I thought it curious but uneventful.

Ice-cold air chillingly surrounded me. I scooted over to the window. Was it open? I thrust my palm to the window and realized as my hand touched glass that it was closed. Muffled noises floated from the outdoors amidst the tapping rain. Frogs croaked from somewhere down below. Crickets strummed their fiddles. The frigid chill enveloping me seemed to be only my own body reacting to being tired. The hauntingly frosty raw chill in my bones was somehow precedent to a strong sense of unease. Rubbing both arms for warmth I wondered if Holli's bedcovers would be enough to keep me snug. I looked over my shoulder to Holli's study desk against the far wall. I thought about dragging the croissant-colored wood chair at her desk across the floor. Bringing it up to the window I could set the chair down there. A stiff cringe crinkled through my muscles as I imagined the chair screeching miserably in wood chair scraping against wood floor. Surely the scraping sound would wake Holli up. My eyes turned for a moment to the sweet nocturnal light playing upon the ceiling in rounded gold patterns. I sat on the edge of the bed and looked through the window to the lovely disc moon. I heard a faint noise that sounded like the disgruntled purr of a cat edging on anger. The sound streamed into a low hoarse voice whispering my name. "Sssuzanna." Startled, I jumped.

Looking to my right, I felt fear. My bones only five years on this earth felt as though they'd gone soft. Bones inside me seemed barely able to hold up my body. I felt like I might faint. Squatting on the floor next to me was…what? A man? A spirit? Demon? My imagination ran wild. Was I sleeping and he was a dream? Oh, but little did I want to know, he *was* a man. Muscular body on him; and was that a mask? Skin dappled perhaps by the moon into looking slightly greenish. Eyes dark like an angry animal. Two growths from his head like grotesque tumors curling. A terrible, scary, mask. He came out of the darkness in a squatting position. *How long had he been there?!* The man pointed his long thin finger at my heart. His eyes strenuously fixed upon my own gaze with violent intensity. Pounding in my chest my heart sped with a rhythmic scream. My mind struggled to stay conscious, as I felt faint.

The man growled as he spoke: "You belong to *me*!"

Muscles regaining strength, I scrambled across the bed. Yanking the covers and floating them up in the air and over my body. I huddled under the bedcovers in fear and confusion. Pulling the dull-white sheet tightly around my head I let my eyes fall to Holli's sleeping self beneath the covers next to me.

"Holli?"—I whispered. I shook her shoulder. "Holli?"

Holli mumbled in her flickering moment of fatigued consciousness. "You sounded weird. What do you mean 'you belong to me'?" She had heard the man also? Holli breathed heavily. I believe she fell back asleep.

Seeing only the parachute-like envelope of the sheet surrounding me, I shuddered. My breath stopped short in my lungs. Inside my chest it felt as though my heart was pounding hard enough to rattle my ribs! Bones vibrating around my lungs with the rapid bunny-rabbit thumping of my heart muscle. Completely covered with the sheet I felt a little bubbly giggle bobble from my throat. Inexplicably I was somehow suddenly struck with amusement by these proceedings. What if it was actually Holli's brother attempting to play a trick on me? The thought sent a delicious mixture of excitement and fear coursing like tingles through my arms and legs. Like the sparkly thrills you get through your skin when you embark on an amusement park ride. Feeling fear on a ride you consciously reassure yourself that you are actually perfectly safe. Finally safe to feel the fear and though it ebbs and flows, it ultimately drifts clean out of you. I flicked my head quickly to look at Holli, wanting to cuddle up next to her. Find safety in the warmth of knowing 'I'm not alone.' Yet the curious urge to take a peek out of the covers and look at the stranger overpowered me. Sheet gripped hard in both my sweaty fists as I reviewed the situation. It was impossible to resist! I had to take a look! I pulled the covers down just past my eyes yet not exposing my nose.

I didn't see the stranger squatting near the window any longer. Where was he? Was he gone? Was Holli's brother about to pop out and say "gotcha"!? The area was empty. "Who? Who's there?" I stammered. It was too dark to see the whole room clearly. Suddenly the gurgling sounds of the man's guttural growl sounded out! What kind of joke is this? I hope and prayed I was having a bad dream. Frightened I ducked my head beneath the sheet and hid beneath the covers again. I inched myself in little skootches until I was pressed next to Holli's body. There was a sinuous old-house creak from footsteps on the floor. Another footstep creaked upon the floor. Fulminating steps. Creaking sounds within a stones throw now. *Someone else is in the room!*

* * * * * * * *

That night I fell asleep huddled next to Holli and hiding under the covers. Holli and I would sleep unawares to the fact that the coming morning would harbor quite a surprise for the two of us. The worst was yet to come.

T W O

DON'T GO ON THE STAIRS

Cuddled up next to Holli with my fists closed and eyes squeezed tight. I had slept the night in a blank dreamless darkness. Now I struggled not to wake up. Attempting to will myself back into the blank velvet softness of my sleep. Sunshine always comes as a sneaky surprise on Saturday mornings. Holli and I rousing well nigh at the same time. Stretching children observing the manifest radiance of light beckoning from the windows to wake up and play. Suddenly waking up seems like a pretty good idea. Hey, Saturday mornings mean cartoons on television!

Tugging the covers from my eyes and at once feeling soothed by the cheerful sunbeams flying through the pale blue lace curtains and onto the wood floor of Holli's second-story room. Specks of dust illuminated into seeming tiny fairies sparkling here and there in the sunbeam. I'd decided my encounter with the frightening grotesque man in a mask had surely been a dream. Bad dreams of course and nothing more. Or perhaps it had been Holli's brother pulling a practical joke? It was probably Holli's brother, of course. Either way it didn't matter to me now. Holli yawned in mid-stretch with a moment's quick shake of her taut arm muscles.

"I'm hungry", I muttered as my jaws involuntarily widened during another deep breath.

Holli brushed her long silky hair of ebony away from her eyes and forehead. Leaning onto her elbows she answered me with an, "Okay. My tummy's hungry too." Hopping from bed with the excitement of breakfast pumping energy through my veins, I threw the covers into a billowy crumpled heap across Holli's torso. Running barefoot across the cool smooth wood floor. I put on the same clothes from the previous day. Holli quickly followed suit. The day was beginning with friendship, food, sunshine, and cartoons. Ahhh happiness. The only kind of joy that comes from being a child with a best friend. Oh yes, there is no greater happiness than that for a child.

Holli sloughed off her pajama gown and wriggled into a pair of light green hot pants she retrieved from the floor of her closet. Also crumpled on the closet floor was a pink blouse with bell shaped sleeves, which she picked up and slipped on. Looking down at my dress I had an instant desire to have my own hot pants on too, which were a bright purple color. Looking at my bare toes I wished I had my white knee-high go-go boots with me. 1969 was such a time of change. And there can be no greater change than that of ones perception. Society can change its perception on something just as much as an individual can. In this sixties era a big band sound would be thoroughly overthrown in popularity by folk singers like 'Peter, Paul, and Mary', and 'Simon and Garfunkel'. Rock and roll would take a new twist with bands like 'The Beatles'. Fashions would undergo great changes as well. Women would prove themselves risqué with the popular crocheted swimming bikini. Hot pants' would make their debut and the mini-skirt would soon be everywhere in its popularity. In a surprising change of people's perception of fashion many would reject the poofy bouffant hairstyles for a more natural look. The 'shag' haircut was in. Tee shirts and jeans would become increasingly the common mode of clothing for many boys, and girls too. Yes, many changes taking place. Glancing again at my bare feet and wriggling my toes I spoke my thought out loud: "I wish I had my own go-go boots and hot pants. I've got some but they're at home." Excitement over having a day to play with Holli overtook my concerns about my clothing. Holli ran her fingers through her long dark silky hair. My stomach grumbled and growled.

"Last one to the kitchen is a rotten egg!"—I shouted over my shoulder; running through the door. Plopping like a frog down creaky stairs of dark honey-brown wood. Quicker than one could whistle 'woo-woo' and it's Suzanna at the bottom of the stairs looking back up to watch the beautiful young Holli descending. Holli's hand sliding along the rail; I stood tiny-boned and tapping an itty-bitty foot with thrilled impatience. Squiggling the champagne-brown shag carpet between my toes. Holli pounced off the last stair with a wave of both arms and rapidly whooped, "Hey! You wanna watch cartoons?!"

Do I want to watch cartoons? If there's a five-year-old who doesn't want to watch cartoons then this isn't planet earth and we two-legged creatures aren't human! Do I want to watch cartoons?!

I responded--"Are you kidding? We *have* to watch cartoons!"

Television. A magic box of pictures and entertainment. Ready with its magic to take you away into silly giggles, foreign lands and wild adventures, enthralling dramas or dreamy imaginings. We run up to the television and halt for a moment in awed stillness looking down at it. I turned the knob upon the face of the TV to the 'on' position. Leaning down onto one knee Holli flipped the large white channel dial until she had at last found a carton. No one had ever heard of a remote control yet! For it was a time when people were heralding Samuel Beckett for his Nobel Prize in literature. It was 1969 and Yasser Arafat had been elected chair of the Palestine Liberation Organization. Queen Elizabeth in England had just ordained her young son Charles to be Prince of Wales and Earl of Chester. And everyone everywhere had to walk up to their televisions to manually change the channels or turn it on and off.

"Breakfast?"

"Okay", Holli replied, "I'll ask my Mommy." Holli turned in a run towards a slender brown door that stood closed on the other side of the stairs. Treading on her heels I followed Holli through the door and into the spacious bedroom. Light from the room's large window betrayed the mothers desire to sleep, certainly, but having two bouncing hopping little girls shouting "We're hungry!" was the more unpleasant event of the morning for her.

Thin and young with paler skin than Holli's but yet the same luscious dark hair, Holli's mother lay on the bed. Holli's mother raised a shapely arm over her eyes as if its shade would allow her to see better. More than wishing to sleep late on a Saturday morning Holli's mother seemed genuinely exhausted. How old could the woman be? In her mid to late twenties? She groaned and frowned at us. "You're what? Hungry?"—she mumbled.

"Yes! Yes! Yes!" We chimed in unison while bouncing up and down on her bed. Her frown deepened as we 'boinged' in wave like movements upon the mattress. "Ohhhh", she groaned again and covered her eyes with the palm of her hand, "Get yourselves something to eat. Let me sleep."

"But we're hungry!" Exclaimed Holli.

"Hungry! Hungry!" I chimed in.

Holli's mother appeared to swoon against the bed and pillow. Her dark hair fell across her face. She lifted her shoulders first before hoisting her head upwards. Then she raised a heavy arm and pointed at us. "Go!" She swooped her pointed finger towards the door. "Go now! I'm sleeping!"

I was an empathetic and worried child. I was taught to be polite and to cow-tow towards any adult. Oh yes it was with urgency that I grabbed Holli's hand and pulled her out of the room. Closing the door gently behind us. Putting a finger to my lips in a mock 'shush!' Holli nodded and then skipped across that drab shag carpet with both arms swinging, making it look as if she were marching. Her knees raised high. She sat down in front of the television. Running behind Holli my eyes darted from the television to the brown and green vinyl floor of the kitchen. I tagged Holli by leaning forward and stretching out my right arm until at last my fingers tapped her shoulder. She jumped and we both laughed.

I looked toward the kitchen again. Oh, that kitchen floor! It seemed every house I'd ever seen had a kitchen floor just like it. Same boring colors looking like the floor of a school cafeteria. Was everyone afraid of color? Why drown every house in brown, beige neutrals, white, and drabs? I began to fantasize about what colors would cross and swirl the area if the kitchen were mine. Burgundy walls with cream Victorian molding. Black marble counter top. No, make that gold. Tile floors with a light blue shade to it. Holli came into the kitchen and scooted a thick wide bar chair of pecan brown over to a yellow-brown counter top that was just to the left of a small silver sink. I felt amazed at how strong Holli seemed as she lugged the chair about. She had a quality of personality that came across so determined and confident. As if she were somehow older than her five years. Qualities I admired. Looking to the sink I found that I liked the spray nozzle that rose up beside the sink. It could squirt water with just a push of a lever which made it very inviting.

My dark-haired Greek goddess of a friend elevated herself until she was standing upon her knees on the counter top. Stealthily I positioned a small step stool in front of the sink. Humming to the tune of "Amazing Grace" I reached across the sink towards the spray nozzle beside the faucet. Turning on the cold water I tested the spray by squeezing the push lever a couple of times. Aiming the thing at Holli my fingers squeezed the trigger. Water flew in an uncertain mixture of drip and spray.

"Hey cut that out!" Holli quipped disapprovingly. A giggle escaped her lips anyway. Between rising and lowering giggles from laughter of my own, I held my stomach and promised not to get her wet again. "Ohh-ho-ho-kay. Sah-ha-sorry", I chortled. My face was beginning to hurt from grinning so widely. Holli smiled and shook her head before turning back to the open cabinet and extracting something. Holli hopped down from the counter in a single swoop, which I thought looked like a very brave and daredevil thing to do. In her hand she held a box which she raised into the air and shook like a rattle. Pop-tarts!

Now Holli had a brother whom always had a pleasant expression on his face. He was older, thin, and lanky. Spending most of his time riding his bike or at his friend's house, I very rarely saw him. Now Holli's father seemed not only to be good at his career in the armed forces but also to carry an authoritative air that made you think he must have popped out of his mother's womb already in a uniform and marching. He had already left the house to attend work. Most likely it was still dark outside when he departed his country abode. My own personal love for Holli's home was accelerated by its emptiness. Its lack of clutter. Oh how my own parents home (really a minister's parsonage) was sickeningly full of items and scattered clutter. When you're a child you think a place can magically stay clutter-free. Secretly I desired to live in Holli's house. House of quiet. House of calm.

We were two excited children bounding through the house and pouncing on the old tan and gray couch that looked like it were made of tweed. Friendship and cartoons and pop-tarts! How could life get better?

Of course unfortunately I've never been one who likes sweets much. So just one fruit flavored pop tart was enough for me. Holli ate two and a half. Scooting closer to the television eventually became far more important than the comfortable couch. We moved to the floor. Sitting with legs crossed Indian-style on the carpet. "Popeye the Sailor Man" came on the television. Smiling and happy we sang the Popeye theme song repeatedly with very loud 'toot toots!' Having always loved vegetables I was fully prepared to argue the yumminess of spinach to my sweets loving friend. But Holli's like or dislike of spinach never came up. It seemed "H. R. Puffin Stuff" came on TV after Popeye. We watched whatever it was that came on TV with delight. We were enjoying ourselves thoroughly when I looked down at the carpet and saw a most horrifying sight! Quickly jumping backward with a yelp and landing on my feet. "Move Holli!" Alarmed and unsure of what was happening Holli leapt back and landed on her feet. I pointed to the carpet. We both leaned, hands on knees, peering at the carpet. Creatures were swarming and writhing in a pile as big around as a salad plate! They were down into the shag and blended into the carpet color.

"Worms?" Holli asked. She pulled her long straight black hair behind her ears.

I answered with trepidation. "No. Worms don't have feet. These have a bunch of feet."

"Feet?"

"Legs. I know what has a bunch of legs like that."

"What?!"

"Centipedes." We leaned closer. Holli stuck a finger out towards them. It was a huge slithering pile. Nearly a hundred of the creepy things. "No! Holli! Don't touch them!"

"Why not?"

"Because! They're poisonous!"

"Poisonous?"

"Centipedes. We'd better go get your mother."

To the left of the living room was Holli's mother's room. Giving a wide birth to the swarming poisonous bugs we ran on tiptoes. Pushing open the sleeping mother's door we ran shouting towards her bedside: "Centipedes! Centipedes!"

"Ohhh!" Mrs. Hunter rolled onto her right shoulder. Pushing her dark hair off of her forehead with her wrist, she blinked at us. Giving her the benefit of the doubt Mrs. Hunter really was being very kind regarding these interruptions to her sleep. "Oh, I'm trying to sleep! Girls!" To my surprise we did not receive a scolding.

"Mommy, there are 'cindy-peas' on the floor!" Hopping up Holli landed on her knees into Mrs. Hunter's bed.

"Centipedes." I corrected. "They're poisonous." You could tell my mother had me reading and writing at a very early age. I was only five and yet had been reading and writing for close to two years already. Equally obvious was that my mother was a teacher deeply devoted to education. Reading the dictionary was a serious line of advice in my house. "They're in the carpet", I added.

Mrs. Hunter patted her daughter's back gently and lovingly. She peered at us through slightly opened eyes and mumbled: "Why don't you kill them? Vacuum them up." Her eyes closed completely and a soft snort snored from her nose. We laughed at the sound.

"I know where the vacuum is!" Holli headed for the door.

I followed Holli. "We'll vacuum them up!"

"Yea! Yeaaaa!" We both cheered as we stomped out of the room.

"Girls!" Mrs. Hunter's voice sounded urgent as she shouted. "Please *don"t* wake me up again! Okay? Girls? You understand? Let me sleep!"

"We will!" We both chimed.

"And close my door!"

"Okay!" Both of our voices rang together. Holli closed her mother's door gingerly. Once the door was closed we both jumped up and down on our tiptoes shouting out again: "Yeaaa! Yea!"

Hopping forward a few feet from Mrs. Hunter's bedroom door. Crossing carpet to linoleum where the coat closet stood. Holli opened the closet door and swooped her hand and arm in a motion for me to come closer and help. The idea of using the vacuum on the centipedes seemed brilliant! A truly novel idea! Together we pushed and pulled the vacuum onto the carpet up next to the nasty bugs.

"This is gonna be great!" I said.

"Yeah it is! But…"

"What?"

"What if they start to run away when they hear the vacuum?"

"Ummm…"

"Wait!" Holli exclaimed. "Wait right there. I'm going to go get the broom!"

"The broom? What do you want the broom for, Holli?"

"You'll see."

I plugged the vacuum into the electrical outlet while Holli sprinted back to the coat closet. She returned with a straw broom that had peeling dull red paint on its long wood handle.

"What's that for, Holli? We've got the vacuum."

"I'll whap the *peas* with the broom, to knock them out, and then you can vacuum them up!"

"Great idea Holli!"

"On the count of three."

"Okay."

"One…" Joining in I sang the numbers along with Holli--"Two… *three*!"

She whapped. I vacuumed. "Ping! Pow! Boom!"—Holli yelled shrilly as she beat the centipedes with the straw part of the broom. Whap!—went the broom. And Holli hooted: "Bah-bing!" Whop!—of the broom, and Holli simultaneously howled out "Take that! And that!" She pulled back. Resting the broom back over her shoulder and wiping her forehead with the back of her hand while I quietly vacuumed. Suddenly Holli had a restless desire to do some vacuuming. And I'll admit that some broom whopping and some loud, spitting, ping pow bah-bing vocalization seemed mighty appealing!

"I….I…" Holli stammered.

Looking up from the carpet and deep into Holli's eyes I guessed the situation. "You want to vacuum some?"

"Uh-huh."

"Okay. Let's trade places."

Holli and I did a little dance of a circle around the vacuum cleaner and the centipede's spot. She held the broom out to me. I held it with a firm grip. We were both sweating and breathing hard. Centipede whapping and vacuuming is a lot of work! I still couldn't get over how many of them there were. A veritable nest of the ugly, poisonous, slithering, creepy things. Bugs Bunny in the background on the television trying to lure Daffy Duck into precarious peril sang out as we worked.

"Alright. Ready Holli?"

"Yes!"

"High-yah!" I hollered in my best attempt at a broom-welding karate chop. Whop!—with the broom. "Ohhh-ooo-high-yah!". Whap! Whump! More karate moves: "Chop, chop! Ohh-yah!" Whop! Holli carefully but briskly followed my actions with the whir and hum of the vacuum. She then pulled the vacuum back and turned it off. I let the broom fall onto the floor behind me. We leaned over the nest area and squinted hard at the carpet.

"They're gone." I spoke with a hush.

"Yep. We got `em."

Strolling over to the electrical circuit at the wall I unplugged the machine and began rolling up the cord. Together Holli and I lugged the vacuum cleaner. We placed it and the broom back into the coat closet. Closing the closet door we turned and looked at one another with shrugged shoulders and puffed lips. The expressions and silence of 'what shall we do next?'

Holli flattened her hands against her sides and offered a possibility for fun. "Want to go outside and play?"

"I was just thinking the same thing." We nodded our heads in the positive to one another in a confirmation that we both agreed on the next plan for fun. I followed Holli as she ran with the urgency of excitement to the foyer where her shoes sat. Sitting on the floor Holli slipped on her sandals.

"Do you want some shoes?" Concentrating on her shoe buckles Holli spoke without looking up.

"Do I need them?"

"I guess." Holli inspected the shoes on her feet. "I don't know." Pulling herself up off the floor she looked at me and smiled.

Smiling back at her I could hardly wait to play with my best friend outside. *Fun, fun, fun!* "I guess I'll go barefoot." Grasping Holli's hand I tugged her arm. "Come on!" Holding hands we ran back through the house in haste for the back door. Quickly we came to the back door of the house. I dropped Holli's hand to broach the doorknob. Concentrating intently I bit my bottom lip while twisting and tugging at the dingy-gold doorknob. It didn't open so I tugged harder. Yet still the door would not yield.

"Oh!" Holli exclaimed. She licked her lips. "It's locked! That's funny; we usually don't lock our doors."

Dropping my arms to my sides I took a step back and peered at the doorknob in search for the location of the lock. I was visually unable to spot the lock. The knob was smooth. "Do you know how to open it Holli?"

"Oh, yeah." Moving in close to the doorknob and leaning to her left Holli pushed a tiny button just to the left and underneath the knob. The button popped out. It occurred to me that I had never seen a lock like that. Holli tugged at the door and it gave way slightly. She stepped back a moment and looked at me. We both placed our hands on the door to equally pull together. The door opened with a sound like'shhlup!'

We ran outside as if we couldn't begin playing any too soon. I turned around on the thin flat cement patio to go back and close the door. I didn't shut it completely out of some odd and inexplicable sudden fear that it would lock behind me and we wouldn't be able to get back in the house. Satisfied that it was mostly closed I turned back towards the yard to see Holli waiting patiently for me at the patios edge. Eyes blinking in the sunlight I squinted at the slightly mowed yard and the wild overgrown countryside beyond it. "Oh, it's too bright!"

"What?" Holli came to my side.

"It's too bright", I repeated. "Why does this planet have to have such a bright sun?"

"What?"

"Well." I gestured towards the sky where the white sun hung huge and glaring. "Wouldn't it be nicer if there were two or three little bitsy suns? So that it wasn't bright. So that it was maybe always twilight."

"What's a twilight?"

Looking at Holli I watched a gentle warm breeze fluff the bottom edges of her hair. "You know", I nodded. "It's when the sky is purple and orange and pink. When the sun is on the horizon about to come up or go down."

"Ohhhh."

"Everything's very green."

"Yep."

"And there are so many different colors of green. Look, there's that lime green of those bushes over there. And the grass is an emerald green. And the trees back there are a dark forest kind of color. Oooo I like that big rock out there!" I pointed to a sand and cream colored boulder that lay upon the middle right of the back yard. It was huge! "You wanna play like the grass is the sea and that big rock over there is the island?"

"Alright." Holli's hands fisted in excitement. "And pretend the sea has crocodiles in it… and we have to swim through it."

"Yes! And we have to swim to that island!"

"Yeah, and we have to swim to it before the crocodiles get us!"

"Okay!" I began pretending I was swimming. Arms pulling through the air as if in water.

Holli thrust her arms in front of her and swooshed them to her sides as if swimming like a frog. She pretended to gasp for air at the water's surface. Flipping her arms Holli bolted for the boulder while I stayed at the patio. Hopping onto the boulder Holli turned to look at me and raised her arms above her head victorious. "I made it!"—Holli hollered.

Still swimming on the same spot of the patio I paused to clap for Holli's success. "Okay. And Holli? Pretend I had to wrestle an alligator. A great big alligator. And I had to wrestle it before I could get to the island with you."

Holli stood on the huge rock silhouetted by the cloudless baby-blue sky. "Okay. And pretend I built a boat and threw it out to you!"

"Okay."

"What's the difference between an alligator and a crocodile?"

"I don't know! Here I come!" Swishing my arms furiously I ran out into the emerald green grass and pea-green weeds.

Out of pure shock I halted in a completely frozen position. With a slight turn of my eyes I could see Holli building her imaginary boat. Holli threw the boat into the sea of green. She shouted at the top of her lungs, "Here! I'll save you!" I couldn't move. "Grab the boat!"—she yelled. Her face drew in with consternation and she demanded: "Have you already wrestled the crocodile?"

"Holli?!" My eyes begged for Holli's help. "I can't move! My feet are on fire!" I began to cry. Tears welling in my eyes and brushing wet against my eyelashes.

Holli's face twisted in worry. "Stickers?"

"Yes!"

"Try and make it to the rock!" Holli stood in place wringing her hands.

"I can't! I can't move! Holli help me! It hurts!" Large dripping tears surrendered themselves to my cheeks, lips, and ears. Several huge blossoms of tears rolled into my right ear to leave behind an uncomfortable wetness inside the ear canal. My tongue sent confused messages to my brain as I tasted the salty drops pooling at the corner of my mouth. "Go get me some shoes Holli! Go inside and get me some shoes!"

"Oh! OH!" Holli's gaze fell to something at the side of her house that I couldn't see from my position. "It's my brother! I'll go get him!"

"Get me some shoes!"

"Hold on! I'll be right back!" Holli bolted off the boulder. Running at full speed she disappeared around the corner of the house shouting: "Hey! Hey!"

Gathering up my courage I thought that perhaps I could sprint it to the bone colored cement patio. Stickers had plunged their hard needle-sharp points into the flesh of my feet. So running meant to step down on the embedded stickers. My muscles immediately spasm at the very first step I make. Hot searing pain shot up from the bottom of my feet and I lost my balance. In one horrid second I saw myself falling and placed my hand palm down behind me to brace my fall. In the same split second I became aware that I was about to fall down into the stickers themselves and there was nothing I could do to stop it or make it less painful.

"Here he is! He's coming!" Holli reappeared from the opposite side of the house from where she had left.

Squinting against the blinding sun, I looked up to see my friend. "I fell!" Stickers now stabbed into my left hip and left leg. Lifting up my left palm I saw over half a dozen hard round brown stickers piercing into the flesh. Wondering if I should go ahead and pluck them out of my skin I looked up to see Holli's older brother come flying around the corner of the house on his bicycle. His dark brown shaggy hair flowed in the wind created by his anxious pedaling. He wore jeans and a striped shirt with short sleeves. I didn't even have a chance to question how he was going to rescue me. Swiftly he scooped me up into his right arm. Never once pausing in his bicycling! Swerving the bike around in one long smooth motion he rode onto the patio, opened his arm, and let me drop onto the patio. "Thank you", I hollered back to him. He didn't stop riding his bicycle but raised an arm without looking, as if to say 'your welcome'. In awe I turned my gaze to Holli. "Wow! Your brother's like an angel or something! He just flew over on his bike and grabbed me up!"

"He's really strong. You want me to help you take out the stickers?"

"No, you'll only stick yourself." I must have pulled thirty stickers from my flesh. One at a time I placed them into a neat pile. "Why don't we play something else?"

"You don't want to play outside?"

"Not right now." I stared at the prickly pile I had created. "Maybe later."

"Okay Suzanna. You want to go watch some more cartoons?"

"Sounds good to me." I allowed Holli to help tug me to my feet.

"You okay?"

"Yeah, I'm alright. But I am never *ever* going to play in your back yard again without shoes on first."

We walked to the door. Holli opened it and then waited while I walked through. I noticed right away that the television had been turned off. My eyes fell to the Hunter's big clunky record player and stereo. It rested against the far right wall. I walked over to it while Holli closed the door. "Want to listen to a record, Holli?"

"Alright. My mom and dad have some records. What you want to listen too?"

"I don't know." Fingering the face of the black stereo I flipped a switch. Music came pouring out. Filling the empty room with its funky rock and roll.

"Oh that's the radio."

"Yes. I know that." The Mamas and the Papas were singing "Go Where You Wanna Go". Their voices harmonizing: "You gotta go where you wanna go, do what you wanna do…you don't understand that a girl like me can love just one man…" I began rolling the dial to see what was playing on the other stations. Frank Sinatra and Nancy Sinatra were crooning away on the next clear station I found. Pausing a moment, I listened: "…in the night so blue… and then I go and spoil it all by saying something stupid like I love you." No, not that one. I'm in the mood for something else. Turning the dial again I listened for something that would strike me as 'happy.' My ears caught a big band sound and I stopped. Listening I became excited by the sound. Yes! Perfect! I love the music from the 1940's. This was definitely a song you could dance too! It was the 1940's band music "I've Got a Pocketful of Dreams" by Ambrose and Dennis. A shriek of excitement squeaked from my throat as I soaked in the swing sounds. Music so big and brassy and full of trumpets! Turning to Holli I took her hand and began to dance. At once the trumpets honked to a halt. The deep male voice of a D.J. was saying something about the previous selection of music. "Aaawww", moaned Holli and I both. It was a disappointment that the music was over so soon. Before we even had a chance to really get dancing! "Awe, man! We caught the tale end of it!" I stomped my right foot. "I wanted to dance!"

"Me too!"

"Maybe there's something else we can dance too." The thought came to me that perhaps I should search a different station for some dance music. In mid stride toward the stereo the station we were already on began to play the song "Boogie Woogie Bugle Boy". "Groovy", I wriggled my shoulders with delight, "I loooove this song!" Taking Holli's hands into mine. We began dancing. I pulled her forward and pushed her backward in jitterbug dance steps. I twirled her around and underneath my lifted arm. Holli gleefully giggled. I squealed with joy. We pulled into one another, our shoulders almost touching, and we rocked left and right. Pushing her back out again, then twirling her in a circle beneath my arm. Wrapping my right arm around her back I dipped her backward and downward as if I were going to give her a dipped kiss. Holli burst out laughing. Grinning from ear to ear I hooted out a breathy laughing guffaw. Lifting Holli back up from the dip kiss move, I twirled her around in a full circle again. Her hair flew upward as she went round. Clasping both our hands together again I pushed her backward and then pulled her forward in more jitterbug steps. I sang along with the Andrew Sisters: "Well he's the boogie woogie bugle boy from company B. He's in the army now. He's playing revelry. He's the boogie woogie bugle boy…"

"Girls!" Holli and I both jumped in surprise at the sound of Holli's mother's voice. She stood with her long dark hair ruffled and tangled. Her eyes blinking with exhaustion. Shaking her head in disapproval from the slightly opened bedroom door. "That's too loud! Holli, either turn it down or turn it off. Gosh Holli, why don't you girls go play upstairs in your room?"

Instantly I turned the volume on the music down. Then with an after-thought of the situation I simply turned the radio off.

"Thank you", said Holli's mom. She shook her head at us again. Then she skulked back into her bedroom; closing the door behind her. Holli and I stood in silence for a while just staring at her mom's closed bedroom door.

"You want to play jump rope Suzanna?"

"Sure. Where's your rope?"

"It's in my room. I'll go get it." Holli turned in a run for the stairs.

"I'll come with you." Running along behind Holli I was wondering what her rope looked like when she answered my question before I even had to ask.

"It's a really cool jump rope. It's pink and stripy and the handles are pink."

Past the closet which housed the vacuum and around the near corner lay the stairs. We began our ascent of the stairs side by side. I jumped a step ahead of Holli. We were both full of joyous anticipation of the frenzied search we were soon to begin. No doubt a massive search for the rope would be required, and of course the greater the search the more fun and adventurous things would seem. Keeping my eyes on my own steps I was already half way up the stairs when it occurred to me that it didn't feel like Holli was coming up behind me. Stopping my ascent I turned to look back at Holli. She still stood on the third step.

"What are you doing Holli?" Suddenly I noticed that Holli's face had drained of blood and looked pale. Ashen. Her eyes were full of fear. "What is it? Do you feel sick?"

She managed to labor a soft answer from her lips. "No."

"Are you coming up stairs?"

Holli shook her head 'no.' She looked frozen in shock and terror. Her lungs pained in a series of panting breaths. I thought she was going to faint.

I was beginning to feel scared for Holli. "What's wrong?"

Holli raised a shaky arm and pointed beyond me to the upstairs hallway. She gasped and stuttered in the middle of speaking: "The.. the.. the devil!"

Descending back down the stairs I felt my concern for Holli grow deeper. When I reached the stair just above where she stood I cupped her cheek in the palm of my hand and demanded with a slight pressure that she look me in the eyes. "Holli. There are no such things as devils and witches and ghosties or goblins. There is no great powerful god called a devil out running around trying to scare you."

Holli's eyes showed she was seriously frightened. "No", she shook her head in the negative. Raising her arm again and pointing once more to the upstairs hallway behind me she whispered, "The devil." I looked over my shoulder at the hall above and behind me. There was no one there. The hallway stood empty. "There's no one there", said I. "He's gone", Holli said with a tremor. Instantly my mind shot to last night and the man I had seen! Grabbing Holli's hand I pulled her off the stairs and back around the corner until we were standing on the carpet in front of the television. "Maybe it was your brother playing a joke Holli." Biting my lip in the confusion. "I saw him last night like that", I said.

Catching myself gritting my teeth, I forced myself to swallow. Willing my jaw to relax. Unpleasantly, I thought again of the deformed looking stranger I had seen in Holli's bedroom last night. He had obviously been wearing a Halloween mask. Washing over me was the desire for the man to have just been a bad dream. Was he the same size as Holli's brother? It seemed he was so much bigger; more muscle and thickness. Yet perhaps fear caused my imagination to remember the man bulky and formidable in comparison to Holli's brother. My initial reaction was to dismiss the event. Ignore it. No doubt that after all it was simply my friend's brother. Probably snickering to himself even now. Thinking how funny he is, certainly. While poor Holli stood stunned and shaking. Squeezing her hand and wrapping my arm around her shoulders. Rubbing her back. I said, "There should be a law against mean jokes." Holli's eyes welled with tears she fought to pull back into her tear ducts and save her from embarrassment. Leaning gently I kissed her cheek and patted her hair. "Come on….", I encouraged, "It's nothing to worry about."

"But Suzanna, I *saw*…"

She *saw*?! Alarm washed over me again. Calm yourself, Suzanna. "I'm sure if there was anyone there it was probably just your brother." I kissed her soft cheek again. "Come on Holli, let's go get your jump-rope."

"I don't want to go up there."

"We'll just run up and get the rope and then run back down and jump-rope outside. Okay? And if you see anything that scares you we'll run back downstairs and we won't go up there again. Okay?"

"Okay." She nodded timidly then wiped her face with the palm of her hand.

Tickling Holli's ribs I smiled at her. "Can I get a smile?" Wriggling the tips of my fingers softly into her rib bones again. Holli broke into a grin and giggled. "Okay. Let's go get that rope. It'll be alright; I'll hold your hand."

"Okay."

And so holding hands we began to make our way to her upstairs bedroom. Holli paused when we reached once again the third stair up on the stairway. Her eyes flashed with fear. This is the precise stair she had been standing on when she saw what was surely her brother playing a bad joke. "It's alright", I told her, "I've got your hand. We'll just grab the jump rope then run back down stairs. Then later on we'll get your brother *back*." I pulled her past the third stair and onto the fourth. Holli's face tightened with anxiety. I thought perhaps if I could just make her laugh. "And later on we'll grab your brother up and kick him in the shins!"—I teased.

Holli laughed and then asked, "What's a shin?"

Lifting my leg up and pointing to the part above my foot I answered: "It's this lower part of your leg here." She laughed again. It seemed obvious to me by her smile that she was going to be okay. We'd get our jump rope and then play. "Want to run Holli?" (She nodded affirmative.) "Okay!", I hollered, "Let's go!" Holli was smiling and things felt normal again. We sprinted up the stairs and paused at the phone booth at the corner of the upstairs near Holli's room. It was an actual working phone booth in metals coated in red paint. The door to the phone booth could be folded open or closed.

"I love this phone booth! Does it really work?"

Amused at my reaction Holli snickered sweetly. "Yes, Suzanna, it's a *phone booth*."

"So it works?"

"Yes."

"Really?!"

"Yes."

"I mean, can you make phone calls and stuff and have them actually go through?" "Yes."

"Holli, can we go inside?" "Come on." Holli opened the vertically folding door. We slipped inside and I closed the door behind us. We were a perfect fit. With room left over to scoot around and shift positions. I adored the phone booth! A red and gray steel dream come true for a fun loving child. Desire to play with the phone booth uncontrollably flooded through my body causing my toes to tingle and my breathing to tighten. Wanting to play with the jump rope, however, seemed even more exciting. It was a tough decision. "Holli? Can we play 'phone booth' later?" Holli smiled at me with a tense uncomfortable pull to her face. Holli answered--"Yea, let's get the rope now. I don't want to be upstairs right now anyway." She opened the booth door and waved for me to follow as she stepped out.

"Okay", I responded.

Holli glanced over her shoulder at me as she quickly made her way into the bedroom. "The phone booth has a different number so we can call each other from the house."

I was flabbergasted! "Really?!"

Holli ran to her closet and began digging through the toys on the closet floor. Bending on my knees next to her I helped her turn the toys sideways and upside-down. Holli's eyes widened as she reached beneath a pile of dolls and extracted the rope. "Got it!", she proclaimed. Without saying anything else, Holli simply hopped up and ran out of the room. "Wait up!"—I followed after Holli. When I got to the top of the stairway I looked down to see Holli standing on the fourth stair and gazing with trepidation at the third stair below her.

"Holli, are you alright?"

"Evil." She whispered.

"You think that the third stair is evil?" (She nodded yes to my question.) Gently but quickly I stepped down the stairs until I was at Holli's side. "Holli the third stair isn't evil." Placing my hand on her back for reassurance. "It's just where you were standing when you saw something that scared you. Your brother." She didn't budge, and didn't seem as if she ever would. Passing Holli I hopped onto the second stair. Turning back to face Holli I took hold of both her hands. I spoke to Holli with assurance, "I'm going to help you." Holli was still looking down at the third stair in frozen anxiety. "Look at me, Holli. Look up. Look at my eyes." Holli looked up and into my gaze. "On the count of three you jump over the third stair and onto the second stair, with me. Alright?" Without her gaze leaving my eyes Holli nodded. Squeezing her hands tighter I counted: "One. Two. Three! Jump!" Attempting to lift Holli's body with the strength of my arms, I pulled up at her waist. She lifted both knees and leapt onto the second stair. Wrapping my arm around her shoulder I gave her a squeeze and guided her off of the stairs. We ran into the living room. I tugged her onto the couch where we both sat down and looked at each other.

"So Holli." I patted her leg. "You want to go outside to jump?"

"Yes. Can I go first?" Holli rose from the couch.

"Sure." Lifting from the couch I trotted over to the back door. Waiting there for Holli to catch up, I hummed a tune. I let her be the one to open the door. We played jump rope for at least forty-five minutes. Then we abandoned the rope to pretend that we were mermaids and the concrete porch was the deep blue sea. We were having so much fun that only playtime mattered at all; we didn't talk about the man in the devil/demon mask (whom we figured was Holli's brother anway.) A soft and slightly chilled breeze began to blow through our hair on this sunny day in Oklahoma. Baby-blue sky spattered by balls of cotton shaped clouds. We ended playing mermaids laying on our backs on the patio looking up at the sky.

"That cloud looks like an elephant." Holli pointed upward towards the vast sky. "Do you see it?"

"I'm not sure."

"*That* one!"

Scanning the heavens; a large fluffy puffy cloud caught my eye. When I tilted my head to the right I could see it. "Oh! I see it. Yes it does look like an elephant."

"Your turn Suzanna."

"Well?"

"What do you see?"

"Clouds."

"No, I mean what does one of the clouds look like to you."

"Well?" Pausing to consider the different shapes and sizes of clouds overhead. "Cotton balls."

"Cotton balls?!" Holli's voice sounded shrill and surprised in a disappointed sort of way.

"Yes." Turning my head to look at Holli I saw that her eyes were squinted and her nose wrinkled up. The expression on her face made me want to laugh. "Cotton balls."

"Cotton balls Suzanna?"

"Cotton balls."

"Okay." Holli looked back up at the sky. "Oh come on! Look at that one!" Holli pointed to a long wispy one. "That looks like a ship! Now are you gonna lay there and tell me that doesn't look like a ship?"

"Yea, it does look like a ship. That wispy thin part on top looks like sails."

"Exactly"--Holli said with satisfaction. "Now its your turn."

"Turn for what?"

"You know. Now come on. Tell me what the clouds look like to you."

I paused to consider the sky. Squinting my eyes and tilting my head. Shrugging my shoulders. Finally I made my decision and answered honestly: "Cotton balls."

Holli made a snuffling sound from her nose. She looked over at me and shook her head. Folding her fingers together and resting her interlaced hands on her chest. Gazing at the turquoise sky. Holli pursed her lips as we lay next to one another in silence. "Suzanna?"

"Uh huh?"

"You want to play something else?"

"Okay." I sat up and crossed my legs under in an Indian style. "What do you want to play Holli?"

"You wanna play phone booth now?" Holli stood up.

"Yes!" I leapt to my feet and chirped with a thrill.

We were two best friends sprinting to the door and passing beyond it and through the living room. Sliding on our feet around the broom closet and almost a full run up the stairs. We both caught our mistake when we turned to look at each other from the door of the phone booth.

Holli rubbed her nose and blinked. "I wanted to go first."

Unsure of myself in this particular moment I could feel my feet shuffling. "I kind of wanted to be in the phone booth first."

"You can use it after me. We'll take turns and trade places. Please? I want the phone booth first."

That sounded fair to me. "Okay." Swirling around I headed back to the stairway. "Oh! I don't know what number to call."

Holli leaned over the railing to speak to me while I descended the stairs. "I'll call you, Suzanna."

"Alright." Taking a few more steps down the stairs before stopping. Looking back up at Holli above. "Where? Where are you going to call me?"

"From the phone in the kitchen."

"Oh yea!" Now I ran full speed down the rest of the stairs, around the corner, and into the kitchen. The phone in the kitchen was too high up for me to reach it. It was that new kind of phone that could hang on the wall. Grabbing a barstool I pulled it up to the telephone. Climbing onto the seat, I rested on my knees. I fingered the phones long, light-blue, curly cord in anticipation. Then it rang! Tentatively I lifted the handle. I felt so nervous as I brought the phone to my ear. What if someone else was calling and it wasn't Holli? "Hello?"

Holli's voice came through crisp and clear. "Hello Suzanna! Isn't this groovy?!"

"Wow! How groovy! You actually called me! I didn't know you could call another phone in the same house."

"It's a different number. Okay, let's hang up and I'll call you again. Only this time let's pretend that we're neighbors."

"Yea. And Holli? Let's pretend that we live in houses down the block from each other and we always have lunch, so you're calling to see if I want to have lunch. Okay?"

"Okay." Holli hung up the phone with excitement coursing through her veins. This was fun!

I waited for the dial tone before hanging up the kitchen phone. Then I shivered with anticipation. I decided that every house should come with its own phone booth. When it rang I involuntarily jumped a bit. Once again I felt that wild sense of adventure. Was it Holli calling or was it someone else? Placing the receiver to my ear and mouth. I questioned: "Hello?"

"Hello neighbor!" It was Holli. "How are you today?"

"Very fine. And how are you?"

"Just lovely today dear."

"Miss Holli, would you like to come over for tea and cucumber sandwiches?"

"Cucumber sandwiches?!"

"Yes. They're very fancy."

"Oh." Holli giggled. "Yes. I would love to darling. I loooooove cucumber sandwiches."

"Yes daaaarling. And I simply adore tea. Tut tut I say. Tut tut. Shall we make it a tea party?"

"Oh my, yes. We simply must make it a tea party. I'll bring my china teacups. Tut tut to you too…*what does that mean*!?" Holli laughed then choked on her own spit. She coughed and cleared her throat. "What does 'tut tut' mean Suzanna? I mean, neighbor?"

"Ummmmm…" I'd heard it used on a television show. But as far as meaning? I wasn't sure it meant anything at all. Just as I was about to respond a blood curdling shriek pierced my ear and sent an electric shock of fear to raise all the tiny hairs on my arms and neck. Holli had screamed horribly. "Holli? Holli! Are you all right?" There was no answer. Is she just playing? Has she been harmed? Kidnapped? Did someone just kill her?! I felt I was going out of my mind with panic for her. "Holli! Holli!"—I called into the phone receiver.

Holli stammered, "I s..s..saw him again! Suzanna he came out of that room and stood in the hallway! And he looked at me! And then he went into that other room!"

I breathed a sigh of relief at the sound of her voice; but her words scared me. I thought again of the man I had seen last night wearing the demon mask. Holding the receiver in both trembling hands I shouted to her. "Holli! Hold on! I'm coming to get you!" I dropped the receiver to let it clonk against the wall and dangle from its long cord. Suddenly I turned around and grabbed the receiver back into my hands again. Bent over the phone I hollered to Holli again: "I'm coming to get you!" Then I dropped the phone piece again. My heart, which was racing far too fast, felt painfully swollen. I could hear each wet thudding heart beat swoosh loudly like a drum under water inside my ears.

As I rounded the corner from the living room my sense of horror caused me to have the illusion that I was running in slow motion. Gasping slowly for breath, my heart slammed.

The illusion ended when I reached the stairs. Yet each step on every stair sounded low toned and impossibly loud. As if I were stepping one foot after the other on top of an echo chamber! *Thump! Thump! Thump!*

Quicker than I would have ever imagined I flew up the stairs and along the hallway with long reaching strides of my tiny legs. Holli was not in the phone booth! Where was she? What has happened to her? "Holli!" A weak meek 'here' came from the position of the booth. Slamming open the booth's sliding door I barely took in two seconds of seeing Holli huddled on the floor before I grabbed her arm. Holding her shoulders in my left arm I gently pushed and guided Holli in a half-run through the hall and down the stairs. Once in the living room I pulled Holli with me to sit her down on the couch. I sat next to her and gave her a hug. I was angry with her brother. This really had scared us! Scared us both! But remember Suzanna how Holli said the man looked too large to be her brother? You thought the man was too large too? What if it wasn't her brother? I shook the thought away. It was too awful to contemplate just then.

Holli stammered: "I…I saw…"

"Hold on Holli. Don't tell me what he looked like just yet."

"But I'm serious Suzanna! I am not making this up!"

"I know. I believe you." Rising from the couch I walked quickly to the counter near the phone and began to search for what I needed. Pausing, I looked at the receiver dangling from its cord. Picking the receiver up and stretching onto the stool I hung up the phone. Opening a low cabinet I scanned over its contents.

"What are you looking for?" Holli's voice sounded like her hysteria from the fright was beginning to wear away.

"A couple of pieces of paper and a couple of pencils."

"Why?"

"Because I'm pretty sure I saw the same guy last night. But how will I know if we both start talking about what he looked like? I want you to draw what he looked like on a piece of paper, while I draw what I saw on another piece of paper. But we can't be where we can see what each other are drawing. Besides, it'll be fun."

"Will we show them to each other?"

"Yes."

"My mom keeps pens and papers in that drawer there." Holli came over to help me. She opened a thin drawer directly under the counter and extracted a notebook and two pens. Pulling two sheets from the notebook; she gave me one sheet and held on to the other.

"Are you alright Holli? You feel okay?" I felt so worried for her.

Holli nodded. "Yes. I'm alright. I still feel kind of scared though. Are you scared?"

"Actually Holli, I feel a whole lot better knowing your okay…but..kind of…yes." Dragging a barstool to one side of the tall bar table and another barstool far to the other side of it. Walking up to Holli I held out my palm. She put a pen in it. I then went over to climb onto the far barstool to cozy up against the tall table. "Ready?"

"Yea." Holli climbed onto her seat.

"Okay then. Draw what you saw but don't tell me anything about it until you're through." We both began to draw and I thought to myself how very much I liked drawing and coloring.

Who knows how long we drew when time didn't matter to us anyway. Yet Holli and I were tickled and amused over the sweet whimsy of drawing. We both finished our drawings at about the same time.

"I'm ready", I said.

"Yep? I'm done too."

"We'll show each other our pictures on the count of three. One. Two. Three!"

We flipped our drawings to face each other. They looked the same. Sliding off my seat I carried my picture over to where Holli sat. Dragging a close barstool just a foot over I was able to climb up and sit right down next to Holli and place my drawing next to hers. We studied them together. We'd both drawn the same individual. "It looks like the devil", whispered Holli.

Patting Holli's back and kissing her cheek I pulled back a shudder and said, "Yes. Well, it's not."

Breath. Just breath. We stared at the drawings.

Suddenly the phone rang and we both jumped in our seats and screamed at the same time! Then we both started giggling over having screamed at the same time. Holli hopped off the barstool and I followed suit. The two of us went over to the phone and stared at it. It was still ringing. "Answer it", Holli commanded.

Climbing onto the stool next to the wall I picked up the receiver and held onto it as I slid back down to stand on the floor. Holli and I both put our ears together against the receiver and I asked, "Hello?"

A gruff grumbling voice like that which I had heard the previous night came out of the phone and into both of our little ears, saying, "You two girls sure are cute."

Holli and I both screamed for some reason and we bounced up and down on our feet. I shook the receiver out in front of me as if I had just picked up a snake, then I tossed the phone to Holli. She grabbed it. Then Holli shook the phone in a similar way and we both screamed again while bouncing up and down on our feet. Jumping up high and swinging her arm, Holli hung up the phone. The two of us then ran screaming around the corner, past the broom closet, and up to the front door. I slipped my feet into Holli's flip-flops laying near the front door. Holli's brother swung open the front door to walk inside just as we were hustling up to it, so Holli and I ran smack dab into her brother; slamming into his stomach. We blinked at him, then we both started talking at the same time. "Did you have a mask… There's a guy with a mask… Somebody just called… And we drew pictures…"

We stopped talking when Holli's brother grasped Holli's head and playfully shook it. Then he grabbed her neck in the crook of his arm and rubbed at the hair on the top of her head with the fist of his other hand. He said, "You two are dweebs; you dweeby freaks."

Holli pulled at his hips and I pulled at his arm as we shuffled him outside of the open door and onto the sidewalk. Holli and I started talking at the same time again. "He was bigger than you….He had a mask…. Do you have a mask…. I saw him last night…. I saw him upstairs… Then the phone rang…"

"Slow down dweeby freaks!"—commanded Holli's brother. "What's the matter with you two? You little shrimps are dweeby freaks."—he said teasingly. "Go play in the water hose or something." He stepped back inside the house and slammed the door shut behind himself without looking back.

Holli and I gawked at the closed front door for a moment. Then we went and sat down with our backs against the house, feeling disappointed that nothing was going to be done about the situation. It didn't take long however to decide that playing in the water from the water hose sounded like a great idea. We got soaking wet playing games with the water from the hose. After we grew tired of playing with the water, we played around the barn and horse corral. Eventually we both wound up back in the house and on the living room couch. Both of us were feeling exhausted and sleepy as we lounged on the couch. A deep refreshing nap seemed to be calling.

THREE

HELL'S ANGELS AND A TUB FULL OF ICE

"**W**AKE UP!"

The sound of Holli's mother's voice came floating through a cloudy hazy dreamless sleep. What was she saying?

"Hey! *Wake up!*"

Holli and I had fallen asleep snuggled together on the couch. Opening my eyes I blinked up into the face of Holli's mom smiling at us as she leaned forward and alternately shook my shoulder and then Holli's shoulder.

"Wake up girls! Suzanna, your mother is here." Mrs. Hunter turned to make her way back to the front door. Holli and I had gathered ourselves up and were following behind Mrs. Hunter. We were practically on her heels when she shouted, "Suzanna! Your mother…" Turning to look behind her Mrs. Hunter yipped in mid-sentence to see us standing directly behind her. "Oh!"—Mrs. Hunter exclaimed. She hadn't realized we were padding right behind her. "Suzanna", she said, "Where are your shoes?" Good question.

What parent hasn't gone a thousand times to pick their child up from a friends house and a thousand times over asked 'Where are your shoes?' It would be a good five or ten minute search before I found them and my mother and I could leave.

My mother had said that Holli's father was in the military. Was he? She said they move a lot which worried me. I didn't want to lose track of my friend. Especially since my own family also moved a lot. My family are such interesting people. I'm terribly proud of the many strengths my family has. My brother with his curly brown hair and good looks, whom would have the eventual good fortune to have eye surgery and go from legally blind to not even having to wear glasses at all, has strength and stamina that I view as practically super-human. Yes, he's that determined and strong and amazing. As an adult he would come to help a poor New Mexico couple who lived in a forested rural no-where. He would personally be the one to deliver that couple's baby! He would save a man from choking to death by performing an emergency tracheotomy at a local community bar! Also, when he became an adult, he would literally rush into the midst of a horrible multicar crash scene and he'd *save lives* until ambulances could arrive. And after the emergency teams arrived at the accident he would search with a little child whom had survived the crash to locate the child's beloved pet dog. There are people who would not be alive in this world if it weren't for the fact that my brother exists. My brother, who can play just about any instrument and writes his own songs.

My sister would in her adulthood become named Woman of the Year in the state she lived in. She would marry and share with her husband in a prominent and successful law firm. Her children would have her red hair and she would have a lake house that once belonged to a famous ball player. My sister would be such an inspiration to others in her great success.

Yet at this stage of events, it is still around 1969 and my brother and sister are still children.

My family are all highly educated people. My father would study for his dissertation sitting next to a man who would eventually become famous for writing the book "Black Like Me". They would have lunch often. My father would go to school with the singer Roy Orbison in Texas and share Christmas cards with Orbison for many years before the singers death. He would complete his doctorates degree and eventually serve over 30 years as a Methodist minister. We would live in drab cookie-cutter parsonages and move every year or two so that he could help better establish another church. My Dad's mother, my marvelous unconditionally loving Grandmother, was the grandchild of one of Robert E. Lee's daughters…as children we were told stories about that anyhow.

My mother would complete her masters degree and teach for over thirty years. Eventually she would work the regions educational system, even though retired, making or breaking a new teachers recruitment….a mixture of always a 'Southern Belle' yet hard working. She would marry the man who would be my very kind step-father. A man who was a rancher. She would enjoy opera and symphony and church activities. She would give advice like, "You may find yourself poor someday Suzanna, but you don't have to look like it and nobody has to know." And "Except for a smile, try not to make facial expressions. Queens and princess's would use that trick in order not to get so many wrinkles." Or "Never go out in public without looking your best." Good advice indeed. My mother's father, Early, was either the singer Eddie Arnold's older brother or his cousin. Now which was it?

Yes it worried me back then in 1969 that my mother had said Holli's parents moved a lot. How could I possibly bare losing my best friend to a move? But society is always moving along and going through changes isn't it. No-one goes through life without changes coming about and moving our lives and our perceptions. The Vietnam war moved an entire society throughout many changes. In only 1972 the United States would return Okinawa to Japan. Yet not all changes are always perceived as painful. Changes in entertainment can move society along without much hurt or frustration with television shows such as seen in 1971 as 'Star Trek' and the 'Sonny and Cher' show. With music changing beat and adding a new flavor to musical choice. In 1971 such songs as "Riders on the Storm" by The Doors, "What's Goin' On" by Marvin Gaye, and "Me and Bobby McGee" by Janis Joplin, were released into society bringing about some changes in sound. Society can even mourn in groups, as did many individuals when Jim Morrison of the band The Doors died on July 3rd in 1971. For myself, one of the greatest changes in my life was shared with millions of others watching their televisions when man first walked on the moon in 1969.

The moon landing was soon to be televised. Man would walk on the moon! "No, don't change the channel."—I urged to my big sister whom had just come back home from a friends house.

"But it's the news", said my big sister as she raised up and removed her hand from the knob on the TV set. Her nose temporarily crinkled up in an expression of confusion. She placed a strand of her long wavy red-brown hair behind an ear and wiggled her knees that peeped from below the hem of her dress. She would have liked the hem-line to have been much higher. My sister had had quite an argument with our mother about the length of that dress since everyone else was wearing those 'horrid mini-skirts'. Yet my sister wouldn't mind looking 'horrid' as long as she looked horrid along with all her other girl friends. That's only natural. I sat on the couch wearing my bright purple hot pants suit and my white go-go boots. I had settled breathlessly onto the tan tweed-like couch to await the magical moment which would make human history.

"You can't turn it off or change the channel", I said to my big sister. "That's the channel the moon walk will come on. The channel with the news. A man is going to walk on the moon tonight and they're showing it on television!"

"Yes I know, I'm going over to Tommy's house to watch it", my sister said with a shrug. She was seven years older than I. Yet something in the tone of her voice made me think they weren't really going to watch it from his house. From someplace else perhaps? The door-bell rang not long after my big sis' had begun to freshen her face and brush her hair. It was Tommy. I followed her to the door and I remember thinking that she and her boyfriend looked so tall. With a wave of her hand and a quiet goodbye my sister left the house and I resumed sitting on the couch. Watching and waiting. When would the magical moment of human kinds exquisite dive into the waters of science and history come into play? Why was it taking so long? The anticipation was absolutely palpable.

Flying into the house after a mild slam of the door then disappearing into his room quite briefly, my curly haired brother (five years older than myself) replied to my curious wonderment that he was going to a friends house. Leaving as quickly as he came. Dusk began to paint its shadowed veil across the landscape outside. Peering out the window to the right of the couch I could see the delicate softening of the light. Where was my father? Rarely did I see my father except for the actual day of Sunday when he preached with perfect sermons at the churches pulpit. Most of the time he was gone 'on the road', spending any actual leftover time home from the pulpit in his back yard garden. Magnificently green thumbed my father the preacher could grow corn, tomatoes (which he called 'tommy-toes'), cucumbers, rhubarb, and carrots, as if by command. Yet mostly he was gone because of his busy schedule. Was he here or on the road? Tip-toeing cautiously and tapping the small fleshy tips of my fingers together I stood at the closed door to fathers office. Rap-tap-tap.

I heard my fathers voice: "Come in."

Pushing the office door open with the index finger of my left hand and poking my head inside. "You're here?" Such a silly question. An obvious statement really. After-all, I was looking straight at him.

"Not for long", father replied.

Desk lamp illuminating his papers as he shuffled them. He seemed in quite the hurry.

"A man is going to walk on the moon."

"I know that Suzanna."

"Where are you going?" I stepped inside the office and walked over to his desk. So many papers. So many books.

"I'm meeting a man from the church."

"Ohhhh." Glancing at the ceiling then down to the floor. Watching my little toes grasp hold of the brownish green shag carpet. "Do we have any salt and lemons? I'm hungry."

"I don't know." Father still hadn't looked up from his papers as he shuffled them around again. "Why don't you go look in the refrigerator. The salt would be in the cabinet." Father stood up and grabbed his suit jacket, a book, and some papers. He was definitely preoccupied. He still hadn't made eye contact yet. "If your hungry ask your big sister to get you something." He smoothed back his dark brown balding hair with the palm of his hand. Flipping the lamplight off he moved with long strides out of his office and through the hallway.

"But...uh.."—I stammered.

"Honey I've got to go." And with that father rushed out the front door.

Once again returning to the couch, I worried I might have missed the man walk on the moon during my brief stay in father's office. But no, there wasn't enough time for that to happen of course.

Darkness began to spread its soothing night-time blanket across the once bright outside world. The moon began to shine moon-shadows and moon-sparkles upon the trees, flowers, bushes, and grass. Grass still green. Flowers still blooming in defiance of closing up and hiding away their fragrant gifts this evening. Wasn't the moon full that night in Oklahoma? I continued to watch and wait.

Coming in was my mother, through the garage door which led into the kitchen. I could see from the couch, my point of eager ministration where I held silent vigil for the lunar landing, that my mother was hurried and strained. Her face bore a look of frustration. Opening the refrigerator she pulled out something in a round dish that was covered in tin foil. Lifting from the couch I padded over until I stood at the edge of the kitchen and the tiny dining area. My curiosity perked.

"What's that?" I asked. Hunger rumbled my stomach with a fervent biting pang. The munchies had hold of me.

"A casserole."

"Do you eat it?"

"Of course you eat it Suzanna! What else would it be for?"

"But its caster-oil?"

"What? No! *Casserole* not caster-oil."

"What's it made of?"

"Rice. Chicken."

"Can I have some?"

"No, I'm late for a lady's meeting at the church."

Mother exited hurriedly and half panting from the same garage door she had just seconds ago appeared from. Waiting a few minutes before I padded through the kitchen and up to the garage door. I peeked to see if indeed mother's car was gone. I half expected to see her perfectly brushed short brown hair and the top of her blouse as she sat in her car. But she was already gone. The garage stood empty. Breathing a sigh of relief through pursed lips I was happy to watch the lunar walk all by myself. I'd been distraught that certainly some drama would ruin everything as my family members drowned out the historical televised moment with yet another ridiculous row. Alone. Breathing out relief once again. Peace and quiet to watch this magnanimous event. Soon the broadcast would take place! How exciting!

I sat on the carpet in front of the television set and watched the event as it took place! Heart beating.

Beating out great swooshes of precious blood into my veins. Pumping. Pulsing. Tingling rolling up my neck and down my shoulders. Astonishment and awe rolling like waves of heat through my eyes and over the top of my head. Reverence inflaming my soul with its intoxicating thrill. "Oh yes", I thought with heavy smoky amazement; "Someone stands on the moon at this exact moment, while I am watching them here on this planet called earth. How huge space is! Wow!" How huge indeed. It was utterly shocking to me as I contemplated it.

When at last the broadcast was over I hoped and prayed no one from my family would come home before I did one last thing. I wanted this time to myself. Going outside I laid down onto my back in the short silken grass and looked up at the moon. I thought to myself how someone stood on that moon just then and was looking at the planet I was on. Looking at earth in much the same way I was currently looking at the moon. That night I would sleep in my bed filled with a fitful excitement. I could hardly stop thinking about space travel long enough to rest my head into my pillow and get some sleep.

My family would travel from state to state in a cramped car come the next year. Moving from church to church. How much more exciting if we could have moved from one place to another by rocket ship like the astronauts! But no, my family had to travel by car like everybody else. My father would minister in many places during 1970. He would preach at the round outdoor 'chapel' at the Sequoia National Forest. A forest where the magnificent Sequoia grew gigantic for thousands of years. They became my favorite and most beloved tree. We would also see Yellowstone park where my father would similarly minister there. My father would preach and then we'd go for hikes. Our entire family hiking in matching psychedelic print jumpsuits. Ponchos worn when evening waned chilly. Roasting hot dogs and marshmallows on sticks over an open fire. Singing songs. It was a lot of fun!

We traveled all five of us in the car packed like sardines with our half coyote pet dog who continually passed the most outrageously stinky gas ever. The dog, named Soaky, stuck his nose out the car window while passing the noxious gas. Soaky was the only one who could get any fresh air! He had his dog ears pulled back flat against his head and his eyes were wide with an expression that can only be described as apologetic and embarrassed. We were all annoyed by the stink in the car, but couldn't help but laugh uncontrollably at the situation. *What had that dog eaten*!? Perhaps I shouldn't have shared my potato chips with him?

We ate a lot of sandwiches and potato chips in the car when we traveled. We got to see Pikes Peak but not before having to pull the car over half way up the mountain. We had all become sick and dizzy with carbon monoxide poisoning while in the car. Parked on the side of the unbelievably steep drive of Pikes Peak, we waited for roadside service to help us. We didn't let this stop us from making it to the peaks top.

Never will I forget my father pouring salted peanuts in a bottle of cola and how he made it look like it tasted so good. Of course I tried it but found that to my taste it was absolutely awful.

Big Sis', Mabel, and I had a running competition on who had the best suntan on our legs. The competition ended when my sister won by using an instant tanning foam that turned her skin orange and wore off only in misshaped blotches. During this period of history my older brother, Rustle, always called me 'sausage' and he wouldn't tell me why.

My favorite time spent in the car was when we sang songs. Beautiful and sweet trilled my mothers singing voice. Especially when we sang the song "Edelweiss". We were not a happy family, but we did have occasional happy moments. I had thought these travels with my father ministering would end with us going back to stay in Springs. I had been a sparkly winged angel for Christmas at the Springs church. I had been a cheerleader and baton twirler for the pee-wee athletic games. I had rolled down the big grassy hill on the side of the Springs church with the other children. How could we not be going back to stay there? My worst fear of losing my friend Holli Hunter would come with the blow that Springs would be a thing of the past. My father was going to be sent yet again to a different church in a different city, so even more changes and traveling were to take place. My first love had been Juan Sanchez when I was three years old and we lived in New Mexico. Now I would leave both my best friend Holli and also my second love in the move from Springs. My second love was the boy next door to our Springs house. His name was Michael Al and he and I were both five years old. Michael's father had played for a famous baseball team, and they had a trampoline in their back yard. His mother was kind and pretty. With Michael I

experienced my very first kiss and my second serious regret. Michael had jumped hard while we were on the trampoline and I fell on my back and lost my breath. He pounced on me and gave me my very first kiss. I slapped him. This was my regret. I felt so badly that I had slapped him.

My family had traveled away and said goodbye to New Mexico where my brother had gotten so terribly sick (along with many other children in the area) after eating fall-out snow. The result of nuclear testing.

Now we were saying goodbye once again in order to move to Oklahoma City. Having exchanged address's I tearfully hoped Holli Hunter and I would stay in contact. Blood sisters must know one another for all their lives!

While our parents moved the hoard of boxes to Oklahoma City, my sister and brother and I went to stay a few days with our Aunt Net and Uncle Troy. The stay with Aunt Net and Uncle Troy promised to prove interesting and fun. After all, they lived on a ranch in Texas. And they had horses! It was a bright sunny day for travel when we kids transferred from our parents green and pale fake-wood station wagon to our Aunt and Uncle's car. We met them in the middle of the empty Texas countryside of flat land and mesquite trees. My brother and sister sat in the back seat of our Aunt and Uncle's car. I sat in the front seat nudged between my Aunt who was on my right in the passenger side and my Uncle who was to my left at the wheel. Aunt Net's heavy breasts seemed an oddity to me. She had a heavy-set frame which never the less complimented her short brown hair which she wore in waves upon her head. Uncle Troy drove all of us to the ranch without speaking for a long while. Occasionally he would run one of his large hands over his balding head or over his big round belly. My siblings and I would probably enjoy our few days stay at our Aunt and Uncle's ranch. It would be settling into another new house in Oklahoma City that would be difficult.

Uncle Troy sat driving down the vacant Midwest road. Green fields on either side of the gravel and dirt road. A spotting of cows here and there. Bright sunny day. An extremely large bird flying up in the sky. Its gorgeous wing-span perfectly in view from the windshield. I watched it flying from my place in the middle of the front seat. The large bird soaring with the wind for what seemed a long time. Pointing to it my Uncle spoke for the first time saying, "That bird seems almost as if it were flying at the same rate as the car."

"As if following our car from up ahead." Remarked Aunt Net.

"Yep." Said Uncle Troy as we all looked up into the pale blue sky. "Look at that", he continued, "It's a hawk. It looks like it's still in the precise same spot in our view that it had been in since we first spotted it."

"It's been a while." Agreed Auntie. "I was thinking the same thing."

Glancing into the back at my siblings I noticed for some reason that we were all staring at the bird first open-mouthed then closed-mouthed and back to open-mouthed. This struck me as extremely silly looking and I giggled. Uncle Troy looked at his watch. Time passed much more quickly than I would have expected for even though it seemed just a few minutes had passed Uncle Troy looked at his watch a second time and announced that thirty minutes had gone by already. The huge lovely bird was still in the exact same spot of our view as before. Perhaps it *was* travelling at the same speed as the car!

Quietly, I began singing a song for the hawk. A song under my breath of what I felt as a deep love for the bird. A child's love and appreciation of its beauty.

I sang: "And pretty hawk would you teach me all you know so that I can fly in my heart." I continued to quietly sing until I could think of no other words, so I decided to end my song by singing "Amen."

Suddenly the hawk made a quick turn. Its wings were held out straight and unmoving. The bird soared in a perfect unwavering line. Not flying even slightly from one side nor to the other. Not a single wobble. Everyone in the car leaning forward in curiosity and awe as the hawk traveled closer towards our direction. Closer to the car. Closer still. Too close.

Aunt Net screamed. Next came shouts from both the adults. A loud furious hollering babble. Smattering of fear sliding across my spine at the sound of their frightened voices. A primal sound; uncontrolled.

Here is the point where everything took place in complete slow motion for me. Pure slow motion of every movement before my eyes. Staring forward I looked directly into the hawks eyes as it came towards the middle of the front windshield. Eyes the color of clear amber gemstones. We had a mutual gaze the bird and I. Eye to eye. An odd and inexplicable sensation of pure unconditional love and of a mystical awe enveloped me as the hawk and I stared eye to eye. Time stood still. Another sensation that I can only describe as an awed unconditional love washed in a wave through my body and mind, and it seemed to this small child that the hawk loved me back. A sweet sensation flowing through me in this moment frozen in time. The hawk and I still staring eye to eye. Such clear amber eyes. Then at last a slow motion movement as the hawks beak touched the glass in the middle of the windshield right in front of me. In this slow motion I was seeing things in, it looked as if the hawks beak were slowly sliding through the glass. Very slowly. Large and tiny pieces of glass rolled very, very, slowly past the hawk's head.

Shards of glass rolling over and around slowly. Bits of glass suspended and barely spinning. Glass, looking like ice-cubes, held in suspension.

The hawk still looking into my eyes. Freeze frame of its pure amber eyes. The hawk's body remained rigid while it lowered itself.

Slow rolling luster from pieces of glass reflecting sunlight, like crystals hanging in the air. The hawk within inches from my face. Now the hawk's beak touching the top of my nose. Keeping my eyes open I lifted my face upward. The hawk slid in delicate slow motion across my face. I could feel the weight of the huge bird pressing slightly on my face. Feeling the hawk's chocolate brown soft feathers brushing velvety against my chin. Fuzzy warm feathers caressing my lips. Closing my eyes in a slow motion blink. Downy fluffy feathers of the great birds body rubbing across my cheeks and nose.

The magnificent bird pressing its satiny feathered breast against my face. Keeping my eyes open to fully drink in the still life moment which felt like a sweet forever. Laggard flowing movement as the hawk's chest smoothed over my open eyes. I saw nothing but chocolate brown feathers for what seemed minutes held frozen in time. Slowly. Slower still. Brown feathered neck smoothing across my forehead. I reached to touch the hawk with my fingers. Reaching up for the bird with my small hand while I stared at its soft brown feathers. Reaching in slow motion. With my eyes wide open I softly pressed my hand against the bird as it was touching my face. Touching his soft feather underbelly with my fingertips as he flew across me. Pure chocolate colored fuzziness on top of my open eyes. My little fingers swirled into the feathery fluff. I heard nothing but the wind. I was not afraid.

A feeling of all encompassing love and peace flowed and rippled through me as if the feeling itself were something tactile and alive.

Surrounded by slow motion stillness in suspension. Crystal-shine glass hanging like stars all around me in the air.

Stars of glass barely spinning and turning in their slow motion rotation of sparkling suspended animation.

Spectacular span of the bird's *wings* as soft in its touch as a whispered breath colliding lightly against my ears and shoulders. An Indian blanket of warm feathers.

Velvety lower part of the hawk's tender belly against my face. Then a crispier softness of its tail grazing across my forehead.

No sound, save but precious silence. All in slow motion. The last of the hawk's delicate feathers levitated off of my face like a veil being lifted.

The great hawk with its wings out to its sides turned its body ever so slightly to my left as it made its final gentle pass over the hair on my head. Following the hawk's movement with a turn of my head. I looked over my shoulder and watched as the bird flew head-first through the glass of the rolled up window in the back seat. There was no blood and the bird never bent or altered from its rigidly held position. It was like the huge hawk had simply glided through the glass as if gliding through water. Ice cube like lumps and shards of glass dancing in the air. My brother was sitting in the back seat next to the glass window the bird exited from. Slow dancing, shattering, rolling glass, floating in the air. The hawk disappeared upward into the sky. All at once the glass simply fell down from the air with a fast heavy pull. The slow motion was over. Time had snapped back into place. Shouts and shrieks from the other car passengers. Gritting nerve wracking squeal as Uncle Troy slammed on the car brakes. Everyone jolted forward as the car slung to a screeching halt. Uncle Troy turned off the car and said, "That huge old bird went through the front windshield and smack dab straight through the back window!" As if that really needed stating. Aunt Net and Uncle Troy opened their doors and stepped out of the car. "Out!"—hollered Uncle Troy. "Yep! Come on! Everybody out!"—shouted Aunt Net in agreement and with a wave of her hand. We all carefully piled out of the car. I dusted a multitude of glass off of myself. But I didn't have so much as a scratch. No one had been harmed even in the slightest. My Aunt and Uncle cleaned the car as best they could of shattered glass by brushing it out with newspaper. We wouldn't get to the ranch until late.

I would spend my few days at the ranch enjoying both feeding and playing with the chickens and horses.

Once I rode their younger champagne colored pony. Most especially I enjoyed the big home-made meals which looked like feasts. Not once however could I stop myself from thinking about not seeing Holli Hunter or Michael Al again. I would never again trek across the cul-de-sac street early in the morning to Michael's house. Have Mrs. Al ask if I was hungry and when I answered 'yes' have her feed me

something healthy and tasty. I thought about how Mrs. Al enticed mine and Michael's excitement by giving us a vitamin and telling us it was brain food. Michael and I found it oh so sweet that there was a brain food pill one could take and be smarter. I would pitter patter over to their house in the morning and if there was a test at school I would specifically request a brain food pill. Mrs. Al's hair piled high up on her head. She hadn't even scolded us when she found Michael and I naked on the lounge chairs in the back yard. How had she guessed that we were trying to get suntans without tan lines? Oooo, was she psychic? Laugh out loud!

I could still see her in her car taking us to school in the morning with her arm extended out the open window so as to politely keep we kids from breathing in the smoke from her cigarette. (Later on in life it would truly deeply grieve me that such an honestly kind soul had left this world when I would learn that Mrs. Al had died of bone cancer whilst Michael was still young. It would be my mother who would tell me of the news. And we would be moved from Springs, and even two more other cities, before I would hear the tragic news.) And what of Holli Hunter? Would I ever again dance in the moonlight with my blood sister?

1970 came and went. Yet not without leaving an indelible imprint in my mind of the student protesters killed at Kent University. The congregation mourning at the church. My father reiterating over and over again that "President Nixon is dragging his feet in the war."

When we had moved into the new house in Oklahoma City I remember feeling enthralled that it was a two story and not your regular parsonage. It was a regular house. The neighbors to our left had just moved onto the block also. From some big far away place. California? New York? Looking out the first floor window from the piano room of our two story on the very first night I'd ever spent in the house I could see the neighbors laying on their backs in the grass of their front yard. The whole family! Several of them out there laying on their backs in their front yard staring up at the night sky. The visual plethora of stars were a novelty for them.

How did things go in Oklahoma City? Ploddingly! And strange. Waking myself with an alarm to go to school in the morning. Everyone in my family disappearing from the house to begin their day before I had even woke up. Patting the house key in my pocket as I walked to school. Reassuring myself that I actually had it. The blocks I walked were interesting as I saw and met a few kids going to the self-same elementary school. It was at this school that I rediscovered 'breakfast'. I received a breakfast at school only once but it was never the less a rediscovery. This was nobodys fault of course, we were a busy family. The word breakfast reminded me of a kind and beautiful Mexican baby-sitter/nanny I had when I was three years old. She would make the most fantastic meats that tasted like a mixture of mild peppers and chocolate. "Shocolat" she would say. She would hand these meats to me on a plate and say, "have some breakfast" in the sweetest thickest accent. "Halv sum breek-fust."

Wasn't breakfast also my Grandmother Barns cooking thick slices of ham? Or my Grandmother Arnez making sausage, biscuits, and gravy? I walked into the school each morning used to forever being known as the "new kid" wherever we lived. Although the wide-bodied male principle had called me a "transfer student". Past the open doors of the elementary. Moving to my left and passing the principles office. Commencing upon the hallway. Why were all the schools I went to so beige? Couldn't other colors, something more interesting, be incorporated into the educational environment? Wait. Look at the paper hanging on the art teachers door, there to my right. An art class. Extracurricular. To be admitted to a contest. And what is that enticing smell? Sweet. Full of cinnamon. Bacon? *Warm smells*. Peer to the left.

Two open double wide doors. I was usually barely on time for school anyhow but on this day I was early. Walking through the double wide doors. Tables. Chairs. So much more of the color beige. Busy people to the left cooking more food behind other doors. Open door to the right where a woman behind a tall table sat on a stool wearing a uniform dress and some sort of net on her dark brown hair. Oh yes, I've found the cafeteria in my new school. Somehow I'd never seen it before; probably because I was usually in such a hurry trying not to be late. Timidly walking through the smaller door where the woman sat.

"Have you got your card?" The heavy weighted woman asked and scratched at her hair net.

"Card?" Tapping the tips of my fingers together with worry. "Is that food you have there?" Lifting on my tip toes in hopes of seeing what was there.

"Yes."

"May I have some?"

"Give me your card." Her hand stretched out towards me in expectation. Her forehead creased in wrinkled puzzlement.

"I don't have a card."

"You'll have to get one."

And here you see my body. Small and pale and painfully thin. I looked down at my body and was embarrassed. "Doctors think its allergies", my parents had said to questioning parishioners. Yes they had taken me to doctors. One doctor at a children's hospital had held my arm while taking my blood pressure then left the room a minute afterwards. When he returned to the room there were large red whelps raised in the shape of a hand print where the doctor had touched me. For some reason I felt so terribly embarrassed about the whelps. Why? Oh how I will never forget my deepened embarrassment when the doctor looked up from the whelped spot and said with a glance to my parents, "I think she's allergic to people."

Now here I stood in a school cafeteria looking up at a woman who wanted a card. "Well unless you have money", said the plump cafeteria woman. I felt uncomfortable as some strange concern flashed in her eyes. "If you don't have a card you have to pay money."

"Oh." Looking at my feet to evade the woman's scrutiny I began tapping the tips of my fingers together again. I should go. Leave. Ahhh but that warm smell. Yeast and salt came into play in my nostrils as I drank in the delicious smell. Biscuits. Yes. Cinnamon. And butter? Yes.

"Well thank you", I said, relinquishing my hope and turning away to leave.

"Little girl, wait!"

Stopping at the sound of her voice. Turning my eye in her direction with complete uncomfortable uncertainty of what she wanted me to wait for.

"Come here kid." She gestured a come hither with her fingers. As I stepped tentatively towards her she slid off the stool and on to her feet. She reached towards something too high up for me to see on the buffet.

Next she leaned her thick body in my direction and gingerly placed a sweet roll into my hands. "I shouldn't be doing this kid. I won't be able to do it again, so get yourself a card."

"Yes Mam. Thank you Mam. It's very kind of you." I turned away to leave the cafeteria. Hovering slightly over the sweet roll and keeping my eyes down onto the food and the floor. Hoping no one would ask me how I'd come upon this breakfast. Suddenly I thought about the day my parents had taken my siblings and I to the Ringling Brothers Circus. They'd even bought us cotton candy which puffed around a paper cone like a magnificent edible cloud. Women made all the more gorgeous no matter what their shape or size by the sleek glimmering satin outfits in bright colors all coated in fantastic design with large gemstones of yellow and red with dazzling splashes of rhinestones. Feathers like gifts from multicolored peacocks of another planet. Men in coat-tails and top hats appearing debonair and dashing. Lushly romantic. With animals so huge and lovely as to fill a soul with the joy of awestruck humbleness. What sweetness it would be to snuggle my face into the fur of one of those gigantesque cats. It was all I could do to hold my seat and not sprint with every muscle pushing and pounding as quickly as humanly possible to hide in the circus tent curtains and join them! The thrill of the sweet roll had made me think of the thrill of the circus.

I bit into the sweet roll. Mmm and it was tasty. Just a tiny drizzle of frosting on top. Not too much sweetness. Just the way I like it. Crispy buttery outside. Soft tender moist and spicy with cinnamon on the inside. Warm to the touch. Melting on the tongue. Now my thoughts turned to my Grandmother Barns. Thinking how nothing had tasted so completely warming and satisfying since I'd last delighted in her baby biscuits. Grandmommy Oleta Barns pressing the ingredients together with her own plump hands. Oleta's prodigious curvy body in a smooth flower print dress. Grandmommy Oleta so calm and gentle. She was unconditionally loving to her grandkids and always smiling. Round wire-rimmed glasses and a happy glow inside a body like Mrs. Santa Claus. Her golden honey-brown hair in soft curls at her neck.

Smiling and quietly brushing butter onto the little round baby biscuits before placing them in the oven to bake. Oleta and my Grandaddy Barns (JB) had the walls covered with shelves holding every shape and size and color of bottle. Also antiques, especially clocks and a monstrously large and beautiful grandfather clock adorned the walls. An old timey phone with a turning crank that my grandparents had once actually used hung on their living room wall. Ah but not even this scrumptious sweet roll could compare to Oleta's baby biscuits. I realized I had closed my eyes in memory. Opening my eyes to once again view the school hallway. I swallowed the last cinnamon-spice bite of the sweet roll. It would take a bit of time but eventually I would come to feel a small sense of familiarity with my new school.

The biggest news in Oklahoma for that year however seemed not to be the Vietnam war per se as much as the Hell's Angels motorcycle gang. It was a warm Saturday afternoon in 1971. I'd been holed away in my room the whole day through reading yet another book by Laura Ingalls Wilder. If I had my druthers on what to do on my own for a day it was always to read a good book. I'd made my bed and smoothed the covers as usual that morning. Yet I never the less had created a propped up position on top of the bed with which to do my reading. Glancing at the clock. Twenty-five minutes after two o'clock. Thirsty for water I looked over at my empty glass sitting next to the clock. I would have to mark my place in the book I was reading and interrupt my engorgement in the story to get something to drink.

Placing a small ear flap down on the page I was on in the book. Picking up the empty glass and wishing I could quench my parched throat immediately. Walking down the hall I was on my way to the bathroom to fill my glass up at the sink when I heard a noise coming from down stairs. It sounded like a burp and a grunt. Might as well get my water from down stairs and see what the noise was all about. Especially since I did not expect anyone to be home at this time. Walking down the brown carpeted stairs. I stopped to look out the window at the back yard. The day looked hot. Stepping into the living room I saw an open newspaper laying across the short walnut colored wood coffee table. My father was an avid news fan. But my father wasn't sitting with the paper at the coffee table. Seeing the paper laying there I deduced that it was probably my father whom I had heard down stairs. Walking up to the boring light brown couch I sat and looked down at the open newspaper. Even though the paper was open it was still in crisp neat squares. No messy scattered sections tangled here and there. I new this meant my father had only had a glance at the paper and not really read much of it yet. Keeping my eyes on the newspaper I spoke loudly into the air around me--"Dad, is that you?" In response I heard my fathers voice coming from the kitchen saying, "Yep. But not for long."

Sitting my empty glass down on the coffee table I temporarily forgot my thirst due to a headline that caught my eye. There in the newspaper were large block letters saying: Hell's Angels. What does that mean? I sat looking at the words while full of wonder. Could the newspaper be talking about real angels?

"Hell's Angels", I whispered out loud to myself. I felt that this particular news article must be wildly fascinating and full of adventure. What was it about?

Gingerly lifting the newspaper in between my fingers I began to read the article about these odd and unusual angels. No, it wasn't about real angels. The newspaper said the Hell's Angels were a motorcycle gang. A gang that had settled themselves at the city park. A mild wave of disappointment sifted through my skin since I'd been hoping the article might be about *real* angels. Oh well.

Reading on, the news article evoked fascination and interest. What would a motorcycle gang look like? Holding the section of newspaper in my hands I ran into the kitchen with the thought that my father had probably gone out back into the yard to tend his mulch. Stopping short of running into him I saw father in the kitchen stirring a mug of what was most likely coffee. He seemed so tall then as all adults appear to children. Stomach so large and pouchy and his hair receding rapidly. He appeared a countenance of self-absorbed unhappiness sometimes and I felt a pang of sadness for him. Didn't adults ever smile? Ah yes! My Grandmommy Oleta and Grandaddy Barns! Yet they were grandparents and had the precious jolly divinity naturally granted when one became a grandparent. Correct?

"It says 'Hell's Angels' Dad!" I pointed to the paper.

"Yes, I know." He mumbled in the midst of his concentration over the mug of warm liquid he was holding.

"They're here Dad! Where we live!"

"I've seen it already."

"You've seen them?"

"No. The paper. I've seen the paper."

"Can we go see them?" Excitement coursed a flush of adrenalin through my body.

"What?!" He looked up from his coffee mug and in glancing down at me shook his head as if in disbelief. Quiet. I waited. He sipped his coffee. More quiet.

"Can we dad?"

"What?" Father took a long careful swig from the mug.

"Go see them!" Wasn't he listening? "Please? Oh please?" Unable to control an ants-in-the-pants dance my feet and knees jiggled with anticipation.

"Dad?" Jiggle of my knees again. "I want to see what a motorcycle angel from hell looks like! Pleeeeese?"

"They're a motorcycle gang, Suzanna."

"I know. I read that. They all ride motorcycles and none of them owns a car and they all hang out together all the time. Right?"

"That's right."

Father sat the mug down on the stove but left his fingers still wrapped around the handle and studied me for a moment.

"Please Dad? I want to see what a Hell's Angel looks like."

Father must have surmised I thought seeing the Hell's Angels gang would be like taking a quick peek at a real angel or at a parade or a carnival. Perhaps I did. No doubt that I did. A child's curiosity over odd names and titles. He shook his head again with an expression that looked like bewildered perplexity. A hint of a smile slightly lifted one side of his mouth. "I've got to get back to work", was his response. Swilling his coffee with a mild grimace suggesting that the drink was bitter. He strode the two and a half grown up sized steps to the sink on the opposite side of the kitchen from the stove. Checking his blue and white striped long sleeved cotton shirt for any renegade drops of the drink. He then flipped on the faucet and rinsed out the mug. He then set it to rest in the sink. Patting his thick looking polyester dark blue slacks then pulling a set of keys out of the pocket. Father marched with long wide strides through the kitchen and living room and to the front door. My barefoot baby steps pattering quickly to follow behind him.

"Suzanna leave that newspaper on the table. And don't mess it all up." My father gave me this direction and then stepped out of the door.

"Yes Sir."

Turning back to the living room I plucked up the rest of the paper off of the coffee table. Tapping my feet quickly as I ran over the beige linoleum floor of the kitchen I set the entire paper down onto the kitchen table. Patting the sides of the newspaper until I'd accomplished a nice neat large square out of it. Then I ran to the front door and closed it. Peering through the partially beveled glass in the front door to see if my father had left yet. I saw his car zooming off down the street. To be alone in the house was more common than not and wasn't at all disconcerting to me. In fact I preferred to be alone in the peace and quiet. It also meant I could sneak in some time to watch television. I read through the article about these Hell's Angels and then neatly put the newspaper back into a lovely square as it had been before my father left.

Hopping up the stairs I hummed joyfully at having the house all to myself. I was humming a song called "Wendy" and continued to hum it as I made my way into my parent's room. The same color of dark cream carpet covered the stairs, hallway, and all three bedrooms. There sat a treasure in my parent's room. It was the television we'd had since I was four or five years old. It was light brown and square with large clunky dials on it. A rabbit ears antennae on top of it. So fabulous and luscious that box called a television. It had no color to its pictures; it was a black and white television.

My parent's bed pressed against the far wall where two average sized windows looked out upon the front lawn. Our lawn with green grass and a gigantic oak tree. A dresser and mirror leant into the side wall on the left. The television, that miraculous square wonder, sat alone at the wall opposite the parental bed. Turn the knob to 'on' and wheeee! And such a lucky day—I got to watch Star Trek with Dr. Spock giving direction in a cool smooth voice to Captain Kirk from the bridge of the spacecraft. What a spectacular delight to enjoy the pleasurable sorcery of television. I felt especially lucky because I also got to watch the Sonny and Cher Show. Listening to the songs and looking at Cher with her mystical eyes and ebony flowing hair. Everyone saw Cher as one of the most beautiful creatures on earth.

"Suzie!" (I was being called by my nickname.)

Startled! Muscles pulling inward with an instantaneous jerk. It was Mother's voice. Looking up from the world's reverie called TV. Jumping from the edge of the quilt covered bed and hurriedly clicking off the television. Running to the top of the stairs I called down to my mother. "Yes Mam?"

"Suzanna come on! We're going out to eat. Come on!"

I ran to my bedroom and grabbed my shoes made of light blue suede. Sitting down on the bedroom carpet I tugged on my socks that had been tucked inside my shoes. Then I slipped on my favorite suede shoes and called to my mother as I lifted onto my feet. "I'm coming!" Out to eat? That was an extremely rare treat. Both of my parents were always extremely busy. My family didn't eat meals together unless a visiting preacher or other such church guest was at the house. Or unless it was a holiday at the home of one of my grandparent's. To eat out was even more unusual. Going out to eat? Yes! It doesn't take much more than the promise of food to have me jumping to my feet!

Halfway down the stairs while I was holding onto the railing my mother asked, "Got your shoes on?"

"Yes Mam."

"Is your dress clean?"

I looked down at my dress. "Yes Mam."

"Well hurry up! Let's go!"

"Yes Mam."

"Your Father is waiting in the car."

"Where are we going?"

Mother and I made it to the front door and she said, "I think we're going to Big Ed's. They have big hamburgers."

"Oooo! And French fries?"

"Big French fries."

"Yummy!" I followed my mother out of the house and to the car where I opened the farther door and climbed into the back seat. I didn't buckle up. Nor did my parents. It wasn't yet really expected by the law for anyone to buckle their seat belt at this stage of history.

Darkness was already creeping into the waning light. Blanketing blackness draping over the outside world while the sun shied away to hide. Stars already beaming through the tenebrous murk pressing its imperative somber bruise across the sky. Yet as a promise of light still out there somewhere to show the way to weary travelers do stars perform their glimmer and shine. It was that moment in time I loved the most. Twilight.

Mother, Father, and I, ate alone without my siblings at Big Ed's that night. Big Ed's was famous no doubt to every family for its super huge hamburgers the size of a dinner plate. If one individual gets the big burger and eats the whole thing themselves then its free. Now that's big! We got one burger and shared it between the three of us. Thanking my parents for the part of the gargantuan hamburger I ate I was feeling full of both excitement and grace for the food. Extremely tasty and filling. Outside of the comforting false light in the hamburger joint the obese darkness of night settled enveloping and lethargic over the city.

Once the dinner was over and we were back in the car I bounced up and down on the backseat. Leaning my elbows upon the back of the front seat I watched the city lights splash past the moving car. Glassy lights of white, red, greens, and purple neon zipping and changing here and there while my father drove along.

"Mother, do you know that there are Hell's Angels in town? They drive motorcycles."

"Yes"; Mother said, "We're going to go see them!" I was stunned! Mother stated this affirmative quite clearly and nodded her head to the same tune. I looked from my father to my mother trying to judge if it was a joke or they were serious. Yet either way I couldn't believe what I had heard. How could it be?

"Are you joking?"

"No", said Mother.

"We are? We'll see the motorcycle angels from hell?"

Now both Mother and Father nodded 'yes'.

"I talked about it with your mother", stated my father with a blank tone of voice. "We're going to take you to see the Hell's Angels. We're going to invite them to join us for church on Sunday. Maybe do them some good."

"Wow! Really?" Disbelief still edged against my ribs. I expected the car to pull into our driveway and be told it was just a joke. Any instant now they would both laugh. But it was no joke as the car kept rolling onward into the city night. At once it seemed that I knew why my parents wanted to go see the gang. Certainly it would be an opportunity for the preacher in my father to invite gang members to chapel and worship. "Do them some good", as he said. Perhaps an opportune moment to impress upon a child how to reach out to others and be of help. Although that seemed ridiculous since such a lesson was hardly needed; I already cared about helping others. But oh my goodness, how I was excited! And yet my excitement tapered and waned as we got close to the park, and close to the gang.

Ominous worry encroached upon my heart as I saw the park up ahead where the Hell's Angels had taken over. Tapping my fingers together and lifting myself onto my knees to better see out of the window. Long hair on simply everyone both male and female. Men with bushy beards and mustaches. Lots of jeans and leather clothes.

Leather in black and leather in brown. Boots and belts with large buckles. Laughing and chattering voices of the men and women gang members cackling in waves through the air betwixt pounding music with booming deep thuds of base. The car pulled onto the dirt and gravel of the park's road as my father slowed down to an eventual stop.

"We're here!" Said my father.

"Yes. Here we are!" Mother looked back at me from over her shoulder as she also announced our arrival.

My father turned off the engine then opened his door and stepped out. Glancing at me through the open door before he closed it.

"We're getting out of the car?" I asked. Both parents shook their heads to the affirmative. I wondered aloud, "Is that such a good idea?" Inexplicably I found myself feeling uncomfortable. "I thought Mother and I were just going to stay in the car. Or maybe I should stay in the car?"

"Come on." Father stated flatly.

"Lock your door." Mother commanded. Lock the door? We never locked the car doors.

"Lock the door Mother?"

"Just in case Suzanna."

"Yes Mam."

All the doors were locked before being closed. Father walked off in his long strides toward the left of the great crowd of bikers. Mother walked towards the right of the buzzing herd of Hell's Angels. Not sure which direction to follow I stopped at a husky oak tree. Watching my parents going in separate directions I wondered doubtfully if any of these bikers would actually come to Sunday service. This wasn't a judgmental thought just a factual consideration. Uncomfortable with the crowd I circled around the burly oak tree while looking at its mud-brown bark. Running my finger against the trees rough bumpy outer skin. Feeling fascinated at the marvel of trees having so many varieties. Different colors, shapes, and textures. Upon rounding the oak tree to its other side I found myself looking at the large wide feet of a man. First I saw his boots. Then I saw his big full belly. Next his wide shoulders covered by an untucked tan cotton shirt. Lastly I looked high up into an angry face. The face of a Caucasian male with frizzy strawberry/blonde hair? He had an equally scraggly beard and mustache of the same color. He was so tall and so extremely broad-chested. A ruddy faced Paul Bunyan of a man is what he seemed to me. A wide collared shirt. I gaped at him in surprise. I still did not know or understand yet the concept of a 'stalker'.

The man lifted his arms from his sides and he pressed a light brown open bottle in his right hand against a white cloth in his left hand. He doused the cloth with some type of liquid from the bottle. Fear prickled like electricity in a spreading wave down my shoulders and spine then up my neck. Frozen to the spot in trepidation. Continuing to just gape open mouthed, I just stared. In one swift revolution of his arm he clamped the white cloth over my mouth and nose. Instantaneously with his right hand he twirled my shoulder around and lifted me up with his right arm under my armpit. Pressing the cloth very hard upon my face he took a step backwards and began to turn around. At first I kicked my feet against the air. Suddenly I felt my consciousness pull from my body and I saw myself as if I were standing outside of my body. The man holding me with the cloth still clamped on my face. Something in the cloth over my mouth and nose was taking me away from consciousness as I breathed it. My eyes looking wild and confused like an animal realizing its trapped. Then a curious thing happened in that second which felt like ten minutes. Just before passing out into a scary cottony unconsciousness, an odd thought ran through my mind. It was: "Why does everyone in this time of history wear only pants and jeans? How come there are no robes?

No jewels? No brocade?" That was my last thought. That odd thought had to have taken place in a split second. And yes I knew from reading books what brocade was. Who could ever know what haunting reasons cause a person to think such thoughts at the precise swing of tragedy.

Whatever happened be it nothing or something during that space between passing out and my next conscious memory I will never know. Nor do I know how long I was out. A blurry slur of images. Shaking movements like someone holding me and running. Slowly my eyes began to focus. Yes, someone large was carrying me and running. The wind was blowing now as it hadn't before. I got the impression a little storm might be brewing. Blustery gusts slapping my hair from all directions. Flashes of red and blue lights were coming at a fast pace into the park. A whooping ring of sirens were howling. Blinking my eyelids at the flashing lights until the image came clear and my consciousness completely back. Ah yes, I could see now what the flashing lights were. The police. Police cars barreling into the Park. Woozy and nauseous I felt whoever was holding me stop running suddenly and thrust me into my father's arms. My father's face in a tight expression. Wind pushing and shoving my hair while I looked at the flashing lights and winced at the loud sirens from the police cars. My father turned to his left and thrust me into my mother's smaller thinner arms saying, "You take her, I'll go get the car!" My mother's face looked stern and amused at the same time. Police poured in. A huge bonfire raged with crackling sparks of fire spinning out of control as it licked and popped against the wind. Rumbling audacious voices of the Hell's Angels rising upward in a massive jumbled chorus.

Mother walked forward holding me and then stopped several many feet from the edge of the park's dirt and gravel road. Father quickly pulled the car up in front of us within no time at all. An intense or stressed look on his face. He leaned sideways and grabbed the passenger door handle from inside and pushed the door open. "Come on!"—He shouted with a pulling wave of his arm. Then he impatiently hopped out of the car and ran around the other side of it to help open the back seat door that my mother was fumbling with. She plopped me in the back seat of the car and I scooted to sit on the far side. Nausea tugged hard on my intestines. Father was already making his way back around to the drivers seat as my mother slammed the back door shut. Father swimmingly reeled into the driver's seat at about the exact same time that my mother hurtled into the passenger side and closed her door. Moving the car along Father hit the steering wheel in frustration. He was only able to move the car at a snails pace at first and then in spurts due to the chaos from the mass of scurrying people and of other traffic. Soon enough he had the car well onto the park's actual road. The police were swooping in. Many officers were taking charge of the park's road where it met with the regular paved road. An officer walked in front of the car and waved at father through the bright headlights. The policeman stopped our car by holding his arm out and lifting his palm toward us. Squinting against the headlights the officer strolled quickly to the drivers window with a flashlight in his hand. Mother and Father exchanged a short lip-biting fearful glance. Tapping on the drivers side window of the car the police officer motioned for my father to roll down his window. Father obliged.

A glowering sensation leading into a nauseating melting feeling caused in me a complete inability to control my muscles. Without the muscular ability to stop myself I slid helplessly onto my right side, facedown onto the back seat. Trying uselessly to force my arm muscles to work. Trying desperately to lift myself back up into a sitting position. No use. My muscles weakly refused to respond. Now my efforts were bent toward getting my head to turn to the side since it was difficult to breath very well with my face pressed into the car seat. The policeman was shining his flashlight into the car and asking my father who he was. I succeeded in turning my head slightly to face the left and I took a deep breath in through my nose. All at once I slipped like jello onto the back seat floorboard.

I tried to speak and tell my parents something's wrong but it came out sounding clogged and slurred: "Frumpfing grong." What was happening to me?

The policeman had shined his flashlight into the back of the car just at the same time that my body oozed with a slide onto the floorboard. For a fleeting micro of a second I had locked eyes with the policeman.

To my utter dismay my body began to tremble uncontrollably all over.

"What's wrong with her?" The policeman cocked his head at my direction in the back of the car.

Father answered: "Well she has been sick. We're taking her home just now."

"Why were you here Sir?"

"Well..."

For some reason I garbled out as loudly as I could, "So thaw motor angels can go toog perch." I wasn't sure if I was heard or even understood.

"See", said my father with affirmation, "I'm a minister. And I thought I could talk some of the angels to go to church."

Why was I unable to control my speech? Or my muscles? I became aware of a sudden strange soft rumbling sound rolling around down deep inside my ears. The trembling worsened.

"Sir I'm gonna need some I.D."

"Of course officer."

The policeman peered through the window at me again with a swipe of his flashlight. Father must have shown his I.D. quickly for I heard the policeman say, "Alright. Get her home now."

The car lurched forward in movement. No longer able to hold my head up I let it rest on the floor-mat. By the time my father pulled the car up into the driveway of our house I felt like I was freezing cold and I was trembling so badly as to feel like I were practically in a convulsion.

I heard my father say, "We're here." He got out of the car.

"We're home", Mother announced as she also got out of the car.

I couldn't speak. I could hear but I couldn't speak. No specified movement came to my wobbly useless muscles so that I could get myself up off the floorboard. Parents calling again and then peeping through the window. Father opened the door on my side and commanded, "Come on now. No time to play games. Get out of the car."

"Suzanna!" Mother leaned past my father's shoulder to look down at me. "It's late. It's time for bed", she demanded. "Now get out of the car and get to your room."

Still unable to speak as if my tongue and mouth muscles had atrophied. I hoped my eyes would be an overture to a plea. Parents on bended knee now. Mother touching my forehead.

"She's got a fever!" My mother's voice sounded surprised and alarmed.

Leaning to touch my face my father stressed: "She's burning up!" He handed Mother the keys even though she certainly had her own pair in the big purse which hung around her arm. "Here. You open the door. I'll carry her." Father gathered my weak limp body into his arms and stood up with a low exhalation of breath. Mother led the way looking back and forth between us and the front door. She flipped through the keys then pressed one in particular into the lock. Turning the key she pushed the door open and then stepped back for us to come in. Setting me onto the couch he bent on one knee and studied me.

"I'll go get the thermometer." Mother disappeared momentarily into the bathroom that connected to the kitchen. She came back with the thermometer in hand. "Keep this under your tongue", she instructed. Mmmph I grunted. She had to keep her hand on the end of the instrument and hold it in place. Time passed and then she extracted the instrument and read it. "She's 104!"

"What?"

"Yes! Her temperature's 104. Get her upstairs. I'll get the rubbing alcohol."

Father carried me upstairs. He then flipped the light on in my room with his elbow. Gently he placed me upon my bed and then stood up and looked to the door waiting for Mother. She came into the room hurriedly. Taking the cap off the bottle she doused a washcloth with the rubbing alcohol. Then she placed the bottle on my nightstand. Quickly she began sleeking the rubbing alcohol across my arms, legs, and forehead, with the soaked washcloth. Father stood back and watched until my mother said, "Let's take her temperature again." He nodded in agreement. Mother had to hold onto the thermometer again. She kept my mouth closed with the fingers of her other hand pressing against my chin. Time passed again. Mother extracted the thermometer. My father leaning in to see what the temperature was. Their eyes widened as Mother announced it. "One hundred and five!"

"Put more rubbing alcohol on her!" Father didn't wait but grabbed the bottle from the nightstand and began trickling the astringent over my limbs. Using their hands they rubbed the stuff into my skin. Eventually they deemed it time to check my body temperature another time. Father tried with the thermometer. Yet I was shaking too badly for the thermometer to stay in my mouth. "She's shaking too hard."

Mother replied: "Hold her shoulders down while I get it under her tongue." She took the thermometer from his hand. Next she attempted to get the instrument into my mouth while my father held my chest and shoulders down.

"She's shaking so hard!" Said Father.

"I can't get the thermometer in her mouth", Mother said exasperated. "Her jaws are locking shut." (My father placed his fingers over my cheek and jaw.) Mother shook her head saying, "No, no, her mouth won't open."

"What do we do?" He asked.

"We'll have to take it rectally."

"You do it."

"Hold her legs still. Hold them down!"

Father held my legs down and looked away while Mother went about the awful business. I was desperate to shout out: "I can't speak. Yet I can hear you just fine! For heaven's sake please don't put that thermometer *there*!" It was almost comical. I was actually feeling embarrassed. And so worried that it might hurt for the thermometer to go... there. Father continued to hold me down. No amount of mind-power on my part could stop the shaking. After what seemed an interminable amount of time Mother removed the thermometer. Her jaw slacked unexpectedly open as she turned with slow tenuousness to face my father.

"What is it?" He asked.

"It's 106 point 5. And it's not going down."

'It's 106 point 5. And it's not going down' was the last thing I heard her say. A moment passed as I watched them look at each other. Then a swooshing silence filled my ears. My parent's lips moved but I couldn't hear anything they said. If I had gone deaf I honestly didn't care.

Turning my head, I had the sensation of someone else being in the room. So, is this where the hallucination starts? Why should I care? I felt no fear. And there I was looking at what I can only describe as an angel! I felt a profound love for this person. Felt a profound love in return. Peace and calm surrounded me. Floating with her legs pulled up into an Indian sitting position. A glowing white robe all around her with long split flowing sleeves. Long and straight and silky deep dark chocolate-brown hair past her shoulders. Love emanated from her even though her pleasing face seemed devoid of any specific emotion. A calm behind her closed berry colored lips. I felt drawn by a feeling of quiet peacefulness like cascading water. She held her hand out towards me. Beckoning. Suddenly I realized an unusual but not unpleasant sensation in my hands and arms. Both of my hands felt like balloons filled with helium floating up out of my body. Surprised yet unconcerned I looked to *see* my hands floating up out of my body! My arms following suit; lifting out of my body. Then it occurred to me I might also be able to sit up and lift my chest and head out of my body. Sure enough I sat up and out of my body. Looking again to the angel I swung my feet out of my body. Reaching out I took her outstretched hand. Looking back I took in one last glance at my body laying on the bed motionless. Then greedily and hungrily for the joy I felt, I wrapped my arms around the angels waist and hugged her. Petting my hair then standing up from her levitated sitting position. She hoisted me into her arms and cradled me gently. Enfolding my arms about her neck in complaisant relaxed exhaustion.

Encircling me in her arms the angel and I rose upward towards the ceiling. Flying. Then she veered towards the window and together we passed straight through my bedroom wall as simply as if it were water. We were all at once outside. Flying slowly upward in the nights moon and wind and stars.

Feeling the mild wind blowing cool against me. Pleasant blowing chill dancing in my hair. I had complete conscious awareness and pure clear lucidity. Slowly we flew. Rising into the air until we were above the roof of my house. Slowly we descended into a sitting position levitated by only a few inches above the roof. How clear the night sky. How beautiful the stars. Closing my eyes and thinking to myself as if in reverent prayer, "Please. I hope this lasts a long, *long* time." Opening my eyes to the sight of her flowing hair and the bright diamond stars shining beyond her. She rocked me back and forth gently. Holding my head in her hand.

We stayed there in that precious moment for a while but not nearly long enough. In a wispy voice like the flutter of butterfly wings she said to me, "It's time to go back.".

"No. I don't want too", I moaned between complacency and complaint.

We moved downward and through the roof. Closing my eyes for a moment. Then peeking to see, we were floating through the attic. Closing my eyes again. The movement stopped and I felt my legs drop down from being cradled. I opened my eyes to see we were standing in the upstairs bathroom. Why on earth are we here? Why am I not back in my bedroom? "No, no", I pleaded when the angel placed her hands on my shoulders, "Let me stay with you."

She pressed onto my shoulders with what looked like a nudge but felt like a hard push. I lost my balance and fell backwards. There was a tingling stimulus as I fell. Then a pulling sensation as if I were literally being vacuumed back into my body.

There was a 'thwok' noise followed by a high pitched vibration like the quick sound of violin strings being swiped with the bow.

In a swift stiff instantaneous movement I sat up from my head, ears, and lips being completely covered in water. Completely wet and naked in a bathtub full of water and tons of ice. Splashes of water and ice as I spun so violently into a firm sitting position. My shoulders slumped as I gasped in a horrid gulp of air then choked slightly and coughed.

I did not feel cold despite all the ice surrounding me. Deeply pulling in more oxygen into my lungs. Looking at my surroundings I became fully aware that I was drenched and naked in a tub of water filled with pounds of ice.

My father came charging through the open bathroom door and halted as if stopped by a red light. Holding a sack of fresh ice in his hands, he looked at me. Jutting his chin to his left shoulder he shouted back at the hallway behind him saying, "The fever broke!"

Brief pause and then I saw my mother poke her head through the open door and look at me. "Oh, it did." Speechless I blinked at them.

"I guess we won't be needing this", Father referred to the bag of ice he was holding.

"Guess not."

"Well I'll go put this in the freezer." And he turned around, tromping off to find the freezer.

Finger pointing at me, Mother ordered: "Dry off. Put some clothes on. And get to bed." She shut the bathroom door.

I moaned then rubbed my face with both hands. I'm not sure why but at that moment my mother's words somehow seemed poignantly ridiculous. As if it were the weirdest thing a parent could say at such a moment under such circumstances. Again, I didn't know why I had this particular perception. Dragging myself from the tub. Hastily I pulled at the nightgown sitting next to the sink and dressed without drying off first. My stomach lunged and I dropped to my knees while flipping open the toilet lid. Dry heaves.

When the tugging of my stomach up into my jaws had subsided I placed my right hand onto the floor to steady myself. I noticed a small fuzzy tarantula a few inches from my fingers. Standing up I reached high and unlocked then pushed open the small screen-less bathroom window. Carefully picking up the furry black tarantula into both palms I carried it to the cool breeze of the open window. Stretching as far up onto my tiptoes as possible I let the spider drop onto the wide roof close below the window and go free.

FOUR

TARZAN AND BABY BISCUITS

The newspapers would later mention the clash and furry of the Hell's Angels at the park that night.

When I questioned my father about the news headlines he said merely that apparently there was some squabble between the Hell's Angels and some other gang. That was all the information he offered regarding that night. Luckily I would soon find myself looking out a car window at endless flat meadows spotted with complacent cows along the country roads of Texas again. On my way to visit my grandparents! Oleta and JB Barns.

Several weeks after the Hell's Angels in the park I woke up in my bed at 3:am to a calming shine of the streetlight outside beaming across my ceiling. A soothing but curiously indefinable hum vibrating the air with its pleasantly deep tone. My head pressed into the comfortable pillow. Enjoying the play of light on my ceiling. Listening happily with stilled wonderment at the resilient low sounding hummmm. Still sleepy I marveled at the cozy vibration. "What is that sound?"—I wondered.

Lulled by the hum which sounded like two thousand monks holding a sweet low tone to the tune of 'ohm'. Rolling to my right I lifted up and peered out the window at the velvety night sky. Then my bedroom door opened.

"Suzanna. Hey Suzie! Wake up! We're leaving." It was the familiar female voice of my mother. Her body stood in shadowy silhouette from the hall light behind her.

"We're moving?"

"What?"

"Are we moving to live in another city again?"

"No. Dad and I are taking you to your grandparents."

"Your mothers?"

"No. Your father's."

"Grandmommy Oleta and Gandaddy Barns?"

"Yes." Walking to my closet she gathered up some dresses and my shoes and underwear from the make-shift shelf on the closet floor. Placing these items into my small white children's suitcase. Silently she carried this bundle out of my room.

"Mother!"

"What is it Suzie?" She looked back at me and rested her left palm against the gold colored door handle.

"What is that loud… vibrating… hum sound?"

Following my finger pointing at the ceiling her perplexed expression changed to one of recognition. "Oh", she said, "That's the attic fan."

"What's an attic fan?"

"It was hot so I turned the fan on in the attic. It's sort of like air-conditioning but it saves a lot more money."

"Ohhhh. An attic fan."

"Get dressed." She closed the door.

"Yes Mam!" Excitedly hopping out of my bed and making it with the wrinkle-free "hospital corners" as my mother had taught me. Pulling my favorite dress off of a hanger. The all yellow dress with the white ribbon around the waist and four small white flowers like daisies upon the chest. Oh how a lovely dress can make you feel so pretty! I twirled around once before sitting down to pull on my white bobby socks and the white church shoes with the buckles across the top. How wonderful! A visit to my grandparents was like waking to see the oranges, apples, walnuts, pecans, and pretty colored pencils stuffed in your stocking on Christmas morning.

So far I had lived in New Mexico. And in Oklahoma I had lived in Watonga, Springs, and Oklahoma City. I didn't feel any emotion one way or the other about another move. But a visit to my grandparents was exciting! My father, mother, and I climbed into the car. Mother treated Father and I to egg sandwiches and apple slices which we ate with what seemed like great fun, for we had eaten them while riding in the car. Father was dexterous handling both the wheel and his sandwich. That moment imprinted me with a permanent love of scrambled eggs between two soft pieces of bread with a little mayonnaise added for flavor. The sun rose and I napped upon bedding placed in the back of the station wagon. My siblings were not with us. Something in my heart must have known we were near my grandparents home for I slipped from a nap into a blinking full awakening.

"Are we there?" I asked.

"Almost", chimed both parents with grins and a look to each other.

Swiftly placing both palms upon the glass of the window I saw to my delight the sign which foretold how very close to the tiny town in Texas we really were. Tarantulas. Yes, tarantulas. The closer one got to the small Texas town this time of year the more and more you'd see tarantulas out on the road. Could anyone know why the huge black furry spiders felt compelled to litter the road with their bodies? Many hundreds and hundreds of them. Father said they probably just liked the heat of the pavement. I felt better by saying short little prayers for the souls of each big spider that met its fate with the car's wheels. Knowing it would eventually become impossible to pray for all of the tarantulas that blanketed the road in the thousands. How could I possibly pray for each one killed when they were killed in massive sweeps all at once?

"God bless that poor spider and may its soul go quickly back to wherever it comes from. Forgive us, for we can't help but squish them." (Then again.) "God bless that poor spider and may its soul…"

"Suzanna! Stop that!"--Father yelled. You really can't blame him. How many times can you withstand hearing a pattering prayer with constant repetition?

"I feel bad for the tarantulas."

"Oh Suzie", Father remarked, "it's over so quickly they never even feel it."

"Well that's good. Poor buggies."

"Arachnids." Mother corrected.

"Eye-rack-kanids." I repeated carefully.

Yet also how exciting to know I was close to arriving at my grandparents. Pleasure that moment when the parents point a finger at the road-sign announcing the small number of population printed below the town name. Parents saying, "We're almost at Grandmommy's and Grandaddy's." Joy indeed! Excitement mounting.

Small in stature from the front, Oleta and JB Barns's home so small and purely clean white on the outside was really quite roomy on the inside. A huge gigantic iron cauldron authentically from pioneer days when large meals were cooked for the cowboys and hungry families and for the Cherokee Indian family members which birthed their Native American blood-line into my Grandaddy Barns. The massive cooking cauldron sat majestically in the front yard painted orange with black trim.

Inside my grandparents house, covering practically every inch of every wall of every room in the house from its kitchen to bathroom then the two bedrooms to the living room were lines of shelves harboring various items of bottles and other glass in so many different colors! Glass medicine bottles from the 1920's. Beveled blue, purple, green, and clear. Bottles of original coca-cola from its very first introduction ever to the public. Antique stove, and antique hot irons with harness clips for ironing clothes. Real antique phones and antique clocks! Chiming clocks with resonant beautiful sound. Cuckoo clocks with little painted birds inside that would stick their heads out and say "cuckoo, cuckoo" every time the hour turned. Grandfather clocks with deep bass lilts and long chiming 'chong, chong' sounds.

Glass jars with glass lids were always on the kitchen counter and always filled with peppermints, clove gum, and lemon drops.

If you were lucky you were someone who got to be at Oleta's house come Christmas time. Where you could taste from the piles of homemade peanut brittle and the melt-in-your-mouth divinity. Pound cakes and fresh breads. Yum!

Scrambling over the back seat from the station wagon's make-shift bed in back and then practically tumbling out of the car as we arrive. At the exact same time Oleta comes running with her tiny brown dog named Tessie. Out the front door Oleta comes and she runs down the three steps to the sidewalk. This is how we greet each other. Oleta and I meet on the grass in the middle of the front yard and throw our arms around each other. Tessie barking in soft and friendly non-malicious yips. Everyone piles into the house and gathers at the kitchen table for a short visit before my mother and father bid their smiles, nods, and good-byes.

"Guess what?" Oleta smiled down at me beyond her plump round cheeks. She lavishly buttered a generous slice of toasted pound cake and placed it before me at the kitchen table. "Would you like a fork or would you like to use your hands?"

"Can I really use my hands to eat it?"

"Of course. It picks up perfectly."

"Like fried chicken?"

"That's right."

I tried it out. Picking up the warm slice of buttered pound cake and taking a bite. Wonderful flavor! I didn't like that it made my fingers feel sticky. "Actually, I'd like to use a fork please."

Oleta opened a small white drawer and extracted a silver colored fork. Handing me the fork she said, "Here you go Honey."

"What did you want me to guess Grandmommy?"

"Your cousins Lisa and Brad will be coming to stay for a few days."

"Yahoo! When?"

"Day after tomorrow." Oleta sat next to me. Her smile looking so peaceful and happy. "Would you like some fried ham?"

"Oh would I! Or… could I… I wanted your baby biscuits." Ooo, food is the way to my heart!

"I've got baby biscuits already made for you. JB and I are going to eat ham and biscuits for lunch now. It's lunch time."

"So I can have both?"

"Yes! What's ham without biscuits anyway?" Oleta grinned and her thin wire rim glasses rose up and then down for a second on her nose. If her hair were white she really would look like Mrs. Santa Claus. Her personality was sweet and unconditionally loving.

"You made the baby biscuits for *me*?"

"I know you love them. *Here*." She stood up and walked over to a pale green tin bread box which she opened and pulled out a large plastic bag full of tiny home made biscuits. Sitting back down at the table next to me she placed the large plastic baggie on the table directly within my reach. She sat and smiled at me for a while before petting my fine blonde hair and then getting back up from the table to stand in front of the stove. Oleta pulled a heavy iron skillet out from a white cabinet next to the stove. Grabbing a huge hunk of ham from the 1950's refrigerator she placed the meat on a plate and began cutting it with a long wide knife. Slicing several thick steaks of ham, she cut with perfection. Silently placing them in the iron skillet she began to fry the meat. Heavy thick salty aromatic scent of meat.

Can you imagine living here with JB and Oleta and eating not just one fine smelling, tasty, fabulous meal every week or two but instead *three* full melt in the mouth meals every day? Some pleasure that! I enjoyed my meal for every little charming and delectable bite. My grandparents and I eating quietly and happily. Fresh milk to wash it down. We all enjoyed our feast of ham and home made baby biscuits that were made by hand with love from Oleta. Of course love was the secret 'Oleta ingredient' which made anyone else's food taste ordinary. After eating Oleta and I sat about the kitchen table again but for a new and most thrilling surprise of a reason. Grandaddy Barns sat handsome with his Cherokee brown skin and black hair just slightly salt and peppered. Contentedly he watched television in the living room from a comfortable beige and yellow thickly stuffed chair. His feet propped up on a round orange-brown ottoman. Present in his cheerful silent way.

Oleta had disappeared into the walk in pantry and returned with the surprise. Socks. Not just any old socks. She spread out onto the kitchen table thick wool socks colored brown, gray, white, and red. Sewing needles ranged from small to larger than I'd ever seen before. A paper sack full of fluffy white cotton stuffing. She proceeded to let me help her make a sock monkey! Yes! Monkey! Marvelous isn't it? I thought the whole thing to be extremely fascinating. She was going to make the stuffed toy monkey by hand; which I found shocking. Not going to buy the toy but actually make it! I helped to cut and sew. Oleta took a glass jar full of many different buttons and poured it's contents onto the table. From a grand variety of bright shiny buttons and beads I chose the colors and shapes I thought most beautiful and sparkly. Incandescent lustrous buttons and beads for eyes, nose, earrings, and a wedding ring. Dreaming of being grown up and having a family and children of my own as I admired the notable sized glass button that appeared to me an important and generous multi-cut diamond. My own sock monkey created from Oleta's caring hands with my help. That monkey would be cherished and cuddled until one day many years after it had been created it would have to be put upon a shelf as a keepsake due to its well loved ragged state.

The next day I was benefited the rare treat of sleeping late. It was near 10:am when I awoke. Mmmm how my heart soared at being with my grandparents. Spending the morning splashing in the small kiddies pool in the back yard for it was an unusually warm day. Watching awe struck I saw Grandmommy and Grandaddy call their pet turtles out from the back yard garden and from behind the pear trees and green apple trees. Grass velveting the yard thick and lush like carpet.

Come evening my grandparents sat in iron seats behind the chair swing in the grass. They pushed the chair swing in quiet content while I lay upon it. A quilt beneath me and a blanket across my body up to my shoulders. I sang for my grandparents almost every song I knew. Mostly lullaby's and folk songs. I did not sing current songs of popularity. Music in 1972 was flush with bringing in rock stars that had androgyny as their flare. These rock stars would often wear clogs or platform sandals whether they were male or female. Because of my parents I was well acquainted with such musical celebrations released in 1972 as "Cabaret" with Liza Minnelli and Joel Gray. And such stage productions begun on Broadway as Bob Fosse's "Pippin" which introduced the world to dancer Ben Vereen. Thanks to my brother I was aware of such 1972 hits as the song "American Pie" and "A Horse with No Name" by Don McLean. But that particular night I serenaded my grandparents with "One Tin Soldier" and "Eskimo Baby" and "In the Valley" and other lullaby's or folk songs.

Finally I made my way that night to a large comfy bed that was so intoxicating with its softness that I felt as though I melted into it. Sheets so fresh and clean and sun dried as to be crisp and buttery gentle at the same time. Sheets smelling like the sun and a breeze. The best thing for any pain be it mental, emotional, spiritual, or physical, *is sleep.* Hey, the pain is gone.

Saucy surprise when I awoke from my safe sleep (even though I knew they were coming.) My cousins arrived! Oh my what fun we'd have! Oh yes, come out and play! Brad and Lisa walked through the door. Brad my age and Lisa a year older. Each of them were sanctified with some of that Cherokee color to their skin. Honey brown hair. Lisa however had a lighter if not completely green set of eyes while Brad had dark brown peepers. Younger than myself by just a few weeks Brad never the less was taller and stronger. Lisa as the oldest had the greatest strength and height. How powerful and capable our muscles were would be of great importance of course when it came to playing our favorite game. Tarzan! Tarzan in the television series we loved lived wild and free in the jungle. Tarzan's grievance was to be a good Samaritan no matter what the outside world thought of him. Tarzan's pleasure was to love and care about Jane, Boy (why did this child have no name?), and Monkey. How many people decided to have a pet monkey simply from watching the Tarzan television series?

"Do you want to play outside?" I asked my cousins.

"Okay", said Lisa.

"Yes!" Responded Brad with a thrill.

I began to run. "Race ya!"

Brad followed suit running past me through the kitchen. "Last one there's a rotten egg!"

"I guess I'm the rotten egg", chuckled Lisa as she gleamed and then heartily laughed. "I just don't feel like running."

"Have fun!" Oleta chimed as Brad and I spun past her. She patted the still lingering Lisa on the back.

Grandaddy Barns had just recently come out of the bathroom to the side of the back door. He watched us with widening eyes. "You kids listen for the ring of that dinner bell outside so you know when it's time to come in for lunch." Grandaddy Barns instructed and smiled with pleasure at the three of his grandchildren. The dinner-bell he referred to was a real bell. It was big and loud and crystal clear in its ring. They had attached it outside on the white wood wall next to the screen door.

"I won!" Announced Brad as he swept past me down the outside steps.

"Oh no!" I said smiling and hopping like a rabbit on both feet down the last few steps. I couldn't help but turn and playfully tease my older cousin. "Hey Lisa! If you're the rotten egg, does that mean you'll smell like one? *Ha ha*!"

"We'll have to buy her deodorant!" Guffawed Brad.

Lisa grinned and rolled her eyes. "Oh hardy-har-har and very funny."

I swung around to face my cousins with a brilliant idea. "Hey! Do you wanna bring out the turtles? Grandmommy and Grandaddy did it yesterday."

Yes indeed Brad and Lisa wanted to bring out the turtles! We were all still young enough to experience turtles as somewhat mythical and mystical. Dinosaurs with houses on their backs that roamed the grassy knolls in unspoken wisdom and slow methodic reproach for their priestly journey. And if one were careful enough it seemed a turtle or a frog could grant you court and you'd be gifted to hold them and look into their eyes, and maybe just maybe their unfathomable judicious 'sageness' that they've kept in secret memory would float from their eyes and fill your brain. And you too would understand the eons that these creatures harbor in their dinosaur like countenance. It is an honor for a turtle or a frog to let you touch it, even better yet to hold it.

"Come here turtles!" We all called. "Turtle, turtle, turtle! Here turtle turtles!"

Climbing down onto my stomach I peeked into the bushes. Deep underneath I saw a turtle. I began to sing to it. "Sleep little Eskimo *turtle…*" The turtle strained its head, then it turned its head to the side in lulled curiosity. My cousins searched other parts of the lush green yard. Laying my arm under the bush I continued to sing to the turtle. Stretching my hand palm up with fingers splayed. Entering the next song which I made up as a song of honor. Patience, child. "Sweet precious turtle, you have calmly seen the years. Sweet precious turtle come to me and you will hear. A song of thank you for your gentle slow self like a gift from up above. Come to me little turtle and I'll sing to you of love." Ploddingly but unafraid the turtle came to me and laid its head in my hand. Its tail poking out from the other end made me think of a puppy dog's tail. The weight of its head against my palm seemed magical; I gasped with excitement.

"Alright! Suzanna found one!" Brad screamed.

I lifted my head to see Brad leaning over my shoulder and looking into the underbrush. He reached in to touch the turtle and the turtle pulled its head and limbs inside its shell. Lifting to my feet I watched as Brad got onto his stomach and stretched his hand into the brush. Bending down to look I could see that the turtle was quite quickly walking away to hide. Stretching farther Brad touched it with his fingertips and the turtle pulled in its head and limbs again. There was no stretching any farther. The creature was too far away for Brad to grasp a hold of it.

"I think I see one over here!" Shouted Lisa. "Come here!" Brad and I ran to her side.

"Nope!" Exclaimed Brad. "It's a rock." He pushed past the geraniums and picked up the rock to show to his big sister. "See?"

"Oh", groaned Lisa in disappointment.

Brad began seeking the garden of flowers and herbs as though it were a clandestine forest. Lisa and I searching the same area with eyes roaming about the nearby pecan trees and green apple trees. We converged the three of us to scout about the large shed. The magnificent shed. For it had its very own flushing toilet and was roofed with steel. To listen to the rain as it hit that steel roof was like bearing witness to a pleasing symphony of cymbals and metal drums. Alas no luck for a turtle near the shed.

"Where are they all hiding?"—asked Lisa.

"Perhaps they've run away?" Gasped Brad.

"Or gotten lost?" I chuckled and mused.

"I don't think they'd have left", said the older wiser Lisa, "because this is where they know Grandmommy and Grandaddy feed them."

"Let's go try and get the one that Suzanna found!" Brad began to run in that specific direction.

Lisa and I followed him. I suggested, "Why don't we go get Grandmommy to give us some of that lettuce she feeds them." We all looked at one another in surprised agreement in the idea of the lettuce and then each of us sprinted for the back door. Making it to the top step I reached up and rang the dinner bell. Brad ran and met the concrete stairs to the back door with a glance over his shoulder at his big sister. Lisa trotted with a Glimmering shine in her eyes. We all stopped at the top step where the dinner bell sat attached to the wall near the screen door. Of course Lisa and Brad also had to ring the bell before we went inside the house! The bell had a low hollow sound like a cow bell.

"Grandma!" I called holding the screen door open for Lisa and Brad to come inside. Leaning back around I was surprised to see Grandaddy standing there smiling down at me. "We want to bring the turtles out. We've got to get lettuce."

"What about carrots?" Chimed Brad.

Lisa came up from behind. "You're a silly little brother. Rabbits eat carrots."

"I think a turtle might eat one too." Grandaddy Barns faced the kitchen. "Oleta! Don't you think turtles might eat carrots too?"

"I heard", responded Oleta with a laugh in her voice. Oleta appeared through the entrance from the living room and walked into the kitchen. We all smiled at her. She reached into the old timey refrigerator and grabbed some lettuce. "Here JB, hand this lettuce to the grandbabies, I'll go get some more." Then in afterthought, "Yeah, maybe carrots too."

JB Barns's salt and pepper hair shined lustrous from the sunlight seeping in through the open door. He passed out lettuce equally between us. Popping a small leaf in his mouth he crunched it. As if on cue, all three of us "grandbabies" also flung a bite of lettuce in our mouths and chewed. Oleta returned from her search of the pantry with a hand towel full of lettuce. She squinted at the sunlight pouring in from the open door; her squinting caused her wire glasses to bob as she made her way down the outside concrete steps by placing one foot and then the other on the same step before venturing on to the next one. "Come on baby turtles", she cooed, "Here sweeties!"

Slow, but with stubborn purpose, two heads from two long and leathery necked turtles appeared. Cute wrinkled faces blinking at the sunlight poked through the low growing mass of green herbs and late blooming flowers at the very sound of Oleta's voice. "Oh look!" Gushed Oleta in a rushing whisper. "Over there by the herbs. That's the Momma and the Daddy turtle."

"There they are!" Cheered JB happily.

"Look, look Brad!" Lisa pointed.

"Where?" Perplexed and straining Brad veered his head this way and that.

"There", said Brad's big sister as she placed a hand on his right shoulder with a long outstretched arm. "Right there. See, they're coming out onto the sidewalk."

Placing my hand to rest on Grandmommy's upper back while she leaned down to feed the turtles, I felt pleased with the feel of her cotton dress with the flowers on it. "They know your voice Grandmommy."

"I know it Suzanna. Those turtle babies know I'm their momma. They come a runnin' when they hear your Grandaddy's voice too; but they like me the best. That's it, come on little babies."

"Grandmommy, do you mind if I touch one of your turtles?"

"Sure Suzanna. Go ahead." Oleta cooed again.

"And me?" Asked Brad.

"Me too?" Said Lisa and then thought better of it. "Will they bite me?"

"Just don't go calling them bad names." JB joked. "Bad names are the only thing that'll make 'em mad and then they bite the tips of your fingers off." JB chuckled and smiled wide as he lifted his hand up with the back of it facing us and one finger bent down so it looked like he was missing a part of it. "See here? That old pa-pa turtle went and took the tip of this finger off when I called him a stinky slow poke. I think it was the 'stinky' part he didn't like." Giggles from everyone.

Lisa waved a dismissive arm in Grandaddy's direction. "Did not!"

Bending down next to the turtles Brad tentatively reached out with his pointer finger and then paused. "Will I get bit?"

"No. Those turtles are as sweet as doves", said JB.

"Turtle doves", laughed Oleta.

"Go ahead and pet `em." Grandaddy instructed.

"I don't think I even want to touch one." Lisa dropped a piece of lettuce in front of the turtles and then hopped back.

With the pointer finger of my right hand I scritched the top of the head of the bigger turtle. (A 'scritch' is much softer than a scratch.) I wondered if the old fellow might pull himself smack back into his shell for a full army's retreat. Stretching its neck and turning its adorably wrinkled face up at me the turtle soaked in the likes of me with what looked to be genuine curiosity.

Magical is how it seemed when the turtle leaned into my finger and closed its eyes in seeming pleasure to be petted. Petting the other turtle seemed only fair so I rubbed her little head as well. Brad studied them by laying on his stomach, hands folded palm down beneath his chin. Sunlight glinted in Brad's eyes lighting the brown of them for a moment. I reached out and caressed under the neck of the nearest turtle. The creature leaned into the petting. Seeing this I simply had to indulge my curious affection and stroke beneath the neck of the other smaller turtle. Lisa came forward bestowing another small piece of lettuce at the feet of the reptiles whom ate it more readily than one might have expected.

Heaving their shells they continued their journey towards Oleta. Their dermal plates wobbling slightly side to side with each labored step. Noticing they had what looked like toenails at the tip of their toes, I wondered if I might be allowed to paint their toenails. Perhaps a lovely hot pink. Designer houses on their backs too with polishes of red and blue and orange inlaid in the shells natural ornament.

I day-dreamed of rococo turtles carrying bejeweled houses like rainbow sparkled shields of armor. The creatures moved on their quest as Brad and I spotted their journey with bits of lettuce. Oleta pointed and spoke sweetly: "Oh look! From behind the apple tree!" Everyone looked to the green apple gallows with its long brown branches.

"Well, there's the baby", Grandaddy announced.

Peeking in its small timid manner the littlest turtle made its appearance and the tour de force was complete. Eventually all the turtles came to rest at Oleta's feet to worship her.

Upon feeding the turtles it soon became our own time to banquet. After dining we would indulge in additional play. Peanut butter and jelly were the afternoons fare. Although I can't stand peanut butter and jelly together. I needed them to be separate sandwiches from each other in order to suit my palate. My Uncle Jerry (Brad and Lisa's dad), and also my own father (Bobby), did not need to keep different food flavors separate. They could mix their foods together and claim to enjoy the taste. In fact, Brad was also well known for his enjoyment of mixing ketchup and jelly with his scrambled eggs. Putrid I should think, but then everyone's different and has a right to be so.

Come evening the house was warm and inviting. It was par course for the waning day to play our favorite game: Tarzan! Grandmommy Oleta Barns handed a huge bag of baby biscuits to me and I shared them with Lisa and Brad. We ate the baby biscuits while playing our game.

"Whoever can pick the others up can be Tarzan." Instructed Lisa.

"How come?" This was disconcerting to me. I would give it my best shot but common sense told me I'd never be able to pick up either of them. "Let me try!" You couldn't tell me I shouldn't at least try. Stubborn headed or impracticably hopeful that it might be, I tried. My tiny arms wrapping around Brad like thin white wings while pulling the pressure of his body to rest upon my hips and lift! His feet never left the ground. Never mind, try again and add an 'umphrr' from my vocal cords. To no avail.

"Okay let me try!" Lisa stepped forward.

"No wait! I haven't tried you yet Lisa!"

"Well if you can't lift Brad then you really can't lift me."

"I've still got to try."

"Oh alright." Lisa rolled her eyes and shrugged her shoulders.

Feeling absurdly foolish I nevertheless wanted to give it a try. After all, perhaps Lisa was simply taller than Brad but not much heavier in weight? Brad was so stocky and muscular while she was not. The effort was extreme to envelope Lisa's body with my pale wire-drawn wings. Finally I had my arms almost all around her hips. No use. I knew even before tugging upward. Stepping back I sighed. We all kept munching on the baby biscuits that were in the huge plastic bag as we assessed the situation. Tiny biscuits made with love by the hands of Oleta.

"You can't pick me up but I can pick up you!"--Lisa stuffed the two baby biscuits she was holding into her mouth and chewed hard. Hands cupped beneath my armpits Lisa lifted my body off the floor with great dexterity and pride in her brawn. I was impressed! But what of Brad? He scooted beside his big sister and as soon as she set me down my brown skinned boy cousin locked his arms around my body while I was unprepared. I thought we would topple over onto the floor for a moment. His hands like a belt buckle pressing into the center of my back. He pulled me towards his chest. My body raised to its tiptoes before settling quickly back down to the floor.

"Ha ha! I *am* Tarzan!" Brad beat his two fists against his chest and crowed loudly. Then he popped another baby biscuit in his mouth and did a jungle call with bits of biscuit spitting out. "Ahh-Eee-Ah-Eee-Ahhh!"

"You have to be able to lift me up too Brad." Lisa opened her arms in invitation for his efforts.

Brad tried for what seemed like an inordinately long time to raise Lisa off her feet. He used deep grunts and groans. He used deep whooshing breaths. Brad tried valiantly to lift the bar of his endurance. Yet despite his skill at hoisting me he was utterly unsuccessful at elevating Lisa even so much as a nudge. This was not the end of the battle. For Brad felt compelled to make Lisa prove her ability to lift himself also before she could claim the diadem of Tarzan.

Although we were still very excited about playing the game no matter what, Brad and I were nevertheless temporarily disappointed not to be Tarzan. This called for one more battle!

"Is your Tarzan call as good as mine?" And with that Brad let loose another impressive, crowing, howling, jungle call. "Ahh-Eee-Ah-Eee-Ahhh!"

Lisa did something unthinkable. She stepped up onto the couch. Yes, the couch! With her shoes on! Then with a preparatory deep breath inward she beat her chest and did a most remarkable Tarzan call. The best Tarzan call *ever*! Brad and I were left in awe! Second only to the magnanimous rendition which the actress Carol Burnett made famous, Lisa was good! Naturally Lisa won out and had the privilege to play the part of Tarzan. Brad and I asked her to make the Tarzan call again, and we clapped; hat's off to her! My delectation was in portraying 'Jane' while Brad flipped back and forth in a frolic between the characters of 'boy' and 'monkey'. Brad sure could do a really good monkey.

Brad bent low and hopped up and down and hollered, "Ooo, Ooo, Aaa, Aaaa", and scratched his ribs and underarms in perfect monkey style. He did fabulous monkey somersaults and eventually caused us all to be hungry for bananas; which to our luck Oleta had. Bananas and biscuits, however, taste rather weird together we discovered. Next Brad would stand stately yet wild as he played 'boy' and carried a sacred scroll to a king. Lisa as Tarzan would swing monkey or Jane on long vines from one tree to another tree and over wide rivers! (The floor was usually the river and the trees were the couch and chairs.) Tarzan had to give her remarkable jungle call for Jane to come help get monkey to the hospital because he was very sick; Brad rolled on his back holding his stomach and groaning. But wait! Tarzan has just thought of the perfect herb to cure monkey! Tarzan swings on the vines and picks the precious healing herbs, then swings on a vine back to monkey and Jane…(Lisa does another rendition of her most impressive jungle-wild call)… "Aaaaah-ee-ah-ee-ahhhhhh!"

"Aaaaaaaaaaaawwwwww", we all lament, as JB and Oleta have walked into the room smiling happily at us and holding our pajamas, "Is it time for bed already?!"

*   *   *   *   *

Our family would have one short, small, picture perfect pinnacle at the end of my summer's three month stay, when my cousin's parents as well as my own parents plus my older brother and sister came to visit and we would all spend the night under the same roof. Everyone smiling and laughing. My mother looking so lovely with that rare smile upon her face. Oleta cutting my father's and uncle's hair while her two sons made jokes and doted on her. Happiness seemed to abound in my grandparent's house. I'll never forget how deeply I breathed in a feeling of pride in my family that last night. Looking at my father I felt that same swelling pride which I felt when sitting in a pew and listening to one of his fabulous sermons. Same ballooning in my bosom for my beautiful mother with her fine taste for clothing, jewelry, and just the right amount of makeup to give countenance to her queenly manners and fertile intellect. Pride and love intertwining like a behemothic vine in my heart for my brother and sister, my cousins and grandparents, and all within my family tree.

I would find out later that our creepy spectral stranger had been stalking my mother when she was pregnant with me. This knowledge would help me to think of the stranger in easier words and descriptors. I would come to find it all quite untowardly disturbing this inexplicable troubadour of danger. But all of life is not darkness. I had my summer with Oleta and JB Barns, and there would be more summers to come where my cousins and I could bask in the love of our grandparents, play Tarzan, and eat baby biscuits.

FIVE

ARSENIC AND OLD PEANUT BUTTER

It came to pass in 1973 that I finally gathered up my courage to brace the question of food with my family; but no-one was ever around. This was not there fault, for as I said they were a busy family. And I was proud of their hard working ethic. I had been eating the chicken noodle soup they had in the pantry which I would slowly stir an egg into to make an egg-drop soup. And I had been using the flour and sugar to bake myself sweet-rolls. But I guess I was just sick of eating soup and sweet-rolls and crackers. I felt I needed someone to teach me the what and how of cooking something else. Perhaps it was simply the timing seemed right as I'd awoke earlier than usual one day and found the lady that went to my Dad's church, whom was cleaning the parsonage, was in the house and in fact standing in the kitchen. It was Mimi. Appropriate indeed one would think for isn't the kitchen the hub of most all cuisine anyhow?

Mimi stood at the gray metal sink rinsing out a thick black and gray heat resistant cup. Warm yellow light poured in from the morning sun through the small to medium sized two-pane window above the sink. The sunlight promised the impressions of a fairly pleasant day. This would prove to be true at a sweet 76 degrees. Mimi's soft chestnut brown hair curled neatly at the neck of her shirt and up over her ears with tightly flowing waves parted on the left and framing her forehead. The turtle neck long sleeved shirt of a matte silvern color was draped with a sleeveless vest of slightly darker color. The vest was a lighter almost silky material that hung loosely at her hips to float against her slate gray skirt. The skirt came to just above her knees. Low heeled black dress shoes on her stocking feet. Makeup gentle and enhancing despite the orange tinted color of her lip stick. The lip color somehow didn't do justice to her pretty green eyes. She seemed calm and happy with a mild smile upon her closed lips. Yes, now would be a good time to broach the subject. Especially with Mimi.

"Hello Mimi. I'm surprised to see you." Silence. "I wanted to find out about something." Time ticking in the quiet. "Mimi, other kids at school have breakfast and lunch at the school. And I'd also like to know how to cook other stuff."

The authoritative head turned its eyes in my direction momentarily with a scrunched nose and a slight sneer, then turning back towards the window and running fresh water into the newly cleaned cup and taking a swallow.

"What I mean is…" Pausing to lift my finger to my lips while choosing my words. "Some kids bring a lunch. And they have a cafeteria. You can actually get a tray and they give you all kinds of food."

Mimi shrugged and swallowed more water. Her eyes narrowed. The quiet was deafening.

"And they have breakfast too." Pacing now and begging my words and tone of voice to sound polite. "How can I have some breakfast? At school? And lunch to eat too? That's what I as wondering. What do you think? They say you can have one if you have a card. How do I get a card?"

Mimi looked to me again yet the muscles in her arms, shoulders, and face, hardened. Horrid grin spreading across her face belying the arch of her eyebrows and coldness in her eyes. I recognized that look. That expression. The grin. The frightening shine in Mimi's eyes. What was I thinking? Obviously this was not the correct timing! Not daring to tell myself from where I recognized that look despite the fact that it seemed as if Mimi had become a different person. I'd seen this happen to her before yet because of my young years it always came as a surprise. Terrible sound to her voice with a stare in her eyes as if she meant to bore holes through me.

"Do you want to embarrass your family?" Mimi contended. "How dare you suggest going around carrying some card for the poor!" The sheer volume of her voice was as much a surprise as her change into such angry behavior. I actually jumped when she spoke. She continued: "That's for poor people! Do you want people laughing at you? Laughing at your family? Talking behind your backs?! You want people to think your family are poor? You'd like that wouldn't you? So you could be hurtful!"

I felt the unearthly lifting of my breath as my brain sent messages of something strange and beyond dangerous going on. I was frightened. The look in her eyes was so angry and overbearing that I felt as if I'd become less than an inch tall and she could metaphorically squish me under foot at any moment. I wanted to say, "Hold on! What is happening here?" Where did her anger come from? Yes, I'd seen that expression in Mimi's eyes before. That hardened demeanor of the body. The hate filled inflection in the voice. What is this all about? It made me think of that night. The night at Holli's when I saw that person like a demon? Like a ghost? The guy whom might have been Holli's brother that was wearing the mask? So much more frightening to say 'like a mad man.' The similarity of voice and demeanor was terrifyingly uncanny. Yet thinking myself a child of reason I simply backed up a few paces so that the kitchens bar stool sat between us. I then tried to reiterate my question. I should have kept my mouth shut!

"I mean, I was just wondering. I was just wondering how the other kids get lunch?" Straining to make my voice sound soft and pleasant. Keeping my chin down with my eyes lifted upward.

Brow furrowed, with eyes squinted and gleaming, Mimi's voice came out sounding more like a growl than anything else. The sound of her voice as if she deeply hated me; perhaps she did.

Mimi pounded two steps forward. "You want lunch? I'll give you lunch!" Thin cabinets suspended from below the kitchen ceiling which required a 5 foot 6 inch woman to stand on her tiptoes just to barely reach the top of the shelf. Mimi extracted from this shelf a half loaf of bread and a bottle of peanut butter that was down to the bottom of the jar. Seeing this was like a secret revealed. How long had that been there? I watched in a wonderment of fear and curiosity.

Tearing a sheet of paper towel from its roll and laying it flat with a hard thunk of her palm. Throwing a piece of bread onto the paper towel. Constant scowling angry face, yet a self satisfied smile creeping up the corners of Mimi's closed lips. Creepy creeping grinning mouth. Eyes that shone pure hatred for me. Swathing peanut butter onto a slice of bread with a knife which was carelessly tossed into the sink after usage. Then bending to open the cabinet beneath the sink. I knew that cabinet. The underneath the sink cabinet. My father had opened it up and shown me two cleanser bottles, one jug of vinegar, and a white thick cardboard type canister.

All of these I was not supposed to touch. But especially not to touch the white canister. My father had pointed to the white canister and said, "Especially don't ever touch that one. It's rat *poison*. It's poison. See that symbol? If you see that symbol than you know it's poison."

Mimi snatched up the white canister and opened it, then she turned it upside down and shook it , shook it, shook it, over the open faced peanut butter sandwich.

"What are you doing?" I tentatively asked.

"Putting rat poison on your sandwich", she said flatly. She said it so matter of fact. So decidedly. The sneer of hatred and distaste still narrowing her eyes and crinkling her forehead. Speechless, I watched her place a second slice of bread on top of the powder coated peanut concoction then wrap the sandwich in clear wrap and plunk the whole thing in a small brown paper grocery bag which she'd retrieved from the pantry. Folding closed the top of the paper bag twice. She then handed it to me. And I took it.

"Thank you", I said. For ironically isn't that the proper response when someone has given you something? Mimi snorted then wheeled around and grabbing her purse off of the kitchen counter made her way out the front door and to her car outside. Standing there unmoving and still holding the bag until I heard the soft rumble and purr of her car leaving the driveway. Then at once I went to the cabinet beneath the sink, fully expecting the canister to be something other than what my father had shown me. No such luck. It was without a doubt the same canister of rat poison with its little symbol of death. A skull and cross bones plainly visible in black and white. I told myself that obviously they must have used up the rat poison. And being the economical people that they were my father or mother must have rinsed the canister clean and reused it to contain something else. Mimi must have known this. Some other white powdery substance. Perhaps flour or sugar? Or talcum? Surely that was the explanation. And so I closed the door to the cabinet below the sink and shrugged. Carrying my dull-brown paper bag lunch with me to school.

Come lunch time I sat at the far left end at one of the long foldable tables in the middle of the cafeteria. My back to the door I sat where I could look out the window at the furthest wall. Not close enough to see anything of particular essence; that didn't matter. For after all I could still see the sky. Dim dismal gray-blue shrouded sky. Which was actually easier on the eyes than a glaring blinding sunlight. Smiling and kicking my legs beneath the table in an excited rhythm. I was filled with an uttermost happiness to have something to eat inside the cafeteria like all the other children. I didn't have to go home and eat crackers or bake sweet-rolls. Placing my brown paper bag upon the table very clearly so the other kids could see it gave me a feeling of normalcy and belonging. I have something to eat in the cafeteria at lunch time! I'm just like the other kids now. Opening my bag and removing the sandwich.

Carefully pressing the paper bag flat. Placing the sandwich on top of the make-shift place-mat of brown paper. I unwrapped the sandwich. Picking up the sandwich with both hands and examining it. Reminding myself that it was most surely only flour or sugar or talcum that had been put in the rat poison canister and now lay in a thick coating on top of the peanut butter. Mimi was certainly kidding by saying that it was still rat poison in the canister, right?

Because of eating something in the cafeteria I will also look like the other children sitting at the table. Fitting in and looking like the other kids seemed more important than actual hunger. I was actually proud to have a lunch. Lifting the sandwich to my lips. Opening my mouth.

Suddenly someone screaming my name: "Suuuuuuuzieeee!"

I would have literally taken my first bite at that precise moment had I not heard Mimi's voice screaming my nickname loud and frantic just at the exact second I was opening to sink my teeth in. The timing was strangely uncanny.

"Suzie! Suuuuuzzziee!" Came Mimi's voice shrieking at the top of her lungs as if a fire had just broke loose around me.

Foregoing my bite with mouth still poised open, I turned to look over my shoulder at the cafeteria doors behind me. I was shocked to see a screaming Mimi, a woman who was always so deeply concerned about how she looked to others, come running and panting disheveled and shouting my name into the cafeteria. Surprised and apprehensive as to what would cause Mimi to enter a room without her usual poise sent my heart pounding in an adrenaline surge of sirens in my mind. To warn me that something really was very wrong.

Standing up; sandwich still in my hands. I stepped towards her as she practically skidded to a halt in front of me and vocalized a short shrill high pitched shriek. Instantaneously and with a jerk of her arm she quickly yanked the sandwich out of my hands so that it dangled between her forefinger and thumb. Then she tossed it into the trash can that was only a few feet from where I stood. Copiously startling was to see her hunched and panting while leaning her left elbow on the edge of the trash can.

Mimi's troubled eyes were full up with worry. She was sweating. Mimi was obviously worried, and she obviously cared about what would have happened if I had eaten that sandwich. Perspiration was spotting drops across her face like early morning dew. Gulping in air she spoke in a breathless struggle. "I…I just remembered that the meat had gone bad", she said very loud; loud enough for everyone in the shocked and quieted cafeteria to hear. She fained a smile.

Rapidly my eyes jerked to my right to look at the trash can which contained my peanut butter sandwich. Somehow it seemed appropriate to stay quiet and not dare mention that there never was any meat in the sandwich in the first place. "I'm sorry", she said loudly again. "I had to throw it away. The meat. I'm sure it was bad." She looked around at the others in the cafeteria while she was talking, and fained that smile again. She patted at her hair as if to straighten it.

Of course she knew it was peanut butter from a jar and not meat. But she also surely knew that I would hold my tongue and not contest it. (A good idea.) It was already painfully obvious to my senses that she was trying to save face for having run in with such a screaming flurry. Fearing her, I wanted her to feel she'd saved face and so I simply nodded.

Oh how a mountain fell that day at that exact moment. For now I knew as I watched Mimi patting her hair and catching her breath next to the trash can that it had not been flour or sugar or talcum powder replaced in the canister. Without a shadow of a doubt *I knew*. *Rat poison*. And a lot of it. This event was actually positive for me as it turns out. Very important and very *positive*. As far as I'm concerned this event *needed* to happen. The reason this is of importance is because it had the profound effect upon me to start questioning what life is all about, and to question what death is all about. It got me thinking on a deeper level. It would be an event important towards making me work on my Laws and Theories.

Screaming Mimi would eventually give me a debilitating pervasive fear of people however. My heart and any trust I may have had crumbling into an enormous shifting ocean of salty tears and doubt. It would take a lot of work to overcome screaming Mimi.

Mimi reached into the receptacle and pulled trash up over the sandwich, then pressed it all down. "Well, since I'm here I might as well buy you lunch." She looked around at the other people in the cafeteria and smiled at them.

"You're gonna buy me lunch Mimi?" Excitement at having my own tray of food thrilled me. I was very young.

"Yes, but you'd better wash your hands first! Anyway its good manners and good hygiene to wash your hands before eating any meal."

Looking at my hands. "Yes Mam."

Mimi looking at her own hands--"I'd better wash also. Come on."

Mimi and I made our way to the restroom and properly washed our hands with soap and water. Mimi scrubbed especially hard and used a lot of soap; which she directed me to do as well. Then when we'd washed and dried our hands I followed Mimi out of the restroom door and over to the kitchen area of the cafeteria where they served the hot lunches. We got in line behind several children. As we inched down the cafeteria food line I found I was unable to satisfactorily continue down the line without watching Mimi's hands. She stood beside me *and* behind me in line. Was it possible she could have something poisonous in her hands and put it into my warm school food while I was looking away? I purposely exerted effort to sweep the tugging thought away, yet found I kept looking at her hands. The plump cafeteria women in hairnets and wearing clear plastic gloves served their portion of food then passed the tray down to the next person to serve their portion of food, and so on. Pears with syrup, then pass the tray down; beans, pass the tray; mystery meat loaf, pass the tray. The last woman in the serving line picked up a roll with her plastic gloved fingers and set it on top of the mystery meat loaf then handed the tray to me. Keeping a glance from the corner of my eye on Mimi's hands I took the tray offered to me. I was so grateful to have the food that I knew I would eat every bite no matter what it tasted like.

I held my tray back as Mimi paid for the meal. Then Mimi and I walked just past the kitchen doors to a long table that stood fairly empty in the cafeteria; she pulled out a chair and sat down. I sat my tray down on the table but scooted it away from where Mimi sat, and then I pulled a chair out for myself and sat down. I tugged my tray up close to me. I knew I was supposed to say 'thank you' to Mimi for having bought the meal, but under the circumstances I did not wish to speak at all. Yet I fought my fears and told Mimi 'thank you for the meal', because I'd been taught that saying thank you was what people were supposed to do. I also knew I should say a prayer before eating but I did not want to close my eyes to do it while Mimi sat next to me. Thus I began a habit which I would keep through out my life of praying with my eyes open. Folding my lily white hands together and keeping my eyes open I said, "Bless this to the nourishment of my body."

I slowly ate with worry and a sickness in my stomach over the rat poisoned peanut butter sandwich I had almost eaten. I kept feeling like I would throw up, so I had to breath very slowly and deliberately just to push back the tide of nausea that kept wanting to heave. Yet oddly and despite the knot in my stomach I also ate with pride that I had a lunch like the other kids; I looked around me to see if the other children noticed that I was eating just like they were. It was not just hunger that motivated me but the desire to fit in. Later on in the school year I would spend my lunch time in the library just so that I didn't have to be embarrassed at not eating with the other children. Mimi nibbled at the food on her tray a moment but did not sit long with me on this day. To my relief she scooted back her chair, stood up, and said loudly, "Well, I've got to go. Enjoy your lunch!" I didn't eat another bite until I saw her leave the cafeteria. Then I stood up and carried my tray to a far table next to the huge window at the back of the cafeteria. Sitting down near the window I ate quietly by myself while looking outdoors at the lemon-lime colored grass and slate-blue sky. Patches of gray clouds undulated in the lofty windswept slate-colored space outside.

The grass looked like it was struggling to stay alive. A singular dandelion arched its yellow petals back and forth in the tug of the wind.

*   *   *   *

That particular evening in 1973 I would have the chance to watch some television but found nothing of particular interest. Flipping the dial on the black and white set I watched some news. Newscasters were vividly animated in their terribly serious manner to distribute the country's current dramas. Britain had graciously decided to grant independence to the Bahamas. Juan Peron had been elected as President of Argentina. Failing to enjoy my world and my nation's real life dramas I elected to go listen to the small radio connected to my alarm clock. Thumping my thumb on my knees and tapping my toes I found solace that night in singing along with the radio music. Cher sang "Half Breed". Tony Orlando and Dawn sang "Tie a Yellow Ribbon". Finally I became tired enough to turn off the radio and rest for a while. Nightmares plagued me all the night long. How fragile the human soul. Yet at very long last, every part of your soul you lost comes back to you. Even if your left wondering why so long.

I mentioned that I thought Mimi was dangerous to my Father when he was home one Sunday evening. He bent down towards me and pointed his index finger at me and said angrily, "Don't you ever say such things about your elders, or I swear someday somebody's going to beat you clear into next week." That was actually a fairly common remark for a parent during that time in history. I nodded and slunk out of the room. Well that didn't work, I thought to myself.

S I X

THEIF IN THE NIGHT

It was an ordinary school day. Lessons taught and hopefully learned, this particular day at school was coming to a close. A fond warm degrees of seventy-one gave all the school children a longing anxiousness toward warmer days of summer. Stuffing my books into the thick gray knit cap I'd brought. No need for the cap to be on my head. The books were kept neatly together in a tight bundle. Bell ringing in announcement to all classes that the school day had come to an end. Tammy came to my home room in school to greet me. I stood next to the table where my books and cap sat. Tammy, who was both my age and my friend, came running up beside me. "How come you don't take the bus Suzanna?"

"Oh Tammy I just live several blocks *that* way." Pointing with my finger. "Its not that far. I can walk it. Want to come over to my house?"

"I'd have to ask my Dad. You wanna come over to my house?"

"Oh, you know what? I think we actually have a supper and youth meeting at the church tonight. Want to come to church with me tonight?"

"Nnnn…no." Tammy physically squirmed at telling this truth.

"That's okay."

"Wanna come over to my house Suzanna?"

"I'll ride the bus with you. Maybe. Will the bus come back near the school?"

"I don't know. I think so." Tammy rubbed her head and fluffed her thin straight sunlight blonde hair. Her sky blue eyes blinking and complementing her smooth creamy peach skin. Taller than I she also bore a *healthy* type of body shape.

Tammy pointed to my books stuffed in the gray knit cap. "Will that thing really hold your books?"

"I guess I'm about to find out." Grabbing hold of the book strap poking out. "Yep! It works. See? I've got a book strap that covers the first two books on top and the cap stretches over the whole thing and holds them all together."

"That's neat. I've got a cap." Tammy produced a red knit cap the same style as mine. "Can I put my books in mine?"

"Why not?" I began helping her stuff her books inside her red cap. Stretching the cap to pull over them. I was helping Tammy stuff and stretch her cap on the room's arts and crafts table. The table was a long, short to the ground, semi-circle of a dark honey-brown fake wood. It was my favorite table in the room because I loved that if you got your school work done early you could go over to the arts table and color or do crafts. Examining the book stuffed cap I found it met with my approval. Lifting the bundle up I set it into Tammy's waiting arms. Tammy tested it out by holding it from the top edges of the red knit.

"Wow! I can't believe that works!" Her voice sounded pleased and full of wonderment. "Okay, hey I hope it holds! I've got to hurry! I've got to catch the bus!"

"Catch it."

"What?" Tammy turned around to look at me.

"Nothing. Just 'catch' a bus. Sounds funny. Like someone's going to toss the bus and your going to catch it in your baseball glove." We both laughed.

"I've got to go Suzanna. Are you coming?"

"Yep."

"Well come on! We've got to hurry!"

"Do you think they left without us Tammy?"

Making our way out of the classroom and into the hall which opened to a myriad of doors. "I don't know", concern crossed Tammy's cherub face. "I'm supposed to go to the bus right when the bell rings."

We automatically began walking with a faster pace.

"Do you always take the bus?"

"Uh-huh."

"This will be my first time to ride a bus."

"Really?"

"Yes. Which way do we go?"

"This way." Tammy pointed to the hallway on the right which led away from the school's front door.

Confused that we wouldn't be exiting by way of the front door I paused to look around. "Are you sure we go this way?"

"Yeah. We go out the back door."

"I didn't know there was a back door."

Walking, I saw that at the very tail-end of the hallway was a sign on the dull brown double door. A fire exit. "I thought we weren't supposed to ever use the fire exit except in a fire."

Tammy patted my back reassuringly. "It's where the bus riders go."

My eyebrows raised at this information. Not only was the fire exit door a dull color, the entire school was dull! The walls a dirty dull beige and the ceiling although the same color had a yellowish colored stain to it. When Tammy opened the fire exit door an entire world I'd never seen before lay forth. A field of concrete. Children gathered in collective bunches that seemed utterly purposeless until the buses pulled up.

The wide yellow monsters rolled their wheels in a slow and plodding manner, with a sputtering hum of filthy smelling exhaust.

"This one!" Tammy pointed out her particular bus and pulled me. Tugging on the shoulder of my dress she broke into a run; I followed her.

"We'll make it", I hollered as the children began filing one at a time into the bus. The yellow school bus seemed so big, wide, and strange. "Do you have to sit in a certain place?"

"No. But the first kids on the bus always take the front seats. Makes me mad. Cause if you wanna sit up front you have to ask if you can sit with them. They'll usually take up the whole seat to themselves anyway." Tammy grumbled her words.

We panted from our sprint. The day seemed actually warmer for the exercise. Annoyingly, the children stood in line without even an inch between them. Resisting the urge to make space between the child in front of me and the boy and girl holding hands behind me, I simply bit my lip and stayed patient. The two behind me were waddling side by side like Siamese twins.

Stepping up into the bus on steps far too tall to move either comfortably or to politely ascend, I felt myself blush; I was wearing a dress after all. Pushing down at the hem of my brown dress, covering my knees with my fingers, I was afraid of showing too much whilst climbing.

Pulling in the complete image of the hippie that was driving the vehicle, I received a full clear impression that although he was scruffy he was also kind and sweet and not to be feared. "Where do we sit?" I asked the driver with the long brown fuzzy hair. He had ebony eyes and a five o'clock shadow of stubble on his face.

"In a seat?" He offered with a mildly serious expression that flashed for a moment into a harmless silly grin. Sizing up his long, torn, bell-bottom jeans that hung completely over his moccasins. Only the tip of his soft shoes were exposed as his feet rested upon the pedals. His teeth were amazingly straight and white which was somehow a surprise to me. A tie-dyed tee-shirt poked through on his chest beneath his soft, blue, hooded jacket. Shrugging, I kept upon my trek following Tammy down the charcoal colored isle.

Tammy cupped her hand to my ear and whispered, "See? Those two boys right there, they took up whole seats all to themselves. Now we're going to have to sit in separate seats."

The solution seemed perfectly obvious. Although making the switch itself gave me doubt since the boys cooperation would depend upon their personalities and basic temperament. I took on the furthest boy on the right first. Leaning in to speak with him and making sure I had eye contact. "My friend and I would like to sit together. I'm going to ask that boy over there…" I pointed to the boy on the left second seat. "…if you can sit with him. If he says yes will you sit with him so Tammy and I can sit together?"

He tilted his head to the side and pursed his lips in thoughtful consideration then shook his head in an exaggerated 'yes'. Oh my! The logistics involved in school bus travel!

Stepping back towards the second seat on the left I again engaged eye-contact but added a quick gentle touch on this other boys red sweater shoulder. "My friend and I want to sit together. This boy has agreed to sit with you so we can sit together. Will you let him sit with you?"

Bobbing his shoulders up and down. "Okay", he said and scooted over towards the window.

"Thank you. I appreciate it very much."

"No problem."

Back to the previous boy. "He said you could sit with him." The boy stood. "Thank you. It's very nice of you to let Tammy and I sit together." Leaning back so he could get by. "I appreciate it", I added. The silent boy nodded in affirmation that he had heard me and kindly went to sit with the boy who was in the left second seat. Tammy and I plopped into our seat together. She was next to the window. Sitting at the edge of my seat I looked around at the children and the driver. Then I looked out the window of the bus and back at Tammy. Back and forth I looked again; just taking in the scene. The jury were in with a definitive verdict that riding a school bus is kind of fun. Suddenly I wished I *owned* a school bus; you could take out some of the seats and put in a couch!

"I wonder how hard these things are to drive", I said.

Tammy looked at me. "You mean the bus? To drive the bus?"

"Yes."

"Why?" Tammy asked with a perplexed frown crinkling up her nose.

"I was just wondering because I thought it would be neat to have one. If you owned a bus you could practically live in it."

"It'd be fun to play in."

"Sure would." A thought hit me. "Oh no!" The bus was already humming down the street. I didn't even realize the precise moment the driver had closed the bus door.

"What is it Suzanna?"

"I forgot to ask the driver if the bus will come back by somewhere near the school!"

"No, no! Don't get up!" Tammy nudged me back down in my seat. "You'll get in trouble if you get up while the bus is going."

"What do I do?"

"Ask him when he stops the bus again."

"Oh. Well yes, that makes sense." Of course waiting made each second seem to last forever. "When is your stop Tammy?"

"I'm one of the last."

"Oh." Waiting. Waiting.

"Are you gonna play?"

"I'd better get home. It's groovy to ride the bus with you though." Watching. Waiting. Passing old oaks and rows of cookie cut square houses in various dreary nondescript hues of beige. Sunshine peeping in and out of low masses of flat clouds. Each time the bus stopped I turned expectantly towards Tammy. I would wait and ask my question of the driver when Tammy's stop came. Children lined up to exit at their stop, the bus becoming more and more hushed with each departure. Tammy looked at me and gave a long blink and a slow nod as if to say: 'Wait. Not yet.' Patience; patience.

Although it couldn't have been more than twenty-five to thirty minutes Tammy's stop seemed exceptionally lengthy in the coming. It was fun to ride along however; especially with my friend sitting next to me. Cogs and wheels groaning as the bus pulled to a corner stop sign. An old rusty moan as the door opened once again. Only a few children were left on the bus.

"This is my stop." Said Tammy. "Call me when you get home."

"Okay." Following down the isle I waved her goodbye before sitting on the cool green plastic seat nearest to the driver at the front of the bus. Leaning forward I asked the driver, "Will you be going back by the school?"

"Yes", said the school bus driver, stretching the word out in a long drawl. "I'm on my way back that direction now. I've only got one more stop." He grinned a goofy hippie grin. I grinned back.

I settled into my seat. Looking back I counted how many children were left; three boys. Somehow it felt special to sit in the front first seat, although why this should be who knows. Moving faster than before the driver sped so that the bus came quickly to its final stop. It was indeed on the way back to the school. I recognized the neighborhood from previous explorations and knew the school wasn't too terribly far away. Allowing the boys to step out of the bus before me, I simply sat and grinned back at the happy hippie. Only when the bus was completely empty did I stand up and walk towards the door. Placing a hand on the bus driver's shoulder to make sure he knew I was speaking to him, I said: "I'm going to get out here. I know where I am."

"You don't usually ride this bus, do you?"

"Nope."

"You sure you know where your house is from here?"

"Yes."

"The school is just over there."

I nodded the affirmative at his pointing finger. "I know where we are."

"Yeah?"

"Yes. Thank you."

A shout came from outside of the bus and thus I instinctively jolted my head in the direction of the noise. "Get him!"--Came the young male voice of one of the boys who had just left the bus. A 'woomf' sound followed the shout. Taking a step down the stairs of the bus I saw the two boys that had been sitting together piled on top of the fatter, quieter, boy and pounding him with their fists. Looking back at the driver I waited open-mouthed for what he would do. A shake of his long frizzy brown hair and he shrugged his shoulders. "I stay out of it", he said.

Without even thinking about it I spun around. Bounding down the exit steps and onto the grass. Hearing the buses moaning and groaning as its door closed and its wheels took it away. In one swollen pounce I wrapped my arms around the back and shoulders of the bully closest to me and threw him into the grass. Both bully's were taller and older than I was but somehow I had greater strength than usual. Next I grabbed hold of the second bully in the same manner and threw him into the grass as well. They wobbled up onto their feet with a genuine look of shock upon their faces. An incongruous surprise for their eyes to feast upon, I stood puny in comparison to either of them. They may both have been stronger, thicker, and taller, but I had a pounding unshakable advantage of outrage heaving my chest with each breath. Outrage beating wildly in my veins and beaming from my eyes.

"What religion are you?" It was the first thing that came to my mind. I aimed my words bluntly and powerfully at the first bully I had extracted from the child's back.

"What?" Fright and confusion flashed through his eyes as this bully shifted his weight from one foot to the other and back again. Confusion cleared quicker for the child who had been beaten. He drank in one last look at his tormentors then bound to his feet in an instant run. I saw the beaten child run behind the shelter of a semi-porch that gave coverage from rain for the front door of a house. Instantly I assumed this was probably where the boy lived although I noticed he didn't enter the house.

Sizing up the two boys remaining I noticed they had similar features with very round faces and strong jaw bones. Large pale gray inset eyes on both of them. Blondish-brown, short, buzz-cut hair on their heads. One boy, slightly taller than the other, wore a puffy green vest with zippers around the arms where the sleeves had obviously been removed. Momentarily I felt worry for the shorter boy not having a coat. It had warmed during the day but had been cold this morning. Sliding aside my worry for his not having a jacket, I took a hard swallow and kept to my objective. Bringing my voice down to a stern calm. Knowing they wouldn't catch anything I had to say *if I were to yell at them*! Letting my eyes and stern calm voice keep hold of them. "What religion are you?" I demanded once again to the first and taller boy who wore the vest.

"What?" He reiterated with genuine confusion.

"Do you or your family have a belief system of some sort? Or a religion? Are you Buddhist? Jewish? Christian?" I stopped short in an odd-feeling sudden lack of memory for other religions. 'Oh!'--I thought to myself, 'A Taoist! That's another one!' Yet before I could say this out loud the boy spoke.

"I'm Baptist." Said the vested boy.

"We're brothers." Said the shorter one.

"So you're both Christians."

Looking at one another then back at me they both chimed: "Yes."

"What are your names?"

"Jimmy." (The shorter one.)

"James." (The taller.)

"Well, Jimmy and James. I'm Suzanna." I shook their hands. The boy's faces stayed perplexed. The shorter and presumably younger brother Jimmy wiped his forehead with the back of his right hand. James nervously flapped his arms up and down so that the flattened palms of his hands patted against his blue-jeaned thighs. "Jimmy. James. You're Christians. Okay. Do you know that means your belief system follows the teachings and sayings of Jesus?" They both nodded. "Most all the major religions have some format for kindness, lovingness, and treating others with care and respect. Did you know that in your religion Jesus said to 'Do unto other's as you would have them do unto you?' " Both boys nodded affirmative and seemed embarrassed and uncomfortable.

"Well do you believe what you've learned from your parents and from your church in what Jesus said?" Again an affirmative nod from the boys and I had a sudden urge to also talk about similar things said by Buddha and Confucius but swallowed the urge knowing it might mute my point for them. "James, Jimmy, according to your religion do you believe you're supposed to live your life by what Jesus teaches until the time comes when you die someday?" I was trying to make a plea with something they were familiar with. The older boy's breathing turned ragged and they both silently nodded again. "Well someday when your old and you've lived your life, when you finally die do you want to look down at your body and know that in your life you beat up on some little kid? A child?"

"Our dad beats on us and says we're sissy's if we don't fight back."

"Shut up Jimmy!" He glared at his brother.

"Well are you two grown up yet or are you two still just kids?"

"Kids."—The boys said at the same time.

"Jimmy, I'll tell her!" He let out an exasperated humph. "We're kids."

"Of course you are. And I am here to tell you two boys that what your father did was wrong. You ought to tell your teacher or your preacher at your church. It's wrong James what your father did. It's wrong Jimmy. And you two are going to have to be smarter and stronger than your father."

The boys gave me sly, pleased, smiles as I continued to speak. "Maybe your father got beat by his own dad when he was young and so now he does the same thing to you… but that doesn't make it right does it?" James and Jimmy shook their heads 'no'.

"Does it feel good when you get beat on?" Head's shaking 'no'. "I'm gonna ask you to do something that's going to feel different and may seem hard at first. I'm going to ask you two kids to be more of a man than your father ever has been. I'm going to ask you to be stronger and smarter. When you get the urge to beat up on that little kid your going to imagine Jesus is right there looking at you and you want to make Jesus proud and you want to be better and stronger young men than your father is."

Placing my hand gently on Jimmy's arm. "Jimmy I want you to feel that desire to beat up someone and imagine that Jesus is standing right next to you. Looking at you. Can you do that right now Jimmy? Can you see it?"

"Yes."

"Okay, you too James." Removing my right hand from Jimmy to place it softly on James' upper arm. I instructed them to close their eyes, and they did! "See it in your mind, that little boy kind of tubby and afraid and it makes you mad and you want to hit him. But then you see Jesus next to you; and you see your father hitting you and you know it's wrong. So both of you boys remember at that moment that you're gonna be stronger and smarter than you've ever been; and you just keep walking. You get off that bus and you go straight home.

You don't beat him up." Pausing in silence to let them see it and think about it before continuing.

"You won't beat that boy up ever again. When you get the urge to beat him up you are going to take a deep breath and say, 'I'm going to be smarter… smarter than my own father!' And then I want you both to feel proud of yourselves. Feel that pride right now."

"Feel that urge Jimmy." Walking around behind them, I pressed my palm against the middle of Jimmy's back. "Feel that desire to beat that boy up. Do you feel it?" (A nod yes.) "Now say it! Say, I'm going to be smarter. Smarter than my own father."

"I'm going to be smarter than my own father."

"Now see yourself not beating the boy but just walking home and imagine you see Jesus next to you. And you feel proud. Take a deep breath in and just feel proud of yourself."

"Yeah!"--Exclaimed Jimmy with a huge smile. The response surprised me.

Putting my palm against the small of James' back I repeated the exact same things to him that I'd said to his brother. James also repeated out loud and with powerful conviction and in fact seemed thrilled when I brought him to the feeling proud part. "You are healed. Now, remember who *you* are." I ended by saying, "You can both open your eyes now." They opened their eyes.

"It makes so much sense when you say it like that."--Said James. "I *like* that!"

"Now I don't want to see you beating up anyone ever again. Especially *that* kid. I want you two to have more control over your own behavior. Okay?"

James: "Okay."

Jimmy: "No problem."

"Good. I'm proud of you." The two boys gleamed when I said that.

Waving them goodbye I took off in the direction I'd seen the beaten child run. Crossing the yellowed dry lawns I made my way toward the front door's rain shelter at the square beige brick house. The house seemed short and had no contour, it was completely flat on top. Shielding my eyes from the sun with the back of my right arm I looked at the house for the slightest of moments before heading towards the front door. There was a complete surprise waiting for me on the other side of the roofed wall that served as a rain shelter. The boy. Legs pulled up to his chest. Elbows on his knees. He covered his face and head with his arms and hands. An overly round pudgy shaking mass of flesh huddled against the brick wall sobbing. My heart went out to him. His muscles heaved and quaked as each rolling sob washed through him. A gurgling choking sound sputtered in his throat and I knew he was trying to keep me from knowing he was crying.

"Hey", I lulled softly, "why don't you go inside your house?"

"I... I can't"

"Why not? Have you lost your key?"

"No."

"You still have your key?"

"Yes."

Sitting down next to him I raised my right arm and lightly placed the tips of my fingers on his shoulder. "Well then why don't you go inside?"

"Because I don't live here."

I had assumed it was his home and I nearly laughed out loud when I realized why he couldn't go inside. Fortunately I caught the laugh before it escaped. I felt happy the boy wasn't looking towards me at that moment while I flattened and smoothed a small smile which had crossed my lips.

The tips of my right hand fingers were still on his shoulder. I placed the tips of my left hand fingers upon his bowed chin and pulled delicately, gently, upward. Feeling his facial muscles give way without any resistance to my touch I breathed a sigh of relief at the ease with which he lifted his face towards me.

His face was streaked wet. His eyes blinking at the sunlight pouring from behind my back onto his forehead. Looking at his face I saw that he was a handsome boy. "You're very nice looking", I said. He shook his head 'no'. "Ah, but you are." His shoulders shrugged and his gaze fell back down toward the cement beneath us. "If you'd been horribly ugly I wouldn't have said a word about your features. So you believe me that I'm telling you the truth. The bridge of your nose is a smooth line leading into its tip and nostrils. Your jaw is strong and blends well into your chin. Your forehead is neither too high nor too low." Pausing. "My forehead is a high one. See?" Lifting my blonde feathered bangs from my forehead. He looked up to see. Sunlight glinted shiny and sparkly into his eyes.

"Oh and your eyes. What a beautiful silver-gray. Your lucky to have such a color for your eyes. My eyes were blue when I was born but changed to hazel. Which means their brown sometimes and a dark forest green sometimes. See?" At this his troubles seemed to melt away for a moment while he gazed and squinted at my eyes. Then a bath of puzzlement washed over his face for an instant. He bowed his head again. I sat down next to him. Lifting my legs I rested my wrists upon my knees.

"My name is Suzanna. What's your name?" (Mumbling from his throat and lips.) What did he say? Did he say 'Billy'? Not pressing the issue I breathed in deeply and sighed. "How old are you?" (Mumbling again from the angel faced boy.) "I'm nine years old", I stated, "I was born in January." Pausing again. "Did you hide your handsome face from me because you thought you should be embarrassed for crying?"

"Yes." He finally spoke.

"Never feel embarrassed Son for anything human. Feelings are just part of being human. Or better yet remember that feeling embarrassed is human too. As you grow you'll learn to control your emotions and pick and choose what you feel and when and why. And you'll even be able to say to yourself not to be embarrassed about being embarrassed! Ha! How about that?" I smiled and nudged him slightly with my elbow and a short crisp laugh escaped him.

"What are you saying?" He asked softly and clearly, with a mixture of amusement and bewilderment.

I looked past the rain-guard to the trees, the sun, and the sky. Breathing deeply again. "I'm saying. Don't be afraid to be who you are." Nudging him with my shoulder again. "Who you are is just as amazing and miraculous as anybody else." With my right hand I gave a brief reassuring pat on his back before returning my wrist to its resting place upon my knee.

"Right now you've got the problem of these bully's, don't you?"

"Yes."

"You could learn to run faster. Get another mode of transportation. You could learn to fight back and give one of those boys a good punch in the chops." I swung a punching move into the air with my fist. "You could tell grown ups about it until you get help; which I think is a good idea."

I gently bumped him with my shoulder and took a deep breath. "I talked to those boys, and although I might be wrong about this, I get a very strong feeling they won't be bothering you anymore." He shrugged and choked again in a tearful whimper.

"Remember to breath. You shrug your shoulders every time I speak, so can you remember to take a deep breath every time you shrug your shoulders?"

He nodded 'yes' and shrugged yet again. And whilst I looked at the sunlight trickling through the trees I got an idea. If I could get him to relax and expand or alter his point of view. Squatting with my weight upon my tiptoes now. Placing my entire right palm upon his shoulder as much to reach him as to keep my balance.

"Can I get you to imagine something? To see something in your mind; like when you are day dreaming." Ankles aching, I shifted my position to sit on my bottom in front of him with my legs crossed Indian-style. "So you'll imagine something for me? Promise? I need you to actually say it out loud, yes or no."

"Yes."

"Good answer." I gathered together the memory of a church camp I had gone to where the church counselor had guided we children through a visualization to relax and focus. With this memory and a burning intuition inside me about what I desired to say I took a soothing gulping breath and began. Then I asked him to imagine a warm bright white light like the sun shining through his brain, mind, emotions, muscles, and bones. Speaking gently I said, "I want you to know now as your bathed in the white light that you have choices, to keep going, to choose to live. To remember every moment of every day that ten years from now time will have washed away much of the sting and pain of today. I want you to feel now in your body and mind that Good really is just as powerful as Evil. And everyone has a right to be who they are. But they are different. And the Good must remain safe. And so a control and a redirection of ones impulses must be applied. You have a right to be who you are. And you now feel your own strength and your stamina of your own power of who you are. Your ability to just relax and be there; be yourself. You allow change to take place and you choose to live, for the ten years from today when things have changed."

Standing up I looked to a tree and the sunlight trembling through its wind blown lime-green leaves. The boy looked up with a visible brawn glowing in his face that had not been there before. As if all the energy he had lost in his life's painful traumas had left those past events and the energy then finally came back to him. He stood up with such a gleaming renewed vigor.

"I feel better", he said with a hint of surprise in his voice.

"*Here*. I give you a hug." Wrapping my arms around his soft shoulders and passing on tender warmth. Backing away from the hug and waving, I said, "Bye", and leaving him with a smile I simply turned and left. I wanted to get back home. Walking back the way I came, I turned at the street corner where the bus had stopped. I heard the boy behind me shout out a 'thank you'. Looking back I smiled and waved again. Rounding the corner and turning right onto the next block. Passing the houses by walking through their front yards. There were no sidewalks there. Stepping upon and beyond driveways. Most of the cars gone this early in the afternoon. What time was it now? Around four or four-thirty? Puffy fluffing clouds hung like white cotton candy that you could just pluck from the baby blue sky and pop in your mouth to melt on your tongue. A pair of filthy browned sneakers hung from a telephone line and I paused to look up at them and wondered why and how someone got their shoes up there. Continuing to walk I pondered at the promise of green grass poking here and there through the yellowish and slightly crisp lawns. Sucking air into my lungs as if I could breath in the beautiful patches of green. Wind blew my downy blonde hair. Thinking of my hair I thought of my stretchy knit hat. And thinking of my hat I recalled my school books I had stuffed into it! Slapping my thighs and looking behind me I realized I had left my school books on the bus! "Ah!", I thought, "Nothing I can do about it now. They'll probably be waiting for me to claim them in the principles office when I go to school tomorrow. I hope."

Walking further along I spied a marvelous pine tree with small blue-green berries on it that were coated here and there with a chalky looking white film. Branches thick and full with the deep green needles of the tree towered way above my head. Having wandered over to the gorgeous tree I reached out and petted the hard round berries. Pulling at the long rotund pine needles I let them slide across the palm of my hand and fingertips. Suddenly I filled with an inexplicable longing which I could literally feel as a weight upon my chest and a fluttering in my belly. A longing to live where I was surrounded by pine trees and cow-towed by mountains. Memories pictures floated into my mind of pine trees everywhere when our family had gone skiing. We had met another preachers family late into the dark night at an all-night café and truck stop. There we had all eaten. I had pancakes with extra butter yet light on the syrup. Then like a caravan we all drove to the cabins we would stay at while on the ski trip. As I thought of the ravishing beauty of the pine trees and the mountains beyond the cabins I remembered a different time with my family in an altogether different forest. This other forest we visited did not have any snow until the last months of our stay. Nearly six months were spent in the seasons of the Sequoia National Forest. Spending most of my time outside among the pine trees was such a treat. My father was the Chaplain for an outdoor symposium of worship services several times a week. Ah how the look and smell of the Sequoia trees made me feel as if I were 'Home'. Not any place on earth, but my soul's Home. Yes, I loved the Sequoia with their huge trunks as big around as a house. I terribly missed the Sequoia trees suddenly as I viewed and touched the blue-green pine in front of me.

At once I heard a sad whimper. A small high-pitched cry. Yet wait, not a cry of distress, but much softer than that. A mewling. Looking down I heard a louder more excited sound like the peep of a happy infant. Walking around the right side of the tree I made an effort to follow the noise. Corny as it sounds I felt at that moment that if angels could exist and could sing a single pure and lovely note then they would have done so at that very moment when I gazed down upon the sweet fragile beauty before me. The way the light played sparkling upon her dark mane only added to the eternal instant as if gazing upon the holy grail. For there at my feet with large round amber colored eyes and black fur mussed this way and that was the most precious creature. A creature whom seemed in need of someone's time and help. Might as well be my own personal time and help, right? It was a little fur-fluffed baby black kitten.

"Your so beautiful", I spoke out loud to the kitten as I bent on one knee. "You're a perfect black. You should be called 'Black Beauty'. Never-mind the story where Black Beauty is a horse!" Picking up the kitten who had come to me as if I'd already been her owner, we gazed at one another. "Horses are magnificent creatures, but no black horse has anything more beautiful than you. Ohhh such a soft baby."

Lifting to my feet with the kitten cradled in my arms I made my way to the front door of the person whose yard I'd found the tiny cat. Ringing the doorbell I needed only wait patiently for half a minute at the most. Opening the door was a brownish olive-skinned old woman with more white than gray in her curly topped hair that was folded into a bun in the back. Baggy blue-jean shorts came to her old knobby knees.

Flat pink house shoes with no back to cover the heels were on her feet. She wore a crisp, white, long sleeved shirt with a firm collar and a vest embroidered with blue, cream, and red. No make-up on her face as she crinkled her wrinkles about her nose and forehead.

"Yes?" The old woman asked as she opened the glass screen door.

"Is this your kitten?"

"No", the woman said with slow thoughtfulness, "but I've seen it about."

"Do you know who owns this kitten?"

"Nope. Aint got a clue. Ya might try next door." She pointed a shaky finger in the direction of the house to her left.

"Well, I wanted to keep it. But I didn't want to make someone sad if this were their kitten and they wanted to keep it themselves." Suddenly I wondered why I felt the need to explain my actions. Wasn't it Audrey Hepburn whom said, "Never complain. Never Explain."? Wise advice. "Well, thank you Mam." Smiling and giving a wave I began walking to the house I'd passed. The house the old woman had pointed toward.

"Your welcome. And good luck!" Said the grandma type lady while she closed her glass screen door and turned to go back and continue whatever she'd been doing before I rang her doorbell.

No one answered the doorbell at the home next to the elderly woman. Nor did anyone answer the door at the next three houses as I made my way back towards my home. I cooed to the kitten purring in my arms. Singing her a lullaby I'd learned from my own mother: "Sleep little Eskimo baby…"

Stopping in my tracks I looked upon my mother's forest green and fake-wood station wagon parked in the driveway. She usually didn't get home until late. Wondering for a moment how I'd missed seeing her car in the driveway as I was walking up. But of course my attention had been upon the kitten. Patting the house key in my pocket and hesitating. Usually no one was home when I came in from school. I already knew what the answer would be when I walked in with the baby feline and asked if I could keep it. No doubt about it. The answer of course would be 'no'. "Even if I know the answer will be 'no' it still doesn't hurt to ask", I say to the kitty as I scratch her ears. Thus I gave my legs courage to carry me into the house and I went in to ask this question for the sake of asking it. Knowing I'd be taking the kitten back to the fully flossed pine tree.

I whispered to the tiny black feline, "I'll still call you Black Beauty, so you remember your name for when I come calling to visit you at the pine tree." I kissed her head.

Yes the front door was unlocked. I walked in to the foyer. Feeling slightly foolish for having asked the small fluffy animal to remember her name. I walked into the house. Halting my day dreaming, I rounded the corner towards the living room. Passing the couch and stopping at the wall at the back of the stairs where the encyclopedias and dictionaries sat stuffed full of tasty information. Looking to the left into the kitchen. My mother was washing her hands. She dried them on a small towel and then quickly moved past me out of the kitchen and into the living room where she retrieved her purse from off the couch.

"I found a kitten Mother."

"I see that."

"Her name is Black Beauty."

"Oh. Like the horse." Mother raised her purse to her shoulder. "That's a good book; Black Beauty. You should read it."

"Mother can I keep the cat?"

"Mother *may* I?" She stated firmly but politely.

"Mother may I?"

"Yes you may." Mother smiled.

"I can?!" I was flabbergasted and excited at the same time. Was she joking? "I can keep the cat?"

"Why not."

"Thank you!"

"Your welcome. By the way, I cleaned your room. I don't see how you could stand it so unorganized."

(I didn't think it was unorganized but I knew better than to say anything.) Mother began walking towards the front door. "Your Father and I have a dinner to go too. Your Sister should be home soon."

"Okay." Petting the kitten again while I watched her step out the front door. Waiting at the window until I saw that she had backed the car out of the driveway and taken off down the street. "Wow!" I looked down at the kitten. "You are my cat!" I could hardly believe it! Turning away from the window I ran through the living room and up the stairs with the kitten still snuggled in my arms as if she and I were old pals. Halting at the open door to my bedroom. Mouth dropping open I stared into my room with a paralyzed coldness pouring through my nervous system. I stood silent and still. My room had not been just cleaned it had been slicked spotless. At first I noticed there were no toys or stuffed animals. Next I plodded as if my feet were in quicksand to my closet. It was mostly bare. Five of my best dresses were the only clothes. They hung nicely in a row on the closet bar. One pair of shoes on the carpeted floor. I unzipped my small white plastic suitcase. It contained five pair of socks and seven underwear. What about my diary? My address book? Letters from Holli? Panic ran through me! Sprinting, I ran to the white Victorian child's study desk against the wall opposite my bed. On top of the handsome desk sat my alarm clock and nothing else. Would I find my things still inside the desk? Opening the drawer I looked down in consternation. Inside were two pencils and one pen and nothing else.

I looked at my bed which was well made with hospital corners like my mother always insisted upon. One always made ones bed first thing after getting out of bed. Tucking the corners tight through a certain particular pattern: hence 'hospital corners'. Instantly I soaked in the well tucked bedspread and realized I couldn't remember if on this specific morning I had made my bed or not. Adding it all up in a matter of seconds. I could understand why everything was gone. I had surely forgotten to make my bed that morning. What had I been thinking? Except for a few clothes, a pair of shoes, and two pencils and one pen, everything had been thrown away. (Later in the week my mother would confirm that everything had been trashed.) Oh well; I should have made my bed that morning. She was only doing her best to keep my room clean. Sitting on the end of the bed I felt tears come to my eyes because I no longer had my address book. All my letters had been thrown away so I couldn't retrieve any address's from that. I would never again be able to locate my friend Holli Hunter!

I began to cheer up as I petted the soft black kitten. Then with excitement I remembered that the last time I was up in the attic I had left a pen and my diaries and the sock monkey my Grandmother Barns had made for me up there! I had my regular diary for writing about life and then my dream-diary where I wrote about the dreams I'd dreamt while sleeping and where I also wrote my short stories and poems. I'd better go look and make sure they're still in the attic. The cat mewed and tried to climb up the front of my dress. Black Beauty made it as far as my chin, which she rubbed with the top of her fluffy head before sliding back down to my arm. "Poor kitty, I'll bet your hungry."

Slowly I walked back downstairs and into the kitchen where I located some powdered milk which I mixed with water and fed in a bowl to the cat; I drank some of the powdered milk mixture myself. The kitten licked the drink eagerly with her tiny rough pink tongue. Purring outrageously! You'd think she'd choke herself purring and drinking at the same time. A milk-drinking kitten ventriloquist!

Scrounging about the kitchen drawers I found some scratch paper and a pen. Making four notes on the scratch paper I stated my name and telephone number along with the question of whether or not I had their black kitten. I left the kitten in the house. Hurrying outside with the notes and some tape in hand. Quickly taping a note to the doors of the houses where no one had answered when I knocked. Running back inside my house I felt worried that the cat might have gotten stuck some place I couldn't find her.

Sweet surprise to see the kitten waiting patiently beside the nearly empty bowl of milk. Grinning with her whiskers turned up and her eyes slightly shut she looked very happy and satisfied. Lifting her into my arms I carried Beauty upstairs where I gathered a chair from my parents room and set it under the attic door that was in the ceiling of the upstairs hallway. Setting Beauty on the carpet next to the chair. Crawling on top of the chair I lifted onto my tiptoes and reached for the knob on the attic door. Catching hold of the knob I tugged open the attic door. Then I grabbed on to the folded attic ladder attached to the ceiling door and began unfolding it as I backed down off of the chair. Standing on the carpet I unfolded the last bit of the ladder. Taking the chair back to my parents room I placed it in the exact spot I'd taken it from. Picking up my kitten and holding her under one arm I ascended the ladder. Placing Beauty in the attic I climbed the rest of the way and then turned around and began to retrieve the ladder. Folding it back up until I could reach the attic door and pull the whole thing shut behind me. I was in the attic with my new cat! Thanks mom! Black Beauty and I sat quietly and contentedly alone in the small triangle-shaped attic. Light poured into the musty dusty attic from a round window that looked like the type of circular window one would find on some great ship.

Beneath the crooked slanted plain wood ceiling, and tucked neatly into a crevice of the floor made of plain unpainted wood slabs, lay my sock monkey, a pen, and my diaries. Right where I had left them! Too bad I hadn't left my address book up here. The only other objects were a soft bed pillow and a small thin blanket which I had also brought into the attic. The attic smelled so good, like sunshine and earth and wood. Resting my head upon the pillow I picked up my pen and diary and began writing about my day. Black Beauty settled into a warm purring ball upon my abdomen.

"Dear Diary,

"August 9, 1974. You know diary, how I was telling about what my father said? That President Nixon was dragging his feet in the war. It's in Vietnam, someplace far away, but guess what? Nixon is no longer President! I think the war is still going on?---seems like forever, I still think of the flower children talking about it when we lived at the (Sequoia) forest. With the big trees. Only they weren't children. They were grown up so I don't know why they called themselves children. Anyway at school we didn't have to do school work! Yea! Well mostly anyway. We spent most the time talking about Nixon, and our new president. We all watched TV at school and it was in color! We watched the TV and President Nixon resigned because he did something bad and got in trouble for it. Something about a water gate. We got to see the new president raise his hand and I think his other hand was on a bible and he became president. His name is Ford. I got my own cat today!"

On and on I wrote. About finding Black Beauty. About riding the bus. The boys and the one that got beat on. I wrote everything down. Next I picked up my dream-diary and thumbed through it wondering if I felt like writing another poem. No. I felt like napping. Cradling Beauty with my hand so that she didn't fall I rolled onto my side and pulled the kitten up against my chest. The pillow was comfortable under my head and the blanket felt good covering my shoulders. Breathing in that comforting wood smell of the attic. The softness of Beauty purring against my hand. I rested along side my napping fluffy kitty. Safe enough to close my eyes and possess a peaceful slumber. When I awoke it was to the sound of my name.

"Suzanna! Suzie? We're home!" It was my mother's voice calling me. She sounded as if she were in the hallway directly beneath the closed attic door. Moonlight shivered its silver rays through the round window. At the very least it was late evening already. Waiting for the sound of footsteps descending the stairs before cracking the attic door and peering down at the hallway beneath me. Empty. The perfect time to sneak out of the attic, but quickly! Don't get caught or you'll give away your secret hiding place!

Barely creaking, thank heavens, I let open the ladder and practically hopped down the whole thing leaving the last rung still folded. Hurry, push the ladder and the attached door shut and pray it doesn't make a loud noise! The kitten complained some underneath my arm and I shushed her. Surprisingly the ladder and door snapped back quietly. And if quiet wasn't enough, I was pleased that the attic door shut with just a mere shove upwards so I didn't have to get a chair and force the rest of it closed! Tip-toeing with keen dexterity at my fastest possible speed into my bedroom; the kitten cradled in my arms. Opening my window which faced the lawn and street I let the kitten out to sit on the rooftop protruding from the living room below. A tall thick tree had branches hanging upon this part of the roof so I knew the cat could easily climb down without any difficulty. Both my parents abhorred having animals stay inside a house. Quickly I closed and locked that window. Then I checked that my other window in my room was locked before slipping under the covers into my twin sized bed. Checking that my windows were locked had become a common ritual before I laid down to sleep. Hearing rumbling voices from my parents as I closed my eyes, I somehow fell back into that same peaceful sleep I'd been experiencing in the attic. This sleep changed at some point in the night when I began having a bad dream. Witches cackling as they flew through my room. Waking up from the bad dream with a grunt from my throat to find I was sweating terribly. Sitting up and swinging my legs over the side of the bed I thought I might go get a glass of water to drink. Rubbing the strands of hair off my sweaty forehead I looked to the bedroom door and it occurred to me that the only light on in my bedroom was the small glowing night-light I had inadvertently left on that morning. Thank goodness for night-lights!

Suddenly a loud crashing of breaking glass caused me to practically jump out of my skin! A burglar breaking dishes down stairs? The sweat beading on my forehead stopped dripping as I felt cold with an instant drop of my body temperature. Instantaneous chill. Shuddering in the now freezing room with the hairs prickling all over my body from the ugly fear enveloping me. I went to look out the side window when I stepped painfully on something sharp. Lifting my foot I saw a sliver of glass in my big toe. Blood pooling up around the sliver. I pulled it out and held the sliver to my eyes in the moonlight coming from the window and examined it. Looking down at the carpet I instinctively walked with extra care to the window and opened the light blue curtain. Immediately I saw that the window was broken! *That was the breaking sound I had heard*! Of course the window had not been broken when I checked the lock earlier before climbing in bed to sleep. A great hole gaped in the glass pane with cracks running up and down around it. Cracks like etched lightening bolts or spider webs were slithered through the glass. Peering out the window where the ground was brightly lit by a mixture of moonlight and the big street lamp that was standing near and glaring florescent.

Gasping at what I saw below I instinctively jumped back and choked on some of my own spit. Coughing, I willed my lungs to breath evenly. Pulling open the curtain. Peering back outside the shattered window I looked and gasped again. A man in dark clothes with a head and face like a demon. *It was him!* Horn type protrusions like tumors growing up and out against the bald grayish-green head of the mask. He stood there looking up. Bolting like lightening from my room I ran into my parent's bedroom just down the hallway.

I screamed my words in a panic. "Someone's breaking in! A burglar! They broke the window!"

My father was instantly on his feet with an apparent rush of adrenaline. He sprung from the bed with a great swing of the bed covers. Mother leapt up more groggily and stared at me with perplexity before looking to her husband.

"What?!" Boomed my father.

"A burglar! He broke the window!"

"Where?"

"In my room! Come quick! I'll show you!"

Father walked in anger with large strides as he mumbled under his breath, "They better not be…" I led the way while mother followed along behind us. Halfway into my room I stopped and pointed to the side window. Father and I then went over to the window. My father lifted the corner of the opened curtain as he gaped at the window. "Why he sure did break the window", he said.

"Oh no!" Exclaimed Mother as she saw the shattered broken window. "We'll have to replace it!"

Father and I gazed down at the ground outside the window. The man still stood there! My father's eyes glared attentively as he roared out "He's still there! *Hey you!*" Anger flushed my father's face red and his breathing became fierce. He thundered: "I see you! You punk! I'll teach you to break into my house!"

"You see him?" I asked feeling frantic to hear what he had viewed.

"Of course I see him! Damned punk! He's a thief!" My father turned with angry tensed muscles. A determined tight-faced expression furrowing his face. He marched out of my room. I padded anxiously by his side. Mother followed worried and silent.

"What did he look like Dad?"

"Some kid I'm sure! Some teenager wearing a mask!"

My mind toppled overboard for just an instant. I knew it had to be a mask but to hear somebody else say it felt like realizing the situation all over again for the first time. I craved more information! Now! So I continued to question my father as we swooped down the stairs. "What kind of mask, Dad?"

"A Halloween mask! Like a devil or something!" His elevating anger caused his face to bloat up as it turned a bright beet red. We all curved around near the bottom of the stairs.

"Did it have horns?"

"Yes!" We reached the last stair. Then he pounded through the living room and I had to run to keep up. "What color was it?"

His hand now grasped the front door knob. Father halted for a second to look me straight in the eye. "Gray like…or…green! The thief!"--He exclaimed with anger.

My breath caught in my throat for some reason and I couldn't speak. At some point Mother had turned on the light in the living room. Father flew out the door and into the front yard with Mother and I following close behind. My father stormed around to the side of the house that sported my bedroom's window up above. Words pounded with a deep tenor anger from his lips. "You're going to jail for this! You punk!" Then my father flung his arm with a fast gesture from me to the house. "Get inside Suzanna!"

Didn't he understand I couldn't stand to go inside? Not yet! Pausing and nervously patting the tips of my fingers together. I mentally noted how exceedingly bright the street light seemed against the burgeoning night. The air seemed warm as I swallowed down an embarrassing realization that we were all standing outside with my mother and I wearing our nightgowns and my father in his boxer shorts. Father disappeared around the side of the house and I ran to catch up with him. "Auuugh!"—Father grumbled. I reached where father stood shaking his fists, "He's not here!" Father shouted and moaned with an angry

frustration as he looked around. My eyes searched furiously around the empty yard and squinted with suspicious straining at the dark black shadows around the bushes and trees. "Get inside Suzanna!" Father looked all about the house and yard for the man in the mask. Begrudgingly I obeyed his command and went to stand just inside the house at the screen door where I could still peek out somewhat at the goings on. My father's voice came from the opposite side of the house in a heated exasperated groan. Mother stepped back inside with my father following behind her. He closed and locked the front door. His voice still wrathful as he groaned, "A thief ! That nasty little thief! Come here to rob us!"

"What should we do?" Mother questioned with a tremble in her strong voice.

"Well, he's gone now! I'll call the police and report it tomorrow! I'm tired! And I've got to get up at 5:am!"

"That was scary." Mother's powerful voice still tentatively shook. "It reminds me of that man that was stalking me."

"Who was 'stawking' you mother?"

"Stalking." Mother corrected as any good school teacher might. "It's spelled with an 'L'. S-t-ε-*L*-k. Stalk."

"What is a stalk?"

"It's a stalker Suzanna."

"Sorry Mother; what is a stalker?"

"Look it up in the dictionary if you want to know what it is."

Father spoke with empty frustration and exhaustion as he moved towards the stairs. "I'm going to bed."

"Goodnight Suzanna. You need to get back in bed. Turn the light out as you come up." Mother instructed.

"Okay. I'm just gonna get a glass of water. I'll turn the light out." I didn't bother to watch my parents ascend the stairs. I turned to step into the kitchen and turn the light, then I gathered up the stepstool so I could reach the cabinet. My heart was still pounding with fear. Pulling myself up to sit on the kitchen counter I opened the cabinet and pulled out a mug that said 'MSU Mustangs' on it. Similarly I scooted the stepstool over and stood upon it to run some water from the faucet into the mug. I drank eagerly and with genuine thirst although it felt like I was just stalling for more time. Wanting my parents to be in bed already I drank more water; I also didn't want to go back into my room. I was still shaken and scared.

When I felt my parents were most likely already back in their room I snuck over to the books lined on the shelves just between the kitchen and the living room. Pulling the dictionary from its place beside the encyclopedias. I turned to the section marked 'S' and looked up the word: stalker. Air caught in my tensed lungs as my eyes read and reread all about the word in the dictionary.

"to pursue by stalking….

1: to pursue quarry or prey stealthily"

One word stuck out among the others. 'Prey.' Looking up the word 'prey' a liquid sense of terror caused my legs to feel weak and shaky.

"prey a: to commit violence

b: to seize and devour prey, as by a predator"

SEVEN

THE HERITAGE
PART 1

Again I dreamed a dream that was so lucid and loud that I would never forget it. My nights were fraught with nightmares. I had dreamt of war again; *yet again*. Waking up I looked at the window curtain and wished I wouldn't have these constant nightmares. My cheeks and neck were wet with tears I had cried in my sleep. The sunlight of morning was streaming through my windows and brightening my room. This was during a year when the U.S. Supreme Court would finally grant female teachers their right to maternity leave. A first aid technique for choking called a "Heimlich maneuver" had just been discovered and announced. Out of a wide-spread fear of new diseases and also out of the most frightening thing to the current public, the fear of artificial intelligence and artificial life, scientists pulled a screeching halt to genetic engineering. Not to mention the cold war! Laying on my back in the bed, I crossed my arms underneath my head and thought about the cold war. This particular morning my waking would be different; I jumped to the sound of my mother's voice.

"Okay! Wake up!" It was my mother poking her head through my bedroom door.

I was startled. "What?"

"Wakey, wakey, eggs and bacony!"

I glanced at my clock. "Why aren't you at work?"

"We've got to get your allergy shots testing done and this is the only time the doctor had when I could take you."

Falling back against my pillow and moaning. "Ohhh noooo."

"Come on Suzanna. Get up. We have to go as of now."

Hopping to my feet I turned to pat and tuck the bed neatly with hospital corners. Spreading the top cover smooth, I yawned. Running to the restroom I washed my face with soap and water. Brushing my teeth with an extra large swab of toothpaste and rinsing with tap water, I then grinned into the mirror to look at my clean teeth. Brushing my hair was quick and easy. Then I returned to my bedroom and selected a clean dress from a hanger. Slipping on my socks and my light blue suede shoes with the buckle straps. Gathering my school books off of my study desk. I went downstairs and announced to my mother whom was standing near the front door, "I'm ready."

We stepped outside and immediately I felt the chill of the morning air. I winced at the cold as I held the front door between open and closed. My mother asked, "Are you cold?"

"Yes. Just let me step back in." Turning back inside and opening the coat closet just opposite the front door I grabbed my sweater. Carrying my sweater across my arm I waited until I got into the car to put it on because I needed the chance to set down my school books. Mother started up the car and suggested we put on our seatbelts since more people were starting to wear them now. As Mother backed the station wagon out of the driveway I asked, "Can I turn on the radio?"

"Okay."

I flipped the radio on. "Oh I love that song", I exclaimed as I turned on the radio to catch the last half of Barbra Streisand singing "The Way We Were". This was the newest song to be sung by Streisand and very popular all across American radio. Singing along with it in my mind as I watched the car passing houses and streets. It was a disappointment for the song to be over and to hear the radio announcer speaking.

"Guess what America!" Blared the voice on the radio. "As you probably already know, there's been another streaking! This time the nude man seen running…"

"Mother why do people do that?"

"Do what?"

"Streaking. People are taking off their clothes and running all over the place naked."

Mother took a long thoughtful moment before answering. "Because they're a bunch of low-class nuts who don't think before acting."

"Yes." I agreed. "You'd think they'd be embarrassed."

"Not to mention how rude it is." Mother added.

"Oh I know. It's very rude. There's a reason people call their privates private, because it's one of the few things they have that they can *keep* private. Or something like that. Besides I don't want to see someone else's 'business' all hanging out for all to see. It's just gross."

"Well Suzanna I agree."

The radio D.J. was now talking about how some stage show in London called "The Rocky Horror Picture Show" might be made into a movie and come to the U.S. sometime the next year in 1975. More talk on the radio of a new movie, this one by Mel Brooks called "Young Frankenstein."

"Mother?"

"Yes?"

"You know that night when you mentioned your stalker?"

"Yes."

"What was he like?"

"What?"

"Did he have blonde hair or red hair or brown…"

"Brownish."

"What?"

"He had a brownish color of hair."

"Was it dark brown or light brown or auburn…"

"I don't know."

"What about his skin?"

"Why don't we just listen to the radio Suzanna?" My constant questions were perturbing her.

"I want to know."

"I don't know what you're asking Suzanna."

"Was he white or black? Was he American Indian? Or Mexican?"

"He had tan skin."

"Like an olive complexion?"

"Yes. Like an olive complexion."

"A born tan like an Indian or a Mexican? Or a natural tan like a white person gets from the sun?"

"A natural tan. Maybe. What difference does it make?"

"Did you know that what causes color in the skin is actually how much or how little pigment you have under your skin?"

"Suzanna you are really starting to get on my nerves."

"Sorry."

The male voice on the radio had just finished talking about the weather and had now started talking about the latest news. It was distracting so I asked my mother if she'd mind if I turned it off. When she said she didn't mind I proceeded to click it into quietness.

"What did he do Mother?"

"Who?"

"The stalker."

"He would call me and tell me what all I'd been doing for the day. It was very scary. I was really worried about you. I was afraid he might hurt you. Or hurt Mabel or Rustle. I was pregnant with you when it started."

"You were pregnant with me when he stalked you?"

"When it started, yes; it lasted for a very long time." There was a quiet hush in the car for a moment. "Then of course the police came up with a plan." My mother, Peggy, tapped her fingertips against the steering wheel.

"Did they get him?"

"No."

"When did the police do their plan?"

"After you were born Suzanna."

"Did he keep showing up?"

"Well there was that one time. You were talking. You were standing up in your crib and just carrying on. A complete conversation. I thought I heard whispering too. I guess you were about three and a half years old. But it really scared me. I could hear you from the other room and I'd swear you were holding on a complete conversation. Answering questions and asking questions. Finally I was just terrified and so I went up to your door and asked you who you were talking too. You said, 'That man'. And you pointed.

"I was just so scared I almost called the police when I first heard you talking to someone. But then I decided to walk on in your room. And when I walked in there was nobody there. But your window was open. I asked you who you were talking too and you said, "That man", and you pointed to the window. It didn't have a screen on it. I never have liked keeping a window open like that ever since then. And never liked a window without a screen on it since then either."

"I remember that. There was a guy there; he went out the window. But I thought he was an angel. That's weird."

"Yep. Weird." Peggy sighed. "Well you probably just imagined it. Well, I probably just gave you too much cough syrup"; she laughed.

Occurring to me for the first time like never before was that I wanted desperately to know about the lives of my family, so I asked a lot of questions. My mother would spend our time together today telling me all about my family. "Mother, I want to know about your life."

"Okay."—My mother Peggy tapped her fingertips on the steering wheel some more.

"And about my Dad? And my grandparents? And…"

* * * * * *

That morning my mother told me a lot of stories about her life and my father's life. Stories about my grandparents and the heritage of my family. It was a morning that got me started asking many questions of my family about our heritage and their individual experiences in life. I found myself hungry to know. This day as my mother and I made our way to the doctor's for more allergy testing marked the first time in my life I began asking in depth about my family. *The following two chapters called "The Heritage" have been created out of such stories I listened too; stories told to me quite often over and over again by various family members. Some of it has also been created from interviews and direct quotes. What you will read is what I personally „imagine" these stories I"ve heard to be like.*

As the story has been told, everything began with a *terrible fight* in the home of the Barrett family. Unrest stormed the Barrett's home. It is rumored that the trouble at home comes straight from the Barrett's of Wimpole street. It was the mid 1800's.

Here it must be noted that it is rumored that the Barrett brothers were apparently very handsome. Indeed they would pass their stately good looks, their strong chin and jaw-line, their handsome noses and wide beautiful eyes on to other generations of lucky Barrett men.

Yes, it began with a terrible fight. The male parental figure of the Barrett home felt that everything except blindly following him was insolence. Yet these two young brothers, the Barrett boys, found ways to protest. They'd both grown their hair past their shoulders which they tied back at the nape of their necks with ribbons. While a great many at this time considered this merely an old fashioned and common hair style the father figure in the Barrett household found the boys long hair as both poor taste and an embarrassment to his family name. And the boys scandalous behavior! Dining with lowlife's and no doubt making themselves the hub of nasty gossip that can taint the Barrett name!

In the temporary leaden quiet of this era one would hear the scratchy rustling of women's style of dress for the day; dress's heavy with a bustle and stiff petticoats. It would be an era common for men to gather away from their women and sip brandy, stopping to smell the fiery sweetness of the drink. Men would smoke cigars with pride! There were plenty of these and many other pleasures easily financed in the Barrett household. Why then on earth would the Barrett brothers give away a set life in England? Why embark upon what should most likely be a perilous adventure?

Yet the young men nevertheless did seek out adventure, and so it was that this became the weighted moment which would change their destiny and the destiny of future generations. Perhaps any fear of a bold quest that might even mean a perilous courting of danger had been quelled by the fact that they had enough money on them to provide a fine and comfortable ship ride. They had enough monies to resettle themselves and to dine as often as they wished on bread, cheese, slabs of well cooked salt cured bacon, and to drink plenty of wine.

The Barrett boy's would pack their dark black frock coats and waist coats; their fine striped trousers and stiff high-collar white shirts. Tapered trousers and box pleat tweed jackets, all packed. They would promenade away on a wooden planked walkway at port where the docks would smell of dead sea creatures and the scent of salt. They would tap their canes on the boards of their ship and watch the sunsets take them to America. These two venturesome dandy's would land port into the muddy wet streets with the smell of rotted water plants and the wafting lemon of the salty breeze in a city called *New York*.

It is rumored here that the Barrett brothers became enchanted by a pub they found which drew them in with the webbing sounds of laughter and violin music amid a thick New York slanged chatter. It is said that it was here in this pub that the brother's would each decide upon a different place to live, and thus parted ways never to meet again.

One brother chose to stay in New York; he'd been intoxicated with the city. The other Barrett brother chose that day at the pub to go to New Orleans and then after that on to Texas. It is with the brother that chose to leave for New Orleans that our story continues.

Our story goes that the young man Barrett met his wife in New Orleans and from there the happy couple moved to Texas where he became a Methodist Preacher. His wife would give birth to a son. (*Another handsome Barrett boy had been born!*) They would name their son: James W. Barrett; but the bouncing baby boy would grow up being called 'J.W.'

Now it is around this same time in our story, in the 1800's, that another family would see the joyous birth of a child. The daughter, Annie Carter Lee, of the famous American Robert E. Lee would give birth. Through the generations there would never be any information passed down on whom was the father. It is said that Annie Lee wouldn't even look at her baby daughter without first reaching for her dark sunglasses and putting them on to cover her lost eye. Poor Annie Lee had lost her eye when she poked it out in an accidental fall after running with scissors.

Annie Lee named her brand new baby daughter: Bertha Emily Lee. Annie Lee *encouraged* Bertha to be tough! She encouraged her daughter Bertha to be a gun shooting, tobacco chewing, spittoon spitting, tough young lady. It is rumored that Bertha Lee would grow up to be able to hit a spittoon on the inside edge from *ten feet away* and shoot it into the brass so that it made a metallic 'ping'!

It has also been said that Bertha Lee could place a row of apples on top of the necks of brown bottles, which in turn had been set onto a wooden saw horse. Bertha could walk far away from the apple topped bottles, turn around, aim her gun, and… *POW*! One right after the other! The bottles wouldn't have moved a bit, but the apples would be blown to smithereens!

James W. Barrett, known as J.W., would grow up in Texas where his father from England had settled. Like his father before him he would also become a Preacher, ministering to the faithful flocks that came on Sunday's to worship. It is here in our story where Preacher J.W. Barrett meets a magnificently beautiful young Cherokee Native American girl. The beautiful young Cherokee girl's name was: Allie Baker.

Preacher J.W. Barrett was a pioneering and independent thinker for he was fully in favor of equal rights for women. This was during a time when the wild fire news spread in 1864 about a woman named Rebecca Lee whom was the first black woman to receive a medical degree from a college. In 1886 a book would be published by female author Emily Dickinson. But there could be no woman more fascinating for good old J.W. than Allie Baker once he first set eyes on her. Yes, the story goes that Allie Baker and J.W. Barrett would fall in love at that church picnic. It was the summer of 1907, and a perfect day for the church to picnic down by the water tank.

One can imagine Allie with her long black hair pulled into a bun sitting on a blanket at the picnic watching the young girls wearing their sleeveless black swim-dresses and leggings, splashing the young boys and giggling. The young boys would wear white sleeveless tops and brown knee-shorts. One can imagine Allie Baker "the beautiful" sitting next to friends with a bowl full of grapes and sliced cantaloupe in front of her.

"What are you reading?" Allie's friend might ask her.

"It's a different author"; Allie might say, "Mark Twain. He just published this one. It's new. I like it so far."

"So Allie", her friend might continue to chat, " what do you think of that man that's so popular these days? Everybody's talking about him. Strange man really. Sigmund something."

"Sigmund Freud." J.W. Barrett might answer as he bends down and hands picked wild flowers of red and orange, yellow, and purple, to Allie "the beautiful." The fields about the picnic would be frothy with flowers this time of year. A sugar scented breeze of blue bonnets, sunflowers, and butter-cups, would bauble everywhere across the grasslands. Mesquite trees, Juniper, and Oak trees would scatter their shade in this part of Texas in the summer.

"What do you think about this new man, Albert Einstein?", Allie's friend might say in idle chit-chat.

Then someone else might say, "Our good president Theodore Roosevelt is a man among men! He stands for a very strong morality. A "fundamental fight for morality" our president said."

"I like President Roosevelt's daughter, Alice. She's so cute!" Allie might respond.

"Do you see? Here?" The friend might question as she lifts the tie at her neck. "This tie I'm wearing is just like the tie Alice Roosevelt wears. Same color exactly." Then she might puff proudly.

The men at the picnic would sit in their knee-cropped tapered trousers and tweed jackets. The women in this era would be in ankle length skirts, which show their pretty pointed boots. You could imagine

Preacher J.W. Barrett and Allie Baker both reaching for a piece of cantaloupe at the same time and their hands *touching*! A glancing eye's exchange taking place between them, and *ahhh mad amore*! They fall in love!

In 1911 Allie and James W. Barrett bring a son into the world whom they name: JB. The letters 'JB' do not stand for any names of any kind. But it is here in the story that we find for family differences the name Barrett changed to Barns; which I find most unfortunate. Yet one can change a noble name to a strong name and have it all be just as well and just as good.

Now meanwhile in this family's history, in the year 1914, Bertha Lee would give birth to a child. She would give birth to a beautiful baby girl and name her Oleta Marie Geaslin. Oleta was born in a year when the very first transcontinental telephone line had been completed. Cleveland, Ohio would bring about a healthy change that year for their new-fangled idea of using a red-green traffic light.

JB Barns and Oleta Marie Geaslin would be next in line to meet, in this heritage, in this tale of love!

So it is in our story of this family that in the 1920's JB Barns and Oleta Marie Geaslin would find themselves being educated at the same small school. JB quietly and sweetly and romantically carried Oleta's books for her during the entire term of U.S. President Warren Harding, and throughout the presidential term of Calvin Coolidge. JB wore his hair slicked back with hair crème and parted in the middle. Oleta wore her brown smock dresses. Their teacher taught all classes regardless of age in the same small schoolhouse room. They would meet on the small sloping hill in the center of a meadow that lay in between their two homes. A patch of trees on the side of the meadow. One lone tree on the hill. The two teenagers usually said nothing to one another except for one word. "Hey", JB would say. "Hey", Oleta would respond. Then there came a special day on the hill as they stood looking at one another with only the wind blowing between them and the sun sparkling in their hair. Their hearts beating like the meadow larks flitting through the trees. Magic furling down around them and upon them as the two beautiful innocent's delicately smiled into one another's eyes. JB said to Oleta, "I've got a good job now that makes good pay and it's secure. I could make you a good husband." JB would press his brown cap deeply with his fingers before the magical moment when he got down onto one knee of his brown tweed pants to ask, "Will you marry me Oleta?"

Oleta would then open her mouth within her endless eternal smile and say, "Yes." The two teenagers would next gleam at each other, clasp hands, and continue walking on to school that day.

Oleta and JB Barns would have two extremely handsome sons. Jerry Barns born in 1936 was the youngest Barns child. Rustle Bobby Barns who was the oldest was born in 1935.

JB Barns at 94 years old would say, "Oleta and I were married over there in Hamilton county. We were married in the Methodist church on Vista Mountain. We were married all our lives since we were married young, and we always got along. She was the love of my life."

* * *

It was literally around this precise same time during the 1920's when another different budding love took place. To be exact, the year was 1926. Pauline Jones with her dark hair and light skin could be seen riding her bicycle from the schoolhouse. Bicycling past the gristmill and the barns and the water wheels. A mule-drawn cotton stripper in the robust fields giving a much needed end to picking cotton with sore tired fingers. Pauline was posted to teach at a rural Texas schoolhouse.

Pauline Jones was boarding at the Arnez's home while teaching. Mrs. Arnez's son, Early, had watched their boarder Pauline and fallen in love with her. She married him and Pauline and Early had three daughters. Nedett Arnez born 1927. Deana Arnez born 1929. And their youngest child, the beautiful Cora Peggy Arnez, born in 1935. *In 1942 a terrible tragedy would fall upon the Arnez family; what I reiterate is from what my mother, Cora Peggy, has told me; this narrative is what I imagine what I''ve been told to happen as follows:*

"Are you about washed Early?" Pauline questioned at the closed bathroom door. She would hear the water make a final splash and hear the reply, "Yep."

Early had removed his dust-covered overalls and bathed. The whole family was about to go to town and make some needed purchases. The 'Dust Bowl' had rolled across the poor American people who had had to endure it. America was completely changed with the marvelous development of the railroad. Many changes had been taking place in America.

Pauline padded barefoot in her stockings and her slip to check on the girls. "Nedett? Deana?" Pauline called as she checked the bedroom. "Are you ready? Is Peggy ready?"

The girls had on their sweater sets with the flared-knee narrow skirts. Deana was just helping little Cora Peggy into her cuff socks and loafers. "Yes", chimed the children as they looked up at their mother. Deana plopped down on her bottom finally to grab a better hold of Peggy's bare foot that still needed its sock on.

"Alright girls. I'm going to finish dressing."

"Yes Mam", the children toppled over each others voices in reply.

Pauline went to stand in front of her bedroom's dressing mirror. She took the popover dress she had sewn for herself off of the bed where she'd lain it out. The broad shoulders of the blue and gray flower-print dress had shoulder pads underneath. She'd sewn these pads in herself. It was tapered into a lovely well-tailored waist and hung just below the knees. Leaving her feet, ankles, and stocking calves showing. She slipped on her low-heeled thick soled black strap shoes.

Looking into the closet Pauline almost chose her Lily Dache` hat but then changed her mind after holding it in her hands. Putting the Lily Dache` back on the shelf she chose instead her smaller brimmed dark cloth hat with a bow that was her favorite.

Turning from the closet and placing her favorite hat upon her head she looked up to see Early freshly washed and almost fully dressed. He still needed to put on a tie.

Since they were going to town, Early had chosen his gray flannel suit with the flaps on the pockets and the small lapels. He wore pleat-less pants and his crisp white cotton shirt was buttoned all the way up. He had already put on his narrow, gray, pinched-crown hat.

"No tie Early?" Pauline inquired.

"That's what I came in here for." He peered at his ties hanging neatly in the closet and passed his fingers softly through them. Finally he decided upon a slim striped one. "What about this one?" He showed the tie to his wife. "What do you think?"

Pauline set her eyes upon the tie and sized it up. She replied with a smile. "Yes. That goes well. You picked a good one."

Smiling, satisfied, Early nodded and began to pull the tie around his neck. Pauline left the bedroom with the instruction that she and the girls would be waiting in the living room. It wasn't more than five minutes when Early emerged with his tie perfectly done. "Alright girls! Get in the car!"—Early announced as he reflexively touched his hat. Pauline led the way with the girls following behind her in a line like little ducklings. Early closed the door but didn't bother locking it since they lived so deep into the empty flat Texas countryside. They piled into the car with the girls in the backseat. "Off we go!"—Early happily stated with a lilt in his voice.

The partly cloudy light-blue sky with its sun beaming bright belied the unhinged doom which crept ever closer to this family. The unimaginable horror that would crumple their hearts was as of yet still unknown to the three grinning girls who were singing songs in the car. Excited as they were to be going to town.

They crossed the miles of crops and the fields of happy lazy cows chewing their cud. The Arnez family entering into the small town with Deana proclaiming, "Woo-hoo! Look! We're here! Can we have some ice cream? Pleeeeese?"

Early parked the car close on the side of the town's five and dime store. The family poured out of the car and onto the sidewalk. Squinting against the sunlight and thrilled at the trip.

"I've got to go to the Feed and Grain", announced Early as he headed in the direction of the store he had in mind. The girls bounced and skipped at the side of their mother's dress. They followed her into the only place the town offered as a department store.

Walking into the store the bell above the door jingled to exclaim the entrance of Pauline and the children. Pauline looked about the store quickly while the children scattered this way and that to view all the interesting items. Finally Pauline walked over to the counter where the old cash register sat. One employee was perched on a chair with an antsy kicking of her crossed legs. The other employee was a gentleman with whitening hair who had been fiddling with the radio.

"Leave it there"; said the female employee impatiently, "You keep flipping the channels around!" She looked up at Pauline. "Yes Mam, may I help you?"

Pauline asked the question which was most on her mind. "Do you have the new Harper's Bazaar?"

"Yes Mam." The lady set down the book she'd had laying open on her lap. The new one written by Franz Werfel, "The Song of Bernadette." She stood up and grimaced at the gentleman turning the radio dial. "All I Need Is You" by Dinah Shore began flowing its music from the radio. "Oh leave it there!" Exclaimed the lady employee with annoyance throwing grit into her voice. "That's Dinah Shore singing! I love that Dinah Shore!"

The man turned the radio dial yet again ignoring the Dinah Shore song.

"What am I going to do with you?" Said the heavy-set lady with breathless exasperation. She turned to Pauline. "Come on dear, I'll show you." And with that she moved from behind the counter to show Pauline the Harper's Bazaar.

All three girls surrounded their mother at that moment, keeping her from following the older lady. They spoke with delighted enthusiasm:

"Can we have some peppermint Mother?"

"No! I want the hard honey kind candy!"

"Can we please? Pretty please?"

Pauline looked at the girls. "Maybe", she said. She tried to scoot past the children to follow the female employee. "Girls, you're under foot! I said 'maybe'."

The man at the radio had tuned in to a current news talk program. Leaning in as if possibly somewhat hard of hearing he turned up the volume and listened intently. The radio blared and he jumped back: "In Washington D.C. twenty-six Allied nations came together for a sole purpose!" The dark male voice booming from the radio paused a second then continued: "This includes the U.S. and Great Britain. A pact that none of them would make any separate agreements with Germany. You folks have all bought in to the use of this 'pact' as a means to divert our attention away from the truly important issues!

"American people are you hearing what I'm saying? I want to ask, 'what about this terrible tragedy on our U.S. navel base in the Aleutian Islands when our own kind were attacked by Japanese aircraft?!

"What are we going to do, and should we do anything, about the German troops in Stalingrad? You've got to know people, and I quote, Hitler says he has Stalingrad 'firmly in German Hands'! Now what I…"

"Turn that thing to something else!"--Admonished the sales lady. "Life is hard enough without hearing all that depressing news all the time!" She looked the older gentleman square in the eyes from where she stood. He shrugged helplessly then began turning the radio dial again.

The radio spoke with a different voice: "British scientists announce the new discovery they're calling 'penicillin'."

"Music! Music old man!" Demanded the sales woman.

"Alright", he replied and began turning the dial again.

"Now what I like is music", said the lady to Pauline as she began to lead her across the store. "I like that song 'Daybreak' with Tommy Dorsey and Frank Sinatra. Oooowoowoo I tell you that Frank Sinatra is just dreamy! He could sing me to sleep any night!"

Pauline blushed at the woman's comment. The children were tagging along. The oldest child Nedett wouldn't stop tugging on her mother's dress.

"Howdy, now that's a good one!" Exclaimed the sales lady looking from the corner of her eye to the man behind the counter who had just proudly stolen her chair to sit in it himself. She spoke this with an ardor as if he had been the one to sing the song that was blaring through the radio himself. Bing Crosby warmly and smoothly crooned out the new hit song "White Christmas."

"I like the movies", Pauline said in response to the saleswoman.

"I do too!" The sales lady was loud in speech and just a little annoying with her animated habit of talking with her hands and stepping heavy. "There's a good one out now too. Its got that man in it. That Humphrey Bogart. Now what is the name of that movie? It's just come out. It's…"

"Casablanca?" Pauline offered.

"Yes! That's it! Have you seen it?"

"No."

Young Deana pointed to a picture on the wall and pulled on the sales woman's dress. "Lady Mam, who's that man?"

The sales clerk looked at the picture then bent forward some in talking to the child. "That's Denton T. Young! They called him 'Cy'. Don't you know your baseball little girlie? Old Cy was put in the Baseball Hall of Fame!"

"What's a 'fame' Mother?" Asked Deana.

"Girls!" Pauline exclaimed. "Let me get my shopping done!"

"Right here dear", complied the sales woman to Pauline, "now what was it you were wanting to look for in the Bazaar dear?"

"Well I…" Suddenly the sales lady befuddled Pauline completely.

"Heavens to Betsy! What am I thinking! Now I remember where I put it. Follow me dear." The sales clerk began walking back towards the front of the store and ushered Pauline to follow.

"Mother! Mother! Can we go outside?" The children begged Pauline while bouncing all around her.

"What?" She asked of her children.

"Can we go outside?" Said Deana speaking up for the excited lot.

"Yes. Yes! Go on outside. I'll be with you in a minute." Pauline watched the children run out of the store. The New York World's Fair had introduced a new-fangled gadget in 1939 called a television. Such advances this modern society was making! A store just a few spots down the block showed off a brand new black and white television in its store-front window. It was the newest latest fascination and simply everyone had at least heard about them! No doubt the girls were beside themselves with excitement to go over and take a look at this new wonder in entertainment.

Pauline Arnez picked up a pound of sugar as she made her way back to the counter in following the sales clerk. The sales lady was now busy fumbling through a drawer behind the counter. A drawn image of a lovely dress caught Pauline's eye. She picked up the packet with the dress drawn on front. Picking it up and flipping it to look at the back and then the front again. Inside the packet was a dress pattern. Feeling it was a good choice Pauline carried the packet along with the sugar to the cash register. She was thinking of the list with the Harper's Bazaar award winning dresses in it. At once there was an unnatural screeching that sounded out from somewhere in the street. Pauline had an instant's reaction to reach up with her right hand and grab her hair. She saw from the corner of her eye as her hat toppled from her head and fell in slow motion to the floor. A sound like a hand-bell ringing one long constant high-pitched note seemed to vibrate in the air. Somehow she had the piece of mind to set down the pound of sugar on the counter. The dress pattern followed suit but missed the counter floating in a time-altered slowness like a snowflake drifting down to the ground.

Although she knew she was running Pauline experienced each step of her feet to take place in a slow motioned beat of her heart. Thump. Step. Thump. Step. She heard that heartbeat loudly in her ears. Nedett was standing on the sidewalk stiff as a statue with her arms petrified into two straight wooden inlets ending in blood-stopping tight fists. She was screaming. Screaming and screaming. Precious little Cora Peggy Arnez had been hit by a truck.

For those who are squeamish you might want to skip over the next few sentences which end this paragraph. Cora Peggy's skull was split open exposing the brain. Oddly enough the blood was flowing away from the brain blessing the puffing brain tissue to be free of coagulating blood clots. The flesh beneath the skin of her legs was beyond torn so that if you reached out and touched it, it would feel not like muscle but like jelly. At least like a benediction of grace Cora was completely unconscious.

Cora was rushed to the hospital. The doctor would comment to Mr. and Mrs. Arnez in horrified awe that it would be a miracle if the child pulled through. Hours of tenuous surgery upon the little girl's head. Cora fell into a coma.

(As told to me, Suzanna, by my mother Cora Peggy--)Cora watched the surgery take place from outside of her body. She stood and waited. Occasionally floating from one side of the operating room to the other. She knew it was her body they were working on. Cora saw one of the attending nurses drop something which fell to the floor beneath the operating table. Something shiny. A key? A small short pen?

Although the hospital were letting Cora's body heal in its coma the doctor had prepared the parent's with the facts. "She won't make it", said the doctor. "You need to prepare yourselves for her death. If somehow she survives for any length of time she will never come out of the coma." The doctor scooted to the edge of his seat. How his heart ached for this family and the dear poor child.

Pauline and Early were sitting in chairs listening to the doctor. Holding hands and crying. Being a 'man' with little emotion meant nothing when faced with losing a child and so Early let the tears fall from his face.

"But what if she came out of the coma?" Asked Pauline. "It could happen, couldn't it? What if she came out of it?"

Placing his hand briefly on top of the parent's clasped hands, tears came brimming to the doctor's eyes. Wiping his eyes he cleared his throat to speak. "If she did come out of the coma she would be nothing but a vegetable."

"Oh!" Cried Pauline. The parents visibly flinched at this information.

"I'm so sorry Mr. and Mrs. Arnez. In all my years I have never seen such severe and terrible injuries. The head trauma is worse than anything I've even read about."

"We will do what we're able. And we'll do everything we can to make her as comfortable as possible. But it's my duty to tell you the truth. Your daughter Cora is going to die. You need to prepare yourselves."

Time passed. The hospital wished to do some testing on the comatose child but she would need to be brought to the downstairs level. The attending physician himself picked up Cora Peggy and cradling her in his own arms he carried her down the flight of stairs. Cora felt such a powerful sense of love and concern and tenderness coming from the man that she thought it must probably be her own father whom carried her down the stairs in his strong arms.

Pauline and Early had already gone to the nearest local cemetery and picked out the plot that would be their daughters grave. They were in the process of sketching out how they wanted her head-stone to look like and what they wanted it to say.

The grief stricken parents went to visit Cora Peggy at the hospital. Standing at the foot of their baby girl's hospital bed they clasped hands and began to cry again. The doctor who had seen the child through everything and had attended to her so tenderly stood to the side of the parents and wept as well.

Suddenly a shock to the system like bolts of lightening shuddered through each attending adult. The child Cora opened her eyes from the coma and looked straight at them. Feebly the child raised her arm as far as she could force it and she pointed her finger at her father. "You carried me down the stairs Daddy, didn't you? I saw it."—Cora Peggy spoke.

Feeling the electric bolt of shock the adult's faces drained white as ghosts. Open mouths and tear-blurred wide eyes stared back in disbelief at the child.

"The…thah..that was *me*", stammered the doctor. "I carried you down the stairs." Surprise still buzzed its frozen stiff-bodied magic on the grown-ups. Then at once the doctor spoke breathlessly to the child: "How? How could you possibly *know* that?"

* * *

Joyously and earnestly it was officially declared by the attending physician (and in fact by everyone who had worked in the hospital) that a true miracle had occurred. Yes it was a miracle. Cora Peggy Arnez would grow up seemingly unharmed. She would walk and play like any child. She would go to University; get her Masters degree. Have children of her own.

EIGHT

THE HERITAGE
PART 2

As a child Cora Peggy Arnez would take piano lessons from a Freida Locks of 'small town', Texas and she would be introduced to her soul mate. Although at ten years old she wouldn't know that the older boy (Elton Locks born in 1928, who was Freida Locks's brother in law) would be the man she would eventually marry and enjoy sharing a happy relationship. Elton Locks would grow up to marry and divorce and have with his first wife three children: Dora born in 1965; Bart born in 1967; and Jenna born in 1968.

Cora Peggy Arnez would grow up to meet her first husband, Rustle Bobby Barns the eldest son of Oleta and JB Barns, while attending University. This eldest son would go by his middle name of Bobby. Interestingly Cora Peggy Arnez would also go by her middle name of Peggy.

* * * *

Summer still broke into the mornings early light with a glistening upon the pointy lime-green tree leaves and spiky forest-green bushes. Birds twittering as always in a chorus of over-lapped languages in tweets, whistles, and chirps. Small tiny birds flicking their heads from side to side as they land upon a baby tree's new branches. Fluffing yellow down under their necks and the grayish-brown feather's across their bodies.

Birds in the sky flowing as a team as if in a synchronized bubble. A black and white tom-cat charges the lowest branch of a tree. A hawk far up in the sky glides in figure eight's as if swooning to the wind. Cora Peggy Arnez had graduated from high school just the day before. Only one day had passed since Peggy took her high school diploma in hand and smiled to high heaven along with all the other relieved and rapturous graduates. Parent's had watched with chests puffed with pride. It was especially a day of magnificent joy for Mr. and Mrs. Arnez since they were watching the graduation of their miracle child!

A mere one day passing after graduation and Early was helping his youngest daughter pack up so he could take her to McMurry University. Father and daughter would ride alone and in silence to McMurry. Pauline had stayed behind. The switch to dormitory life would seem lonely and scary for Peggy during her first 48 hours there. The peanut butter and crackers Early had bought as a snack for his baby girl became her dinner that first night in the dorm at university. She hadn't yet figured out the how and where of the campus cafeteria.

On that first night in the McMurry dormitory Peggy sat lonely in her fairly empty room. She set a few pictures of her family on top of the dresser to stave away the fear and loneliness of being in a new place. Quiet had a resounding presence. A pressure of silence that filled up an entire room and pressed down upon the heart.

Suddenly there was a shift in the air. A tinkling of notes as if from a piano; and the sounds of laughter. It was coming from outside the dorm room and Peggy was surprised at the realization that she was hearing not just female voices but male voices as well. Were men allowed in the girl's dorm? Curiosity and encouragement from the music made the young Arnez girl smile. She felt it wonderful that there was a piano playing and singing going on. Lifting off of the small rectangular bed she smoothed away the wrinkles on the sheet she'd brought with her from home. Giddily Peggy tip-toed through her small square drab-brown room over to the door. Although why she was tip-toeing she didn't know. As stealthily as possible Peggy turned the door knob and cracked the door open just a bit; leaning her ear into the opening. Laughter erupted within the singing and piano playing from somewhere down below. There was a new song out this fine year of 1953 that had become very popular. Everyone simply fell in love with it. It was that song by Pattie Page called "Doggie in the Window." A sparkling of notes from the old ebony and ivory while young voices broke out again in song. It was the new song "Doggie in the Window" they sang. Peggy tightened with excitement. "I love this song", she thought to herself. She exited the dorm room closing the door quietly behind her. Peggy snuck down the stairs but quickly. She peeked around the corner and saw the group of young student's singing while gathered around the dorm's lobby piano.

Young Miss Arnez relaxed her facial muscles and pulled her shoulders back straight. She put a smile on her face which was easy to do in her excitement. Finally she swallowed down a huge gulping breath of courage. She cleared her throat.

Then at last Miss Peggy Arnez turned around the corner. Walking with a slight bounce of happiness in her step she made her way over to the singing group with all the purpose of having every right to be there as any of the other students. She joined in the singing. Nods and smiles of welcome and approval wafted across to her from the singing and piano playing youngsters. It was a relief to see that most of them had their beenie hats on. It was the "slime cap." A green beenie that every freshman had to wear to signify that they were new to the university. And unless you wanted some good humored hazing you'd better have your beenie on! "Ah-oh", thought Peggy in mid song, "I forgot to put my beenie on!" Worry momentarily threatened to ruin her composure. Knees and hands trembled. Then a calmed feeling soothed liquid throughout her mind as she made the accurate assumption, "They don't know me. As long as I act confident in my right to be here they won't know I'm supposed to have a beenie on!" And with that the brave and beautiful Cora Peggy Arnez smiled again sweetly and continued singing; with good humor. Calm. And at least the imitation of confidence. And when it comes to confidence who can tell an imitation from the real thing?

Summer of magic. And the magic is: friendship, the beauty of the campus, and doing something enjoyable. Cora would get an enjoyable job singing commercials and more at a local radio station. How the beautiful Cora would become so famous among the students for her beautiful voice. She had a fabulous talent for playing piano too. Yet her true acclaim was so much more than that. She would become well known on campus for having the singing voice *of a nightingale*.

Summer drifted away, as summer's always do. Maple trees spread the color of fire through their branches. Old oak trees lumbered their heavy cargo of leaves and nests. Then at last the trees shook themselves of its weight a little at a time. Autumn dancing in like a woodland fairy on the breeze. Leaves turning from yellow to gold; from burgundy to caramel.

The smell of smoke and fire from the chimneys of neighboring houses would once again drift into the pleased noses of passers by. Sweet and pungent fragrances of summer flowers fading into the smell of campfire-like smoke and ripe pecans. Wind snaking through branches and slithering smoothly over buildings. Whispering that their blustery gusts would soon turn colder. Autumn encroaches like a beautiful Queen.

It took a while as Cora Peggy settled into her newly assigned dorm room for the fall semester. She had rather hoped she'd have the same dorm room she had occupied during the summer session. How easy would it be to locate the whereabouts of her summer friends? During the summer she hadn't had a roommate and was looking forward to the experience. It was a slight disappointment when her originally assigned fall roommate had vied for the right to bunk in a different dorm room with someone she already knew. Peggy wished she had been the one who had already established a roommate. Things turned out very well indeed however with yet a new roommate that had been assigned in replacement. For the replacement mate shared Peggy's love of church service and piano and singing.

*   *   *   *

One of the female dorm residents whom had made friends with both Peggy and her roommate opened the door and stuck her head inside. "Hey girl's! A bunch of us are going down to the Dixie Pig and get 7-up floats. Wanna come?"

"Yes!" Peggy and her roommate cheered out in unison. They covered their mouths and giggled at their own enthusiasm. Peggy looked out the window. Light was filtering from a bright sunny day into gray shadows outside. Suddenly thinking better of it Peggy asked, "But it's getting dark."

"Oh my goodness don't worry", said the girl bouncing in the doorway. "We'll go back before curfew! Don't worry Peggy."

"Ooo I'd hate to get locked outside the dorm." Peggy grimaced at the scary thought. "I'd hate to have to ring the bell and have to face the dorm mother."

"No kidding", agreed Peggy's roommate.

"Oh we'll come back in time! Come on! It'll be fun!" Their friend positively gleamed as she leaned against the door handle and kicked her foot back and forth between the door's archway.

"Okay", said Peggy with inevitable excitement. Her room mate giving a solid nod downward in happy assent.

"Yall girls hurry up, we'll be waiting for you in the lobby." And thus their host whom had so kindly invited them gently closed the door behind herself.

Bells rang outside the window from the nearby chapel of the church. Pigeons fluttered back and forth from their outside roosts upon the dorm windows. Evening began spreading its dark shadows like the smooth roll of a knife against half-melted butter. A light breeze rapped upon the windowpane. The wind was beckoning like an uninvited guest for anyone to let its cooling chill inside.

Peggy and her room mate hopped to their mirrors for a last minute check and primping. Both girls puffed some peachy colored powder onto their cheeks, foreheads, and noses. Peggy blotted an orange-red dab of lipstick onto her lips while her room mate dappled her mouth with a bright red color.

Both girls were wearing simple yet nicely tailored white blouses with peter-pan collars. Peggy had white gloves which she slipped onto her hands and up to her wrists. Her room mates gloves were a common light pink. The girls each had on wool sheath skirts that hung just over their mid-calves. Peggy twirled slightly to check her light blue and gray wool skirt from the back and duly tuck in her blouse around the waist. Then she slipped on her clutch-coat jacket that was of matching color and material as her skirt. It was the jacket without any buttons. She bent down to straighten her bobby-socks which had begun to sag slightly as she'd been sitting in the dorm chatting with her room mate. Peggy still had on her white saddle shoes with the wide caramel-brown stripe across the top of them. Her feet ached for having worn her saddle shoes all day long.

Peggy's room mate sat on the edge of her own bed and looked down at her bare feet. She wiggled her toes. Somehow the toes wiggling caused both girls to start giggling. Then the room mate brushed her fingers through her short wavy lightly red hair and sighed. She said, "I wish I could just go to the Dixie Pig without any socks or shoes on!" More soft laughter and female giggles.

"I can just see you walking in your bare feet!" Peggy laughed.

"Hand me my bobby socks will you?" Peggy tentatively lifted the socks from the chair, wondering how anyone could leave stinky worn socks laying in a spot people would want to sit. Peggy decided to tease her friend and pinched her nostrils with her thumb and forefinger. Holding the socks with her arm as far out from her body as possible she dangled them from the very end-tips of her clenched fingers.

"Very funny", the friend laughed with a bob of her reddish waves of hair. She snatched her bobby socks from the giggling girl's fingers and then bent to slip them on. She put her saddle shoes on also. Only hers had black stripes across the tops. She put on her straight shortly cut wool jacket of red. It matched the color of her sheath skirt which had a poodle emblem on the side.

Peggy checked her hair in the mirror again. Peggy's hair was swept back off of her face and cut short in the back so that it came to the nape of her neck. Her soft hazelnut colored hair folded in waves and ended in gentle curls all around the edges. She thought of the freckles on her arms. She thought of the gentle texture of her hair. She powdered away freckles on her nose. Sadly Peggy didn't realize she was absolutely beautiful. Her false self-image of plainness was incorrect. Peggy falsely thought one could see the scars over her head and underneath her hair. Scars from where she'd been run over by a truck and had to have extensive surgery when she was little. The thought of her time in a coma after the accident still sent shudders down her spine, haunting her. Cora Peggy Arnez was beautiful.

"Ready Peggy?"

Turning to face her room mate Peggy smiled. "Yes. As ready as I'll ever be!"

The two friends put their green "slime beenies" on their heads. Leaving their dorm they went downstairs to the lobby that held the piano.

"My mother just loves root-beer floats", said Peggy's friend as they walked and chatted.

"Yes, but it always makes me think of beer", Peggy smiled. The two girls giggled.

"Maybe we should have them make 'beer' foats", her room mate teased. The two girls giggled again as they rounded the corner to see the other two girls and one boy waiting for them.

"There you are!" The tall dark haired girl who had invited them exclaimed. "We've been waiting! I thought I'd have to come up and drag you down." Her straight hair bobbed at her jaw-line that sported two heavy waves on the side of her head to keep the bangs off of her face. Her bobby socks matched the color of her light green sheath skirt and short cropped heavily textured clutch coat perfectly. Her blouse and gloves were white. Her smile showed lovely white teeth but she wore no makeup except for a dab of bright red lipstick. Her eyes were so dark they looked almost black.

"We were just talking about this book", the shorter girl gestured to the tall thin boy with them. This girl was unsurprisingly pudgy with her short stature. She adjusted the hairpin holding the green slime beenie to her very dark hair. A long thin silk ribbon pulled her straight bobbed hair away from her face. Her dress of thick cloth was a slightly different color of brown from the stripe on her saddle shoes. The lipstick and blush she wore was a cotton candy pink. The blush layered thicker than it should have been. Pulling her glasses out of her handbag she put them on. She wrinkled her nose like a bunny rabbit a few times before pushing them farther up the bridge of her nose with her pointer finger. Gesturing with a wave of her arm she invited everyone to go ahead and leave with her. "Come on! We ought to get to the Dixie Pig before they run out of floats!" She giggled. "Of course what I really want is the ice cream."

"I hear you on that one", said the young man as he held the door open for the ladies to walk through first. All five of them stepped into the light breeze of the waning day. Making their way along the sidewalk in a collective bunch.

"What book was that?" Peggy asked the young man.

"What?" He felt confused. His pecan-brown hair was almost a crew cut and had obviously been slicked a bit with pomade. His pale blue cotton shirt was buttoned to the top of its wide collar. With a slightly darker blue knit vest on top. A thin trim tie of yellow and blue stripes lay finely knotted at his throat.

"The book she said you all were talking about", explained Peggy. They were all happy and continued to smile and talk as they walked to the Dixie Pig.

"Oh, this!" He flushed a bit from a quickly passing fever of embarrassment. "I've got it in my hand", he chortled. He lifted the book in his hand up high. Two short laughter snorts escaped him as he fained a slap to his forehead with his left hand. Swallowing a little hard he showed the book to Peggy as they walked along. "It's one of the new ones from that writer, Ernest Hemingway."

Peggy leaned towards his arm to read the title of the book. The words seemed to jiggle from the movement of their continued exercise towards the malt shop. Finally her eyes caught hold of the title and she read it out loud. "The Old Man and the Sea."

He nodded then tucked the book against his ribs with the bend of his elbow. "It's good", he flatly declared.

"Oh yes, I know that one", said Peggy with a bright smile. "Did you know that the author, Hemingway, he's up for a possible Pulitzer Prize for fiction?"

"I'd thought he had won one", said the taller dark haired girl as she absently flapped her light green skirt back and forth with the grasp of her hand.

"You think?" Inquired Peggy.

"I'm not sure." The tall girl widened her eyes and shrugged her shoulders.

"I haven't read it yet." Pushing up her glasses with a finger the shorter girl in the pink cotton candy skirt gestured towards the boy. "You are gonna let me borrow it aren't ya?"

"Well now…" He put his arm around the short girl's shoulder and made a tsk tsk sound. "I don't know…"

"Don't tease!" She pushed her glasses up again then elbowed him in the ribs.

"Ouch!" He teased and rubbed his ribs. "Okee-dokey." He laughed then pulled his arm back down to his side.

"So when am I gonna hear the nightingale sing again?" The tall dark girl posed the question to Peggy.

"I don't know." Came the reply. "I guess when we're all standing around the piano again." Peggy smiled and turned her green eyes to the sky above. It was clear enough and dark enough for the moon and stars to already begin showing their beauty.

The tall young man with the pecan colored hair was the one to open the door when they arrived at the Dixie Pig. No-ones legs were tired from the walk. Or if muscles were achy no one noticed. For the scenery of the campus and small shops combined with fresh air, idle chit-chat, and the excitement of being a university student was far too enthralling. All the girls politely said 'thank you' to the young man holding the door.

There were other students in the Dixie Pig already seated as the group made their way to a booth. Yet of all the people there was one man in particular that caught Peggy's eye. She had never seen this handsome guy before! She soaked in as long a glance as she dared and felt some odd momentary sense of heightened awareness. It was as if all the sound in the place had stopped for a minute; although of course it hadn't. Clinking utensils on thick hard plates. Pinging sounds of glasses full of soda being moved about. All of this came back to Peggy's ears as she turned her eyes away from the handsome guy. She heard music and conversation. Turning to follow along with her friends she didn't give the moment another thought. Although, she must admit, she had sat where she could see him if she wanted.

Peggy and her room mate and the other friends all squeezed onto the softly stuffed seating of the booth. Promptly the waitress with her fuzzy brown bee-hived hairdo marched heavily up to their table to pass out menus. The waitress then looked at the group with a slightly sour expression and sighed. She continued to chomp rather nastily on her gum while she rubbed her pencil up into the hair beneath her cloth Dixie Pig waitress crown. She was somewhat dumpy with extremely large breasts. A few dry wrinkles in her rusty red face gave tell that she had a few years on her.

"I'll have a 7-up float", said the taller girl.

"Me too." (Agreed the shorter girl, pushing up her glasses with a finger again.)

"A whole round of 7-up floats!" The pecan haired young man exclaimed happily.

"And you too?" The waitress pointed her pencil at Peggy and made a popping sound with her gum.

"Yes Mam, thank you." Peggy Arnez smiled at the waitress after her reply then moved her green eyes upward in an attempt to steal another glance at the handsome young man sitting at the other booth. She stared longer than she meant too. But how could she help it? Peggy Arnez wanted to laugh. The good looking guy in the other booth was in the midst of what looked like an extremely heated conversation. But he kept looking up and smiling at her with his perfectly straight white teeth. She looked away modestly towards the window at the right of their booth. For modesty's sake Peggy determined not to look at him again. Yet she had snuck a long enough glance to make out the name on his green slime beenie. It said: Bobby. Now she knew his name.

The jukebox flipped another record. "Don't Let the Star's Get In Your Eyes" with Perry Como and the Mitchell Ayre's orchestra began to play. Bright ceiling lights shown down upon all the youth crammed into booths and chattering away. The 7-up floats came quickly to Cora Peggy Arnez's table. Never before had a frothy soda ever tasted so good to her.

Sitting at the far booth the handsome guy enjoyed argumentative conversation. Bobby Barns loved to argue politics, religion, and current events. His two male friends sat at the booth with him. They also enjoyed getting fired up over a topic. The bee hived waitress plopped a hamburger down carelessly to Bobby Barns's friend sitting across from him.

"More coffee please", said Bobby while pointing at his empty mug. The waitress rolled her eyes and stuck her pencil in her hair and left it there. She sauntered to grab the coffee pot and popped her gum all the way back to Bobby Barns's booth. She filled his mug with coffee and sighed.

"Thank you Mam." Bobby Barns gestured with a smile. The waitress shrugged her shoulders and rolled her eyes again. "Anyhow", Bobby continued with his conversation, "the United Nations has been having these international disputes ever since the end of World War Two!" His face was becoming red again with the excitement of debate.

The freshman boy opposite Bobby Barns who was not eating anything said, "It's because Fidel Castro has just come into power!"

"No! No!" Bobby Barns banged his fist against the table. "That should have nothing to do with it! And what… Fidel Castro has been in power now for what…three years? I'm telling you the problem is with proper mediation!"

"Okay, but say we determine a method of mediation that…" His friend continued to speak but Bobby Barns became aware that he was now just half listening as he looked over at Peggy Arnez again.

"Come on. Come on." Bobby thought to himself. "Look up." Sure enough the beautiful girl wearing a slime cap with the name "Peggy" on it looked at him for an instant. He flashed her a great big toothy smile. She giggled and looked away, sipping on her soda float. Looking at her Bobby decided instantly that he was going to marry her. He had seen her before; many times. Yet he hadn't ever gotten her to notice him. Until now. He didn't think she remembered him saying "Hi" to her the other day when they passed each other in the library. She had seemed so busy in the library that she had hardly looked up at all in her automatic response of "Hello" back to him. "Heck", he thought to himself, "I knew I wanted to marry her from the first day I saw her." He had been hoping for an opportunity to pursue her.

Before Bobby could even complete his thoughts a huge gale blew the door to Dixie Pig open. It made a huge loud thrump which caused everyone in the place to either jump or turn. The door stayed open and a violent wind blasted through every nook and cranny with a howling sound like a small hurt animal screaming.

Dust and dried bits of grass circled through the establishment, riding upon a continuous colossal huff and puff of the winds breath.

A young boy who was most probably a student was sitting in the booth closest to the open door and he stood up to close it. His short black hair looked greasy and he wore blue jeans rolled up at the bottoms into wide cuffs. He closed the door and a few of the patrons clapped.

Lifting and turning, the jukebox lowered its needle to play another record. Notes flowed from the bubble-windowed jukebox. The tune wafted from the jukeboxes lit up shiny purple sides. Nat King Cole was singing "Pretend."

Peggy blinked. The guy with 'Bobby' on his beenie cap was grinning at her again. He's so cute! She politely smiled back. What was this feeling? "Perhaps I need some real food in my stomach", thought Peggy as she pondered the cause of the feeling. A feeling like giddiness. Heart beating much too fast.

She felt like being silly. Her tummy fluttered. It happened every time she looked at this guy. Turning her eyes to the window she could see her reflection. It was pitch dark now outside.

Boom! The wind pounded the windows all at once sounding like fists on glass banging frantically. So loud as to make everyone jump was a magnanimous spiriting of thunder. Instantly it seemed, rain angrily pounded against the glass windows with an assault of savage fury. Crackling, breaking, like the breaking of bones, the lightening scorched the sky over and over again. Relentlessly.

Alarmed, Peggy and the rest of her group jumped up. Standing and staring out the window with fear and awe. Everyone burst into a slow short wave of laughter at how jumpy they'd all been. The girl with the glasses pushed them back up her nose again and asked, "Is it a tornado?"

"My! We'd better get back! We'd better get to the dorm!" Said the taller girl with great concern. Her dark hair bounced as she turned her head. Raindrops patted at the window.

"We'll make a run for it." Stated their male friend with the pecan hair.

Watching Peggy Arnez's group at the other side of the room Bobby Barns could tell they were about to leave. "Gotta go!" Bobby announced standing up.

"Nahhh. Sit down." Said Bobby's friend who'd had the hamburger.

"Yea", coalesced Bobby's other friend, "Sit down. Wait out the storm."

"Nope!" Bobby still had his eyes on Peggy and her group. They were moving towards the door! He moved, rather lunged, a few elongated strides and was next to Peggy.

Peggy tugged at her blue wool clutch coat wishing it had buttons. It seemed a good opportunity to take in that long drink of what the grinning young man looked like. "Yes!"—She thought to herself after glancing to double-check that it was 'Bobby' printed on his cap. She had the name right. Trying to appear casual she tipped her green eyes to the left to better see him. She liked what she saw. He was so very handsome. A crew cut for his hair. She focused quickly on the color of his eyes. Then she looked away again. "Such pretty blue eyes", she thought. Peering casually again as if to take a look at the Dixie Pig about her she sought another visual sip of the handsome man. Truthfully she had looked him up and down so quickly as to be hardly noticed. He had on a cotton broadcloth shirt that was pale blue and buttoned up to the collar with both cuffs buttoned at the end of the sleeves. His shoes of black leather which lifted at the toe and ankle looked well cared for. "Well, he certainly seems to take care of how he looks", Peggy thought approvingly. She took in one last peek and saw him grinning and pressing his arms into the raglan sleeves of his short, wheat-brown, tweed overcoat.

Looking now at the storm Peggy got a wet-spray surprise in her face. The Dixie Pig's front door walloped open and stayed that way. Once again a multi-pitched wailing like a vengeful banshee came swirls of wet circular gusts of wind. Instinctively the crowd pulled together. Bobby Barns was now hyper aware that his upper arm was *touching* Peggy Arnez's shoulder! He felt a tingle.

Cora Peggy's mouth opened with insurmountable surprise at the raging storm. Bobby leaned in a bit of pressure against Peggy's shoulder so that she would turn to him. She did turn her head to him! She looked him square in the eyes! He felt a thrill of heat. He spoke loudly to Peggy: "Looks like we'll have to make a run for it!"

"No kidding!" Responded the pecan-haired young man standing in front of Bobby and Peggy. "On the count of three! *Ready*?!"

Every single person standing in front of the open door and squinting into the wet wind counted together. In unison voice and smiles on their faces they counted with a shout: "ONE! TWO! *THREE*!!"

The group ran in a laughing shrieking herd out the door. Leaving the door open behind them they piled outside. Once within the storm everyone realized the weather was far more foul than they had already expected. Large outrageous pounding drops of rain beat on them like a million tiny angry fists. So much rain that it was blinding. An earthy wet ozone smell wafted through their lungs and nostrils. Cold rain pelting into their eyes.

"I can't see!" Peggy laughed with consternation.

"Here!" Bobby cupped her shoulders in the palms of his hands to stop her from running. She stopped.

"What?" Peggy shouted above the noise. Thunderous rolling booms faded only slightly before giving way to a smashing blast that was so jolting as to be like a bomb reverberating tiny vibrations under the skin. Electricity causing the hairs on their arms to stand up instantly.

The other people in the group were starting to get ahead of them. Peggy covered her eyes to protect them from the tumultuous pelting rain. Bobby took hold of the front of Peggy's beenie with a pinch of his fingers. He pulled it down so that Peggy's eyes were practically completely covered by the cap. Did he mean for her to follow him blind?

"My goodness! Ha!" Peggy Arnez bent in laughter for a moment. Grinning she said, "Well, I still can't see, but it feels better!" She noticed the rain had a metallic taste upon her tongue.

"Yeah, the rain is so hard it hurts", affirmed Bobby Barns. "I've rarely seen such a fierce downpour!" They were having to shout at each other just to be heard over the deafening bellow of falling water and roaring winds. Plus there was the ear-splitting blasts of thunder. Bobby took her hand and planned to continue in the run when he felt a solid tug from Peggy pulling him back.

"Hey!" She hollered.

"What?"

"I said 'hey'!" She pointed to the wool beenie covering her eyes and said: "What a way to pull the wool over my eyes! Ha!" She laughed at her own joke. They were both soaking wet already as they stood there.

Bobby cracked up laughing and replied, "Yes, ha! I guess I really did! You've got a sense of humor. I like that." Grasping her hand tightly he hollered: "Just hold on to my hand! I'll lead the way!" Thus with Bobby leading the way the two of them ran. Running past trees bending in submission to the overpowering winds. Running past the shops. Sprinting as faithfully as their feet would safely take them. Occasionally inextricable yelps and shrieks followed by laughter would escape the youngster's throats. More silvery metallic tasting raindrops flowed into their mouths each time they laughed. The muddy grassy smell of ozone grew more powerful.

Lightening bolted in daunting shocks of light which could be felt on the skin like a tremble in the surrounding air. They made it to a sidewalk of the university campus. Holding hands they ran in the rain!

They each had to keep hold of their beenie caps with their free hand just to keep the thing from blowing off! Flashing electrified illumination ripped across the sky. The lightening felt much too close. Its burning streaks leaving a trickle of light to fall into their eyes before they could even blink. The sky again curdled. Unleashed rumbling percussions echoed.

Something warm and friendly was igniting between the two students. The kind of feeling that makes you forget your actually strangers. Bobby Barns and Peggy Arnez arrived at the door of Peggy's dormitory. They were underneath the shelter of the awning now. She pushed her beenie cap back off of her eyes. They stood at the doorway holding hands for a lingering moment. Both of them experiencing a heightened awareness of the touch. Timidly they pulled their hands apart to rest at their own sides.

Lightening pulled electrical at the hairs of their arms. Thunder crashed as bass drums. Yet the two young students stood in complete silence, grinning at each other. Rain flowed down upon them; soaking the grinning sillies.

At last Bobby Barns cleared his throat to speak. "Hey, maybe we could go see a movie sometime." He still had to speak loudly just to be heard over the chaos of nature's noises around them.

"I'd like that!" Peggy Arnez suddenly felt that tumbling sensation in her stomach again. Heart pounding faster. Beating harder. A warm tingling in her sides. Pound, pound, pound went her heart ever deeper, and dragging her breath away with it! She could actually feel the hot hammering in her chest.

Bobby's heart also thumped wild beats with warm impassioned thuds against his ribs. "Okay. Maybe tomorrow?"

"Yes."

Bobby willed his brain to recall what movies were out in the theaters. "That one movie is showing. That one with Burt Lancaster." He paused in thought. "And Frank Sinatra."

"My, I like Frank Sinatra."

"So does every girl!" They both giggled. "It's called 'From Here to Eternity.' The movie I mean."

"Yes." She could see his tank undershirt beneath his drenched pale blue cuffed shirt. It pleased her that he wore an undershirt.

"So your name's 'Peggy'." He pointed to her name printed on her beanie (which was sometimes called a slime cap by the students.)

"Oh yes. Its my middle name."

"I go by my middle name too. Its 'Bobby'."

"Yes. I noticed." She pointed to his cap.

He blushed and flashed her a smile. "Oh yea, and there's that other movie showing." He pressed his lips together. "Its called… its called…" Pressing his lips together again only harder. "I can't remember, it has Audrey Hepburn in it."

"I love Audrey Hepburn!" Rain kept pouring down around them and spraying them in wet wisps of the wind.

"And Gregory Peck. I think it has Gregory Peck. I really like Gregory Peck." He felt like he was stuttering. This feeling caused him to blush again. Next they both spoke at the exact same time and pointed their pointer fingers at each other. After initial gasped breaths they both spoke on top of each other saying, "Roman Holiday!"

"Yeah", nodded Bobby as he continued his thought. "That's the name of the movie. Roman Holiday."

"Okay. Well I better get inside now."

"Yes. You better."

"Bye Bobby." She opened the door and began walking into the dormitory.

"See you later Peggy." He lifted his hand in a short wave. Bending his knees with his left foot lifted onto the toe of his shoe. He watched her walk inside. The door closed behind her. Then he looked up into the rain without minding it splashing into his eyes. Raising his arms all the way up high in the air he fisted his hands. Like a boxing champion he tensed his fists. "Yes!"—He exclaimed with a smile of excitement. "Yes! Yes! Yes!" He had gotten a date with the nightingale. He shook his raised arms one last time before turning into the rain and jogging away. He had a kick in his step.

Does thunder explode warnings to young lovers in love? Lovers never heed such warnings. Yet wasn't it the storm that had brought these two together? If so then the thunder would be like a living thing with the heart of a fool. Couldn't the wind push people apart and the lightening flash out 'Stop!'? If so, then the wind and the lightening have turned out to be buffoons screaming hopelessly at the intoxicating promise of being loved. We are all, after all, only human. No human being has gone through life without at least once ignoring tumultuous signs. If indeed such 'signs' even exist. Oh how deeply we all stand equal as human beings when it comes to matters of the heart; even if only for a moment.

Indeed the two star-crossed youngsters would go to see a movie together. As they walked back to the university's dormitories after the movie was over the couple were followed by an odd and ominously nasty smell. Of course they couldn't have been expected to be able to pay much attention to the movie. Not when they were sitting so close to one another! Not when their hands had met and were held for a lingering instant during the picture! But what was that smell following them? They each tried to sniff at themselves and the air without the other one noticing. They peeked unpretentiously at their shoes. Ah-ha! Peggy saw something brown and sticky on the heel of her shoe. Dog poo! "Uh, why don't we walk on the grass. It's such a nice evening, we can see the stars better from there."—Peggy suggested. "Alright", responded Bobby. And the couple moved off of the sidewalk onto the grass. Peggy walked by scooting her feet and pressing her shoes into the grass. She stopped and pointed to the sky, "Isn't that Venus?" What Peggy didn't know was that Bobby had thought he was the one who had stepped in dog poo. The two of them looked up at the sky and they both scraped their shoes into the grass as inconspicuously as possible. As they continued to walk Peggy squirmed her heel every step or two into the ground and wondered, "Does he notice the dog poo?" Bobby did the same thing wiping the bottom of his shoes into the grass and wondered, "Does she notice the dog poo?" They both wanted their first date to go on without either one of them having to mention dog poo. Later on in their lives they would laugh about this incident.

Mad amour! *Mad amour!*

*   *   *   *   *

Cora Peggy Arnez and Rustle Bobby Barns were married in 1954. He would become a minister and she would become a teacher. They would bring three wonderful children into the world. Mabel Peggy Barns born in 1958. Rustle Bobby Barns Jr. born in 1960. And me, Suzanna Marie, born in 1965.

Rustle Barns (Jr.) would have three children: Cory born 1983; Mabel Anne born 1988; and Mona born 1988. The eldest child, Mabel Peggy Barns, would give birth to a daughter named Jaida in 1983. She would also give birth to two sons: Mick born 1991; and Bill born 1993. I, Suzanna, would have one wonderful daughter, born 1998.

<u>N I N E</u>

<u>ENTER THE STALKER</u>

The following was written by Cora Peggy Arnez Barns Locks in the year 2006. Other than a couple of words removed, it is reproduced here in full. **Some names have been changed in this book to protect the privacy of those individuals, this letter is reproduced with that in mind.** *It is about Peggy's first recognition that she had a stalker.*

Written by Peggy Arnez Locks/2006: "Remembering an unhappy story in my life is hard for me because it is too much like digging up a skunk—one always wishes they had left well enough alone! It reminds me of a pastor who said, 'Why would we pray, God take these burdens from me, then keep holding (on) to them?' I recall the time of obscene (phone) calls then.

"Our family lived in a small house on Idaho Street in (removed), New Mexico—a street with through traffic so all acquaintances in the neighborhood were the ones on our side of the street with even numbers. About the only time Mabel age five and Russ three were allowed out the front door was to walk to the car. The chain-link fence around the back yard gave very little privacy for family activities and children's play. This did not bother too much because the one child just east of us would see playing outside and would soon come out to join the fun. The greatest problem was the midsized thin dog that was a part of the family could leap right over the fence with only the slightest effort, fortunately he would not wonder far---just had to be frequently brought back into the yard.

"About one and a half years living on a busy street, child number three was on the way to making the house seem a little smaller. The pregnancy was mostly uneventful after the months of morning sickness and on some occasions feeling faint. Before the arrival of the new family member a disturbance, that boggled my mind, occurred. Being home and caring for two small children, keeping a clean house, being sure that a four year old little boy (Rustle Barns Jr.) and now a six year old kindergartener (Mabel Barns) were clean and presentable, well prepared meals for family was a pretty big job. That was only a part of it, being a ministers' wife involved me in the music program of the church plus an active participant in women's groups, and an active part with the children's ministry. All of these were truly a blessing and around caring supportive church members.

"A phone call was a welcome diversion from normal duties so when the phone rang about 10:00 o'clock (a.m.) one midweek day I gladly answered, but was in heated shock when a voice on the other end began making disgusting remarks. I quickly slammed the phone on the phone cradle and walked into the room where my son was playing and sat trembling watching his block building. In a few minutes I regained my composure, went into the kitchen to start early preparation for lunch for my husband and son. I had just begun when the phone rang again, being sure it was my husband, I picked it up to tell him about my unhappy experience but heard a familiar sounding voice but not the sound of my husband who often called before coming home. It was the voice I had heard less than an hour earlier, which filled me with fear as he repeated the same comments. Again I put the phone down quickly with maybe a little less force; this time not only did my hand shake but so did my whole body. I got my four year old in the kitchen to 'help me' prepare lunch, brought the dog in the house and locked the doors; all the while being careful not to let my son see my stress. It was not long until Bobby, my husband, pulled in the drive. I told him about the calls and how nervous it made me. He said for me to call him anytime the calls came; I assured him that voice would never be unrecognized in my mind.

"The next day, almost exactly the same time the phone rang again and it was the caller from the day before still saying the same kind of 'sick' statements again, I would hang up quickly. The difference the second day was that Bobby was out of town and the caller called three times this day. By this time I was not only afraid for the two of us at home plus the unborn baby, but my daughter at school for fear that while such a 'creep' may just threaten me he might be more aggressive with a child.

"Several days went by without the calls so I thought whoever that was probably had gotten it out of his system or moved on to someone else. The flash of heat to my stomach every time the phone would ring had almost stopped. That did not keep me from making sure I was at school early every day to be sure I was there as soon as the children left the building. Before the calls, the crosswalk guard would walk Mabel across the street to the church where Bobby and/or the secretary was until I got there to pick her up. Somehow I was not too sure that someone more sinister might intercede between the guard and her father's office.

"Then it happened again, but I got up the courage to ask, 'How do you know my name?' He answered, 'Oh I see you all the time, when you take your children to school, when you hang out clothes. I watch you all the time.'

"Months later, that was the worst! Finally one day I called Bobby who called the police. The police called me right away and said they were sending out a detective to talk to me the next day. Somehow I felt relief and concern, 'What if I had to tell them the exact words the stalker said?' Sure enough the next morning the detective and a policeman came---my son was staying with the next door neighbor. Just as I had feared they did have to know all he said to me; I managed to get them out but I now have few memories of the exact words he said, other than that he was watching me and my children, and that he had a very strong interest in my unborn child. I remember the words he said were threatening to me, leaving me afraid I might be raped. The stalker told me everything I did and everywhere I went too. I don't want to remember all the stalker said and I will never try to bring them back because there is no purpose to inflict that kind of stress on myself. Once I told the detective all the trash, that was enough! The officers said I was at risk and they were going to watch the area around my house until after the baby was born.

"When it was only three weeks until due date it did give me some comfort because every morning the police car was parked about a block east of our house. They also told me when the stalker called, not to hang up—just lay the phone down and go next door and call them to keep the line open. They also had me to get him to talk more and try to set up a meeting time---after the baby was born. He did keep calling and about three weeks after I gave birth, I did get up the courage to see if he wanted to meet me and where. But he realized he was being set up. The detective planned for me to sit in my car at the designated place (to meet the stalker) and as soon as anyone started toward the car I was to drop the keys out of the window--- the police would have me surrounded and move in when the keys dropped. The stalker must have become aware that he was in trouble, and we were unable to succeed at the set-up.

"I did feel suspicious of some people, but most of all a fellow who was very mentally slow who lived about two blocks east of us. There were two worship services every Sunday; Bobby had to leave before eight o'clock (a.m.) for the early service, but the children and I got ready for Sunday school and church and just a few minutes before we would leave, the fellow down the street would be waiting at the door for a ride to church. He would never look at me in the face. I told Bobby of my suspicion so he told the fellow he needed to find another ride to and from church.

"That was a dark memory. I had many hang-up phone calls for years where whoever was on the other end of the phone and had called would not speak. But I felt a lot better when we left (removed), New Mexico. I did love the people in that church and the community."

End written statement by Peggy Locks/2006.

*   *   *   *   *

Diapers during this new era of the 1960's consisted of safety pins and cloth. When the cloth diaper was dirty you had to rinse it out in the toilet before washing it in a mixture of laundry soap, vinegar, and bleach. Truly and endless and unpleasant task. Peggy had just put a fresh diaper on little Rustle and was preparing to go to the store. Peggy grabbed her purse along with Rustle in her arms and walked out of the house. Rustle placed the pointer finger of his right hand straight upon his mother's nose. She opened the car door and placed Rustle in the backseat. Then she proceeded to hop in the drivers seat and turn the ignition. The car was such a big bulging light-blue boxy creation. Full of chrome and truly fabulous.

Rustle was not belted in at the back of the car. Which was not unusual since some cars in 1964 didn't even have seatbelts. Although it was becoming of notice to Americans that front seat belts were well on their way to becoming a standard in the design of United States cars. How magnificently sweet the style of most cars in 1964! Vehicles had low silhouettes. Slightly gaudy but mostly beautiful combinations of chrome and paint. Wrap-around windows topped off with terrifically bulbous bodies. Sharp white-wall tires. Smoothly sculpted fins. Barracuda's caught the eye and raised the eyebrows then. Plymouths found hungry automobile consumers throughout the U.S.A. But it was for the Mustang which the public swooned with titillation for more than any other car. Peggy clicked on the car radio: "Lady's and Gent's and all you Cat's, I have another favorite from Dean Martin", the radio announcer was saying. Peggy smiled. She liked the soft comfortable tone of Dean Martin's voice. She hummed along as Dean Martin sang "Everybody Loves Somebody." The song rolled by like a lullaby and little Rustle had fallen asleep on his side with his mouth open and sweat matting his soft light brown curls. Sunlight poured down through the car windows onto his freckles but it wasn't the sun which made him sweat. For some odd genetic reason baby Rustle sweated in his sleep no matter what the temperature or the outside circumstances. Rustle's father, Bobby Barns, sweated profusely in his sleep also. And Bobby's mother Oleta swore that her own father was a sweat-sleeper as well.

Now Roy Orbison began trilling his tonsils on the radio with the song "Pretty Woman" as Peggy pulled into the grocery store parking lot. She tapped her fingers on the steering wheel in time to the tune. Lady luck led Peggy to a parking spot directly in front of the grocery store. Fluffy puffs of clouds baubled about like spun cotton sprinkled upon a baby-blue baby's blanket. A tranquil translucent sky.

Peggy parked the car and swept out of the driver's seat. Purse in hand. Clopping in her high heel closed toe pumps around the front of the car and to the backseat door. Opening the door Peggy took a moment to sigh over how cute little Rustle looked sleeping in the back. Definitely a freckled little cherub.

Scooping Rustle into her arms he began to cry with an initial wail so loud that Peggy's right eye squinted and twitched. She closed the door with a push of her hip then said, "Shhh sh shhh", to her son. He became quiet. Mother and child entered the grocery store. She picked out a cart and put little Rustle into it.

House-wives and women working outside the home all alike pushed their carts most often with kids in tow. The beehive hairdo was no longer the odd style you might see every now and then in a gum chewing waitress. It was the style! Practically every female you'd look at in this modern world had either a beehive or a bouffant. Women in straight trim dresses of gentle pastel colors that fell to the knee studied produce; squeezed the produce; smelled the fruits and breads. Peggy made her choices of healthy fruits and vegetables quickly. At the check-out counter Peggy chose a pack of clover gum and added it to the items.

After paying, Peggy politely thanked the cashier and courteously toted her own cart with both groceries and Rustle inside to the waiting car. She put the groceries up front in the passenger seat and Rustle in the backseat.

She pulled the car up to the small brown square parsonage where they lived. It felt good to be home and the shopping for the day over. She brought Rustle into the house first then went back for the grocery bags. She caught a glimpse of her reflection in the car window as she was opening the door and reflexively raised her right hand and patted her hair. Rustle waited uninterested inside the house as Peggy grabbed the two medium-sized brown bags of groceries from the car's backseat into her arms. Bumping the door with her hip, it closed with a slam. Walking to the house she breathed in deeply of the fresh New Mexico air. There was a faint scent of wet earth and ozone as if a rain were coming. Distinct smells of Mexican food with thick heavy spices wafted upon the breeze. Someone nearby was busy cooking.

Stepping inside the parsonage she closed the front door with her hip in the same way she had closed the car door. Peggy walked into the kitchen and set the grocery bags down on the counter near the telephone. Once her arms were no longer burdened she clip-clopped in her heels back to the kitchen light switch and flipped the light on. While walking back over to the groceries the phone began to ring. Peggy reached for the phone with her right hand and pulled the receiver off of its cradle. The twisty winding phone cord wrapped about her elbow momentarily. "Hello", she cheerily chirped, "Barns's residence, Peggy speaking." Telephone manners were very important to her. Prim and proper do count.

"Hello Peggy", came a deep breathy intense voice.

"Hello. Who is this?"

"I know you went shopping." A man's voice.

Peggy bent her head to her right side to hold the phone between her ear and her shoulder. With her hands free she pulled the grocery bags closer to her and reached in. She plucked out the rather large meat department packaging of raw chicken. "Who is this?"

"I know you bought chicken. But you didn't get a whole one this time did you?"

"What?!" Pausing. Peggy looked at the package of chicken in her hand. She chuckled slightly and said, "Well, that's a good guess." Setting the meat down on the counter she reached back in and pulled out the fresh green beans.

"And I know that you bought green beans. And squash. Getting ready for supper are we?"

Peggy felt suddenly strange as she looked at the bag of beans in her hands. "How may I help you?"

"You also bought a bag of flour. Who taught you to cook? Your mother?"

Peggy felt a chill flow over her shoulders and down her spine. She leaned forward slightly to peer into the grocery bag. Straight as an arrow she looked directly at the bag of flour sitting at the bottom of the grocery sack.

The man's voice purred low and deep. "That's an awfully cute little boy you have. Little Rustle. But I know a secret about you. Peggynnnn."

Peggy's personality was always one of manners and etiquette. She had a tamed and healthy pride of the blood-line running through her veins. Her parents were successful people. Good people. Peggy therefore had an air of good breeding and higher education about her. Rather like a 'southern belle' or a socialite. Consequently it did not occur to her to be rude in any response to her caller. Plus this could be one of her husbands parishioners. "How may I help you?"—she repeated.

"You want to talk to me about your secret? Peggynnn?" He drew her name out like the growl of a dingo. "I know it makes you sick every morning. I know it makes you faint." There was a breathy pause.

"You're pregnant aren't you Peggy? Who is that growing inside of you? Peggynnn? You know I'm very interested in that baby growing in your womb. Talk to me about it. What are you going to name it?"

Without even being able to think clearly Peggy blindly answered. "Suzanna Marie if it's a girl. Rusty Dietrich if it's a boy." She was so rattled she didn't know what to do or say.

"Interesting." The sound of a low breath being sucked in. "You know I watch you all the time? I like watching you. I see you even when you think nobody is watching. I know what you do when you're alone."

"Who is this?!" Fear filled her with a rising alarm.

"I see you when you take your pretty little girl to school. Such a nice name she has; Mabel. I'm there when you hang your laundry out to dry. I watch you all the time."

"*Who is this*?!" Peggy demanded.

"I know all about you. I know your smell. I could even tell you what color of underwear your wearing, right now."

She gasped. She grit her teeth together in an open-lipped grimace. Peggy looked at the receiver in her hand and gripping it tightly shook it hard. As if trying to strangle the phone. She slammed the receiver down; effectively hanging up. A trembling shaky feeling rose from the base of her spine and spread throughout her lower back and down her arms. Pressing her thumb and forefinger to the bridge of her nose. She closed her eyes. Letting out a long stressed sigh. The phone rang again. Peggy jumped and looked at the telephone as if it were a poisonous spider. Brrr …ring. Brrr …ring. Sweeping the phone off the hook and pressing it to her ear she was horrified to hear herself rudely shout: "What?!"

The low growl dingo voice sounded out again. "Strange. Isn't it?" It was the same breathy hungry voice. The same caller. "Strange", the voice paused, "Strange." Another sucking inward breath. "Strange isn't it? Peggynn."

Peggy clobbered the phone back down again. A swarming prickly swirl of fear overwhelmed her as she'd hung up the phone. Instantly she went to the back door of the house which was closest to her and locked it. Then she moved waveringly to the front door and locked it also. Her heart was pounding, and fear felt like a living creature vibrating under her skin.

Breathing hard as she stepped back into the kitchen she picked up the chicken and practically threw it into the refrigerator. Next she rinsed her hands and briefly dried them on the hand-towel. Peggy was terrified the phone would ring again. Stomping into the room where Rustle was playing she said "Hey" to the boy and then sat down on the large orange ottoman. It felt as if she were collapsing. Every inch of her body was shaking uncontrollably. The thought ran through her mind that she was glad it wasn't someone she knew or someone from the church parish whom had called when she'd answered the phone so rudely with just the word 'what'!

*   *   *   *   *

Unknown to Peggy this event was simply to be the beginning. The phone calls would keep coming, and coming. The stalker was both enamored and 'concerned' and menacing regarding the new baby growing in Peggy's womb. This mysterious man was following her everywhere and then reporting to Peggy everything she had done during that day. This young preacher's wife told her husband about the phone calls and the stalking. Finally he called the police. Yet even Mr. and Mrs. Barns themselves didn't realize how painfully long term this terror would turn out to be.

*   *   *   *   *

When the time finally came that Peggy found herself in her living room talking to the police about her stalker her belly would be quite obviously baby-swollen. Her ankles were swollen as well. And she had to go to the bathroom so often that it wasn't just annoying it was embarrassing. The day the police came Peggy had pre-made some coffee and snicker-doodle cookies for them. Peggy paced the living room floor uncomfortably. Occasionally she rubbed her belly swollen with life. She was trying to be polite with the visit of the police and was glad they liked the coffee and the snicker-doodle's, but she couldn't hide her nervousness and fear no matter what she did. Why couldn't 'the man' just stop stalking her? Why couldn't he just give up? The police were saying that sometime after the baby was born they could have her set up a time to meet the stalker so that the police could hopefully nab him. Peggy prayed that 'the man' would stop this horrible nonsense before she gave birth to the baby. She didn't want to *meet* him!

The two policemen sat on the couch with a crouching awareness clenching their muscles. As if they were ready to pounce a bad guy at any minute. Both policemen had politely removed their hats. The one policeman with the crew cut hair had placed his hat on the table to his left which displayed a lamp with a boxy over-sized lamp shade. The other officer had short hair that had been carefully combed and lightly greased to primly part on the side in a dapper line.

"Mam", said the crew cut officer with a gesture of his hand, "My partner and I are in agreement that you're under danger." He cleared his throat and shifted in his seat. "Now what we can do, and this is what I recommend we do, is that we keep an officer out to watch your house. We can use an unmarked car. And we want you to call us immediately any time this man calls you."

"That's right", agreed the other officer. His hand was hanging tentatively over the plate of snicker-doodles on the coffee table. He's had eaten several already. He lifted his mug of coffee to his lips and sipped as if wetting his mouth rather than drinking it. He continued speaking. "And it's very important you don't hang up right away when he calls. You need to talk to him. Keep him on the line. See if you can get him to give away some information about himself." He snatched up another snicker-doodle. Raising his eyebrows with a pleased expression as he bit into it. "Then you need to call us immediately afterwards."

"Ohhh", thought Peggy to herself apprehensively, "How can I stand to talk to *him*?!" The very idea made her sick to her stomach.

Despite everything, the calls kept coming. The stalker kept right on stalking her. And the police seemed no closer to finding out who the man was. Now just the *sound* of the phone ringing made Peggy feel sick and queasy. As the months slipped by The Man remained ruthless. She could still recall the grip of the policemen's hands that first evening as they shook her hand and thanked her for the snicker-doodles. And saying to her how good the cookies were. Somehow this parting scene with the policemen kept repeating itself over and over again in her memory. Couldn't they have said something more about the stalker? Couldn't they have come up with some sure-fire plan that would completely reassure her they would catch this nut-ball?

Come the morning of January 22, 1965 Peggy's water broke, signifying the eminent birth of the baby she'd been carrying in her womb. And still the police had not yet nabbed the stalker. She knew she'd promised the police to set up over the phone a meeting with the stalker sometime after the birth of the baby if they had not yet caught him. Deep in her bones Peggy feared this possible meeting far more than she'd feared the process of giving birth! There was no way to hold things off now, the baby was on its way.

At the hospital Bobby sat in a chair next to his wife as they prepared her for the birth to come. Peggy's contractions were full-blown and very close together now. Bobby's nose was buried in one of the latest popular books to have freshly hit the press. He was reading the new book "Little Big Man" by Thomas Berger. Although she would never admit it to her husband Peggy was somehow annoyed that Bobby was reading a book. It wasn't long however before the doctor checked Peggy's progress of cervical dilation and announced, "It's time!" They rolled the aching woman into the room set aside for giving birth. In 1965 quite a few husbands were doing the radical and staying in the birthing room with their wives. Not sure he wanted too Bobby nevertheless donned a gown that tied in the back called scrubs. He slipped a thick white cap that reminded him of a hairnet over his head and he put a mask that tied in the back over his mouth.

The birth had terrible complications. It had gone awry when the doctor discovered that the baby was breach. Unfortunately the pain was so intense that Peggy screamed out loud and then passed out. Peggy woke to a nurse with a mask on her face waving smelling salts under her nose. She yelped as she woke up from her faint.

"Mrs. Barns", said the doctor staring down into her face and tapping his elbow against her shoulder. "Mrs. Barns, the baby is breach. I'm going to give you something that will make you sleep."

"Thank heavens!" Responded Peggy. "Let me sleep! Go ahead!"

*   *   *   *   *

My mother's version of my birth is this: "There was only *one* knot in your umbilical cord! And the only comments anyone made about you (Suzanna) were the nurses saying that you didn't like to have your feet uncovered!"

Reverend Bobby Barns, my father, would relay to me his version about my birth as follows:

"(Suzanna) came out screaming but it was not a screaming like I had heard either of my two previous children make when they were born. Not a screaming like any of the parish members baby's made when I've gone to the hospital for their baby's births. The screaming was blood curdling. In fact, the doctor said he'd never heard anything like it either in all his years of birthing babies. The doctor turned to me and said, 'This baby is screaming bloody murder!'

"And as if that wasn't horrible enough the doctor showed me that the baby (Suzanna) had knots tied into (her) umbilical cord. The doctor pulled me over to look at them. He counted eighteen knots in the umbilical cord.

. *Eighteen!* And then the doctor said something that wasn't a real statement, not a literal one, but it was still chilly…the doctor looked at me after counting the knots and said, 'Looks like some devil got into the womb and tried to kill this poor baby! Either that or this baby changed her mind about being born!' I will never be right in the room of a baby being born *ever again*! I can watch the baby being born just fine through the window in the door thank you very much!"

*   *   *   *   *

Sitting in my father's office I listened to him relating his story. I had been enveloped over half of the day listening to my mother telling me stories and had found them fascinating. When my mother dropped me off at my father's office after my allergy testings were finished I continued to learn about my past and my family heritage by needling my father with question after question. It was 1974 and the day was nearly spent. My dad was just telling me about when I was born. I had already heard my mother's version of my birth when we were at the hospital. "So what happened next?"—I asked my father, Bobby Barns.

"After what?" Bobby looked up from his desk and the papers in his hands which he'd been scrutinizing on and off while he answered my questions and told me his stories.

"After the doctor counted the knots in my umbilical cord and I was born?"

"Nothing."

"What do you mean?"

"They just cleaned you off, wrapped you in a blanket, and put you in the nursery."

"How come you guys didn't know I was going to be a girl until after I was born?"

"You should consider yourself lucky; Rustle and Mabel had decided you were going to be a puppy!"

"What!" I rolled off of the office chair and onto the floor laughing. Laying on my back on the carpet I looked up at my favorite picture sitting on the reading table in a plain wood frame. I didn't like the frame however, I wished the frame were made of gold or silver and embedded with colored jewels. I did like the picture very much however. "Can I have a pencil and a piece of paper?"

My father frowned. "What do you need paper for?" He began putting his papers away by stuffing them into a manila folder.

"That picture." I got up and walked over to it. Running my fingers over the glass covering the image. Bobby was a chaplain now at a university. And of all the pictures in the chapel office this one was my favorite because every time I saw it I laughed. It was a close up of a horses face. The horses nose looked big and wide in comparison to its ears and eyes. And it had an impossible wide-toothed smile like he had just eaten all the cookies in the cookie jar. Underneath the horse was the caption: 'Smile it will make people wonder what you've been up too.' The image made me feel happy every time I saw it. "I want to draw the picture on a piece of paper and take it home with me."

"Suzanna we don't have time for that."

"Tell me about when I was born again."

"I've already told you that." Bobby lifted a book from his desk and strode with long steps over to the bookshelf which was stuffed to the hilt with all sorts of books. He slid the book from his hand back into the jammed shelf.

I loved looking at the books filling his shelves and always wished I could read them all in one gulp. Walking up beside him I placed my hand upon a delectable leather bound book sticking out among the others on the shelf. "Tell me about when you met my Mother at McMurry."

"I've already told you that too."

"Well tell me something else."

Bobby retrieved his black blazer from off of the dark wood coat tree and slung it over his arm. "We don't have time for that Suzanna, we've got to go meet Peggy."

"We're meeting Mother?" I wiggled my feet out of my shoes.

"Yes. Put your shoes back on, come on! Let's go!"

"What about a copy? Can you make a copy of the horse picture with the copy machine?" Copiously I pressed my feet back into my shoes.

"Honey we'll have to do that some other time." He opened his office door and waved me through it. "We've got to hurry so she's not waiting on us." He began walking quickly and I had to scamper to keep up with him. He opened the chapel door letting in the late afternoon sunshine.

Squinting my eyes at the sunlight I watched Bobby slip his arms into his blazer. Following behind him I asked, "Why is she waiting on us? Where are we going?"

"We're going to grab something to eat and then we're coming back here for the opera."

"Ahh!"—I gasped with excitement. "I'm going to see an opera?" What could be more exciting?!

This day marked a change in my life. It marked the moment I began to pay attention to the fact that I had family around me. That they had hopes and dreams, and experiences and a history of their own. Yet it also marked a fabulous addition of aesthetic value. That night I fell in love with opera! I'd sat with breathless awe watching "The Mikado." As the orchestra hummed and the huge thick red curtains opened on the stage I was stunned and mesmerized.

Throughout the entire production I wanted to be the orchestra and the actors and singers and also the audience all at once. That night in my bed I had such a craving to clandestine up into my precious hiding place in the attic. The attic with its round 'boat' window where I could look out at the night sky. Clandestinely I could hold my sock monkey! Black Beauty my kitty-cat spirited away with me in my secret hiding place! To lift my pen and my diary up to the shine from the streetlight glowing through the round window and write about my day would be fun. Whispering in ink to my thirsty observer called paper. In my diary I had written how when I first heard "Adagio for Strings" by Barber I had closed my eyes listening to it and wept. Now I wanted to write in my diary about the opera and my day's events. I wanted to put everything into my diary. I fell asleep thinking of the event Peggy told me about in the car on our way back home from the opera. She had reiterated at my endless request and told me once again about the event when I was 3 ½ years old and the stalker had sneaked into my bedroom. (When she thought she'd given me too much cough syrup and I'd therefore possibly imagined the man.)

During that year my mother and I would go to see many fantastic productions at the university performed on the stage. Opera. Musicals. Symphony. Ballet. I was dipped into a realm of entertainment that was like magic. Like being graced with some dreamy ability to watch the bud of a flower open up to you. My heart filled with a longing and my soul with a hunger for this entertainment. I'd spent dreamy hours pouring over books. And now the unearthly euphoric kingdom of live performance. Actors and singers. Stage sets and orchestra. Beautiful people in beautiful clothes gathering at the theater into their plush seats and falling into a spellbound hush. I firmly feel that for the human soul to be truly healthy one needs entertainment as dearly as safety, food and water, and sleep.

T E N

LITTLE DRUMMER DANCING, EVIL'S ON THE PHONE

Dreams of the ilk which you can never forget maneuvered their way into my slumber. I'd had the same dream several times. It was still the 1974 school year and tonight was just one night of many in which I'd had the repeated dream. This had to have been the seventh or eighth time in a row. I'd been having it for over a week. I would come to have several repeating dreams over the years; some good, some *not*.

Not suspecting I would become enveloped in this dream yet again I had gone to bed just praying for nothing but some peaceful rest. I begged for a child's sleep. My mind pulling downward wafting in gentle steady circles as I lay under the bed covers. Circling down into a darkened bedroom lit merely by a small night-light. Circling down closer to see the shape beneath the covers. The child.

I lay on my side in the twin bed with the covers up onto my cheeks out of some odd panic causing an inability to sleep without my ears covered. My favorite blue and pink long sleeved nightgown pulled tight over my bent knees. Looking a little closer at this scene you would see that I am sweating profusely while my eyes are moving back and forth beneath my shut eyelids. Closer still, and you are privy to the fevered dream burning inside my mind.

Finding myself an adult. Already grown-up and wearing a long, loose, long-sleeved white dress. Aware in the dream with an uncanny lucidity and sitting on a huge rock. Perhaps a small boulder? Wind sweet and fragrant blowing through my long hair. The rock I sit upon is a smooth beautiful gray with natural flecks of gold and pink in it. In a meadow of dark and pale greens. Marvelous mountains truly pink and purple and blue-gray in pastel shades that flow within the mountainous rock.

Staring in awe at the serene lake of aqua and turquoise and baby blue. So clear you can see to the bottom. The water flowed at its farthest edges in brilliant colors of maroon and bright orange that lapped at the shore in curves. At least thirty feet high, fountains shot brilliantly from the middle of the lake. Mesmerizingly beautiful the fountains shot in different layered spouts. Each spouting layer was a different clear bright color. Purple, yellow, pink, and more.

Beautiful beyond words towered the rising mountains peaked with snow on the other side of the lake. Majestically scattered throughout the mountain's rock the soft precious color of lavender sparkled like glitter.

Leaves of trees trembled in a light breeze. Soft thick moss and low-growing grasses rolling in waves of the gentle sweet-scented breeze. Mind numbing beauty! The greens of the landscape practically glowing in lime-green. Dark blue-green. Vibrant, pure, green. Ah, the brown sprinkled here and there in chocolate and mahogany. Glittering shining beauty as to be beyond the capture of any artists brush!

Such stunning and glorious attractiveness as to still the soul and quiet the mind of any other thought than the beauty it beholds. My eyes drink deeply into my soul the splendid beauteous attractiveness and sublime colors of the terrain. Peacefulness and a deep abiding love filled my heart and mind with each liquid breath I took.

Tapping on my shoulder. A tapping that made me wonder what it was that would disturb my ecstasy. Looking with a turn of my head I saw a small oriental boy with thin dark eyes and dark short hair. He stood tapping my shoulder. Now as I looked I saw several children. All of them wearing white smocks over their clothing. Children, one representing each of the orient. Also an American Indian child with long black hair. A white child with long blonde hair in wafting waves. Another white child more peachy than not with short brown hair. A child from India with amber eyes. A child with deep brown skin. Another child with skin so black as to be purple, with fluffy flowing curly hair. Boy children and girl children. There was a child for each race on earth. Touching their faces gently with my hands while they gathered around me and clung sweetly to my sides. I felt such a deep love for them all! Gazing again I looked at the marvelous splendor of the orange, magenta, and maroon tips of color in the water as it lapped against the shore. "There", the children said, pointing to a shining spot that literally seemed to emote love in the mountain peaks just beyond the waters, "Take us there."

Next in the dream I began to hear myself snoring: A snorting sound piped from my nose and throat and immediately I opened my eyes, thinking I had awakened myself. Sitting up in bed it occurred to me that I no longer felt like sleeping. Swinging my legs over my bed I went to stand up when it became apparent I was still asleep and having a very lucid dream. My nightgown looked different. My arms and hands and feet were bigger. Sauntering to my mirror I looked in it and saw that I was in a body all grown up. Turning to look at my bed I saw my child's body laying under the covers still sleeping. Yes. I was still dreaming; I knew it. Gazing back into my mirror I studied myself and wondered if that's how I'll really look like when I'm grown up.

At once a great wide beam of shining white and pale blue light shone down through my bedroom ceiling. The light seemed inviting and sparkled as if it were filled with soft glitter. Walking into the light so that it beamed down upon me I raised my arms up and felt of it with my hands. There was a slight tingle in my fingers and palms. Swinging my arms I leapt up into the beam of light and let it carry me upward. I could see nothing but the warmly inviting glitter sparkling tunnel of light as I traveled through it. The shining tunnel brought me to a door made of gold that had a curved arch to the top of it. The doorknob was a giant carved ruby surrounded by gold lattice. Placing my hand around the doorknob I turned it and to my excitement it opened.

I stepped into a room made of old logs like a cabin. It was basic and plain and not fancy but comfortable. The back side of the door was not gold with a ruby handle, it was old wood and an iron knob. The room seemed extraordinarily familiar. It was *my* room somehow. In it was a large flat wood desk with a book lying closed on top of it. Also on the desk was a big feather quill standing straight up in its holder. To the side of the quill were two medium sized plain looking wooden bowls. Underneath the table was one small wooden sliding drawer. There was absolutely nothing else in the room but these items. There was however a very small rectangular window lined with darker wood. This small window had no glass pane or screen but was instead open to the outside. Perched on the window was the largest black crow I had ever seen. (At least I think it was a crow.) It was huge and had shiny feathers so black as to have a purple undertone to them. The crow was looking at me. I walked up to it with happiness to see it, and I gently petted its wings. It seemed we were old friends.

I took a moment to look out of the small rectangular open window. It was just big enough for me to poke my head through. On the other side of this window I saw a world so beautiful as to be miraculous and breath-taking. I recognized this world as my Home. Love flowed between myself and my Home

Looking down at my white gown clad self I thrilled at seeing myself in an adult body. I knew at once I had work to do. Sitting down at the desk I pulled one wooden bowl to me and held my palms over the bowl. Two wounds opened without pain in the center of my palms and blood poured from the wounds to fill the bowl up. My wounds healed up instantly.

Opening my extremely large leather book that was trimmed with gold I paused upon the first page. Picking up the big feather quill I rolled it in my fingers. I dipped my quill into the bowl of my own blood. With this quill I wrote in the book with my own blood. Then I paused putting the quill in its holder.

Opening the small wooden drawer beneath my old desk I extracted an antique box full of the worlds finest and most delectable creamy chocolates. Placing the chocolate in my hands I pressed my palms together and let the warmth of my own body melt the chocolate. Opening my palms over the second wooden bowl I let the chocolate I had warmed with my own body pour in to fill the bowl up. Once again I lifted my quill and I dipped it into the soft melted chocolate and then continued to write in the book.

Alternately I wrote in the book by dipping my quill into my warm blood and then back to dip into the warmed chocolate. At last the work was finished. Closing the book, I left it upon the ragged wood desk. I stood up from the old plain wood desk and walked to the door to leave. As I was reaching for the door it opened and a man with thick blonde curly hair and wearing a white gown walked in. He was an angel I thought and somehow someone that I knew well.

As I looked up at him my smile faded upon the realization that I could no longer remember what I had written into the large leather book! How could this be?! I had just written it! At once a terrible panic soaked through me. I asked this angel, my friend, "How can I not remember it!? I just wrote it! How can this be?" Fear coursed through me. I meant to walk on through the door and into another tunnel of glittering light that veered up and away from the original tunnel from which I'd come. But the angel took hold of my shoulders and stopped me. "You'll have to live it first", he said.

"What?" I gasped. "What do you mean by 'I have to live it first'—*what does that mean*?!"

I made a leap for the tunnel of light and swept my arms as if swimming; I felt sure this tunnel that went upward would lead me to my Home.

My old friend the angel leapt upward and grabbed me around the waist. We struggled. Yet he swung me back into the cabin. I jumped for the door again but he blocked me and I wound up in the silliest position with my hands and feet up high against the edges of the door. Suddenly and with exasperation we both pulled back and bent forward placing our hands upon our knees. We were both panting hard and the humor of the situation brought a half laugh from both of our lips.

We both stood up straight and the angel placed his arms around me in a gentle hug, and I allowed him to fly me out of the door and through the original tunnel of light and back into my bedroom. I walked to the bed and saw my child's body sleeping soundly near the edge of the mattress. I turned to the angel with a thought to say something. Yet before I could speak my glowing friend said, "Get back in your body!" And he pushed me so hard that I fell backwards. A strong suction with a sound like a 'ZIP' pulled me into my body. I dreamed then that I had my own wings made of light, and that when I fell back into my body I hit myself smack in the nose with the edge of one of my own wings. The dream was over. I sat up awake but had lifted so quickly into my sitting position that I tumbled sideways. Grabbing onto the sheet I tried to stop myself from falling off of the bed. Too late. I rolled and fell off of the bed and onto the floor on my back with the sheet piling on top of me. Then my pillow which had been caught into the sheet fell with a plop onto my face. All the other times I'd had this exact same dream I had never fallen off the bed!

For some reason I lifted my arm up with my finger pointed toward the ceiling. With the pillow still on my face I said out loud, "Very funny!" Pulling the pillow off my face I spoke out loud again saying sarcastically, "Weird dream, thank you very much."

My nose was runny. Without thinking better of it first I immediately wiped my nose with the back of my hand. I thought perhaps it was the shadowy quality of the nightlight but the snot on the back of my hand looked dark. I wanted to wash my hands good with soap immediately. Getting up I turned on the light switch. Wiping again at my very runny nose. It wasn't snot. Looking into my mirror at my face I was surprised to see that I had a bloody nose. Lifting my head up and placing my hand under my nose to catch the bleeding flow I made my way down the hall and into the bathroom. I washed my hands and face then stuck toilet paper up my nostrils. That seemed to do the trick.

Stepping into my bedroom I checked the clock to see what time it was. Three o'clock a.m. Not feeling sleepy at all it occurred to me this might be the perfect time to write in my diary. Carefully and quietly opening the door to my sister Mabel's bedroom I tiptoed in to borrow a chair. I heaved the chair to just underneath the attic door in the hallway ceiling. Once I'd successfully let down the attic ladder I returned the chair back to my sister's bedroom and shut her door. Climbing into the attic I pulled up the ladder and closed the door behind me. How amazingly quiet I had come and gone. Moonlight and streetlight flowing in through the round 'boat' window seemed like it might not be enough for writing. So I braved it and turned on the attic light. Reaching for my dream diary first I wrote down that I'd had the same odd recurring dream again. Then I opened my life diary to pen all the events of the last twenty-four hours. I began by writing of the event my mother had told me while we were riding in the car through the nights darkness, coming home from the opera. "Dear Diary, When I was little……"

* * Toward the end of 1968 in the month of December little Suzanna Marie had a slight cold causing a runny nose and a cough. Peggy had measured a based dosage of children's medicine. And that seemed to keep the cough away. Otherwise it was an ordinary evening. Bobby and Peggy Barns were in the living room just down the hallway from the small sewing room where Suzanna was in a crib. The Barns's had not yet saved up the money to buy an actual bed for their growing youngest child. So the crib still

sufficed. When nights were warm in this part of New Mexico it was a great money saver to simply leave the windows open. Let the breeze stave off the stale air. The window on the left wall as one walked into Suzanna's room did not have a screen on it to protect the inside room from any flying insects. It was a room with drab dark blue carpet and free from any clutter. Toys were kept in the closet. In the closet was baby Suzanna's favorite Gentle Ben teddy bear. Pull a string attached to a small round ring and the teddy bear would actually talk saying, "Hello. I'm Gentle Ben"!

Bobby and Peggy were sitting on their beige rectangular couch watching the news on the black and white television. Bobby had several habits incongruent with Peggy's particular predisposition. He would collect tin cans and glass bottles to turn into companies as a means of recycling. But he wouldn't take the items in until he literally had an entire garage full. Leaving little room for tools and brooms in the garage much less the car. He would grow beautiful African Violets in the house but couldn't stand to have just a few. He would fill up nearly every room in the house with the violets...very pretty! He had the proverbial 'green thumb'. One time he grew rhubarb in his backyard garden and filled up three shelves in the one and only small pantry with jellied rhubarb, pickled rhubarb, stewed rhubarb, spiced rhubarb, jalapeno rhubarb. Bobby also always had notepads in his lap and papers all around him because it really is a lot of hard work to write a Sunday sermon.

"Do you hear that?" Peggy questioned of Bobby.

"Yea, Suzanna's talking away with someone." Bobby said absent-mindedly while sitting on the couch with notes for his sermon scattered from his lap to the couch to the coffee table.

Peggy got up and turned the television off. "Who's that talking with her?"

"It's Rustle or Mabel." Bobby pushed his glasses up his nose thinking nothing interesting of the situation.

"Rustle and Mabel are in bed asleep."

"Oh don't worry Mother'. Mabel or Rustle got out of bed to use the restroom and so now they are in there talking with Suzanna. Don't worry. He or she will go back to bed on their own in a few minutes."

"But does that sound like Mabel or Rustle's voice?"--Pondered Peggy. There was something very wrong; Peggy could feel it. And the voice talking back with Suzanna didn't sound like a child. "I'm going to go check on Suzie." Stopping at the beginning of the short hallway for a moment, she had a sense of fear keeping her from going any further. "Suzanna?"—Peggy asked. The door to Suzanna's room was open so Peggy could see most of the crib from where she was standing. She could see Suzanna standing up in the crib and talking to someone in the part of the room not visible from the open door. Her youngest child had been talking and answering questions just like anyone would in the midst of a conversation. Peggy could also hear the lower toned voice speaking with Suzanna but it was now in a hushed whisper. Confusion and anxiety kept Peggy from walking directly into the room. Instead she took a quick left to the adjacent hallway where Mabel and Rustle's rooms were. The doors to the older children's rooms were both cracked open slightly. She peeked into Rustle's room. He was there in bed sleeping with sweaty wet hair. His covers kicked off of him. Peggy closed his door. Then she softly walked to Mabel's room and stealthily peered inside. Mabel's auburn hair was tousled about on the pillow where she slept soundly. Peggy closed her daughter's door.

Softly Peggy walked back to the entrance of the short hallway where she could look through the open door and see her youngest child standing in her crib and looking directly at someone and talking. The low-toned whisper had suddenly stopped. "Suzanna? Suzie? Who are you talking too?"

Peggy decided to go ahead and walk into Suzanna's room after a few moments hesitation. Suzanna looked up at her mother. The child pointed towards the open window at the other side of the room and stated flatly: "That man."

"What man?"

"*That* man!" Suzanna pointed again.

Peggy stayed in her spot. Quiet and unmoving. Unsure of what to do. Suzanna cried out, "You scared him away!"

"What do you mean I scared him away?" The breeze was blowing through the wide open window that had no screen on it. Slowly Peggy walked to the open window and without getting too close reached out and closed the glass pane. Quickly and nervously she locked the window. *" I don"t ever want a window without a screen on it ever again"*, she said, and Peggy kept that sentiment the rest of her life.

* * *

I'd spent my time writing upon the pages of my diary in fairly short crisp notes of my experiences and had digressed at last into doodling little pictures all around the paper. I'd fallen back asleep in the attic. Sunshine now poured liquid warm hues of amber, salmon, and magenta through the round window as I began to wake up. The showering rays peaked my remembrance that my parents would be waking soon too. Pressing my lips together I lowered the attic ladder with as much gentility and quiet as possible. Climbing down the stairs the ladder creaked twice and I stopped in mid movement to cringe. Folding the ladder up slowly, I took in a breath of courage. Then a final push to make the ladder click and the door of the ceiling attic snapped shut.

Stepping into the bathroom upstairs I ran a few inches of water into the tub to soap up and wash quickly. Washing my face and hair with the same hand soap. Trying to count off my time by repeating one through sixty five times so that my bath was a 'military bath' as my father always insisted I should take. It saved both water and time he said. Slipping my nightgown back on. Opening the lower shelf beneath the sink I snatched up my tooth brush, squeezed some toothpaste on it and brushed my teeth thoroughly. I couldn't have spent more than eight minutes in the bathroom. And just in time too! I could hear my parent's alarm clock ringing in the new day. Sprinting from the bathroom so as to avoid any confrontation with my family, I closed my bedroom door and sat on the bed. Which dress should I wear today?

Unsurprisingly I chose my yellow flowered dress to wear. It was after all my absolute favorite. My white buckle shoes over white cotton socks. I had completed the work in all of my school books a week in advance so that I could spend most of my hours at school doodling and reading. I had expected it to be an ordinary day at school. But it was not!

I had asked my teacher, Mrs. Johnson, if I could go into the media room to read. I had already shown her my books with my work in all the subjects having been done a week in advance. This wasn't unusual for me. The media room was just a large open room with black boards on rollers and a television and a projector. She said 'yes' again as expected. So I found a little niche in a corner behind a blackboard and commenced to reading another interesting book by Laura Ingalls Wilder. Becoming absorbed by the book I was scarcely aware of the time. It turned out to already be lunch time when I received the first disturbance to my reading. Looking up from my book, around the side of the blackboard and out the door. I saw the two bullies and their victim whom I had come across on that first bus ride. They were pointing at me, talking, and nodding their heads. It was then I noticed a young boy I wasn't familiar with listening to them and looking at me nervously. One of the bullies' waved for me to come over to them. Setting my Laura Ingalls Wilder book face down so as to hold my place I stood up and walked into the hallway. Turns out the former bullies and their former victim had been telling the other kids about me. Telling them I could help them. I did not know what to make of this, yet sometimes it is most prudent to go with the flow of events.

Once I made my way into the hallway I saw a medium sized group of children both younger and older than myself gathered in a huddle and looking at me. It was break time for the children. Inquiring as to what was going on I soon learned that each one of them had a problem of some sort that they wanted help with. One at a time I took each child to sit with me in my reading spot. I asked what was wrong or bothering them. I listened. I tried to raise their self esteem and brandish courage in the children. (No matter who they were.) It was shocking to me how many of them needed help with a feeling or an experience. So many! This process went through lunch and gym and into the next class; no teachers came looking for me, nor I assume, for the other children. This continued for the couple of years I would go to that school. Most of them were experiencing depression from their parents divorce. Using a visualization helped with most of the children to feel and deal with and not be controlled by their emotions. Yet a couple of them I felt needed to see a physician and I suggested to these that they speak to the school counselor. The two 'bullies' had stopped their bad behavior I'd found out. They, plus their former victim, were the ones spreading the word that I was someone a kid could talk too and trust. I couldn't possibly express all of my surprise at this.

*   *   *   *   *

Walking home on that particular day from school at about halfway to my house I noticed the neighbor girl I played with now and then, Mary Vorheis. Mary's home was the house on the corner just up from my own. She liked wearing dresses just like me. Right now she wore her red and black plaid dress with a cream turtle-neck underneath. Through Mary I had met Lisa who lived across the street on the other block. Lisa was a year older than I and Mary was a year younger. Mary had pale white skin and dark black hair cut into a 1920's bob around her jaw-line. Seeing her up just a house ahead of me I called out to her, "Hey! Mary!"

She turned. Upon seeing me her face grew into a smile. "Hello! I didn't see you behind me."

"That's because I was *behind* you." We both laughed.

She walked over to me. "So what are you doing?"

"Just walking home from school."

"Me too."

"So Mary, you wanna come over to my house and play?"

"Okay."

We walked past the big oak trees up the last half of the block to my house. I wanted to show her Black

Beauty. Yet to my disappointment the cat wasn't currently around. Placing my key in the front door I was surprised to see that the door wasn't locked. Had I left it unlocked this morning? Had some other member of my family been home and left it unlocked? I worried about it for only as long as it took Mary and I to get inside the house.

"What do you want to play?" I asked. Then I noticed she didn't have any school books. "You didn't bring your school books?"

"I didn't want to carry them so I left them at my desk."

"That's funny. I did the same thing." We walked into the music room and sat on the bench in front of the piano. We both played on the piano. Rather, we pretended to play the piano.

"It sounds funny. What kind of piano is this Suzanna?"

"Oh! Isn't it cool? It sounds like a harpsichord. That's my favorite instrument next to the violin. The harpsichord."

"Is it a harpsi-thing?" Mary began plunking out a metallic sounding and simplified version of Chopsticks.'

"No. It's a regular piano. My brother put tacks into the hammers." I lifted the lid of the piano and showed Mary the row of softly coated hammers with tacks stuck in them. We plinked a key note here and there while watching the tacks hit the strings. Lowering the lid I concluded, "Makes a neat sound. Like I said. Like a harpsichord."

"Did your brother get in trouble for putting the tacks in it?"

"No. I don't think my parents know about it yet." Giving this consideration I decided I had an opportunity to keep my brother from getting in trouble. "Mary, you want to help me pull out these tacks?"

"How come? I thought you liked the sound."

"If my parents don't already know about the tacks then if I pull them all out then Rustle won't get in trouble." I was already busy tugging at the pressed tacks trying to wedge them out.

"Uhh, I guess so." Mary began pulling at the tacks. "They won't come out."

"Yea, they are in there pretty good aren't they?" Pausing and contemplating the tacks. What would help get them out? "Hey! I've got an idea." Turning and running into the kitchen I opened a drawer and extracted two butter knives.

"What is it?" Returning to the music room I held out a butter knife to Mary. She looked at it with confusion. "We can get the edge of the knife under the tack and then pull it up!" Wiggling the tip of the knife under a tack I lifted up to add pressure. Sure enough! The tack popped out! "Hey, I got one!"

"Me too! It works!" The knives made the tacks pop out easily and quickly. It couldn't have taken more than ten or fifteen minutes to get them all out. Of course this left us with a big pile of tacks. Not knowing what to do with them I scooped them into the skirt of my dress then padded to the large green plastic trash can in the garage and dumped them in there. Mary had followed me to the garage and we both went languidly back into the music room. Sitting at the piano we both played "Chopsticks" together. "This is fun Mary!"

"The piano sounds so different!"

"Yea I know. It really does." Lifting my fingers from the keys. "You wanna listen to some records?"

"Okay. Want to dance?"

"Yes." I closed the lid to the piano. Over in the corner of the room was the record player. Not more than eleven records leaned upward against the record stand. "Most of these are Rustle's. But I've got a Christmas record. Want to hear my favorite song Mary?"

"Okay."

"Even though it's a Christmas song?"

"Yea. I like Christmas songs!" Mary began hopping up and down on the balls of her feet and singing. "Jingle bells! Batman smells! Robin laid an egg!" (I joined in singing with her.) "The bat-mobile lost a wheel and the Joker got away! Hey!" We laughed and sat down on the carpet in front of the records. I picked out the Christmas record and pulled it out of its large square sheath. Holding the record carefully with a finger through the hole and the fingertips of my other hand at the edge. I stood up. Balancing the record on my finger inside the record's plastic hole in the center. Lifting the lid of the record player. Then I gently placed the record down on the player's perfectly round spot. Turning the knob of the player to 'on' and then softly pulling the arm forward until the needle was placed in the record's fifth groove. I had guessed correctly in finding the groove where the song I wanted began. I turned up the volume. Drums and people singing "Purrumm" came flowing with the liquid music through the sound speakers. Mary bounced to her feet just as I cheered, "Let's dance!"

The song "Little Drummer Boy" was pouring loudly through the air in the music room. Mary and I faced each other lifting our right arms high and clasping fingers. We stepped in and bumped our stomachs together. We stepped out and nodded our chins at one another. Slowly making a circle around the fairly small room. Scooting our feet on the carpet. Holding fingers and stepping in to bump our stomachs. Stepping out and nodding. Suddenly we broke our clasp and both began waving our arms. Hopping and swaying, we next danced free-style.

We were in the middle of adding a few Swan Lake style ballet leaps when the sound of a man laughing interrupted our dancing. The record skipped and scratched irritatingly across the record. The deep laughter came again. It sounded like someone was in the next room. The record continued to swirl in a circle with the needle at the edge scraping with each turn. The laughter was such a surprise that Mary and I both bristled and felt scared.

"What was that?" Mary asked.

"Sounded like laughing. Sound like laughing to you?"

"Yea, like a guy. You heard that?"

"Yes, of course I did." I put my hands on Mary's arms. "Hold on." Swiftly striding over to the player I twisted the knob and turned it off. The scratching record halted.

Mary looked as frightened and surprised as I was. "Suzanna what was that?"

"Shhh." I put a finger to my lips and lifted my head listening.

"It stopped. Who was that? I thought we were alone."

Placing my right hand on the middle of Mary's back. "Don't worry Mary. My brother must be home. Or my Dad." Taking Mary's hand in mine. We walked into the living room still feeling frightened by the surprise. "Rustle? Are you home?" I called through the living room and over to the stairs. "He's probably playing a joke", I said to Mary. "Rustle? Dad? Who's home?!"

With trepidation we went upstairs and checked the rooms. No one there. Descending the stairs much more quickly than we had ascended them we ran into the kitchen. No one in the kitchen. Then I opened the door that led into the garage to check for a car. The garage was empty. Back in the music room I looked out the window to check the driveway and see if any cars might have pulled up while we were dancing. No cars or persons in the driveway outside.

"The house is completely empty." I said to Mary.

"Well then who was that laughing?"

"I don't know." The phone began to ring. Thank heavens! It was probably one of my parents! Or maybe it was my sister or my brother! Still terrified I picked up the receiver of the phone with the excited anticipation of a familiar voice that could give us some reassurance. "Hello?"—I asked into the telephone.

"Strange isn't it?" An unfamiliar male voice.

"What?" I asked stunned.

"Strange. Strange, isn't it?" The voice sounded menacing and wicked.

Mary said, "Who is it?" For some reason I can't explain I handed her the telephone. She took the receiver and leaned in pressing her ear against it. Her eyes widened and her face went pale and blank. As if shocked into a stupor she slowly handed me the receiver back. I put it to my ear again. The man on the other end was still saying the same words. Over and over again. With breathy pauses in between. I heard from the phone, "Strange." Clomping the phone back on it cradle. Fear zinging through me like prickling needles.

I began to feel somewhat nauseous. "Mary, let's go sit down." Mary followed me into the living room where we sat on the couch. Such a bummer, our fun had been spoiled. Before I could think of anything to say or do I looked up at a terrifying sight. Standing there in the living room just a couple of feet from the foyer to the front door. The man! He had the greenish-gray demon mask on! We was wearing dark blue jeans with work boots on his feet and a dark blue long sleeved button shirt. The skin beneath the shirt was tan.

"Aaaa!"—I shrieked in frightened surprise. Mary looked over in the direction I was staring. She screamed a shrill squeaky high pitched shriek. The man said nothing. He did nothing. He just stood there; glaring horribly at us. Then we both screamed together and I grabbed hold of Mary's arm. Dragging her into the kitchen and over near the sliding glass door that led into the back yard. "Is that your brother playing a joke?"—Mary whispered.

"No. Too big. Wrong skin color." I whispered in reply.

"Are you sure?" Mary whispered again.

"Yes." We kept our voices soft and quiet.

"What do we do?"

"Get out of here."

"Good." Mary turned and headed back through the kitchen. She was going for the front door! Running up behind her and taking hold of her elbow I pulled her back. "No, no!" I continued to wisp. "Not that way!" Dragging Mary along with me back towards the sliding glass door. I felt such a sense of urgency. "Through the back!"

Grabbing Mary's arm I took her along with me. Undoing the latch I opened the sliding glass door as quietly as possible. We stepped outside slowly and then all at once broke into a run. We ran across the back yard patio and around the side of the house. Fumbling with the lock on the tall wood fence I felt rushed and anxious. "Hurry up!"—Mary urged. Speechlessly I shook the lock loose and opened the gate of the fence. Mary and I flew through the gate and into my neighbor's front yard. Both of us panting while running hard up the block. "Where do we go?"—Mary asked with fear piercing her voice.

Glancing at Mary briefly as we ran, I said, "To your house!"

Silently except for our heaving breaths we sprinted to her house. Stopping at the white columns seemingly holding up the roofing over the patio of Mary's front door. Mary collapsed onto her rumpus on the left side of the cement step of the patio. I leaned against the right side column. Pressing my hand deep into my left side ribs in the hopes of sending away the painful spasm twisting the muscle. We huffed heavily as we spoke and tried hard to catch our breaths.

"My Gosh! We just saw the devil!" Mary wheezed.

In gasping breaths I said: "No, it wasn't the devil! There is no such thing as the devil…not if you believe in God anyway…not if you believe that God is the one that's all powerful! There is no magically empowered devil running around trying to scare everybody!"

"Then…" Mary gulped in air as her lungs began to calm down. "Then what was it?"

"Not *what*." I rubbed at the stitch in my side. It was starting to feel better. My breathing was still labored and heavy. "Not what. '*Who*'." I took in a long drink of air. "It's a person."

Mary's eyes were starting to let go of some of their wide terror. "Then *who*? Your brother?"

"No. My brother has lighter skin and his hands and neck have freckles all over them."

"*Then who*?!" Mary demanded.

Looking at her squarely. Breathing deeply. Slower gasps. Wishing I had the answer. Looking at the ground and then next at the wind blowing harder around us. The sky was darkening. Finally my lungs relaxed. Taking in a last deep breath I looked her in the eyes and answered her question. I said, "I don't know." The clouds in the sky were bulging and turning ashen gray. "Come on", I said walking over to Mary. Taking her hand I helped her to her feet. "We better get inside."

Mary opened her unlocked front door and we stepped inside the house. We had practically opened the door into Mary's mother's face. She had just been descending the stairs that were close to the door on the left. "There you are", her mother exclaimed. "Your father won't be home for supper. He has to work late." She was obviously trying hard to hide a feeling of disappointment and perturbed frustration that her husband wasn't going to be home to share dinner.

Mary looked at her mom as she stepped up onto the stairs. She didn't respond to her mother and for some ridiculous reason I felt compelled to respond for her. "Okay", I said, "We're going up to Mary's room to play. Is that okay?"

Mrs. Vorheis wrung her hands together and her head wobbled. "Of course", she said, "I'll be in the kitchen. Finishing supper….*maybe*." She walked away with quick clomping steps of her high heels.

I followed Mary to her upstairs bedroom. She was so lucky. She had tons of toys. Even a small plastic play cottage in her room. In her back yard she had swings and a slide. We both clambered on top of her big bed and looked out the long stretch of three wide windows above it. Wind whipped the trees unmercifully. Deep gray darkness swelled throughout the air and sky.

"Wow!" I exclaimed. Delighted at the thought of a storm. "I love storms! Thunder happens to be my favorite sound! Lightening is great because it's just like watching fireworks!"

"Yea, really!" Hooted Mary.

Just then rain spit against the windows. We stared at it in awe and wonder for a while. Then at last we decided to play. Mary and I played 'grocery store'. The cottage was our store. She even had really cool plastic fake food! This game we played until we had both performed as cashier and shopper equally. It was fun. Once that game ended we pretended we were at a drive in movie. Pretending to sit in our car and eat popcorn and sip soda's while we watched the movie. This game didn't last too long. After all, how long can you pretend to eat popcorn and sip soda before it becomes just plain redundant?

Finally we pulled all of Mary's dolls and stuffed animals out of her closet and arranged them on her bed. We played 'orphanage'. Which was highly more interesting than playing drive in movie. We fed the children and bathed them and sang to them. We were in the midst of throwing the children a grand huge party when the sky crackled and boomed in what had turned into a vicious storm outside. We watched the cacophony from the windows for a while before Mrs. Vorheis entered Mary's room franticly. "I think you better get home *now* Suzanna", Mrs. Vorheis sputtered, "We're in the middle of a tornado warning!"

Mrs. Vorheis placed newspaper in my hands and instructed me to hold the newspaper over my head as I walked home. Thus I walked in the storm holding the newspaper in both hands over my head. The wind pushed at me; whipping my body. Pelting cold rain fell into my face. I held the newspaper over my head as I was told to do but it really was a useless effort. The rain was massively pouring and the wind was throwing it in every direction. No one was home yet when I got to my house. It was just as I'd left it. Rain had been thrashing into the house through the sliding glass door that I'd left open. I ran through the house, looking to make sure nobody was there, then I locked all the doors. I mopped up the rain-wet floor with a towel. When finished cleaning up the wet mess I wafted up the stairs and into my bedroom. Black Beauty was standing on the roof outside my bedroom window meowing and wet. Poor thing! Opening the window I brought my cat inside to get warm and dry. She purred in my lap and watched the storm with me. To me a truly good storm is like watching fireworks and listening to the symphony. Lulled by the raging, booming, sparkling storm. I fell finally into a dreamless sleep with my kitten in my arms.

ELEVEN

MYSTERY OF THE LIBRARY MUSE

The red and blue Viet Cong flag flew over its palace in April of 1975. The Vietnam War was officially over at last. President Minh broadcasted to pained ears a message of unconditional surrender.

The American nation were swimming in disco music, mood rings, and pet rocks. Everyone was amazed that anyone could make money selling rocks while secretly going out and buying one of the painted-face rock cuties themselves. The year of 1975 would see interested audiences everywhere thrilling over boxer Muhammad Ali 'floating like a butterfly and stinging like a bee' when he went fifteen rounds in the boxing ring with Frazier. And the movie "Jaws" by Spielberg scared plenty of people into having panics while splashing around in just a swimming pool! Meanwhile, readers got to taste Vladimir Nabokov's new book "Tyrants Destroyed."

On this particular day in gym class the kids had been chosen for teams by two of the teacher's favorites and a full scale basketball game was underway. The gym teacher was a tan muscular woman with sandy blonde hair she always wore in a pony tail. Her treatment of the children she deemed unworthy could be appalling. Many of these children had sought solace talking to me about it. Today the gym teacher was going farther than she ever had before. Much too far.

Picking out the weaker students she berated them whether they were playing the game well or not. "John! Move your feet! You fat dummy! You want to know why your so fat and ugly? Because you never move! Look at you! You don't even go for the ball when it comes your way!" The teacher got up off the bench and onto the court where she placed her mouth less than an inch from the ear of a small skinny oriental girl who wore thick big-rimmed plastic glasses and screamed: "And you! You know why you have to wear those stupid looking glasses, Ms. Four eyes?! Because you don't keep your eyes on the ball! Keep your eyes on the ball! Your not *that* blind are you?!" It really was appalling.

I cringed with every terrible word that came out of the gym teacher's mouth. Why did she have to be so cruel to these children? The ones who were weak or fat or small or different. You could see she was cutting them to the quick with her awful words. She thinks she can motivate them by making them angry no doubt. But guess what? Such a thing never works. My shoulders pulled in and my ears actually hurt every time she said something else horrible to another one of these children. I tried to encourage and sooth these poor singled out kids by running up next to them and telling them not to worry about what she was saying. The students who were seasoned basket ball players also winced and cringed as they listened to the teacher lash these kids. I exchanged glances with them wondering what they thought should be done; only to get a shrug in response. These were nine and ten year olds she was yelling at!

"You're pathetic Smith! What's the matter with you, you lazy piece of crap?!" (Did the teacher really just say 'crap'?) "You're nothing! You know why? Because your scared! Look at you! Your scared of the ball! What kind of stupid lazy wimp are you!? You wanna stay a wimp? Huh? You wimp?!"

All of a sudden I absolutely lost it! I couldn't stand it! I was very small and thin in stature but you probably wouldn't have thought it just to hear my voice on that day. Outraged I pointed to the children in a full sweeping movement and nearly ordered them to all sit down. "You too", I demanded of the teacher who was on her way back to the bleachers as it was. To my profound surprise everyone complied. Everyone, including the teacher, all took a seat on the bleachers and turned their faces at me with a near cowering and shocked look. I was still too horrified at the teachers behavior to be fully aware of how strange the situation was.

Pointing at the teacher I boomed with the outrage in my voice. "You have done nothing but berate the children! They look up to you for everything because you're a grown up and their teacher! And you may think your motivating them by calling them names and being mean to them! But all your really doing is just calling them names and being mean! How dare you treat any child that way! I should go right now to the principle and tell him exactly what you've said to these kids! He should hear it *right now*!"

In a flash my mind became fully aware of the fact that I had the entire class along with the teacher listening to what I had to say. The teacher appeared aware of how she sounded and what she'd said at this point. Tears were in her eyes and I thought for a moment she would cry. Breathing in deeply I thrust out a huge sigh. Assessing the situation. How did I do this? Good heavens! My parents believed children were to be seen and not heard. So was I really expressing horror to my teacher about her behavior? I was! Wiping my forehead with the palm of my right hand I said to the gym teacher in the calmest voice I could muster, "You know, I could, and probably should, go to the principle right now and tell him the names you've been calling these kids. But maybe what I should do is just go to the library until I cool off."

The teacher and I were looking into each other' s eyes. She looked sad and even frightened of me. Nodding her head in the affirmative she said softly and politely, "Maybe you should just go to the library until you cool off."

Nodding my head to her. Then I walked closer to the bleacher where she was sitting. I pointed to her and spoke softly, "Be careful what you say to these children. Please! They believe everything you say to them. And it can become a self full-filling prophecy when you are cruel."

"What you want to do is mold these kids into the best adults they can be. Not call them names and bring them down so that they become unhappy and screwed up adults! Please! Watch what you say. Be very, very, careful." Letting out an emotionally exhausted sigh I said, "I'm going to the library now." The teacher acknowledged what I'd said with dignity. Walking to the gymnasium doors I opened one of them and slipped away into the hallway. What a weird day.

First I went to my locker and pulled out my notebook and a pen to take with me to the library. I stopped walking when I got to the glass front doors of the school. Placing my right hand on the long silver bar of the glass door I looked out at the sunshine glaring in the empty sky. I saw the browned grass with the name of the school in big letters atop salmon colored bricks. There was the sensation of someone behind me, watching me.

Turning around I saw a small young girl about my age standing a few feet from the girls bathroom and staring at me. She looked stunned. "Are you a ghost?"—she asked me.

Startled by her question I looked down at myself. I knew what caused her thought. "No. I'm not a ghost. I'm way too pale. And I don't weigh enough."—I smiled; she still looked scared. "It's because my hair is so light. Is it because my skin is so white?" The girl nodded 'yes'. "I'm anemic", I said, "It makes me look like snow. Do you still think I'm a ghost?" The girl nodded 'yes' again. "Well I'm not. I can prove it."

"How?"

"Here; I'm going to move closer to you. And I'm holding out my arm. Just touch me." Slowly I stepped up until I was within arms length of the girl. Holding out my right arm I patted my skin with my left hand. "See? Just touch me."

Her mouth opened and with fright still in her eyes the girl reached out little by little until she had touched my arm.

"See?" I said. "Flesh. I'm a living person."

"Ohhhh. Your so white! Why are you so white? You scared me! I thought you were a ghost!"

"I know."

"You need to get a tan or something."

"Yep. Maybe I will." Turning around I began walking back to the glass doors. Leaning back I waved once at the girl and said, "See ya later."

I heard her say goodbye as I pushed down on the silver bar to open the school door. Walking outside I clutched my pen and notebook under my arm. I had placed it under my arm when I'd moved toward the girl. Now I shuffled my items so that I carried them in both hands. The day seemed too warm to me. The sun too blindingly bright. The library was a mild walk across a field from the school. It was big and square and made of light brown brick. I liked the large size of it. I liked the turn-style you pushed through after just walking in the door. The old leathery soft wood smell of books delighted me. Walking to a table inside the library I looked around me and I felt blessed to see so many books. So much information and entertainment contained in this fabulous place called a library. Sitting down at the table I opened my notebook and looked at the blank pages. Chewing on my pen.

"Can I sit here?" A soft pleasant tenor voice.

Looking up I saw a grown man in a black blazer and black slacks with a deep blue checkered button-up cotton shirt underneath. He wasn't wearing a tie and the first two buttons of his shirt were undone. His skin was naturally tan. Sort of a dark orange-brown. His thick hair was black and neatly cut and parted on the side. I wasn't afraid of him at all. He had kindness in his eyes.

"Sure", I said.

He sat down at the table in the wood chair next to me. I went back to chewing my pen and looking at the paper.

"So", he said with a thoughtful politeness in his voice.

"So." I responded without looking up. I thought about drawing a flower. Instead I drew a swirling spiral. "It's better you know. Things are better. I mean, we don't feed people to the lions anymore. We don't think its okay to just kill each other in a duel just because of a fight. People think things are worse now, but they're not…if they had television and radio way back when…people would be appalled to see that things are just about the same now or in fact *better*." I sighed and began coloring in my spiral with soft pen strokes. "You know. Like the song, 'Israel in 4 B.C. had no mass communication'." Looking up at his face. Such kind eyes. "You know the song?"

"Yea", he spoke so gently. "So. What would you do to help someone out there in the world if you could?"

"Help clear away one of their fears maybe. I hate fear. It feels so awful. It makes things so bad."

"What fear would you hope to ease?"

Now I began to doodle a flower. Big luscious petals, a straight stem, and wide leaves. "Have you ever been so scared in a situation because you thought you were going to die?" I looked at him. He shrugged and nodded affirmatively. "Well I wish there was some way to prove that consciousness survives death. Like scientifically so there could be no doubt. That would help me if I knew that. But it's impossible."

"Well then, that's what you should do?"

"I don't know. I'd need all kinds of books."

"You're in a library", he spoke sweetly. Such a kindness emanated from this man. "There are all kinds of books here."

"No. I would need to know what *kind* of books to look in. What kind of science books. You know?"

"You could start with anatomy. Or physics."

"Oh yea?" I was interested. "Spell that for me." He spelled 'anatomy' and 'physics' for me as I penned the words down on my notebook. "Thanks!" I tore the sheet of paper out and jumped from my chair. Now I had something to do! Excitedly I went over to the long semi-circle of a desk where the librarian sat. Her auburn hair in a bouffant. Her cotton dress short sleeved and dowdy with a cloth belt around the middle. The nice guy who had helped me followed me to the desk. "Mam?"—I called to the librarian. Her chin was still down as she turned her eyes at me. She gave me the impression I was an annoyance to her. "Mam? Can you help me find some books?"

She raised one eyebrow as she closed the book she'd been reading and left her chair to come up to the desk. She had a scary grimace on her face. Although she didn't say anything to me she did make a 'hrumph' sort of groan in her throat. I got the feeling she didn't even like kids.

"Can you point me to some books about these?" I waved the piece of paper at her. "See these? Books about these? Anatomy and physics?"

Looking partially over her shoulder and waving her thumb sideways the librarian said, "Those would be that way. Against the wall."

"Well can you show me some books in particular? Please?"

"I can show you." The gentleman said as he stood behind me and to the right.

The librarian eyed me with a frowning, downward, crease of her mouth. Looking first to the man and next to the librarian I said, "Okay. Thank you." Back to the librarian I said, "Its okay. He can help me find them. Thank you mam." I watched the librarian lift her chin with a quick movement then turn to go back to her chair as she shook her head.

"This way", the gentleman said politely to me as he opened his arm in a wide gesture towards the far side wall of the library.

"Thank you." I followed him to the brick wall covered with books. He began pointing to every type of science book, which I pulled down, occasionally I had to use the library step-stool. Books on the body.

Books about the mind. Physics. And so much more. I was so excited! Absolutely thrilled! Sitting at the table I poured over the books. Enjoying each tasty morsel offered by the pages. I wrote and wrote into my notebook. Full of an impassioned enthusiasm I looked up from my notebook and the books surrounding me to where the kindly gentleman had been sitting at the table. I'd been so consumed that I hadn't noticed him leave.

Getting up from my chair I walked the length of the single floor library looking through the isles. He wasn't there. In fact the entire library was completely empty. Walking back to the librarian's table I saw that it was dark on the other side of the glass doors. I walked through the turn-style and up to the door. Placing my hand on the glass I looked outside and realized it was dark because it was night-time. I let my feet lead me to the librarian's desk. "Mam?"

The librarian's smile halted into an instant bland frown; as if she had a bad taste in her mouth. She stared at me with a look of annoyance.

"Mam, I was wondering if you knew where that nice man went?" I paused. "The one that was helping me."

"There wasn't any man in here. There's been no one in here but you all day." She lifted a pink knit sweater off the back of a chair and began pulling it on. "In fact its closing time." She pointed to the clock above her on the wall then glanced back at me. "In fact, it's past closing time! Five minutes past! You got to leave now. You gonna check out any of them books?"

Speechless, I just stared at her. Then I sucked in a deep breath of disbelief and I put my left hand on my hip and stretched my right arm out straight as far as it would go and pointed towards my table with my pointer finger. "That nice man that helped me… certainly *was* here!"

The librarian put both hands on her hips, which pulled her pink sweater forward, and said, "There's been nobody here! You seen anybody here? This is the *school* library! It's always empty like this, less some teacher comes here with her kids! You gonna check any of them books out?!"

In my mind she might as well have had the word 'LIAR' printed across her face in big block shadowy letters! She was lying! How could she lie! Pattering stiffly to the table I gathered up my pen and notebook. I didn't even bother to put the books back on the shelves where they belonged; I was mad. Of course that man was here; how could she be so ridiculous?! The librarian's rude lie made me so angry!

Glaring at the librarian as I walked past, I looked her in the eye. Keeping my eyes on her I noticed she had a change of expression on her face. As I passed through the turn-style I said to her flatly, plainly, and clearly, "Liar." I turned my eyes from her as I pressed open the glass door and left the building.

"How could she not have seen the man, honestly!"—I thought to myself as my anger went away. Suddenly I felt terribly guilty and down-hearted that I had called the librarian a liar---what if she was telling the truth? Stopping in my tracks in the cool night air, I laced my fingers together and said a quick prayer begging forgiveness for having called the librarian a liar.

The night was chilly with a slow cold breeze. The sky was pitch black so I was grateful for the street-lamps. Hands dropped to my sides I lifted my head up towards the night sky. Looking to the heavens I wondered where the moon was. No moon in sight at all. "Must be a new moon", I thought to myself. "Must be a new moon."

TWELVE

THE BISHOP CALLS

1975 flowed off into the river of time bringing about the United States bicentennial year of 1976. My school performed the musical version of "Let George Do It." My father had promised he would come.

During the entire program I stood upon the first bleacher on the stage and scoured the audience for my father. He was too busy of course, and intellectually I understood. Yet the disappointment was palpable for me. I was still a child. I would have to become a grown-up and give away my childhood thoughts before I could fully understand.

Time would pass and we would move and live in several different parsonages. The year 1977 would bring about a huge craze over King Tutankhamen whom scientists suspected had been murdered. A toll began to fall on my parents marriage from the many phone calls where whoever was on the other end just breathed and refused to speak. Suspicion regarding the phone calls ran rampant. A bitter decay burrowed into the family Barns. It had actually been decaying for a long time now. With mass communication now at hand in the world's human drama, this decay of family seemed to be very, very common in most American families in the nineteen-seventies.

Mr. and Mrs. Barns both were very hard workers. My mother threw herself into her work and into getting her master's degree. My father, whom had his doctorate, was gone all the time which was usual for the way he did his job anyway. Mr. and Mrs. Barns would divorce. My older sister Mabel was enjoying dorm and sorority life at university. My mother had told me that my brother Rustle was living with a friend. As for myself, I kept working on the notebook(s) I had been filling up ever since that unusual eve in the library.

I put the information from my notebooks onto large pages of paper so that I could use it as a visual aid when I gave my seminars…or classes, or presentations, if you prefer to call it that. I first gave a seminar for the young adults group and the kids in my youth group at my church regarding my work. Through word of mouth the news of my work and my seminar spread throughout the communities churches. Soon I was giving the seminar at all the churches in the city regardless of religion or denomination. People kept calling me and asking me to show my work and do the seminar for them. Word spread and for the next three years I ended up being invited to many churches and social groups to show my work and do my seminar. I was eleven years old when I first started giving the seminars on my work. By the time I was 13 and about to be a freshman in high school I got an exciting and unexpected phone call!

"Hello?" It was dark outside and I was the only person home. "Barns's residence. May I help you?"

A happy sounding male voice introduced himself. It was the Bishop from the church! "So I hear you give a remarkable seminar from some work that you've been doing. I've heard a lot about you! Good job Suzanna!" *(Wow!)*

"Thank you."

"I have an opportunity for you. I'm sorry I'm calling so late but it has been a busy day."

"Oh that's okay. It's really not that late."

"So I'd like to know if you would teach your seminar at the region church camp this summer. Would you be interested?"

"Oh!" I was so excited. It was the Bishop and he was asking me to teach my seminar! "I'd love too! It would be an honor! Thank you for asking!"

"So I hear you're about to be a freshman."

"Yes."

"Well that's a bit young. Most of our people have already finished graduate school. These are people going for seminary mostly. Would that bother you?"

"No."

"Okay! Well I'll send you the information."

"I'll give you my address."--I began scrambling for a pen and piece of paper when I realized in my thrilled flurry that I didn't need them for anything.

"Oh no, that's okay. I've got your address. I know your father."

"Well I'm really excited. I can't tell you how much I appreciate your asking me. I'll be on the look out for the camp information."

"We'll do. Now you take care! Goodbye."

"Goodbye." After hanging up the phone I called my Grandmother Oleta and Grandaddy JB Barns. I told them about teaching the seminar at the camp! When I ended the conversation with my Grandparents I hung up the phone feeling glad to have heard my grandparents voices. Suddenly I missed Oleta's baby biscuits and wished I had a bag of them to nibble on and savor.

I was thirteen years old the summer before my freshman year in high school when my mother drove me to the regional summer camp. I had flipped on the car radio once and Rod Stewart was singing, "Do Ya Think I'm Sexy." "Turn that thing off", Mother had said and she reached and turned it off herself. The ride was quiet after that. Each mile closer to the camp brought more forest and wilderness. When we pulled up into the camp there were adults everywhere laughing and chatting. Mother parked the car in the grass. Getting out of the car I noticed that I didn't see any children at all. "Hold on Suzanna", said Peggy having made the same assessment. "I'm coming with you to check in."

"Okay." I took my suitcase from the backseat. I had packed just enough. Lumbering my work for the seminar and also my suitcase I made my way to the table set outside with people sitting behind it in chairs giving name tags to the grown ups as they came up from the line. I waited for just a moment as two people before me signed in and got their name tags.

"Yes?" Said the nice looking young man sitting in the chair behind the table. "Need to sign up?" He was looking at my mother.

"Yes", I said, "I need to let you know I'm here. My name is Suzanna. I'm teaching one of the classes here this week.

The man, perhaps in his late twenties, looked at me with a mixture of surprise and confusion. Then he saw my serious expression and began to file through the papers on his clipboard. He stopped in the middle of the second page and placed his finger halfway down the paper. "Oh yes! I see it. I've got your name right here. Are you sure that's you?" He looked at me curiously.

"Well of course I'm sure that's me. It should say *Suzanna*, that's me."

"What I mean is…you look so young…you look…" He paused and took a breath. "The majority of the people here attending the classes, well, most of them, have already graduated from a university and have their masters degree. A lot of them are in seminary. Some of them have their doctorates."

"The Bishop called me. He knew I was going to be a freshman this year."

"Wow! You look too young. So you're a freshman in college?"

"No. I'm going to be a freshman in high school."

Peggy waved a hand in front of the young man as she spoke with gestures. "You know, that's what I thought. When we pulled up and I saw everyone I knew there had been a mistake."

The handsome guy smiled at me. "Obviously they thought you were going to be a freshman in college."

"Well I knew it", said Peggy. "Come on Suzanna, let's go."

"Go?"

"You're actually supposed to teach one of the classes", the young man stated with a lilt as if it were more of a question.

"Yes sir. I've got all my stuff here. If the people don't mind my being so young I can still teach the class."

"You think that you can still teach it?" He looked at me. "Even though they're so much older than you?" He lifted his brown bushy eyebrows upward.

"Yes; I can. But only if you think they won't feel it is rude that I'm teaching it and yet I'm younger than they are."

"Well now", he said to my mother, "if she thinks she can teach it then she's more than welcome to do so. Someone thought she could or she wouldn't be on my teachers list here."

"Mother I'd like to stay. I've been looking forward to it. I can do this."

"What ever." Mother waved me away and turned to leave. She had a slight scowl on her face. "Don't go calling me to pick you up. Because I'm not going too!"—Peggy hollered over her shoulder.

"I won't. Don't worry."—I responded. Turning to the man I grasped the pen he was holding out to me and I signed in.

I was excited to walk among the many trees and smell the pine. I was looking forward to seeing the heavens at night and watch the star's glowing brighter than jewels. I wanted to smell the delectable scent of campfire and watch the flames flicker. The air *tasted* like pine as I breathed inward, and I licked my lips. Stopping at a bench I sat my baggage down and looked at my little black and white map. I'd received the map at the welcoming table where I signed in. There was an 'X' on the map where I was to teach my

class. There was another 'X' on the cabin I had been reassigned too. It was a cabin in the far back of the property that I would have all to myself since all the other cabins were co-ed.

Checking around to make sure I had my bearings I stood up and took my luggage to the far cabin. I found the cabin easily which truly surprised me. I had full well expected to get lost on the property a couple of times before I found it. I left my suitcase and seminar materials in the cabin. Then I took off down the trail with the map in hand. In search of the chow hall!

I found the chow hall, it's doors open and welcoming. Walking into the hall I was immediately drawn to a table that sported bread, butter, and water. I spread butter onto two pieces of bread and then pressed them together like a sandwich.

I took my map and my bread with butter and walked along a hiking trail until I came to a quaint outdoor chapel that was tucked into the woods. Sitting down at a table in the chapel I ate my sandwich happily. Listening to the birds twitter I felt at peace in the spot. Watching the tree dappled sunlight sprinkling through bushes and branches was a delight. Two squirrels scampered and chased one another on a large oak at the edge of the chapel. It was serene; beautiful.

Soaking in the warming beauty I thought about my brother Rustle and sister Mabel. I thought about when we were in Watonga, Oklahoma just before we'd moved to Springs. I was thinking of the month of March in 1969. Mabel had been jazzed because come March 24th, 1969 Mabel would turn eleven years old! Bobby and Peggy would lot each of their children one birthday party during their growing up years. It could be a slumber party if the child wanted. Mabel decided since she would be turning the impressive age of eleven that it would finally be the perfect time to choose her one birthday party. Of course she chose a slumber party! Everyone was so happy!

I was remembering when my siblings and I were getting the house ready for Mabel's 11th birthday party by picking up the dirty laundry. Happily bustling with hopping popping energy while we gathered up the dirty clothes. Mabel and Rustle were carrying me around the house each holding opposite ends of a dirty sheet pulled off of one of the beds. From each bedroom and also from the bathroom my siblings would empty the room's laundry basket onto the sheet they carried me in. Gathering the dirty laundry and hauling it in the sheet was one thing but Mabel and Rustle thought it fabulously hilarious that they were dumping the dirty laundry on top of their little sister! I was having a great time!

With the blessedness of cheerful delight, Mabel and Rustle helped each other pick up the full laundry basket from the corner of the bathroom floor. "Heave!"—Mabel and Rustle shouted as they lifted the green basket and emptied its contents on top of my head. I sat in the middle of the sheet on the floor and raised my arms with glee as the dirty clothes tumbled over me. I found it great fun to be doing something with my older siblings.

"You're nuts!" Mabel bellowed down at me with a laugh.

"That's so gross Sausage." Said Rustle with both a smile and bewilderment. "How can you like that? That's dirty clothes, Sausage!"

"Why do you call me sausage?" I asked of my older brother. Looking at my big brother's shaking head and disgusted expression I asked, "What's gross?"

Mabel and Rustle exchanged glances and then stomped their feet and giggled hopelessly.

"The laundry, Sausage!" Rustle answered. "It's dirty! Remember?"

"It doesn't smell bad." I insisted on picking up a sock and smelling it. Eyes widening with the realization that the sock really was stinky, I bellowed with laughter. Mabel and Rustle laughed so hard!

Mabel and Rustle held on to the sides of the sheet and with a mutual lift they carried me to the last room on our journey, both the sheet and the dirty laundry, *with me riding in it*. We had made our way to Rustle's room.

Setting down the sheet with me their little sister laughing in it, my older siblings shook their heads and grinned. Mabel and Rustle helped each other lift and carry the laundry basket that was sitting in a cardboard box in Rustle's closet. They carried the basket over to me and the sheet. Thumping the basket over, they let the dirty clothes fall again onto my head. "Bombs away!"— Rustle shouted. Squealing with glee I once again raised her arms in the air and twirled my hands around. A huge smile on my face. I was so happy! My siblings were spitting with laughter!

"Ooo", sneered Mabel before a big guffaw of ha-ha's blasted from her lungs. "Man! Suzie! You're going to smell like dirty socks and dirty underwear for my whole party! You'd better take a bath! You're sooo going to embarrass me!"

"What!" I giggled and grinned from ear to ear. "I looooove getting laundry with you guys!"

"What an embarrassment!" Mabel rolled her eyes. "Mother! Suzanna's gonna smell like stinky underwear for my whole party!"

"Now I know why you're stinky, *Sausage!*" Rustle laughed and clapped his hands.

It was a very happy memory. I thought about that memory of March 24th, 1969 when my siblings and I had gathered up the dirty laundry. I caught myself chuckleling out loud. Finishing my bread with butter I realized I was grinning hugely in my revelry of memory. The Bishop had called, and now I was about to teach my seminar at the camp…I didn't care about the age mix-up. Watching the sparkling sunlight as the squirrels scampered and played, I took in a happy breath. It was such a pretty day. Rising to my feet I decided to hike back to the chow hall and ask when supper would be served! It was going to be a fun and successful camp in the beauty of the forest.

The regional seminar church camp would turn out wonderfully. I did a great job. I taught my classes to people ranging in age from their late twenties to their early sixties and every one of them gave me great feedback and were very positive. I was grateful.

THIRTEEN

HANG ON FOR DEAR LIFE

French psychoanalyst Jacques Lacan, 80, died in 1981. Francois Mitterrand was elected President of France. Britain finished building the longest suspension bridge in the world called "Humber Bridge". Most people would remember this time for when Iran released 52 American Diplomats held hostage for 444 days. Or remember the year for the astonishing fact that President Ronald Reagan in the U.S., and Pope John Paul II in Rome, both survived assassination attempts. As for myself, I would recall these events later on in my life as being primarily concerned with crossing one of the most trudging bridges…*high-school!* Once I entered high school I no longer had young people coming and asking me for guidance or help. I was compelled to have fun with my friends and enjoy school activities such as theater and flag corps. Peggy and Bobby divorced; which for all its pain was the best thing. Come 1980 my father had remarried to Mindy who had a three year old girl named Carla whom he adopted. Both Mindy and Bobby were pack rats. They both preferred a similar relaxed and comfortable mode of dress. They were simply alike in all the small little ways that made them properly compatible. This turned out to be a blessing in disguise for Peggy. For Peggy was reintroduced to her true soul mate. It was Elton Locks. Her piano teacher's brother in law whom she met formally one day at a piano lesson when she was ten years old. Peggy and Elton were also alike in all the small important little ways that make for a compatible marriage. They both appreciate a more tailored mode of dress. Similar interests in entertainment. Both of them loved playing 42 with friends once a week. Similar manners. Alike even down to both of their both enjoying just a sandwich for supper at night!

I moved to a small town in Texas I'll call 'small town' when my mother married Elton. I was blessed to receive step siblings through this marriage. I'll never forget staying up late on Christmas eve with my stepsisters Jenna and Dora and my stepbrother Bart; we played board games and drank creamy eggnog while the stockings hung on the fireplace. Dora read to us from a fabulous book of hilarious little known facts; we all laughed and chatted about the fun information in its pages. Jenna and I hid food in her room for late night snacks and chats. As a family we would all sit down for supper every night at the table and eat. It felt like a real home.

On a couple of weekends I went to a small town establishment for dancing with my friend Ray and we would do a great rendition of the jitter bug. One evening when the night was particularly dark I called up Ray and told him I had a surprise. Something I had to show him. Could he come out and play?

"Yes. I can come out. What's the surprise?"

"I can't tell you Ray. If I do it won't be a surprise."

"Can you pick me up?"

Elton had a remarkably old car that he'd taken care of and still worked. Between Dora and Jenna and Bart and I we would take turns driving it now and then. I knew the car sat unclaimed for the evening. "Yes. Yes. I can pick you up. I'll be there in five minutes. Okay?"

"Alrighty; I'll be waiting."

Grabbing hold of my purse and pulling the keys to the old car off of the key hook I left the house. I slid into the car, buckled up, and started the ignition. Driving the several streets to Ray's, I stopped the car in front of his house. Ray beat me to the quick and was already out the front door of his house and walking in his long legged gait towards me. "Hey! Come along!"—I said to him with a wave of my hand.

Ray climbed into the car and buckled his seat belt and looked at me with curiosity and a smile. "So what's the surprise?"

"Ooo, you know I can't tell you. But you're going to love it. I swear to you it's something you've never seen before, and you'll never forget it for as long as you live. It's something beautiful."

"Okay." He laughed.

"I'm serious. You're going to love this."

Ray was tall and long legged. He had bright red hair and freckles and wore glasses. He was also a kind and thoughtful friend with a great sense of humor. He grinned at me and inquired, "Can you tell me where we're going at least?"

"We're going to the lake."

"What have you got? Fireworks?"

"Even better than that!"

"Alright. You've peeked my curiosity!"

Flipping on the radio I moved the channel around until I heard some clear music. It was hard to get a decent radio station in such a small town but soon I found one that was fairly clear. I turned up the volume as a band called Devo began singing their song "Whip It." Ray and I rocked our shoulders and tapped our toes and fingers to the music. The night was so black. The moon and star's were hiding in the darkness. It felt like it didn't take more than ten minutes to get to the first lapping shore of the lake. Not a streetlight or house-light for some miles. Parking the car I turned on the inside light so Ray could see me. We undid our seat belts and turned to look at each other. "It's fireworks isn't it!"—he stated feeling certain of his assessment.

"No. Oh no. This is something so wonderful, so beautiful, that you will never forget it for as long as you live. Are you ready? Because this is *magic*!"

Turning off the inside light of the car.

Turning off the headlights of the car.

We were enveloped for a second in pitch blackness so thick you couldn't see your hand before your face. And this is the moment; the moment in that split second when your eyes are wanting to adjust, you see something beautiful! Up against the windows and all around the car were so many *millions* of lightening bugs that the brain struggled with the illusion that you were looking out into the universe at stars and planets so bright and close you could touch them!

"Oh my gosh!" Gasped Ray. I heard him physically gasp with an inward draw of air that was stunned. The sound of true awe. "Look at the lightening bugs! There are so many of them!"

"Millions! There are so many that it looks like your staring at star's, doesn't it?"

"Yes!" Ray gaped.

"Now for something truly incredible. Come outside!" I opened my car door and Ray followed suit. We closed our doors and walked tenderly into the swarms of glowing yellow lights blinking on the back of the bugs. Ray climbed on top of the car hood. Leaning back with his arms crossed behind his head. He said, "I've never seen anything like this before in my life! You're right. I'll never forget this as long as I live!"

I danced into the millions of blinking lights like star's come down from the heavens just for me to dance in. Dancing in the star's! The lightening bugs filled ones sight from all directions with their sparkling blinking shine. Flowing my arms out to my sides I twirled around in circles amidst the millions upon millions of glowing lights. Dancing with a sway of my arms in the middle of them. The velvet ebony darkness of the night a back drop like the vast universe to the glimmering, lustrous, blush and blaze of the lightening bugs. I danced and twirled and swayed with my arms out from my sides into the air and imagined the music of Pacabel's Cannon in D playing in my mind. We watched the beauty of the lightening bugs until time forced us to feel that we had better get back home.

*   *   *   *   *

My dear friend Kristi and I spent a lot of time together during this era. We climbed the ladder day or night up into the attic of the school's stage. We met there to take turns reading a most scandalous and delicious book. Vladimir Nabokov's "Aida"! We *ooo"ed* and *aw"ed* over "Aida". We giggled and were shocked as we read the book. Kristi and I, climbing in whispers to clandestine up to our secret meeting place. Exchanging turns reading, we knew this must surely be the most exquisitely savory and alluring words ever put to paper. We discussed the chapters we read. Tantalizing! Shocking!

On the next good day when I was privy to the old car our new household of kids shared I went to Kristi's house to pick her up. Sitting in her bedroom I felt truly amused at how messy it was. She apologized over the mess. But I told her several times it didn't bother me in the least. I was happy just to have her delightful company. She pulled out a record of a band called "The Police." A band we both liked. She played the music and we discussed what to do for fun.

"Want to go to the park?" Kristi asked.

"We could take a picnic. Swing on the swings a while." I shrugged my shoulders.

"We could take a picnic to the lake." Kristi offered.

"I like that idea. Or I could drive us to Wichita and we could go see a movie."

"I think I want to be outside. But we could get our picnic stuff in Wichita." Kristi's brown skin shined with a natural born glow. She was fabulously gorgeous. Her hair was an earthy brown spun sand and gold. Her large water-blue eyes framed perfectly with long dark lashes. She had a natural amber scent to her skin when she perspired. A copper goddess. With a spicy sweet personality that was kind and romantic. "Heyyyy", Kristi purred. Her eyes sparkled suddenly with a surreptitious mischievous grin. "We could get one of those little magazine books that have explicit stories of romance in them. Or *maybe* we can. You may have to be 18 to buy them!"

"You mean a 'nudey' magazine?"

"No. It doesn't have pictures. It has stories."

"Yea! We can take turns reading them out loud. Are the stories as scandalous as Nabokov's books?"

She leaned forward with a smile like the cat that got the mouse and giggled. "Even more so!"

Picking up a square pillow out from under the pile of clothes I was leaning upon on the floor I tossed it at her. She caught it and laughed.

"Okay girl", I got up on my feet. Then I impersonated the voice of the cartoon character Yogi Bear and said: "Let's go get some pic-a-nic goodies for our pic-a-nic baskets, yey hey Boo-Boo!"

Kristi and I piled into the car and I drove the fifty minutes to Wichita. The band called The Rolling Stones sang the song "Start Me Up" on the radio just before the news hour began. There were so many things being talked about in the news these days. The young ones of the time, especially teenagers like myself and Kristi, would sit up close to their televisions and watch with sheer fascination as a new show took place on television. A show that would call itself MTV. This new and interesting entertainment would broadcast its very first show in 1981 with a tantalizing video from a band called the Buggles with a song called "Video Killed the Radio Star."

Finally the fifty miles drive had passed and we parked at the closest grocery store we came too. Leaving the car for the grocery store we had a true sense of excitement over being alive and going to have a picnic at the lake. Entering the store we strode up and down each isle while I pushed the grocery cart. "Oh!"—we both exclaimed in unison—"Fortune cookies!"

"Okay", I said, "We definitely have got to get some fortune cookies!"

"Most definitely", exclaimed Kristi. She grabbed a box of the sweet fortunes and tossed them into the cart. It seemed we'd found our niche on the specialty isle.

"Caviar?" Asked Kristi with her sweet shining smile.

"We have to have caviar."

"Which kind?"

"Believe it or not they each have a different taste. Get the black lump-fish caviar. It's the best."

"Are you sure Suzanna? I kind of like this red one."

"The red caviar is prettier, but I don't think you'll like the taste. It's best used in cooking. But go ahead and get it. We'll get them both."

"Yea!" Kristi tossed both the black and red caviar into the cart. She picked up an item and waved it in the air. "Smoked oysters?"

"Put it in the cart!"

We looked into the cart then at each other. "What else?"—Kristi inquired.

"Cheeses."

"Mmmm." Kristi's blue eyes flashed and she did a little dance. "Ooo, I want the little round ones wrapped in their own mesh!"

"We need crackers too."

"They're right over here." Kristi walked farther down and pointed. "I wonder which kind of cracker we should get."

"Butter crackers."

"Mmm, that sounds good." She excitedly picked out a box and held it up. "I want these!"

"What kind are they?" Walking over to her I looked at the box. "That looks like a great one. The picture makes the cracker look crispy, browned, and salty. Good choice!"

Kristi set the box in the cart and we continued to stroll the isles. We passed some fine chocolates from Holland and both agreed it was a necessity for our picnic. Next we made our way to the cheeses and Kristi picked out some savory looking gouda. We were both happy about our choices and eager to taste them. On our way back to the front of the store we passed an array of beautiful looking bottles filled with red wines and champagne. "Oh! I wish we could get champagne!"— Kristi looked longingly at the pretty champagne bottles with sparkly gold and silver tinsel tops.

"Yea, but we're not old enough. They'd card us for sure and wouldn't that be embarrassing!" We continued looking longingly at the fancy titillating bottles. "I've got the perfect thing!"—I said and walked just a little farther along the isle. I picked up a bottle with a gold sparkly tinsel top and showed it to Kristi. "See Kristi? It's non-alcoholic champagne!"

"I want the pink one!" She said with another cat's smile. "Pink champagne sounds so… I don't know." She placed her hand on her heart and laughed. "It sounds so pretty and…sparkly!" She laughed again; she had a beautiful laugh.

"Great! We'll get them both! Put the pink one in the cart."

We bought our goodies and placed them in the car. On our way out of town we stopped at a gas station to look for any small books of steamy soap opera romance. We found one! We were both so ready for our picnic at the lake that not even once did either one of us think about getting our swim suits. We were too busy thinking about the sunshine and the cotton dappled blue sky! Driving home with our groceries and book of romantic tales we turned the volume up tremendously loud on the radio. We rolled the windows all the way down so that the warm wind whipped and swirled through the car and through our hair.

The day was sunny. Yet even if it had been a cloudy day it wouldn't have mattered. Friendship was our sunshine. The kissing wind felt so good flowing through our hair. In our peace of mind the over 60 miles to the lake flashed by like ten minutes. Rolling the car slowly to park on a deserted shore surrounded by trees. There were no other people in sight at the lake. We tugged our goodies onto the sand beside the water and realized we hadn't brought a blanket to place the food and drinks upon. Ah well! Does not matter.

We tenderly ate our caviar and cheeses and read our fortunes. Both of us were surprised that the smoked oysters tasted good. The crackers were crisp in texture and tasted salty in the back of our mouths. Our 'champagne' bubbled against the roof of our mouths and tickled our noses in tiny sparkles. The chocolate melted creamy on our tongues.

We cracked open the fortune cookies and nibbled them. Perhaps we'd find a special fortune. Perhaps we'd find a fortune that would read, "Votre message pour-quoi vous mon petit bonbon champignon et fleur Anges, non quelque-chose se-passer, vous avoir le place devoir aller après mort depart votre corps."

All the while we took turns reading from the steamy book and found ourselves rolling with laughter at how outrageously cheesy the stories were! They were so bad they were hilarious! It was great silly fun!

"Oh I wish we'd brought our swim suits." I felt a longing for the flowing lapping body of water.

"What I really wish is that I had a speed boat! I'd take us flying so fast across the water we'd feel like we had wings! The wet spray on our skin! Just the speed of the boat itself!"

"I can't believe we didn't bring our swim suits." Kristi stood and looked around with a frown. "You know there's nobody around?"

Standing up and walking to the water's shore I looked around the lake. "Looks like we're the only ones here alright."

"Think we could get away with skinny dipping?" Kristi's brown skin was shining in the sun.

"Well?" I looked over the lake again. No one in sight. "You know? I think we could get away with it. There's not a single person at the lake today. We're the only ones!" Looking into Kristi's happy blue eyes. "As long as we hop into the water quick who's to know?! I'd love to go swimming."

"Yea! Let's go swimming!"

We giggled and laughed with nervousness and uncertainty as we became sky-clad. Once our clothes were shed we both ran screaming as fast as we could into the water. Sinking up to our necks instantly by bending our legs to hide our state of a certain swim suit absence. We splashed and swam. Enjoying the cool water completely.

At last getting prune skinned we decided to get out of the water and get our clothes back on to read some more from the ridiculous but funny book and eat some more fortune cookies. *Read* our fortunes too, and wonder what would the world lay ahead for us when we grew up.

"Come on Kristi, let's go have some more fortune cookies and caviar!" We stood up from the water to walk towards the damp sand at the shore.

"This was fun. I've never skinny dipped before."—Kristi spoke with a smile. Out of the entire lake completely empty of others one lone car drove down the slight gravel trail where our own car was parked.

"I've never skinny dipped before either. It really *was* fun!" I had just stepped out of the water at the exact same time Kristi had; we hadn't noticed the lone car yet. The car parked behind our own and three strangers got out of the car. Kristi and I had not seen the strangers coming to park behind our car. We looked up in time to see them walking down the rest of the trail toward the water. It was a mother and her two small children. The mother looked up to see us naked and shook the towel over her arm and screamed. Standing naked Kristi and I also screamed. The mother screamed again. Kristi and I screamed again too. Grabbing her children's arms she pulled them back around towards their car. Kristi and I dove into the water still screaming. Kristi went completely under the water to hide. I ducked down so only the top of my head and my nose poked out. I shimmied behind a tree growing into the water. Kristi came up for air and swam up next to me to also hide behind the tree. Peeking past the water and the tree branches we waited until we saw the woman drive away.

"Of all the places in this entire lake that lady had to pick right here?! When she saw our car why didn't she guess there was someone at this spot already!" My anger and embarrassment caused my voice to quake. I looked at Kristi and we locked surprised eyes. *We burst out laughing!*

"That was so embarrassing Suzanna!"

"Way embarrassing! I tell you what, let's never *ever* go swimming again unless we have our swim suits!"

"Agreed!"

We laughed until we could hardly breath! I splashed Kristi with the water. She splashed back.

"Okay, okay." I said as we splashed each other and laughed. "On the count of three we run for our clothes! Okay?"

"Yes!" (We counted together.) "One… Two… *Three*!" Screaming and laughing at the same time we sprinted for our clothes. Picking them up in a flurry and straining to get them on quickly!

"You want to go to my house and listen to some music Suzanna?" We were both successfully dressed thank goodness!

"Okay." Looking over our picnic I lifted the sacks they came in. Handing Kristi one of the sacks while the blue sky shined above. We opened them and started putting the picnic items back inside. Once we were packed up we walked back to the car. The sacks went in the back seat. Hopping in the car ourselves; droplets of water rolled down from our wet hair. I backed the car out of the grassy trail and onto the gravel road. Kristi turned on the radio. We left the windows down to ruffle us with the warm wind. "I can't believe about that lady! Of all the spots on this empty lake for her to choose!" Kristi put her hand out of the window to catch the air with her fingers. The car rolled across the unpaved road as we both laughed while the sunshine poured down upon our faces.

*   *   *   *   *

During the 1981-1982 school year our high school one act play "Alice in Wonderland" was the District AAA champion. Everyone was so excited! Students were thrilled. Teachers were proud. Especially proud of course was the high school drama teacher Mrs. Pasek. I played the part of Alice. Kristi was the hookah smoking caterpillar. Kristi and several other cast members such as Sara and Rhona graduated that year. Yet the Manhattan Project Version of "Alice in Wonderland" was so much fun that it had become a favorite. So the next year in 1983 we did the same play! Not only were we champions, we took the one act play all the way to state this time! More thrilled students and proud teachers.

The state contest was held at the University of Texas in Austin, Texas. Dora K. won an All Star award. I won an All Star for playing the part of Alice again. It wasn't awards our cast were interested in really. It was the good time we were having that made performing the play so great. Everyone had so much fun. How did our drama teacher Mrs. Pasek keep her patience with our raucous energy?

The charm of the play was Lenny. In the one act play Lenny played the part of the baby who kept sneezing from his mother's overuse of pepper in the soup. He was a big guy and played the part hilariously in a huge bonnet and with a gigantic baby rattle. He was not just big. He was tall with large thick arms and broad shoulders. Lenny was part in parcel of the cast as we took the high school play to the state competition. Everyone was thrilled to stay in a motel in Austin for the contest. The motel was next to a Mexican restaurant and the dead end for a bridge that was a road and walkway over a very busy highway. On the other side of the one-hundred foot bridge was a small convenience store and gas station. The one act competition was over but we were going to go ahead and stay the night and leave the next morning. Thirsty for a soda and munchy for some chips I had headed for the convenience store at the other end of the bridge. I had walked almost all the way over the high bridge from the motel that our cast was staying in when I heard my name being called.

"Suzanna! Hey Suzanna! Wait up!" Lenny was running toward me on the walkway on the left side of traffic.

Stopping and turning around I saw Lenny coming my way. I waved at him and waited where I was for him to catch up. When he reached me he was out of breath from the run. I patted him on the back. His dark brown afro looked a bit misplaced since he was a Mexican American. His dark skin was dappled with sweat.

"I've been looking all over the place for you Suzanna! I was going to ask you to walk with me on the bridge."

"Walk with you on the bridge?"

"I mean.. the.. I meant the… uhh…the…"

"You're flustered."

"I mean to go to…the…the gas station there. The… to get a…something to drink."

"Well Lenny, you're in luck. It just so happens that's exactly what I was doing. Come on." I waved him forward and we took off to the gas station's little store.

Inside the store I went to the candy bar isle and thought a moment about something salty and sweet with nuts. But no. Not interested in candy just now. What about the other isle? Walking around to the other isle I stared at the snacks trying to decipher what my mouth wanted. What would taste and feel the most pleasing on my tongue?

 Cheese puffs? Maybe something salty and crispy and made from corn? From potato's? Yes, something made from a potato. Something buttery and crisp. No, wait! Ah-ha! Just the thing! Cheese crackers with peanut butter in the middle. I picked up the snack I had chosen and made my way to the refrigerated drinks. Deciding on what to drink was easy. I wanted a bubbly cola. Grabbing the soda I walked to the front of the store where I place my two items on the counter. Pulling a couple of dollars out of the pocket of my khaki shorts I paid for my snack; happy that there wasn't a line I had to wait in.

I suddenly realized Lenny was following me around the store when I turned around to look for him; he was standing right behind me. I stepped to the side and waited for Lenny to move forward. He didn't. I looked at his hands and realized they were empty. "Aren't you going to buy anything?"—I asked him.

"No. I'm fine." Lenny smiled but looked terribly nervous. This was odd. I'd never known him to be nervous about anything before.

I shrugged. "Do you need some money?"

"No."

"I'll buy something for you. No problem."

"No. I'm fine." Lenny gave that funny jittery looking smile again.

Why was he acting so strangely? I shrugged again. "Okay. Well. Let's go." I walked out of the store and Lenny followed behind me. As we walked across the bridge Lenny kept lagging behind. I had to keep stopping and waiting for him. I had opened my soda and taken a sip then screwed the lid back on. Currently I was contemplating if I wanted to go ahead and open my peanut butter cheese crackers. Open them now, or wait until I get back to the motel? Stopping and turning around I waited for Lenny to catch up again. "Come along slow poke", I said playfully. We were now directly in the middle of the very high bridge with extremely heavy rush hour traffic going 75 miles an hour down below. Lenny stopped walking and so I stopped walking as well. He looked at me and waved his hand at my soda.

"Suzanna. Can I have a sip of that soda?"

"Sure. Of course you can." I handed him the cold soft drink.

Lenny took the soda from me and we both stood still as he opened it and took a small quick sip. He screwed the lid back on then sat the soda down on the walkway of the bridge. This confused me.

Why did he do that? I was just in the beginning of asking him: "Why did you set…" Lenny stepped forward and swept me up so that I was elevated sideways in his arms. I was completely confused and a little bit alarmed. "Lenny, what are you…" He turned around and stepped up to the edge of the bridge. Holding his arms out he dangled me past the railing and into the empty air directly over the traffic. He stretched his arms out as far as they would go. My package of crackers fell out of my hand and fell over one-hundred feet into the highway traffic. Looking down after it I saw the snack get smashed into oblivion by the tires of a zooming car. Suddenly the cars were honking. As I stared down in terror I saw the honking cars swerving to keep from hitting my body. A semi-truck began honking and honking and also swerved out of the lane to keep from hitting my body.

Looking up at Lenny I grabbed hold of his t-shirt and twisted it around my tight fists. When he dropped me perhaps I could hang on to his shirt. Hang on for dear life! Lenny squeezed his eyes shut and grimaced; he was about to drop me. Then he let out a long breath and opened his eyes as if he couldn't do it. Lenny began laughing! It was an ugly horrible laugh. I was so terrified I couldn't even scream! I placed my head against his chest. My fists still twisted into his shirt. I closed my eyes and clenched every muscle in my body tightly as I waited for my death. I couldn't get out of it. If I struggled I would cause myself to fall the long distance into the speeding traffic even sooner.

A minute passed. A very, very, long minute. Then Lenny backed up so that the safety of the walkway was beneath me. Then he set me to my feet on the concrete. I sprang from the walkway away from him and cowered on the side of the road. Grabbing at the asphalt with the palms of my hands; my head was swimming with fear. Lenny was laughing again. It was a horrid sound. Forgetting completely about my cola I leapt to my feet and began running. I ran and ran. I ran as fast as my feet would take me. Willing my legs to run faster. Pausing just a second at the end of the bridge I looked both ways to make sure I didn't run out into a car when I crossed the road. It was clear enough to run across. Bolting across the road I headed towards the motel. A sense of relief swept over me as I felt my feet running through the motel parking lot. The feeling of being close to my motel room and of having ground beneath my feet were a relief. Sprinting up to the door of my motel room I breathed in gulps of air. I was shaking so hard I thought I wouldn't be able to get my room key out of my pocket without dropping it. The key trembled in my hand as I pushed it into the keyhole. "Come on! Come on!"—I whispered under my breath. The latch turned. Bolting into my motel room I swung the door closed and immediately locked it. I slid the chain lock across so that it was locked too. Spinning around I ran into the bathroom and closed the door behind me. I leaned against the wall then slid down with my shoulder against the wall until I was in a squatting position. Tears burst from my eyes. Choking sobbing gasps and gulps came from my throat. Finally I fell back onto my bottom and buried my face in the palms of my hands and cried. Where were the angels when you needed them? I was still shaking with fear. The tears flowed.

Come the last day of school I braved approaching Lenny and broaching the subject. I asked him: "Lenny. I wanted to ask you. I wanted to know…. Why did you do that? Why? Why did you hold me over that bridge?" He looked me in the eye but his face was squelched as if worried or embarrassed perhaps.

Lenny answered: "I talked to my grandmother about it. She said the evil eye had been put on me or I wouldn't have taken the money and done that."

Money? What money?! Who did this? *Who did this!* Ask him! Ask him Suzanna! Have him describe this person! Ask him about it! I was too confused and stunned to find my voice. Speechless! *ASK HIM*! Who paid whom for what? What did this person look like? He then told me a man, some man he didn't know, had paid him.

I wanted to ask questions; I felt tears in my eyes. There was no hope for my vocal chords to work. I was literally too stunned to think or speak. I simply left him. I left him and hoped I'd never see him again.

From that day onward I would be inflicted with vertigo. The vertigo would make me feel dizzy and as if I were falling even if I wasn't. It would hit at odd times. I could fly in an enclosed airplane without feeling it, only to have the vertigo hit when simply riding up or down on an escalator. I could strap in and ride on a roller coaster and because of the strap not feel the vertigo. But I would never again be able to climb a tree.

FOURTEEN

WHEN THE ANGEL SINGS

During the year of 1982 I had tried a job working at the small town's Dairy Queen fast food restaurant. It didn't work out. I held the job a couple of months before realizing I was never going to get the hang of turning the ice cream cone upside down to dip it in the hot thick melted chocolate glaze. Every time I turned the ice cream upside down it fell out with a plop into the melted glaze. No matter how fast I was! Each time I'd have to fish the ice cream out of the glaze before it melted into it. Impossible. The poor customer would be waiting as patiently as they could for me to get their dip cone. I'd enlist the help of another worker if there was one working with me that shift. But that just frustrated the employee as they were trying to get food from the chef to the customers also! I was a customer's worst worry if they had ordered anything that needed to be dipped in chocolate glaze!

Ever since my mother had married Elton and we'd moved to 'small town', Texas I had been going to my Grandmother Pauline Arnez's house during every lunch break from school. My grandfather and Pauline's husband who was named "Early" was either the singer Eddie Arnold's oldest brother of thirteen children or just one of Eddie Arnold's first cousins. Nobody had ever heard from Eddie. The story was that Eddie had a chip hanging on his shoulder over his father's bad temper and had said he didn't want anything to do with any of his family. Coming from thirteen children it seems sad he discontinued contact with everyone. The problem for Pauline was that Early had died years ago.

I had thought one day during the lunch hour that I would go and visit my grandmother and bring her a sandwich. That's when I discovered the problem. Pauline was practically turning into a skeleton because she wasn't eating. But what truly alarmed me was that she had burns on the back of her legs where she'd stood too close to the fire from the gas heater. She'd said she was cold all the time and hadn't even realized she'd burned her legs. Since that day I'd been driving to Grandmother Arnez's house each lunch break to make sure the gas flame wasn't too high, that the back of her legs were staying healed with the salve I put on them, and that she at least ate something.

Eventually it became evident to Pauline's three daughters, Peggy as the youngest, that Pauline needed living assistance. It was then that the difficult decision to put Pauline in small-town's rest-home for the elderly was made. On my first visit to the rest-home by myself a most surprising event took place.

Opening the heavy door to enter the rest-home I thought to myself how amazingly heavy the door really was. The look of the door belied its weight. The place was flat and square on the outside; made of brick. The inside smelled like antiseptic and urine. A repulsive smell. The long rows of fluorescent lights glowed unpleasantly bright. Walking up to the front desk I asked a woman with brown fluffy hair pinned up against her head and wearing a white nurses uniform dress where Pauline Arnez's room was. The head nurse bent down and placed a bony elbow on the long curving desk. She lifted up a few pages of type-written paper before her eyes flashed with recognition that she had found on the paper what she was looking for. "Yes", said the nurse, "Ms. Arnez is down this hall on the left." The nurse pointed with her left arm and pointer finger to the direction she was speaking of. "Just turn left down that hall. Her room is on the right hand side." The nurse gave me the room number then picked up a full clipboard and walked off hastily. She gave the impression with a slight sneer that any visitor to the home was a nuisance.

I didn't wait to see where the head nurse was going. Although I wondered why she seemed so sour. Following the directions she'd given me I walked down the hall looking for the room on the right hand side that housed my grandmother. I found it easily. It turned out the nursing home was a fairly small place. It held just three hallways of rooms in the layout of a cross. I stepped into Pauline's room. Her hospital bed was rolled close to the big wide window that looked out upon a pleasant square of grass. The safety railing was pulled up and in place on both sides of her bed. She looked at me with an expression of pure confusion. Not confusion about me in any way. But a confusion about her being in the nursing home. Her expression wasn't just confusion, it was also a pleading look with her eyes widened. At the right side wall was a plain wooden chair without arms. Picking it up from the back I brought the chair over between Pauline and the wide window. Sitting in the chair I smoothed out the lap of my gray wool skirt. I loved the blouse I was wearing with it. A blouse shiny like silk and full of silver, magenta, and green. It was an outfit I liked to wear because its shininess and splashes of color reminded me of Christmas. My blonde hair was curled with feathered bangs brushed to the side. My make-up was still fresh and I'd refreshed my lipstick in the car before coming into the home.

"Hello Grandmother." I placed my left hand on top of her wrinkled tan hand that was covered in brown liver spots. Why on earth were they called *liver* spots? I wrapped my hand around hers and held onto it firmly but gently. "How are you doing Grandmother?"

She looked but didn't say anything. I had just decided she wasn't going to speak when she said: "I'm alright. They feed me too much here."

"Well I'm glad to see you've gotten some of your weight back. You were skin and bones you know!" Smiling at her. Leaning up and kissing her forehead. "I love you." Sitting back into the chair. I petted her hair with my left hand. Her short fluffy curly hair was matted and tangled. She looked cold in her nightgown under the sparse sheet and blue knit blanket. "Are you cold?"

"What?"

"Are you cold Grandmother?"

"It's cold in here."

"So you're cold?"

"I'm always cold in here. I'm always cold. Is it winter?"

"Is there another blanket in here or do I need to go get one?" Standing up I turned towards the back side wall where the dresser was. Opening the drawers I found only pajamas and house shoes. Tons of nightgowns. "It's autumn Grandmother. But it has been getting colder." I glanced at the window. "You've got a nice view. The grass there is still green. And that's a pretty bush. Is that a rose bush?"

I'd finished rummaging the drawers for a blanket. Pauline looked at me and made a feeble point towards the window. "That bush will grow roses on it come summer. Got to keep the branches trimmed. Got to trim the roses too. Or the new ones won't bud." Pauline looked out the window without raising her head from the pillow. "Sure is cold."

"Grandmother, I'm going to go get you another blanket." She had fallen into a silence. "Okay?" Pauline just looked at me without speaking. "Okay. I'll be right back. I'm going to go get you another blanket. Okay?" I began walking for the door. "Okay? I'll be right back." Stepping out of her room I took a left back towards the front desk. No one at the desk. I walked into the hall directly in front of the nurses desk. I'd only walked a few feet when I saw an office with the door open. Stepping to the door I could see plainly that no one was in the office. There was another office to the right of the hallway with the door closed. On the door it said, 'Office.' So I walked over to it and knocked on the door. Nobody answered so I knocked again. Still no answer.

Well? Say, didn't that one door on Pauline's ward have a sign on it saying janitor's closet? Walking back the way I had come to the start of the hallway that was Pauline's wing. I looked at the door I'd seen. I was correct. It said 'janitor closet'. Attempting to open it I shook and pulled then pushed at the doorknob. No use. It's locked. They probably wouldn't have any blankets in there anyway. For no particular reason I grabbed the doorknob and gave it another shake. In my head I kept singing to myself the new song by a group called 'The Police'.

"Every little thing she does is magic", I kept singing to myself.

"Can I help you?"

Startled, I jumped and looked behind me. It was the same nurse I spoken with earlier. "Yes. My grandmother is very cold. I was looking for a blanket."

The nurse ducked her hand into a white pocket of her white uniform and extracted a medium sized ring of keys. "Well you're not going to find a blanket in there. It's over here." She gestured to the door at the wall opposite the janitors closet. "See?" She walked the few steps over to the door and pointed to a sign on it. "Say's 'linen' on the sign there now doesn't it?" She picked out a specific key. Putting the key into the door's keyhole she turned it. It made a popping sound as it unlatched. Opening the door she gestured for me to take the door. I grabbed hold of it.

"There you go. Just close the door when you're through. It'll lock behind you."

"Okay. Thank you very much. I appreciate it." The nurse walked off without looking back or saying anything. I stepped into the closet. Sheets, pillow cases, blankets. A great pile of thin blue knit blankets. Choosing two blankets from the top of the pile, I turned around to exit the closet. Making sure the closet door had closed properly behind me, I shook the door knob. Wondering as I walked back to Pauline's room why it was so quiet in the nursing home. Too quiet.

Turning into Pauline's room I thought that it did seem a little chilly. Carrying the blanket's over to my grandmother I gave her a smile and a greeting. "Hey there! I'm back. I've got two blankets. Do you want them both or just one?"

Pauline didn't answer. She just looked at me like a little child. "You want them both?" Still no answer. "I tell you what. I'm going to put them both on you and if you get too hot you can just take the other one off. How's that sound? Okay?" It occurred to me that she had probably spoken all the words she was going too. She'd always been quiet. But this was a childlike quiet sort of like wonderment. I fluffed each blanket out one at a time and spread them over her and up to her neck. "Thank you", she said.

"Well you're more than welcome." Sitting back down in the wood chair between Pauline and the window. I brushed the blue knit blanket away to reveal her hand. Taking her hand into my left hand I then petted the top of it with my right hand fingers. "You know I should have brought something to read to you! I don't know why I didn't think of that!" Petting her hand. "I should have brought you a snack too! Something yummy." Patting her hand. "What would you like me to bring as a snack Grandmother Arnez?" No answer. "What kind of treat sounds yummiest to you?" Leaning over and kissing the back of Pauline's hand. "I love you, you know. I'm glad to get to see you. So what do you think? Maybe a candy bar? Does that sound like a yummy snack?" Not only was there no response but my grandmother's expression looked incredibly blank as she looked into my eyes. "Yep. That's what I'll do. I'll bring you a snack next time I visit. And a story I can read to you. I think you'd like that. That would be nice, wouldn't it?"

I kissed my grandmother's knuckles and patted her hand. "How about I sing?" Standing up I noticed her matted hair again. "I'm going to brush your hair for you. Okay?" There was a brush on the top of her dresser. Retrieving it I stepped back to my grandmother and brushed her hair. It was easy to get the tangles out since her hair was so short. Smoothing her hair down with my hand I petted the top of her head for a minute. Then I kissed her forehead. I walked to the dresser and put the brush back on top. Then I strode over to Pauline Arnez's side. But this time I was at the left of her bed with my back to the door. "How about some songs? Would you like it if I sang to you?" Pauline looked at me and said, "Yes. Sing please."

"Alright. How about some Christmas songs first?" I sang: "Have Yourself a Merry Little Christmas", and "Chestnuts Roasting on an Open Fire." I sang "Little Town of Bethlehem", and at least half a dozen other songs. I switched to songs I practiced with my voice coach and had sang successfully at competitions. Songs in French, Italian, and German. At last I thought I had sung everything I could think of except for the lullaby's I knew. But just as I thought my mind was a blank I realized I hadn't sung to her one of my most favorite Christmas songs: "Oh Holy Night."

I sang "Oh Holy Night" as I had practiced it. As I had sung it for the congregation at church. When I had finished the song I felt someone tapping on my shoulder. Turning around I saw that the whole room was full of fragile elderly men and women. Two were in wheel chairs. Everyone who could get out of bed and walk had piled into Pauline's room and they were spilling out of the room and down the hallway. How could I have been so busy singing that I hadn't even noticed them all come in? There were so many. The beautiful elderly woman with the long white hair that had strips of faded gray in it was the one who had tapped my shoulder. She spoke to me with anticipation in her eyes. "Have you come to take us Home?"

I was confused. "What?"

"Have you come to take us Home?" The woman with the long white hair gestured with arm towards the large group of people. "They all think you've come to take them away. To take them „Home"."

"See!" Shouted an elderly man in the back. "I told you there was an Angel in here! I told you the Angel was going to take us Home!"

The crowd started talking on top of each other's voices saying words like angel, home, heaven, free. My confusion faded away as I realized that all these people thought I wasn't human. They thought I was an Angel and that I was here to rescue them from the nursing home and take them to heaven, their real Home.

My lungs convulsed and I choked. My mouth went dry while tears came wet to my eyes. How could I stop myself from crying? I could feel my heart breaking as I attempted to speak over the crowd. "I wish I could take you Home. I really do. I'm so sorry. I can't take you. I wish I could take you Home. I'm so sorry." Oh my gosh! I didn't know what to do! I wiped the tears away as they rolled onto my cheeks

"What did she say?" Questioned one elderly man.

"She said she can't take us now!" Said the elderly woman with the short straight hair.

"Well when will she take us?" Demanded the man in the back. They continued to talk about it to one another.

One frail looking woman with thick fuzzy pink slippers on poked at the woman with the long white hair and demanded of her: "Ask the Angel when she'll be taking us to heaven! You ask her!"

"When will you be taking us from here?" The long flowing white haired woman asked.

I responded with tears that seemed to be welling up inside my chest as well as my eyes. My chest actually ached and I wanted to cry out. I wanted to say: "I'm not an angel. You've got it wrong. I'm sure an angel will take you Home when it's time. But I'm just Pauline Arnez's grand-daughter." But what could I say? How could I speak but with kindness and consideration for their aching longing hearts? I pointed at my grandmother. I said, "She's my grandmother. And I couldn't think of anything to say so I decided to just sing."

A woman from out of the crowd in the hallway pushed her way into my grandmother's room. "Jessie's talking! Jessie's talking!"—she shouted.

"What!?" Exclaimed one old man.

"She hasn't spoken in years!" Shouted an old woman.

Next they were all talking amongst themselves about how Jessie had spoken for the first time in many years. The woman who'd pushed her way into the room and announced this news about Jessie now pushed her way to me and grabbed me by the arm and started pulling me out of the room. "Come on Angel! She wants to see you!" She pushed at the crowd. "Out of the way! Jessie wants to see the Angel!"

There was a rolling flush of murmuring among the old people about how Jessie wanted to see the angel. Once the woman holding my arm had me out in the hallway she stopped for a moment to tell me something. "Angel, Jessie can't get out of bed. She wanted to see you too but she can't move from that bed." Then we walked into the room across the hall. The woman was still pulling me along. The crowd of elderly people were following us. Once inside the room the woman pushed me with her hands on my back towards the woman in the bed.

I walked up to this bed ridden woman who hadn't spoken in so long. Her eyes were wide as quarters. And I could tell by her open mouthed child like smile that she was the happiest right now than she had been in years. Or at least that's the impression that I got. Placing my hands on the smooth silver railing at her bed I smiled back at her. I petted her hair for a while. Then I bent down and covered her face with kisses. I petted her hair some more and I asked her, "Would you like me to sing to you?" Jessie smiled and nodded 'yes'. I sang "Oh Holy Night" again. Jessie looked to the ceiling as if she were seeing something I couldn't; I mean that it was an expression of relaxed concentration. Reflexively I looked now and then at the spot of the ceiling Jessie was looking at while I sang. When I finished singing the song I leaned down and kissed Jessie on the forehead. Now the tears really were threatening to leave my eyes, in droves. Placing a hand on my mouth I turned and ran out of the room. I ran down the hallway. Past the nurses desk. Pushed open the heavy door to the rest-home and flew onto the sidewalk in the bright sunshine of the day. I ran to the car and got behind the wheel. Resting my elbows on the wheel I placed my face in the palms of my hands and let the tears come. I couldn't get the faces of the elderly people in the crowd out of my mind. More precisely I couldn't get that image of the expressions on their faces out of my mind. The look in their eyes. That look! It was a look of desperate *hope*! Desperate Hope. They were hoping with all the faith and desire they could muster that I was there to free them. Their angel come to take them Home. That look had gotten under my skin. I knew that as long as I lived I would never get that look out of my head.

Wiping away at my tears, I sniffled. I grabbed a tissue out of the box sitting on the passenger floor board. Suddenly I had an idea. Opening the car door I got out of the car and closed the door behind me quickly. I walked back down the sidewalk and back to the heavy front door. I opened the door to the nursing home with the same surprise at its weight. Walking past the deserted nurses desk I marched up to the office that had previously had its door closed. The door was now open and I walked in. The head nurse looked up from the newspaper she held in her hands. "Can I help you?"—she asked with a sour annoyance tightening her face.

"Yes." I spoke with the sensation that I was out of breath. "Yes. I want a job. I want to work here."

And so I spent my nights after school working at the nursing home. I worked there on Saturdays and Sundays also. I was a nurses aid called a candy striper. Sadly, the next day when I began work at the nursing home I had gone first to Jessie's room and received some bitter news. She was gone. She had died in the night; it happened some time after I had sung to her obviously. I could not tell if any of the elderly even recognized me from the late afternoon when I sang to Pauline Arnez and Jessie. I wasn't wearing make-up, I had my uniform on, and my hair was pulled back into a bun.

The one woman with the very long white hair with strips of faded gray in it turned out to be named Lilly. She was sweet as can be. She would call to me as I was working and ask me to sit on her lap. She was adamant about having me sit on her lap every time at least once during my work shift. She would pat her lap and say, "Come here little girl. Sit down on my lap and I'll tell you a story." So I was a little girl to her of course. I would balance myself with my hands on the arms of her chair so that my weight was barely on her. I was afraid to put my actual full weight on her tiny thin legs out of fear that I would hurt her. And there, balancing as I was, I would quietly listen to her tell me a story from her life. Over the time I spent working there she had told me stories about her childhood and her wedding day and her children. Each and every story Lilly told to me was a blessing.

FIFTEEN

SINGING FOR GOTTI

1982 had brought into the world the movie "Tootsie" with Dustin Hoffman. Other movies were popular that year such as "The World According to Garp" with such players as Glenn Close, John Lithgow, and Robin Williams. Of course who could forget Attenborough's movie with Ben Kingsley's performance as the amazing "Gandhi"? Kristi and I had gone together to the movie theater and fell in love with Steven Spielberg's "E.T.: The Extra-Terrestrial." Kristi and I continued to swoon over the band called "The Police". Yet 1982 had flown by and was gone forever. Passing away as years do, time keeps ticking away. Life goes on. I had graduated from high school the next year and wanted to get my higher education while also wanting the job I worked to be one that would be fun for me. I could get my degree to teach as I went along and in the meantime work in some fashion with the entertainment industry. What would be better then to go to New York City?

So it was that I found myself freshly graduated from high school and on an airplane destined for New York City. I'd bought my airplane ticket with money I'd saved from working at the nursing home. I'd packed two suitcases. Which was one suitcase too many if you asked me. If I'm going to travel than I'd rather travel light. Yet this was not a vacation. I was moving there! My sock monkey Grandmother Oleta had made me was packed in one of the suitcases I was bringing along. I was finally eighteen years old, and on my way to New York City!

I discovered the loveliness of airplane radio head sets. The stewardess had handed me the blue plastic ear phone set and showed me this little hole in the right arm of the seat that I could plug it into. There was a dial for changing the radio station. I plugged the ear phones into my ears then placed the end plug in the small hole I didn't hear anything. I moved the dial back and forth looking for a radio station but there was not a sound. Perfect silence. Then I noticed the other dial which said 'volume'. Hmmmm. I turned the volume up. Yep, that was it! Adam Ant's voice came bellowing into my ears singing "Goody Two Shoes." "I like that song", I thought to myself. I wanted to sing along with it, but of course I didn't since I have had etiquette drilled into my brain by my mother. So I looked out the window at the darkening sky and enjoyed the song with a light soundless tap of the tips of my fingers. I sat there and wondered if I could get any work in the theater of the stage or perhaps with the movies. 1983 would thrill me with movies. There were so many good entertainments to enjoy. Movies like "The Big Chill", "The Right Stuff", and the visually fun one that was like one long MTV video called "Flash dance." And what about singing?

Perhaps I could get work in some area of that field? Wow! New York City! The Big Apple! The "Goody Two Shoes" song ended and was replaced by "She Blinded Me With Science" by Thomas Dolby. Another good song.

Music from the 1940's might be my favorite but I nevertheless have an eclectic taste. It turns out that the radio station I'd found was thrilling me with an entire plethora of good tunes to tap my finger tips too. "Stray Cat Strut" by The Stray Cats. "Down Under" by Men at Work. The Eurhythmics sang their haunting song "Sweet Dreams." Marvin Gaye wailed soulfully for "Sexual Healing." Men Without Hats chortled wonderfully with an unusual beat in "Safety Dance." I was so pleased with the entertainment in fact that it threw me for a moments annoyance when they stopped the musical parade for the news. I heard through my earphones: "The San Diego zoo announces its first condor born in captivity…" I rolled the dial and changed the station. Accidentally I hit the volume, turning it up. Blaring into my ears "IBM announces the development of a computer chip capable of storing 512,000 bits of…" Turning down the volume I also slipped the dial back and forth for another station. It seemed everything was the news. But on this exciting airplane ride to Manhattan I really wasn't in the mood for listening to the news. Unplugging the ear phones from my ear canals I let the ear phone set fall to rest in my lap.

Luckily I was able to stay with a friend of my sister. Mabel's friend Joni had lived in New York City for some time now. She was sympathetic to my plight since when she herself had moved to Manhattan she'd had to live in her car the first week. Joni turned out to be very sweet and very pretty. Long dark hair. Perfect physical shape and tall. She and her boyfriend had a loft in a nice New York City neighborhood. They were both actors and both waiters at restaurants. I slept on Joni's couch and stayed with her for two weeks. The day after I arrived at Joni's loft I got a newspaper and circled available jobs in the classified section. I got the first job I interviewed for. In fact I started work that day right after the interview! It was a waitress job down in Chelsea at the bistro and bar called Chelsea's Pub. Everyday for a week and a half I rode the bus down to Chelsea and worked. I was grateful for the job. Especially since the job came with one free meal. That one free meal was the only meal I ate in a day but I didn't have to buy groceries which was a huge plus with regard to saving up for an apartment.

I learned right away that its not just dipping things into hot chocolate glaze that I'm bad at. I've got to be one of the worlds worst waitress's. I could never ever remember who had ordered what. Nor could I remember for certain which plates of food went to which table. Unfortunately for me there weren't table numbers to go by. The family that worked the kitchen were fresh from China and just learning English so they weren't much help to me on remembering. The family were nice. And I admired them greatly for their hard work and determination. All of them; the mom and dad and their older children. Every time I worked this family would be listening to cassette tapes teaching them how to speak English. Impressive!

Luckily for me every customer I had liked me a lot. Bad as I was at waitressing not one of them failed to tell me how nice I am. I insisted I was simply using good manners. Was it such a surprise for a New York City waitress to use 'please' and 'thank you'?

After just my first week of working at Chelsea's Pub the Chinese mother and father who worked in the kitchen asked me to marry their son. (They were serious.) "Yes", the mother said, "You very nice. Make nice wife. He work for you. You no have to work. He be very good husband." They were visibly disappointed when I insisted I wasn't ready to get married just yet. But I thanked them deeply.

Come near the middle of my second week working as a waitress I told Joni that I was going to have to look for other work. Waitressing was not my forte. Joni listened sympathetically and then mentioned that I needed to find other work to her boyfriend later that night when they were out with some friends. They came home very late but I was up and awake and writing in my diary. Joni went to the kitchen to get a glass of wine. Then she retired with her glass of red into the loft with a book to read. Her boyfriend paused to sit down on the couch across from me before joining Joni.

"Joni said you were needing to get different work. Are you sure? Waitressing is good money here."

"Yes I'm sure. I make a really terrible waitress. I need to find something I can actually do right."

"Well", he spoke with his thick New York accent, "I happen to know a guy. He's got a job. He offered it to me but I don't want to get messed up in that scene. The job comes with a free apartment. Joni and I have talked about it and have both decided we'd better not take it ourselves."

"It comes with its own apartment? Did you just say that the job comes with a free apartment?"

"That's right."

"I'll take it!"

"Well there's something I need to tell you first."

"What's the job?" "Parking cars. You'd be a valet."

"You're kidding!"

"No."

"Well I can do that!"

"Well just wait Suzanna. There's something I've got to tell you."

"What? What is it?"

"This club has a restaurant on the other side of it. The restaurant is called "Tucano's". The club is… "Club A."

"Yea?"

"Okay. You don't get it cause your new here."

"Yea?" "This club and this restaurant. They belong to John Gotti."

"Okay." I had absolutely no idea who John Gotti was. Was I supposed to know?

"Do you know who that is Suzanna?"

"No. Should I?"

"Okay these people see, they're wise guys. Get it?"

"Wise guys."

"Yea. You know what that means."

"Wise guys?"

"Yes."

"That they're really smart?" "No." He put his knuckle against his upper lip and laughed. "Talk about green", he whispered under his breath. Was I being insulted? He laughed again only a little bit softer. "These guys, you know, they're Mafioso."

"Okay."

"Mafioso."

"Okay. I'll take it!" I thought he was being colorful with his words. Mafioso didn't sound like an actual word to me; I thought he was making a metaphor for seriously hard working and tough working at that….I thought he was mispronouncing the word 'macho'. Never did it dawn on me once what he was really talking about. Besides, all that kept beaming in my head were the words: *Free apartment! Free apartment!!*

I moved into my new apartment that weekend and began my new job the same night. The apartment was a descent size. Empty, but clean. I preferred empty and clean. There was not a telephone; I'm not even sure if it had an *outlet* for a telephone. It overlooked the parade route on 61st and 1st street! The club, Club A, was posh. You had to be a member to go there and memberships started at $10,000.00 dollars. In 1983 a beer was cheap unless you went to this club. At Club A, a small glass of beer was ten dollars. On my first night working there it rained. My boss, a fabulously charming and handsome man named Dean, had given me a black shirt and a black pair of pants. Both of which were far too big for me. I had to roll the pant legs up forever before they reached my ankles. Same thing with rolling the sleeves up to meet my wrists. I opened doors for the cars that arrived. I retrieved cars for the people leaving. By the time this first night in the rain was over I was soaked completely through. That was alright. The job was fun and I kept so busy that it went by quickly.

The next afternoon I met with my boss Dean for some lunch. Then he took me on a cab ride to Bloomingdales where he got me a uniform that actually fit and helped me pick out a pair of thermal underwear. That way the next time it rained during work I wouldn't get quite so wet? He said I'd need them when the weather started to turn cold. His blonde hair was combed back perfectly; his nails were buffed and clean. He wore a black long-sleeved shirt and black pants and expensive black polished shoes. Dean's dreamy eyes were blue as a tropical ocean. As we were on the escalator (which he cutely called the upscalator since we were going up on it) I had felt dizzy with upward movement on the ride to the second floor. Then something magical happened! Dean took my hand! This handsome man and I were holding hands up the escalator! Everything was magical about it! The way my whole body tingled at the mere touch! Was this love I felt? Oh it was! It *was* love!

Dean and I dated during that whole next year. My time spent with Dean were truly happy days. I wanted to sing out: HAPPY!! We went out to eat, went to the beach, took long rides in the limousine that was at his disposal. He enjoyed buying me gifts. And if I was worried about his buying such an expensive gift for me he would smile and say, "Forget about it!" He sang his favorite songs to me! I will never forget him swaying and dancing; well dressed as he smiled and sang...giving me all the attention while he effortlessly came across seductive and gorgeous. I'd fallen head over heels in love with Dean. He was handsome, charming, sweet, loving, and thoughtful. (*Sigh!*)

At Club A one night I saw the actor Ed Asner as he was leaving. Guess what? It was raining! I'd come prepared however. I kept an umbrella with me at work at all times now. Mr. Asner stepped into the rain to hail a cab.

"Oh! Mr. Asner!" I called to him as I came running out opening my umbrella. Holding the umbrella over his head I said: "Mr. Asner! You're a Star! Come back under the awning. I'll get you a cab."

"Are you sure?" He asked politely.

"Certainly."

"You're a *girl*!"

"Yea, I get that a lot. Apparently people don't expect a girl to be a valet. Come. Let me walk you to the awning."

"Thank you."

"No problem at all!" I walked him dryly back to the club's awning. Then I stepped out into the street. A taxi was coming. I waved my hand and called, "We need a taxi here please." The taxi just went on past me. Another taxi turned the corner. Again I waved my hand and said, "We need a taxi here please." This taxi also just drove right past me and this was in spite of the fact that I had made eye contact with the driver! Certainly the driver knew I needed a cab! When the same thing happened with the third taxi that went by I turned to Mr. Asner and apologized. A man up ahead of me half way down the block shouted at the third taxi that had passed me by using his thick New York Accent, "Hey! Taxi!" The taxi stopped for him and let him in! When the fourth taxi came around the corner I called out with as thick and powerful a New York accent as I could muster! "Hey! Taxi!" The taxi driver screeched to a halt for me. "Hey!"—I turned to Mr. Asner—"That works!" Mr. Asner laughed. I walked him with the umbrella to the taxi and opened the car door for him. He handed me a tip and said to me, "You did a pretty good job on that New York accent!"

There were quite a few famous people I saw there when I was at work. The Kennedy's booked the club one night for a party. The famous former 'Beatle' member Paul McCartney came in a limousine with his wife Linda. When I opened the limousine door for them Paul McCartney stepped out first. He glanced at me then did a double take and said, "You're a *girl*!" I smiled and nodded. "Yes. I get that a lot", I said. Was it possible I was the only female valet in all of Manhattan or something? "Wow!"—said Mr. McCartney—"I was surprised to see that you're a girl!" "Yep", I said, "And all this time they thought I was a *Guy! They couldn"t see past the fake beard and fake mustache!"*—I teased. Mr. McCartney laughed and nodded with a pleasant smile. Linda was looking out from the car seat. Her eyes went back and forth from her husband to myself with a look like she wondered if she'd been forgotten. "Oh! My lady!"—I said to her. I took her hand and helped Mrs. McCartney out of the limousine. She smiled. Paul McCartney then wrapped his wife's hand in his own and he began to walk off. I stood smiling at them. Linda whispered something in his ear. "Oh", I heard him speak under his breath. He dug into his pocket and handed me a tip. It was the biggest tip of the year. He handed me a one-hundred dollar bill!

Later in the year as winter had taken hold of the icy city I was greeted with a pleasant and flattering surprise. A handsome older man wearing very nice clothes (a lovely maroon tie with shiny silver streaks in it, a perfectly made and absolutely beautiful suit, and a long black overcoat) walked up to me and introduced himself. He spoke with the best of manners and endearing politeness. His nails were buffed and clean; his hair gently streaked gray and combed back. His voice was soothing and he had a magnetic smile that made you want to smile back. I was struck with how handsome he was for an older man. "Hello. You're Suzanna, aren't you?"

"Yes."

"Well it's very nice to meet you. I'm John Gotti." He shook my hand.

"Oh it's so nice to meet you! You're the owner of the club and restaurant!"

He chuckled. "Yes", he said. I heard that you can sing. That you have a beautiful voice. And that you can sing in Italian? Italian opera?"

"Yes. That was part of my vocal training. I had to learn opera in French, English, German, and Italian. I was a winner at the Nationals contest."

"Nationals! Really? That's wonderful! Congratulations!"

"Thank you Mr. Gotti."

"Well. I have a favor to ask."

"Sure!"

"You see I brought my girls with me. I wanted them to hear you sing a real opera song in Italian."

"Oh sure! I'd love to! How did you hear about me?"

"Dean mentioned you."

"Oh yea, I've sung for him almost every song I have in my repertoire. I was wondering how you knew. I don't go around singing at my job here!" I laughed at the idea and Mr. Gotti smiled warmly.

"They're in the car. Can I have a moment of your time and you can sing them that Italian song?" He gestured towards the car behind me.

"Absolutely", I said. I still had no idea 'who' he was. I just thought he was the owner of a couple of ritzy business' and ultimately my boss. I got into the passenger side of his car. He looked over his shoulder into the back seat and so I looked over my shoulder into the back seat also. The night was darker inside the car but I could see the two beautiful little girls sitting in the back seat. The club's owner introduced me by saying, "These are my girls."

"They're beautiful", I said honestly. Looking at the two precious girls my heart strings tugged. Oh, how I wanted to be a mom and have children! "Hello!"—I said to the beautiful girls—"I'm happy to meet you." Pausing a moment, I added, "I'm Suzanna." I sang for them my contest piece "O Del Mio Amato Bien". The girls were quiet and polite as I sang it. When I'd finished the song I told the owner of the club that I'd better get back to work and that it was nice meeting him. He offered me a drink of Dom Perignon champagne before I left, as a treat for the song. I politely declined. How was I to know I was passing up probably my only opportunity to taste the best champagne there is? Looking back into the backseat before leaving the car I said, "Goodbye girls. It was very nice to meet you. You are very sweet and very beautiful. I hope I have girls like you someday. Yall have a good night." I turned to Mr. Gotti: "Well, I'm flattered that you asked me to sing for your girls. It was a pleasure. Good night." He nodded in the affirmative and smiled. I stepped out of the car and went back to work still not having any idea exactly who I had just sang for. He was just the owner, and a very nice gentleman. Any time I saw him after that he always nodded and smiled and said hello. Next to Dean, John Gotti was one of the nicest men I'd ever met.

That year I sent out what felt like tons of copies of my picture and resume to agents. Never heard a thing from any one of them. I went to a dozen auditions for both the stage and film. Nothing. At one audition for a film I stood on the stage between two girls with their busts pushed up and showing, and their skirts so short you didn't just see their stockings (one of them was wearing garters) but you also saw their panties! This might not be unusual except that the part all three of us were auditioning for was the role of a thirteen year old little girl! I myself had come to the audition dressed as an actual thirteen year old would dress. The director let the two girls on either side of me read the lines for him Then he said, "You and you on the outside of the line. You get call backs." He didn't say a word to me. Unfortunately I couldn't see him from the small stage because he had a spotlight on us so bright that you couldn't even see into the first row of seats! The two girls walked off stage and I still stood there defiantly. The spotlight turned off. Then the lights in the small theater room faded to black. Light came into the room when someone opened the door and left it open. "Hey!" I called. "Please let me read! I can do this I swear! You won't be disappointed! Please just let me read!" No answer. It dawned on me that the little theater was now empty except for myself. I made my way to the door by following the light pouring in from it. What a bummer.

I also spent that year working constantly at the Club A. It got to the point that after a nights work I would go back to my apartment to sleep and then actually dream that I was at work parking cars again! It was getting exhausting working there and then dreaming I was working there so I decided I'd better start accepting days off. My romance with Dean bloomed. I wanted to marry him and have kids!

My last day of work was appalling. I was at the awning as usual. Opening car doors. Retrieving cars for people. It came my break time and I took it. I walked around the corner and into a convenience store on 61st street. It was close by. I bought myself a candy bar. Walking back to the Club A I took my break outside leaning against the wall of the club and eating my treat. First I ate off the chocolate on the bottom of the candy bar. Then I ate the nougat part of it. Lastly I savored the peanuts and caramel with the chocolate on top. Dean walked over to me laughing. He kissed me on the cheek. "You knows", Dean said, "I've never seen anybody eat a candy bar like that!" He laughed again and shook his head.

"I didn't know you were watching me eat it."

"Forget about it! I've been watching you the whole time. I'm thinking, whats'a matter? That girl don't know how to eat a candy bar? Capice?"

"Capice." I said back to him and smiled. He was so handsome! Oh, and what a beautiful smile he had!

Dean looked to his left and took in a breath of recognition. "Yo Sal!"—he said—"You with Ernie tonight?" Dean walked off to talk with his friends. I decided I wanted another candy bar. I usually don't hunger for sweets. Yet right now that chocolate tasted perfect and so I wanted another. I began walking back to the corner where I'd need to turn to the left to make it to the nearby convenience store. I was a little more than half way to the corner when I realized I was walking while looking down at the ground. I lifted my head to look up at where I was going. I couldn't believe what I saw! How could it be? Standing in a long sandy tan coat was the man from the library?! From when I was a child? It looked like him exactly! Or at least it seemed to be him right down to the very last facial feature. The man who had been such a help to me in choosing books at the library that day when I was a little girl!

He looked me straight in the eye. Then he stepped sideways one way and then turned and ran the other way. Dean had run up behind me. I started to run after the man. Dean pulled on my shoulder with his hand. "Hey now!" He said. "What'sa matter?" Dean and I were both coming up on the corner of the street now. He pulled at my shoulder again and I stopped and looked at him. "What'sa matter sweet-cakes? That guy stiff you a tip? He steal a radio from one of the cars? What'd he do? Just tell me I'll take care of it." I shook my head but I couldn't think of what to say. "Forget about it", Dean said, "I'm gonna get that guy." Dean took off running after the man.

"No! No Dean!" I shouted as I ran after Dean. I met Dean at the corner of the street just as he was turning back to look at me. I placed my hand tenderly on his arm. "He didn't steal anything." I paused to catch my breath. "He... he just looked familiar that's all. Someone I knew when I was a kid." I couldn't help myself but step farther onto the corner sidewalk and look down the street for the man who looked like the guy that was at the library that day. I didn't see him anywhere. He'd probably ducked into one of the stores on the block. "Don't worry about it honey", I said to Dean. "My break is almost over. I'm going to get back to work." I took Dean's hand in mine and we began walking back up to the club. When we reached the club I gave Dean a soft kiss on the lips. He said, "Yea, alright. Say I got to get inside. I got to see Ernie about some business." "Okay", I answered him and I watched him walk into the club. It was about one o'clock a.m. and it was a slow night. I walked past the awning to lean against the wall again. Mingee, one of the other valet's walked over to me and said "Go get that Rolls Royce. Here are the keys. The guy's coming out soon." I jogged to the parking lot across the street and got into the Rolls Royce. Starting up the engine I thought to myself how pretty the car was. I drove the Rolls up to the club a couple of feet in front of where the awning began. I stepped out of the Rolls and came around to stand on the other side of the Royce on the sidewalk. I turned and saw a man with curly brown hair leave the club. He pulled his keys from the pocket of his long brown coat and looked up at a taxi parked across the street.

Then I saw a man step out of the club. A hefty pudgy man with dark hair. He reached inside his black coat and pulled something out of it. His eyes grew wide and his face determined. He came up behind the curly haired man fast and swung something at him. It was as if the top of the curly haired man's head had exploded. Blood and flesh flew in every direction in the air. Suddenly the image slowed down into slow motion for me as my mind grappled with what I was seeing. The hefty pudgy man had in his hand an instrument that had a long wooden handle attached to a chain. At the end of the chain was a big round metal ball with spikes all over it. He swung the weapon at the mans head again. Then again he swung it at the mans head and gore flew in all directions. This is when the one moment of the entire event took place that I would never forget and which tore at my heart so deeply. The curly headed man turned and looked me straight in the eye. Our eyes met and locked. That expression on his face! That look! It was the same look I'd seen on the faces of the elderly folk that day I sang at the nursing home! He was looking at me with that look! *Desperate Hope!* He seemed to want me to do something that would help.

I reached for the passenger side door of the Rolls Royce. All at once the scene snapped out of slow motion and back into real time. I opened the Rolls door, climbed into it, and locked the doors. I didn't know what else to do. The hefty man was swinging the spiked ball on a chain over and over again mercilessly. The man with his head coming apart in pieces fell against the hood of the Rolls Royce I was sitting in! Still the pudgy man didn't stop. He leaned into the man bleeding all over the Rolls Royce's hood and continued to batter him with the instrument even harder.

The curly haired man was trying to protect his head with his arms and hands now; he began screaming. Screaming horribly! He lifted from the hood of the Rolls and began running through the street screaming and screaming. The pudgy man followed his victim for a couple of feet while still swinging; then he hopped into a car that had pulled up squealing beside him. The car did an illegal u-turn and sped away in the opposite direction from the screaming bleeding battered man who was running down the street.

Mingee pounded both fists on the passenger side window of the Rolls Royce causing me to jump. I looked at him in confusion. He tried to open the door then pounded on the window again. "Open the door! Open the door! Get out here!"

Dazed, I complied. I unlocked the car door and stepped out of the vehicle. He thrust a pile of terry cloths into my arms. "Get this cleaned up for %!'s sake! Get all that blood up! The owner of this car is gonna be steaming if he see's all this blood all over his #!'ing car!" Mingee pushed me to the car and my arms fell into the pools of blood on the hood. Lifting my arms I looked at them. Looked at the blood on them. I looked at the hood. So much blood! So much more blood than I would have expected. It was a practical lake of blood! I pressed the white terry cloths into the blood on the hood. They soaked up into being pure red instantly. There was way too much blood for these towels to clean up. Suddenly I snapped out of my daze. That poor man! I needed to call an ambulance! I spun around and saw Dean walk out of the club. He looked at me covered in blood and holding the red sopping towels. He went into a rage and pushed Mingee and shouted at him, "Mingee! What's happened here?! What's the matter with you! You gonna have my girl clean up?! Huh!? You gonna have my girl clean up?!" Dean spun around to me and gently placed his hands on my shoulders. "You alright?"—he asked.

I shook my head. "Dean! Dean! That poor man! We've got to call an ambulance! We've got to go help him! He needs help! He needs a hospital!"

Dean hugged me with one arm. "Yea, yea. My poor baby. Oh my baby." He kissed my temple. All at once an ambulance came screaming around the far side of the street. Its sirens wailing and its lights flashing. The siren stopped and the ambulance halted a little ways up the block. "You see that?" Dean pointed at the ambulance. "That guys gonna be all right. He's getting help, right now. They gonna take him to the hospital and he's gonna be all right. Come on with me. Come on. I'm taking you home." I let Dean guide me to his apartment which was not far from my own. We walked up the stairs. Once in his apartment I informed Dean that I didn't think I would be working at the club anymore. I knew that what had happened was not his fault or anyone else's fault. "I knew something bad was going to happen", Dean had said, "I saw that man in the club. The other guy was flirting with his wife. That guy ain't never gonna be welcome into Club A again, I can tell you that!"

I took a shower and Dean went out to get some whiskey and soda. When he came back with the whiskey I was dried and in a bathrobe and under the covers of his bed. He poured me a drink and I drank it. At that precise moment I knew I was probably going to move away from New York. Perhaps I'd go to California. Would Dean come with me?

The answer of course was 'no'. Dean could not come with me. For a long time I kept hope against hope that he might move to be with me anyhow. Our wonderful romance was over but I cried for years over Dean. Love never dies. I went back to stay with my mother and stepfather for a little while which just made things worse since my mother didn't want me married to Dean nor to anybody else for that matter. My younger step-sister Jenna was still at home finishing high school. Bless her heart. She watched me cry for days, *for weeks*, over losing my relationship with Dean due to circumstances out of my control. The FBI called me at my mother's house. The FBI! I was stunned. How did they even get my number? Did I have any information I could give them? No, in fact, I didn't. The man hurt (most assuredly killed….murdered…) by the jealous husband, would have had his case reported by the hospital to the police.

As for Gotti and Dean and Ernie.. did I realize that Mafioso was not a description of character but actually meant the New York Italian Mafia? Yea, I finally got it. I'd figured it out. The fact is, however, not once did I see any of those people ever do anything even remotely illegal. They were all very thoughtful and polite and kind to me. I had spent an extraordinarily happy year in New York City! Save not but the bum cattle calls for the entertainment biz and save not but that horrible last night at work with that poor dear man attacked. Sorrow was nevertheless determined not to be a stranger to my destiny. Danger loomed annoyingly around the purple flower-covered corners of my future fate.

SIXTEEN

ANCIENT FRIENDS

The brownies turned out to be marijuana brownies. Hippy brownies. Groovy psychedelic chocolate yummies. This was a complete and utter surprise to me. Getting ready to go to work at Ancient Friends Bookstore and Seminar Center, I hummed back and forth between two years of popular song. Somehow I was mixing last years favorite "The Future's So Bright I Gotta Wear Shades" by Timbuk 3, and this years 1987 hit "Walk Like An Egyptian" by the Bangles. Both songs were great because they were fun. I found myself singing "Walk like an Egyptian, bowng banga bong bowng, I had a freaky teacher who wore dark glasses, she said my future's so brrrright..I gotta wear shades!" This singing that was such a consistent part of my personality blended with the memories of the weekend.

I had moved from New York City to Hollywood, California. I rode on the airplane with non-stop streaming tears over leaving behind my beloved Dean. I had asked him to go away with me, but alas, he was chained to Manhattan. The last acting "cattle-call" for a movie lead part in New York had ended with yet another slap in my face to remind me that only people who are *someone* and know 'somebody' get into the movies. Thus Hollywood would be my next try in spite of that fact. And so my little 'nobody' and 'no-one' lily-white butt had moved to California and landed a job at Ancient Friends Bookstore and Seminar Center in old Pasadena. Ancient Friends lay on Holly Street. The name reminding me of my old beloved friend, I had walked into the place. Within ten seconds of being in Ancient Friends I was offered a job (by a woman I would come to care for deeply and dearly) who said to me as I picked up a crystal, "You need a job, don't you?" (I nodded my head 'yes'.) She continued saying, "You're supposed to work here at Ancient Friends. You can start...*right now.*"

And so I allowed the woman, named Irene, to show me around the store. Her chestnut hair was thick and cut very short. Her skin had a natural olive tan that flattered her almond colored eyes. She had to be five foot eight tall, and her clothes were lovely. She wore a flapping green Mexican skirt, a long sleeved shirt of shiny gold, green and brown. A cream colored shawl hung over her left shoulder. The jewelry decorating Irene's face, neck and hands were made of turquoise. Also around her neck hung a large crystal that came to a tapered point. She appeared so mystical and lovely.

Anyhow, that was when I'd started my first day of work at Ancient Friends. And I did indeed begin work at Ancient Friends within ten minutes of having walked into the store. The store was fairly narrow and elongated; ending in a moderately sized seminar room. The blue-green carpet that ran throughout the store was covered with shelves that had a variety of mysterious books, tapes, videos, and crystals. The books and tapes promised insight into the strange workings of the universe and the human (and animal) soul.

You're wondering about the brownies, aren't you? Well that chocolate surprise was provided by David, a thin, not very tall, white young man with blonde hair. Over a year ago he had come to one of the seminars I'd taught. I had been giving seminars on the scientific theorems I'd been working on since childhood. Friendship bloomed quickly between David and I. I had a crush on him but he never made any attempts to go past our friendship. We were on our way one Saturday to one of the best California theme parks. David was driving. "Oh phooey", I said, "I forgot to take my vitamins this morning." I had the day off but found myself missing Ancient Friends.

"Oh I've got vitamins." David was driving. His elbow rested on the open window and the blustery wind tossed his hair up and down.

I was surprised by what he said. "You've got vitamins?"

"Oh yeah. I always carry them with me." He took his hand off the wheel for a second to scratch his knee through his faded blue jeans. "They're in that pouch over there in the back seat."

Unbelting myself, I turned onto my knees, pulling my short flowered sundress back over my blue cloth shorts. Reaching over I grabbed the pouch sitting in the back seat. Straightening back out I put my seatbelt back on and unzipped the pouch in my lap.

"Go ahead." David made a singular nod upwards of his chin. "You can have some of my vitamins. I don't mind. I've got some niacin in there. Niacin is really good for you."

"It is?"

"Oh yeah, it's great for the nervous system."

"Okay." I took out a multivitamin, two vitamin C 1000mg, and three 250mg niacin. I popped the entire amount of vitamins in my mouth, took a swig of my bottled water, and swallowed the whole thing. "Thanks."

"No problem."

Now if you've ever taken niacin without eating first, you can guess what happens next. Within ten minutes my skin flushed bright red. Pain seared across every inch of the skin covering my body. I felt like I was on fire!

"Aaaack!!", I screamed. "It feels like I've got a sunburn!"

"Yeah I can see it. You're all bright red!"

"Aaahhh!" I hollered again. "What's wrong with me? Oh my gosh! I'm on fire! I'm on fire!" I took my seat belt off of my shoulder and began bouncing up and down on the seat. Waving my hands over my arms and face, I then pulled down the passenger-side visor and peered into the mirror. I was the color of a ripe red tomato. "Oh do something! Oh help! Aaaaahh! What's wrong with me?" Panic curled, slithered, and thrashed through my spine and in my brain.

"Didn't you eat anything this morning Suzanna?"

Panicking, waving my arms, and bouncing up and down, I answered him in a strained, high-pitched voice. "No!! No!! I didn't eat anything this morning! I wasn't hungry! *WHY!!"*

"Grab that bag in the back seat! It's got some brownies in it. I made some brownies for us to eat. It's the niacin, you've got to get food in your stomach."

"You baked brownies?!!"—I practically screamed. So he was a cook; who knew?

I lunged for the back seat and swooped the bag into my hands. Opening the bag before I'd barely gotten myself turned back around, I grabbed two brownies and literally stuffed them into my mouth!

Brownies filled my mouth past capacity, and I had to try and get some water into it so that I could swallow the thick chewy stuff as soon as possible. Swallowing hard and forcing the sweets down my throat with labored gulps I began to become aware of the odd consistency of the food. I grabbed two more brownies and ate them quickly but without stuffing them in all at once. It didn't take long before I began to feel better. The burning sensation was going away. Chewing slower now, I rolled my tongue around the confection. "Hey", I said to David, "they taste kind of…" How could I find the right words? "They taste sort of like they've got…. like they have…*hay* in them."

"Oh yeah, that's the pot."

"What?" Turning to look at him, I spit what was in my mouth into my hand and dropped the remaining piece of brownie I was holding back into the paper bag. "Do you mean in 'pot' like as in marijuana?" I began to examine the chewed bit sitting damply in my palm.

"Yes. Of course." He took in a long look at me. "You mean you've never had pot brownies before?"

No, I had never had pot brownies before. I wasn't sure what to expect. But I can tell you this… the landscape looked more beautiful than ever before. The sky had never looked so blue, nor the clouds so fluffy and sugary. David ate some of the brownies too. We stopped at a park and just talked, or sometimes stayed silent, for a long time while enjoying the beauty of the landscape and the wind. We never went into the theme park which turned out to be closed that day anyway.

So here I was thinking about my weird weekend and singing songs to myself while I got ready for work. The clock said eight a.m. I was renting the back part of a house that used to be used as a children's day care. The room's two side walls had large windows with no curtains. I had to change clothes in the large closet that had an industrial sized working sink. I heard the phone ring in the living room that I shared with my landlord. I could tell by the shout from the young lady whom was my landlord that it was another prank phone call. Opening the door from my large room I walked into the living room. The phone began to ring, *again*. Jenny, my very skinny landlord, flung her long dark brown hair around and growled at the telephone.

"It was another breather!" Jenny shouted. "I hate that!"

"Here, let me answer it this time." Walking to the side table I picked up the receiver of the ringing phone. The stalker was barraging me with phone calls that had become so common place after so many years that it had become more annoying than menacing.

"Hello?" I asked upon taking the receiver. Pause. Silence. Breathing. "Hello? You know, if you've got a wrong number, or you're just being weird, either way you need to stop calling." What else was there for me to say? I hung up the phone.

"The breather again?" Jenny asked this question with concern on her face.

"Yes." I shrugged. "Don't worry about it. These stupid phone calls happen all the time. I've always had them, everywhere I've ever lived."

"Everywhere?"

"Yes. Everywhere. Since I was a kid." I turned and began walking back through the living room. "Everywhere I've lived that's had a phone, that is. It's probably just wrong numbers." Grabbing the door handle to my room I gave a one hand wave to Jenny. "I've got to get to work."

Closing my door, I turned and stubbed my toe on a trash bag full of clothes and old items I'd been meaning to take to the local shelter. I left my room via the door that opened onto the back yard and drove to work.

Once at Ancient Friends I propped open the front door to the store and put out the welcome stand. The day went quickly as always. There was always an interesting person to meet who came into Ancient Friends. People asked me questions about books or tapes. Some people just wanted to tell their story. Sweet music in flowing rhythm's with whale song and chimes soothed both myself and the customers. Day turned into night time without my hardly noticing. It was to be a long but nevertheless interesting night at work too, since a seminar was scheduled to take place in the back of the carpeted store. About twelve people showed up for the eight p.m. seminar, which was a pretty good amount. Spending most of the night walking back and forth between the store and the seminar room, I was enjoying the atmosphere. Listening to the gentle music playing in the main part of the store was a pleasure.

It was nearly ten p.m. before the seminar about channeling ones higher self began coming to an end. I'd closed the front door earlier that afternoon, and so preparing for the people that would soon be leaving, I went and propped the front door back open again. Staring at the carpet as I walked over to the large chair in front of the bookcase, I sat down. Running my fingers through my shoulder length blonde hair and straightening my yellow dress, I sighed and waited for the people to come out of the seminar room. A big bee came buzzing and zooming through the front door and landed on the back of my chair. The bee made a few buzzing noises and then lunged off the chair, airborne; flying a perfect loop and circling straight towards me. Buzzing right up in my face, I laughed at seeing the bee up so close. Circling my head and buzzing it then came back to stay in the air right in front of my face again. Airborne once more for just a moment, the bee landed on my ear! It tickled. Crawling around on my ear the bee buzzed so loud that even the sound tickled. "Goofy bee!"—I said out loud with a laugh and a smile. It was a big fat fuzzy looking bee. I put my hand up to the side of my head and the bee crawled onto it. Walking around on my hand, the bee looked to be searching for nectar. Scratching on the center of my palm for a while the bee then settled down and stopped moving. Blowing a soft breath on him didn't spur the bee to move.

Blowing again I gained nothing. Finally I used my pointer finger of my other hand to gently nudge him. He buzzed. I nudged again.

Standing up and lifting his head, the bee began to buzz some more. Asleep! The bee had gone to sleep! Looking at him closely I mumbled, "That's interesting. You're a cutie." Airborne once more, the bee made one last circle of the room, then flew out the door into the starry night.

The people from the seminar then began shuffling through the room and out the door. They were all completely silent, which was unusual. Yet it was pleasing that they moved so quickly. I really didn't want to have to hang around and figure out pleasant ways to suggest that they might want to go ahead and leave.

The man who had directed the seminar stood at the door looking up at the night sky. Wearing a very large beige-white shirt that fell past his hips, he also donned baggy pants of the same color and the same soft smooth cloth. One shiny silver ring was on his index finger and a turquoise ring on the middle finger of his other hand. Around his neck a large necklace of beaded raw turquoise stood out against the beige-white of his shirt. He was a slightly balding man whose behavior, voice, and expressions, were all of a very serious manner. Sitting still in the chair, I simply watched him with curiosity.

Yet I soon felt embarrassingly uncomfortable as he walked over to me and asked, "Did you enjoy the seminar?

"Sorry, I missed the last of it", I said. In my sudden embarrassment I realized I hadn't really given much attention to the seminar this time. "Well, I guess it's time to close up." I closed the front door.

"Yes", drawled the man as he clasped his bejeweled hands together, "May I walk you to your car?"

"I guess so", I said without immediately thinking of what else to say. "I need to check on Irene." I walked to the office with the chubby seminar instructor following behind me. The office door was open. I could tell that Irene had already left. "She's gone already. I just need to lock up."

The man followed me as I locked the front door. Then he and I left the store by the back door, which locked behind me. The seminar instructor walked at my side now, our shoulders almost touching. He leaned in towards my face and said, "When you get angry, sad, or hurt, or even unhappy, your blood pressure changes."

There was a long pause so I felt I was supposed to remark on his comment. "Yes", I said, "You can get stuck in your emotions; and it can effect you physically."

He reached beneath his long beige-white shirt and extracted a cigarette pack and lighter from the pocket of his baggy pants. He pulled out a cigarette and put the pack back into his pocket. There was a clicking sound as he rolled the lighter in his fingers and it hit across his turquoise and silver rings. He lit the cigarette and spoke with a plume of blue-gray smoke coming out of his mouth. "It's like having a bad habit when your stuck in an emotional response."

I opened my car door and placed my purse on the front drivers seat. I started to get in my car when I realized I had left my diary in Ancient Friends. "Oh!"—I said. "I left my dairy inside the seminar center. I've got to go back and get it. Thank you for walking me to my car though; I appreciate it."

"Are you going to be alright?" He spoke with another plume of smoke circling from his lips.

"Yes." I waved a friendly dismiss with my hand as I locked my car. "I'll be fine. The parking lot is right here. It's close, and I do this every night anyway." Lifting up my chin I looked at the seminar instructor and nodded to him while giving him a smile. "Thank you." I marched back to Ancient Friend's back door; I unlocked it and went inside. At the front of the store beside the register lay my diary. Picking up the diary and tucking it under my arm I walked towards the back of the store again. Stopping at the restroom I decided I had better 'go' while I was here since I could already feel the fullness of my bladder. So I walked inside the restroom and used the facility, then I washed my hands and reflexively checked my hair in the mirror. Then with my diary in tote I left Ancient Friends by the back door that opens onto the parking lot.

When I got outside the seminar instructor was gone, as I had expected. Then as I made my way closer to my car a horror flooded over me and caused me to stop stone dead in my tracks. It looked like the windows to my car had been rolled *down*! Yet how could it be? I had very specifically locked my car and even had checked that the windows were rolled up before I left to go get my diary. Adrenalin flooded my blood. My heart pounded.

I moved even closer to the car and was stricken to realize both windows were open. Coming up to put my hand on the car door, I looked for glass. There were no broken cubes or spiky shards of glass….both windows of my car had been rolled down! The windows were rolled up and the car had been locked when I'd left it!

Trepidation caused me to tremble as I peeked fearfully into the front seat where I had left my purse. My purse was gone! Purse panic! Frantically I searched underneath the car seat. Suddenly I heard the shaking musical sound of a wooden rattle; as an Indian rattle. I paused for a moment then decided to ignore it. I looked under the car; I was frantic for my purse and wouldn't feel satisfied driving off without having checked about for it. All the while the sound like old shaman rattles used by Native American Indians kept on flowing forth their seedy sound. The sound was creepy but this is California, near Hollywood at that, so I didn't bother myself with the incessant rattling noise. My head hung down as I poised just inside the cars driver seat; I placed my face in my hand with resignation and despair that my car had been somehow broken into and that my purse was gone.

Then I heard a male voice laughing and say, "Poor girl! Sorry! Huh-ungh. It's gone! He's not there, and the purse is gone! Oops; huh?" Confusion wafted through my brain and I lifted up to look and see whom was speaking; I hit the top of my head against the inside of the car. It hurt.

Rubbing my head I pulled myself out from my car to look behind me where the laughing and taunting and rattling was coming from. My first thought was that it had to be a crude joke. But the mask! I stood dumbfounded as I looked at a man (who stood under the street lamp and was in pretty good physical shape) in the alley from the parking lot standing completely naked except for a loin cloth type of *diaper* on his privates. He had two Indian rattles, one in each hand, that he was shaking. And he was wearing a Halloween mask like a demon or devils head. He shook the rattles and laughed! I was terrified and furious both at the same time. Natural instinct tugged me from my fear and confusion and said: *Crazy man !—RUN!!*

Darting in a cold sweat for the back door of Ancient Friends, my heart pounding, I fumbled anxiously with my key ring for the correct key to the lock. I found the correct key and realized disconcertingly that I was feeling light-headed and faint from the fear. Placing the key in the lock I pulled back my key ring into the palm of my hand and shot like a rocket back inside the store. The door would automatically lock from the outside when closed.

Sitting on the blue-green carpeted floor I just waited there until I had relaxed and got my breathing back down to normal. I should call the police! Breath; just breath. Relax your muscles.

As the fear began to trickle away I lifted to my feet and put my hand on the door. Breathing in deeply through my nose I reached hold of the handle and then let the breath come pouring out of my mouth. Opening the door in one quick hard pull I peeked out to look into the alley. The crazy man wasn't there.

Suddenly I got the urge to make it to my car. I took in another breath for momentum. Flying out from behind the door I ran across the very small parking lot, swung open my car door, and instead of hopping in my car seat as I'd planned I simply stood there a couple of seconds and just stared. My purse had been put back in my car in the drivers seat!

Confusion abated as fear of the crazy man with the rattles who was wearing a diaper flooded over me again. Grabbing my purse I flung it into the passenger seat, closed my doors and locked them, rolled up my windows while starting the ignition, and I was out of there. "Oh my gosh that was weird", I said as I backed out of the parking lot and headed home. When I got home I checked my purse; it was intact. Nothing had been stolen; not even the few dollars I had left in my wallet. It would appear I had been frightened and nearly had my purse stolen by a man wearing an ugly mask and dressed up like *a great big scary baby!*

CHAPTER SEVENTEEN

HUSH

My experiences in California led me to the decision that I needed a break. I was running away from the stalker yet again. Or at least running away from something. So I phoned my friend Kristi in Waco, Texas and told her I was going to come live in Waco for the summer so she and I could goof off and have some greatly needed fun.

Oh yes, we did have fun. To celebrate my arrival in Waco Kristi threw a party. I was staying with Kristi in the house that she and her husband shared, and Kristi and I had spent the better part of two hours running about the house putting on make-up and fixing our hair, painting our fingernails, and choosing what to wear for the party.

Night-time fell and hordes of interesting and unusual people I didn't know filled up the house and the front porch, the front yard, and the back yard. Music pounded the house while in the living room many of the guests (myself and Kristi included) read out loud our own personal poetry favorites. Unbeknownst to me I had been purposely watched by a very certain man on the night of that first party. And unbeknownst to me, my life would change forever because of it.

It was a summer of parties and silliness. Kristi and I took picnics. We flew kites in the park on windy days. One blustery afternoon a tree full of summers engorged green leaves took permanent hold of Kristi's kite. We both laughed until it hurt when we saw that the tree had eaten her kite. I was reminded of the cartoon character Charlie Brown who could never seem to keep his kite away from the voracious trees. Oh yes, it was a lovely summer that still held the magic of happiness and true friendship.

I had noticed the huge rickety plantation home that was across the street from Kristi's house was not just old and dilapidated but also empty and abandoned. So I went to the city to find out who owned the aging run-down plantation home. Within one week of moving to Waco I had secured the rental of one of the abandoned homes gigantic rooms. The house did not have a telephone in it anywhere. I knew exactly which room I wanted. The room I wanted was delicious! I wanted the room with the six foot long and two and a half foot deep antique claw-foot tub. Mmmmm, what a bubble bath of pure pleasure and relaxation could that tub give me!

On the day that I was to move into the gigantic room of the spacious home, I waited across the street on the steps of Kristi's porch until my parents arrived with a dresser drawer they no longer needed. My mother and stepfather, Peggy and Elton Locks, pulled their car up in front of the dilapidated home I would be renting a room in; they had the wood dresser on a trailer attached to their car. Running across the street to greet my parents, I gave them hugs and thanked them for letting me have the old wood dresser. Lugging the suit case that I'd had with me when I was waiting on Kristi's porch I stepped up to the front door of my new residence. For the first time since the city had allowed me to preview the home I placed the key the city had given me into the key hole and unlocked the front door to the house. "Come this way", I said to my parents, and they followed me into the house. "I'll show you the room I'm renting. Oh my goodness", I spoke with excitement, "You're going to love this bath tub! You've never seen such a huge and beautiful claw-foot tub!"

We walked up the stairs and turned to the left of the two upper-floor rooms. I then opened the door to my claw-foot clad house-apartment and there was a young man inside standing there. I stared at the man in deep surprise. How did he get in? *When* did he get in? Should I be afraid? Before me stood a man who looked about my age, in his early twenties. He had blonde hair, honey-white skin, and blue eyes.

Dean had brilliant blue eyes and blonde hair. But Dean had manicured nails; brushed back "Italian style" hair neatly cut and combed. Dean wore keen clothes that were upper-class and expensive. Yet this man standing before me had punked up blonde hair that stood out at all ends and looked like he'd asked an eight year old to cut. He wore old jeans and a much too small black tee-shirt with the name of some punk band I didn't know printed on the chest, and the shirt was torn and full of holes. And he was barefoot.

Dean oozed the exquisite quality that he could protect a girl; this punked and tatter-clothed man before me also wafted with the waves of being a man who could protect a woman. He seemed to have an air of authority. I realized I liked him; how very disturbing. Shaking off that thought I tried to think of what would be the most appropriate thing to say to this stranger. He was standing in my house-apartment! *Who is this guy*?!

"Um, are you here for maintenance?"—I offered towards the stranger.

"What?", he asked.

"Maintenance." I glanced at Elton and Peggy who were standing behind me staring at the stranger just as bewildered as I was. "To fix something before I move in?"

"I'm moving in!" --Said the punker and grungy young man whose blonde hair stuck up in several different directions.

"What?" I asked.

"*What*." Responded the punker guy.

"What..what do you mean?" I was a confused spirit searching for clarification. "What do you mean that you are moving in?"

"I'm moving in!" He seemed exasperated.

"Oh! So am I." I still felt confused. "This particular apartment has a great claw-foot tub."

"Yes. It does."

"Well, I'm Suzanna." I gestured toward my parents and said, "These are my parents, Peggy and Elton Locks."

"How do you do." Stated Peggy.

"Nice to meet'cha!" Smiled Elton who was chewing on a toothpick.

We all waited for a moment but the silence held too long. "And what is your name?" –I asked.

The young man was staring at the floor but lifted up his face long enough to say, "Oh. Jay."

"Nice to meet you Jay", I said with a smile. My parents were smiling also but Jay had a stern, very serious expression. I gestured to Jay with my right hand as I asked where exactly he was staying. "So which room are you renting? The room with the balcony?"

"I'm renting this one!" Jay's attitude was unfortunately rough and a bit perturbed.

"You can't mean this one." I was feeling a sense of anxiety beginning to bubble inside me. "Not this one."

"Yes, this one." Jay offered nothing more.

"Well not this one, with the claw-foot tub?"

"Yes! That's why I want it." Jay smiled. "I love that claw-foot tub. It's great!"

"That's why I want it too. I want the tub. Specifically." Moment of soft pause passing as I sucked in a deep breath. "You can't have this one. I've already rented it; I've paid for it already."

"But I've already paid my money." Jay spoke this so firmly.

I was startled. "On this one? This room?"

"Yes. I've paid my money and this room is mine."

"But it can't be. I'm moving in…*today*."

My parents stepped up closer to my side. "Well, there must be some mistake." --Spoke Peggy with a shake of her head and a lick of her lips.

Elton frowned. "We'll just have to find out from the land-lord which one of you has their name on the lease."

"Can't you take the room next door?" I asked. "It's huge, and has a really great balcony." I hoped by mentioning the balcony this Jay guy would take a different room from the one with the claw-foot tub. "And the rooms downstairs! They're gigantic! And one has a big fireplace that works."

"No." Jay shook his head.

"You're kidding me." I wished he would lift his face up a bit more so I could better look into his eyes. Looking around the room I saw absolutely nothing that looked like someone was moving in. No clothes. No boxes. Nothing. "Where are your things?"

"I only have one box…. It's in the kitchen."

"I didn't see you come in."

Elton stepped forward and took charge. Between gnaws on his toothpick he said, "We'll have to talk to the landlord. We'll just go on down and find out."

"Yes. I think that's right." Peggy spoke up. "Elton thinks we should go see the landlord, and I think that's exactly what we should do." She nodded her head as if saying 'yes'. Putting her hand on Elton's shoulder Peggy said as a statement, "Why don't we do that then."

The punker guy and I were getting nowhere just standing there bickering. So I turned to my parents and affirmed the decision, "Okay." Nodding my head towards Elton I said, "I know where the rental agency is."

"I can drive ya." Elton rolled back and forth on his heels and raised his eyebrows. His eyes sparkled with a bit of amusement over the situation.

Peggy looked worried and concerned, and even a bit disgusted at this weird barefoot stranger. "That's it." Peggy placed her hand reassuringly on my shoulder. "I'll take you there Suzanna. Elton and I will take you." She pressed her lips tightly together.

"Okay." I tried to muster a smile for my parents.

Elton shook his head and tisked at Jay. "Come on, let's get this taken care of. I want us to head back for home before it gets dark."

My parents and I stepped back toward the door. Turning back around I questioned Jay, "Do you have a car?"

"Yes." Jay looked down at the floor again.

"You know how to get there?" I squinted at him.

"No."

"No?!" Jay's answer completely surprised me. "You don't know how to get there?!
You don't know how to get to the place that rents the rooms here?"

"No."

"Well", said Elton tartly, " you can just follow behind us in your car then. Come on, let's go." Elton tisked again and ushered Peggy and I out of the room.

He must have made the rental by telephone, I thought as I tried to reason the situation. Jay raised his left arm in the air with his palm and fingers of his hand sideways as if in a karate chop. "Alright", Jay said curtly and followed along behind us until we were all out of the house.

Elton got into the drivers seat of his comfortable boxy car and Peggy got in the passengers seat while I climbed into the back. We all sat looking backwards until we saw the young punker Jay in a loud and dilapidated car behind us. I gave directions to Elton; pointing with my finger. The rental company was only several streets away. We pulled into the cement lot and parked near the entrance. Elton kept the car running until he saw the young man Jay exit his car; next Elton turned off the ignition and we all hopped out and headed for the establishment. Then with a strong thick tenseness in the air Jay and I took the lead to get to the door first. Jay and I grabbed at the door handle at the same time and sort of opened it together. All four of us marched into the medium sized place of business.

At the counter I had the young female clerk with the short brown hair look up the information to find out who paid on the claw-foot tub apartment first.

"I'm sorry", the clerk said shaking her head while gazing into a big heavy book. "But it looks like you both rented the room on the same day." She placed her index finger on a spot of the book and peeped up at us with an apologetic look. The clerk said in a high-pitched voice, "We have other rooms for rent in that house."

"How did you make such a mistake?" Elton asked, coming to my aid.

"I want the one with the claw-foot tub." I vocalized in frustration towards Jay.

"So do I!" Grumped Jay. He and I squinted at one another with anger.

I could see I wasn't going to get anywhere with this. So with a sigh and a bow of my head I conceded. "Okay." I bit my lip and looked at the clerk. "He can have the apartment with the tub. I'll take the one with the balcony." Turning to the stranger named Jay I shook my finger at him. "But I get to use that claw-foot tub sometime!"

Jay shook his head with affirmation and the situation was resolved. Late that very afternoon after I was moved in and Elton and Peggy had left, the young punker named Jay said he'd like to cook me some dinner to sort of make up for what had happened. But he said he'd have to cook in my apartment because, as he said, "Because my apartment doesn't have a stove, but yours does." I had simply responded with, "Okay, I guess I aught to get to know my neighbor anyway."

So on my very first night in my new apartment the guy with the blue eyes and punkish blonde hair cooked dinner for me in my room with a balcony. It was surreal; and I still hadn't completely gotten over my disappointment at not getting the room with the claw-foot tub. This new neighbor called Jay Jared dance-bounced in front of the stove in my kitchen. A grin warming his face Jay said, "I love cooking. Well, when I'm cooking for other people."

I hadn't asked what he was making yet. I wasn't one to talk much if I didn't have too. And if you wait long enough when you're with other people somebody else will say exactly what you had on your mind anyway. So I sauntered to the window in the living room and looked out upon the balcony and roof. I watched the sun setting into early evening shadows for a while before going back into the kitchen to see what he was making for dinner. Wearing a gypsy skirt with rhinestones on it, and a sleeveless black and gray top of light material with brocade, I snuck up behind Jay. I was barefoot; my silver bangles on my right wrist jangled. "What are you cooking?" I leaned past his shoulder and peered into the pan on the stove. "It smells wonderful." He swirled around to face me and with lightening speed quickly kissed my nose. I was stunned. What was my response supposed to be here? Looking from the corner of my eye to the ceiling I tried to think. Then I glowered from the ceiling to the floor. Not knowing what else to do I simply took two steps backwards and turned my observations back to his face. "Ummm, what are you making? It smells good."

"Smell a little cinnamon?" He asked.

"Mmm, yeah, actually. Smells great."

"I almost forgot the onions though. Good thing I finally thought of them before I left the store. I felt so hungry for …I don't know… something different. So this is gonna be a middle-eastern thing. Like something you might eat in Egypt."

I nodded. "Cool." Then I leaned in and closed my eyes and breathed in the intoxicatingly spicy aroma.

Jay nibbled a taste of his fare from a spoon then swung his arms and did a sort of 'happy dance' in front of the stove. "You hungry little girl?"

"Starving." I couldn't help but smile and laugh a bit over the antics of his dance.

"I should have cooked the onions first in the olive oil." He was smiling and pleased with his exotic meal simmering in the pan. "But it'll turn out alright though. Because I added the onions with the tomatoes and red peppers, so the juice makes a kind of paste. Then I put in fresh dates. Started the saffron rice cooking… added the rest of the juices. You know, stirred it in. I love peppers!" He raised his arm for me to inspect. "You see that? You see the hairs raise up on my arms?"

I inspected his arm and indeed the hairs were standing up. "Yes."

"That happens every time I even *think* about peppers. The hair on the back of my neck stands up too!"

"Ohhhh." Cocking my head I leaned in and looked at the back of his neck. "Yes, I see."

"Oh! And garlic. Garlic and cinnamon and cumin."

"Mmmm", I sounded out with approval. "It's scented the entire house."

"Scented it. Oh yes. Like incense. All it needs to do now is simmer. I've got it simmering. Should be good."

We stared at each other. I looked at the kitchen ceiling again. "I think I'd like to put Christmas lights on the ceiling."

Jay also looked up at the ceiling, "Chili pepper lights."

"Hey, I like that! Chili pepper lights would be great!"

"I can put them up there for you if you like."

"Okay…well…", shrugging and smiling I continued, "okay, I guess you could put them up there for me if you like. I'd appreciate that actually."

Jay lifted the pan off the stove. "It's ready to eat!" Jay set the pan to rest just off of the burner. He went over to my refrigerator and peered into it. "I don't know why I'm looking into your fridge again. All you've got in here are seaweed and some lentils. Weren't you planning on ever eating?"

"Actually, I hate cooking. But I think it's great that you do. I wish I liked cooking but I just don't."

"No soda?"

"No. Sorry. But I have some Perrier in the cabinet." Pointing with my index finger I directed Jay, "There. The top one to your left."

"That'll work." He pulled the large bottle of Perrier from the cabinet and set it on the table. "Cups?"

"In that cardboard box on the counter I have some plastic cups and stuff."

"Plates?"

"Oh I've already got them out there. They're paper plates." I gestured towards the counter. Suddenly I thought about the other items in the cardboard box. "You know, I do have a couple of ceramic plates in the box there. And some silverware." In the box I had the ceramic plates, red plastic cups, and silverware adding up to two forks, four spoons, and five knives.

Jay pulled out two plates and two forks and set them on the small table in the little kitchen. He remembered then to turn off the stove and he brought the aromatic pan full of food to the table and scraped it's contents onto the plates in large spoonfuls. Next he placed two red plastic cups next to the plates and poured them full of Perrier. We sat down to eat and I complimented him on the deep cinnamon and saffron flavored dish. It tasted so wonderful that I felt a thrill at the flavors rolling across my excited taste buds. The meal all salty-sweet spice. Succulent. Luscious. Appetite satisfying. It's scent wafting dark and exotic.

"I'll have to make you some of my famous chili."

"Uh-oh", I thought.

"I'll make it with tofu."

"Uh-oh", I thought again but didn't say anything.

"The trick to my chili is the cheese and real butter. And I cook the bell peppers…every single color of bell peppers in beer."

"Oh no!"—I thought. What was I to do? It was as if this man knew that my heart is through my stomach! "I'd like that!"—I blurted out before thinking to restrain myself. I scolded myself; why did I say that!?

"I'll make it tomorrow."

"Okay." I was slain.

"So you're friends with Kristi? Lives across the street?"

"Yes. Do you know her?"

"Know of her."

"So, Jay. Umm, so…" I was trying to initiate conversation. "So what's your favorite childhood memory?"

"Well…" Jay thought about it and took another bite of food. "I think that Michael Lavvy wanted to make a rocket powered car." He laughed. "Bottle rockets and toy cars are one thing", he laughed again. "But it's a good thing we were kids and couldn't make a rocket powered car. We would have blown up the whole neighborhood!"

Now we both laughed. "What about you? What's your favorite memory?"

I thought momentarily then smiled. "Not really a childhood memory but a barely new to adulthood memory. Kristi and I went to a renaissance fair. It was just such a perfect day. Makes it my favorite, you know?"

"Yep."

"So what's your most embarrassing memory?" Smiling, I knew this was a silly question, but it was interesting.

Jay took a few more bites of the luscious food. "Me and some guys were hanging out in the parking lot. This was high school. I had the sweetest car. Sixty-nine camaro. It was stolen…"

"Oh, I'm so sorry."

"Yeah, anyway that's another story. So, we were hanging out in the parking lot. Having a smoke break. And somebody started talking about bombs. And I gave my idea of a really cool bomb. And somehow the word spread around that I had actually made a bomb. And the police came to the school."

"What?" I laughed.

"I had to call my Dad's wife… his wife at the time. He's been married a bunch of times. Anyway, she was a lawyer."

"What happened?"

"Nothing." He took a last bite of his meal then drank some Perrier. "The police figured it out. It was a mistake."

"Wow." I couldn't think of anything else to say for a moment. Then I complimented him on the sultry dark spiciness of the food. "You know I did have a moment that was embarrassing myself…well, I'm not sure if it was specifically embarrassing or just weird." I took a sip of bubbly Perrier. "I was living for a couple of weeks in the warehouse of a theater where they keep all their costumes. I was living there so I could save up money for an apartment. And these other two guys were living there also. It was huge! Costumes everywhere. Anyway, I had bought hot dogs for the night and we all roasted them on wire hangers over a barrel that one of the guys had set on fire outside." I swallowed another bubble filled quaff of the water. "And we ate and then we went back inside the warehouse; we were sitting on some boxes we'd climbed up on; they were piled high. And we were just sitting about for a while talking. On a box down below us was an old cardboard pizza box with some old pizza in it that I know for a fact had been sitting there for over a week. Then here we are talking and this naked guy. Really old wrinkled guy; I mean he looked like he was over one-hundred years old he was so wrinkled from head to toe. This old wrinkly guy naked from head to toe comes walking up pretty as you please like it's no big deal, and he walks up to the pizza box, pulls out a slice, and walks off eating it." Jay and I both laughed. "I asked about it and the one guy I was talking to said, 'Oh, that's Charlie, he's a nudist. You'll see him pass through here from time to time'. Can you imagine!"

"He'd probably been eating old food for so long his stomach was made of steel!" Jay smiled and chortled.

"Yea, right?"—I said. Swirling my fork through the spicy food I then brought a few more bites to my lips and savored the flavor as it burst upon my taste-buds. "You know what?"

"What?"

"When I was a kid…ha..when I was little I used to think that all dogs were the boys and all cats were the girls." Smiling, I giggled at the memory.

"Hey! I used to think that!"

"Really? No way. You're kidding."

"It's true." He looked out the window and sipped a little more from his cup. "I guess one of my best memories is when I was a goofy boy running through the woods and playing games… I used to have this cool fort. We dug a big hole and surrounded it with rocks. We did a really good job. Anyway, I guess I got off the subject…yep! I used to think the dogs were boys and the cats were girls."

"Well what do you know about that… I've never met anybody else before who thought that all the cats were girls and all the dogs were boys when they were a little kid. Kind of weird you thought the same thing I did; when you were a kid." Without thinking I had placed my fingers on his hand when I said this. I realized my mistake and quickly pulled my hand away. He grinned at me. "So", I said thinking. "Sounds like a cool fort you were talking about Jay."

"You bet! We had it all built up. Then when we got older we used to play paint-ball games."

"Oh I've always wanted to play that. It sounds like fun."

"Oh man, we played rough too. We would break up into teams; there was no mercy!"

We talked like this for a long time. His most frightening memory was when his grandfather got drunk and chased his grandmother around with a pool stick; definitely scary. He was into music bands I'd never heard of, like the "Sex Pistols" and the "Ramones." He left for his house-apartment just down the hall from mine late that night with the two of us agreeing that he could make his 'famous' chili using my stove. I was tired but couldn't sleep that night as I lay in bed and read from a book until the morning sun began painting the sky in sprays of yellow and various wispy hues of orange, pink, and blue. Songs of the crickets were still being sung outside, although softer and gentler. The cushy round pillow beneath my head and the silky smooth sheets felt good. My favorite blanket pressed against my side and draping over one arm felt soft and voluptuous. Sleep finally and alluringly called to me at last. This new apartment would bring me peace from the stalker because it did not have a phone. Surrounded by a silence then I allowed myself to sleep. I dreamed I could fly.

The next day in the middle of the afternoon while Jay was out buying things to make his chili, my friend Kristi came over and informed me there were only two tiny kittens left unclaimed from the litter her cat had. Did I want one?

Kristi and I walked downstairs from my apartment and out into the bright sunny day. I immediately wished I'd worn sunglasses. Just then Jay pulled up in his car and he inquired what we were up to. He followed Kristi and I across the street to Kristi's sprawling ancient house to look at the kittens. The two last kittens were in the front yard hopping through the grass that grew to the height of their ears. It was a boy and a girl kitten; both were pure black. Gathering up both mewling fuzz-balls into my arms, I declared them both as belonging to me. I would name them Aida and Ivan. In honor of Vladimir Nabokov's book called "Aida".

* * * * *

Not too much time would pass before fate would find Jay and I as a couple. We moved into an apartment in Austin, Texas. The two sleek black cats, Aida and Ivan, grew up with us together. Kristi would divorce her husband and leave Waco only to discover herself also in Austin. Kristi would have a new love in her life whom in her future she would eventually marry and bear his child. Amour ran rampant then for Kristi and I and it seemed our men loved us back. Because Jay and I had a phone in our apartment in Austin the stalker continued to menace me with harassing and sometimes purely silent calls. It was an unwelcome and menacing result of having telephone service.

I would wake one Saturday morning to see both cats, Aida and Ivan, cuddled across the top of Jay's head. They were oblivious to Jay's freight-train snoring. Stretching as I woke up, I smiled at the sight of the cats on Jay's head. He too woke up then and he saw the cats through his sleepy eyes. He smiled and pointed at the warm fur-balls on his noggin, "Look at this!"

"Yes; I saw." I said to him. "Hey, I wonder if we can find Aida's pet mouse today."

Ivan had brought his little sister Aida a baby mouse. The silly thing was that Aida did not eat the mouse. Aida had made the baby mouse her pet! Yes, a cat with a pet mouse! The last we'd seen of the baby mouse it was wet with cat slobber. Aida had licked and cleaned the tiny mouse as if it were her baby. There wasn't so much as a scratch on the mouse. I had seen Aida carrying her pet mouse around the house by the nape of it's neck. As if it were her kitten she was very careful with it.

Jay and I had both watched Aida cuddle the mouse between her paws, not a claw out. Neither Jay nor I could catch the mouse because Aida would stuff her pet underneath the couch when we came near. She was protecting it. She would bring it bits of her cat food too. We did not locate the mouse that particular morning although Aida was suspiciously standing sentinel at the edge of the couch. So Jay and I took a walk through the botanical gardens that day. All of nature in the botanical grandeur quivered with beauty. Then after we left the gardens Jay bought a bag of oranges from a man standing next to a stoplight. We ate the oranges while taking a very slow hike through the hills. When we returned home Jay was wishing he didn't have to go to work that night. We ambled into our apartment and I went to the kitchen to get a glass of water. "Hey!", I heard Jay shout from somewhere in the living room.

"What is it, Jay?"

"I found the mouse!" Jay hollered with excitement at seeing the mouse and I ran into the living room to check it out. Jay was bent over at the back of the couch. Aida was carefully cleaning it; getting all that loose mouse fur in order to help her dear mouse-child from any unfortunate occurrence of hair-balls. And so it was that when Jay got it into a jar it had neatly sleeked fur, a little wet with cat slobber but nevertheless looking as though it had been keenly groomed. It was just a baby. Jay and I talked soothingly to the little tyke. Jay took the nicely groomed baby mouse outside, and when the jar was opened to the mouse's freedom it was hesitant to leave and only timidly sniffed its way out into the grass. Underneath the evening stars the mouse flicked it's whiskers and finally took off into the world.

Jay and I had seen the end of the nineteen-eighties together with the passing of the cold war with the destruction of the Berlin wall. We had seen the ninety's come rushing in with the wave of change as people became conscious of the internet, cellular phones, fax machines, and pagers, on a wide scale. Yet we received a constant barrage of 'prank' calls from the stalker; he wouldn't end his obsession and leave us alone. I was becoming used to the calls at this point. Jay would fuss and spit every time they happened. The phantom caller seemed to me at this point not so fearsome as just annoying.

Jay left for work that evening after I kissed him goodnight and I expected to spend the rest of my Saturday night lounging and reading a book. It seemed I had barely settled onto the couch with my book to read when the telephone rang. I first thought to let the answering machine get it but then I thought that it might be Kristi so I decided to answer it.

"Hello?" I spoke into the receiver.

"I had to call you." It sounded like a female voice so I did not suspect my annoying caller. Yet it was not a voice I recognized.

"What?" I felt confused. "Who is this?"

"That doesn't matter. I had to call you."

"Who is this?" I switched the receiver to my other ear. "I don't understand. What is this about?"

"Uhhm, I'm from the comptroller's office."

"Comptroller?"

"Yes. You've got to gather up your strength and just write it; write the book."

"Write? What?" I had some sort of loony on the phone.

"Write the book." The woman cleared her throat.

"What book?"

"Listen. There's a church with a little chapel outside with two angel statues in it. Just go there and clear your mind. You'll know what to write."

This was insane. I was beginning to hate the telephone. The woman hung up before I could even think of what to say. Completely perplexed, I stared at the receiver for a moment. "Well that's weird", I said and then hung up the phone. I'd barely begun to settle back onto the couch with my book to read when the phone rang again; I felt angry now. Quickly turning to look in the direction of the telephone I blinked for a couple of rings before hopping up to answer it.

"Hello?" —I asked.

A man's voice frightened me saying, "Strange. Strange, isn't it?"

"What?" I couldn't think of what to say or what to ask; I felt horrified. It was the stalker.

The man spoke in a sinister voice; he kept repeating the same thing. He said, "Strange. Strange. Strange." The man practically growled. "Strange; isn't it? Strange."

I slammed the receiver down in a terrified gulp for air. With my hand still on the receiver the phone rang again. My body stiffened. I lifted the receiver then slammed it back down again. I waited a second then tentatively bent down and lifted the receiver to my ear. I heard a dial tone.

My heart raced as I urgently dialed Jay's work number. He answered the phone with a flustered and exasperated voice, "Can I help you?"

"Jay I just had a really weird call and then a really scary call right after it."

"It's probably just another of those prank calls we get all the time. Look, I'm very busy. I haven't even started the audit yet. Can't this wait 'till later? Look I really got to get back to work."

My heart was thrumming so hard that it was difficult to breath. "Well…I'm…I'm frightened."

"We'll talk about it when I get home; sorry, but I've got to go, I'm really busy."

"Oh."

"Okay, great." He hung up the phone.

He was busy; I understood. But I felt such a wave of fear that I felt literally dizzy. I needed to get some air. Running through the living room I headed for the door; grasping the doorknob, I flung the door open for some fresh air. "OH!", I yelped. There was a man standing there. The surprise of not expecting a person to be there was enough, but the dizziness from my previous fright was overtaking me and I had to sit down right there in the doorway.

"Excuse me", I said to the guy with embarrassment in my voice, "I'm feeling dizzy." I simply assumed he was one of the many people who dwelled in the apartment complex. He looked a lot like the muse I had met in the library so many years ago in my childhood; but it couldn't be the same person of course, there didn't look to be enough years of age having passed on his face.

"That's alright", he spoke with such a medium-deep and warm, mellow voice. He bent down to look at me, balancing on the balls of his feet and two fingers of his left hand touching the concrete. He seemed sincerely concerned about my gulps for air. While I simply felt embarrassed I gravely wished he wasn't there. He had a sly grin and he was handsome. His dark brownish-black straight hair fell over his ears with bangs over his eyebrows. He was young enough; his skin was a healthy olive shade. The man was dressed in black, or a very dark brown; with a trench-coat that hung to his ankles. "You alright?", he asked. You know anything about hypoglycemia? I know what you're experiencing. I've been through it myself."

"Well that would be a coincidence." I said with a bit more sarcasm in the sound of my voice than I meant to express. He smiled, but didn't say anything. "This feeling is horrible!" I kept concentrating on taking deep slow breaths.

He said: "Well I've been through this. It's the most horrible feeling in the world."

"Like you're falling?"

"Yes." Bright eyes sparkling, he smiled slightly. Although he came across with a genuine kindness, concern, and relaxed calm, he also seemed to be amused.

"You think it's what? Hypoglycemia? You have it?" Confusion gnawed at me. It was certainly just fear from the phone calls that I was feeling.

He looked straight up towards the sky and said: "Oh. Uh-huh. Hypoglycemia." He sighed. Swiftly and sharply moving his chin downwards, he looked me directly in the eyes, speaking firmly: "I've been through it. Everyone in my family has been through this."

"Wow. That's weird. Your whole family?" I was actually beginning to feel better already. "They all have hypoglycemia?"

Looking at me sternly, and leaning forward, he said with calm but firm intensity: "The worst thing is not knowing what's happening to you."

Staying relaxed and smiling, he spoke to me with that soft warm deep tone of voice: "You'll be fine. The worst thing is just not knowing what is happening to you." He paused. "You might be tempted to take a warm shower or bath, but don't. You could hurt yourself." The man paused a moment and seemed about to laugh, but his expression merely expanded into a wider grin. "You want to know the best thing for it?" He looked at me so intently. "The best thing for it", he paused as if for emphasis, "is sleep." He shifted the weight of his feet. "You need to eat something, then get some sleep."

Looking across the room from where I sat in the doorway my gaze fell upon a box of cherry cordial chocolates. Hopping up to my feet I went quickly over to the coffee table and picked up the chocolates. Popping a cherry cordial in my mouth I figured that one way or the other it couldn't hurt to get some fast energy into my system. I began to walk back towards the door to tell the guy that I appreciated his thoughtfulness. He was gone already. I was disappointed; I wanted to know who this neighbor of mine was. Grabbing a few chocolate cordials in my hand, I set the box back onto the coffee table, then I turned and ran out the door. I chased after him. I wanted to know his name. I hadn't seen him before; he was probably new to the apartment complex.

I didn't see him immediately so I just followed the sidewalk as it curved past the apartments and beside the creek to where the woods met the walk-way. "Hey!"—I called as I saw the back of his head and the movement of his black trench-coat in the woods. He was holding one end of a leash that was attached to a good sized adult dog. "Hey!", I called again. He stopped walking and I caught up to within about fifteen feet of him.

It seemed odd how he still had his back to me after I'd called to him. Squinting my eyes, I looked at him closer. Then he slowly turned to face me. Looking into my eyes he gestured to me by bringing his index finger up to his lips in a motion of: "*HUSH*"!

Quickly he pulled the clasp of the leash from the dogs collar to set the beast free, and waved his right hand forward in some sort of command. The dog was a hefty healthy wolf-like dog, perhaps a mixture of German shepherd and husky. It bounded it's paws into a run and leapt into the air in such a motion towards me that I thought I was being attacked. The dog leapt into the air as it got close to me and I cowered. Instinctively I brought my arms up to shield my face. But the dog soared in it's leap right past me. My head turned in the direction of the dog and my stomach clenched. There was a man who had been standing directly behind me. The dog went for the man. He was a white man wearing jeans and he had no shirt on. He was wearing a Halloween demon mask; the rubbery kind that covers the entire head. The dog hit upon the guy with no shirt. He hollered and then ran off screaming with the snarling dog chasing after him.

Horrified at seeing the man in the mask, adrenaline zoomed through my veins and shot into my heart. Fear propelled me and I shot into a full run. I ran from the woods to the sidewalk; running hard as I passed the creek and rounded the corner to my apartment. My heart pounded out beats of fear so violently that it was audible to me.

Swirling into my apartment I slammed the door shut and locked it. Then I felt worried that someone might have come into the apartment while I was outside. So I cautiously inspected the rooms and turned on all the lights.

Immediately after discerning that there was no one else in the apartment with me I went over to the phone and grabbed hold of it. Stretching forward I snatched up the phone book. Flipping through the pages I located the number for the local police and dialed it. I explained to the police about my situation, and how the problem of the stalker and also of his prank calls had been going on for years. I was stunned to hear the gruff male policeman say that he couldn't help me unless I had proof in the form of a visual or audio recording. This news led me to stammer and sputter out phrases like "How can this be?"

"You want my advice?" The policeman questioned with a crisp, toughened, Texas drawl.

"Yes! Yes! I'd love your advice. Please!"

"Hire a private detective."

"A private detective?"

"Yes, that'll allow us to come in and do our job. You'll have to hire a private detective."

Dejected and disappointed I thanked the officer for his time. The next thing I did was to go set the alarm-clock for nine a.m. I wanted to hire a private detective first thing in the morning. The lights stayed on, glaring away the nights darkness, while I slept fitfully.

When the alarm went off the next morning I found Jay to be deeply sleeping after having come home from the night-shift. Every single light in the house was still on. Pitter-patting into the kitchen and grasping hold of the phone and the phone-book, I ended up calling one private detective after another. Not a single detective had a price I could afford; and every one of them refused a payment plan.

So life went on. The stalkers phone calls went on. Time passed into an even stronger sense of complacency and desensitization towards the unseemly calls. *What could be next?!*

CHAPTER EIGHTEEN

HANDBOOK FOR THE DEAD

The years struggling to be born into the 1990's would pass from the blockbuster movie "The Lost Boys" in 1987, and the Bangles band radio sweep with a song called "Walk Like An Egyptian." Time passing into the popular movie based on the Anne Tyler novel, "The Accidental Tourist" in 1988. And just at the cusp of the 1990's smashing into human history, 1988 would also bring death.

Death of a loved one can be the most difficult thing to overcome. Even the threat of ones own death is as difficult. Years passing by can help, but oh so slowly. Death walked in as an uninvited visitor whose very presence seemed to bring a universal systemic infection for which there could be no relief. My sweet grandmother Oleta Barns would die in 1988. The news of her death fell hard for the entire family. My big sister had called me and told me about her death. Unfortunately I couldn't even gather enough strength to bare the weight of talking on the phone with Mabel after the stomach-punch of that fatal news. So I muttered some nonsensical excuse for not being able to continue talking on the phone with Mabel, and I hung up the phone. I sat down upon the floor feeling stunned and tried to figure out how there could possibly be a world that didn't have Oleta in it. I went to the wake and viewed Oleta's body with a desire to wake the dead. I sat on a bench at the funeral home. When we all got to the cemetery I was unable to get out of the car; I couldn't handle watching them lower her body in its casket down into the earth. So I stayed in the car during the lowering of Oleta's body at the cemetery and watched as rain-drops fell slowly in the cloudy graying sky, landing with soft thumps against the car windows. Time would flush into the 1990's and take itself year after year down into the Rubicon void.

Although time would still pass streaming with it's sorrows and it's joys down the river of life. You can not avoid life's flowing, pulling, Morpheus current. The stalker continued to flow along with my life; it seemed an eternal unavoidable fact. At this point wasn't he most likely harmless?

One phone call from the stalker quite specifically stood out like a burning red flag. His words were so disturbing. "I've got your cat", the stalker said in this specific phone call. "Your cat's name is Ivan. I can see it on his tag." He spoke with a bit of a southern accent I hadn't specifically noticed before. Red flags rose up indeed in my mind; and fear for the safety of my cat surged forward. "I stroke Ivan's balls", said the stalker, "He loves it when I stroke his balls."

YUCK! My stomach felt queasy as this man's words revolted me so deeply. I thought about the private detective I couldn't afford. I thought about the police and wondered if this call about my cat would constitute as enough for them to take notice and help me; to trace his calls. "First of all", I said with statuesque rage heating my blood. I practically shouted as I wagged my left-hand index finger at the receiver. "First of all my cat's have been 'fixed.' So Ivan has been neutered. He *has no balls*! Second of all I'm having this call traced and if you so much as harm a hair on my cat the police will find you and you will spend the rest of your life in jail! You pervert!"

The stalker laughed. He *kept* laughing! Anger and fear soared through my veins as I slammed the telephone receiver down hard! This stranger's obsession seemed endless. Yet I was growing so tired. I ran to my window and waited with the fearsomeness of Quetzalcoatl, standing straight and still and tall until to my relief Ivan did come home within just a few minutes of my vigil.

*   *   *   *   *

Yes, the years ebbed in the undulation of time's breath. The fleeting wisps of the eternal waters of time brought no relief from death. No relief from the stalker. Nor from disappointment or betrayal. If you're a good soul and sensitive to the sufferings of the world, you have to turn your head and look away just to continue to be of any help to yourself or others.

The cat's became a sort of solace as if they were my children. This just barely curbed my desire for a human child of my very own. The older I got the more my hormones fed the need to have children.

On this particular morning I woke up first and jostled Jay's arm to wake him up. He opened his eyes sleepily. There he was, laying near the edge of the mattress with one eye peeping at me while his other eye tried to pull him back down into sleep.

"Good morning Jay, want some breeaack…" (A burp the size of Montana rolled out of my mouth.) How embarrassing! Yet the burp was nothing compared to the sneeze that immediately followed. "Breeaack..*SNIT*!" A high pitched, nose burning, one hundred pound mouse squeaking, kind of sneeze. "Oh!" I put my fingers to my lips and raised my eyebrows. "Excuse me", I said.

Jay raised one eyebrow and squinted the other eye while giving me a surprised expression. Then he slapped one hand against his forehead and fell back onto the bed laughing; uproariously.

Shaking my head and holding my stomach I laughed out loud from sheer embarrassment. Then neither one of us could stop laughing. Jay started poking fun at me by making the most absurd sounding burp and sneeze noises over and over again. This only made the two of us laugh harder. He giggled and 'harred' then came up for air to pretend a burp and a sneeze. Rubbing my ribs in an attempt to stop the stitch that was forming from laughing so hard, I watched Jay roll back over on his side to laugh again. Our laughter ending, Jay popped up on the edge of the bed with tears rolling down his face. One look at the floor and then he nestled his eyes into the crest of his arm. "Ohhhh", he sighed. Then he looked up at me and smiled.

The day was getting off on a goofy foot. We only thought our outburst of laughter was over. We were now sitting at the edge of the bed together as we watched Aida the cat walk over to the bedroom's door frame. Aida huddled down low against the carpet. It was an odd and ominous position. Fur from the middle of her back prickled up; then the prickled fur rolled forward to her shoulders. It happened again. More prickled fur rolling forward towards her shoulders. The prickles became stiffer and Aida made a 'glack glack' sound as she began to dry heave, poor thing. Her whiskers plucked forward with her chin against the floor. Aida's cat ears strained tenuously flat. Then, *BLAATT*, a big slimy gooey wad of eaten rubber bands regurgitated from her stomach onto the carpet.

"OOOooooooo", Jay and I both said in unison. (Then of course, we had to take a second look.) "AAaaauuugh!"—we both moaned; and then at the same time for a brief moment we both covered our eyes with our hands. (Then we both took an even closer look; of course!)

"Vomit with rubber bands in it has a way of making you look at it even if you'd rather not." I said this while shaking my head. Then I bent down on one knee and began to soothingly stroke Aida's fur. "Poor kitty. Don't worry. When its rubber bands you've eaten, you always have a way of bouncing back." Rubber bands; bouncing back. (Oh hardy-harr-harr.)

"I can't believe she ate rubber bands! Where did she get them?" Jay asked this while staring at the curled mess.

"You know that bag of rubber bands I…" We both started to giggle.

"You left the bag open?"

"Yea…I…oh! Oh! Did I tell you about yesterday?"

"I don't think so Suzanna."

"When I went to clean out the litter box, I was nearly scared to death! There it was, half hanging out of a doo-doo…all rubbery and long. I thought for a moment that Aida had gotten a really bad mongo case of some seriously huge worms!"

"And it was the rubber bands!"

"Yes!"

"Well, I guess she's alright!" We both glared with precarious disgust at the pile of regurgitated rubber bands. "Just great…" Jay smiled and coughed and patted his chest., "…do we get to draw straws for who gets to clean it up?" Jay sprang to his feet and went to the bathroom only to return with a swath of toilet paper. He picked up the regurgitation in the toilet paper, then he dropped it in the bathroom trash can and washed his hands. He came back to sit on the edge of the bed with me.

Patting his leg I said, "Thank you." We looked at each other and pressed our shoulders together giggling. Then we both fell over onto the mattress laughing.

Not but a few minutes later we went over to our little girl-kitty and petted her; cooed at her. We fed her some cat treats and massaged her ears. We gave some cat treats to Ivan too; he'd been watching us with the treats the entire time we cooed over Aida.

Jay and I got dressed. Jay put on jeans and a tee-shirt but I had to admit his choice of clothing was at least better; he had also taken to wearing his hair very short and neatly trimmed. I pulled on a light cotton flowered dress. Jay put his hands on his stomach and made a growling sound, then he tugged at his shirt a couple of times as if examining it.

Strolling in hefty muscular steps through the apartment and over to the sliding glass door, he opened the sliding glass and looked outside. He gave a weather report. "It's starting to cloud up! Look at that big one over there. Man, it's huge!" He pointed up into the sky. "Coming this way too. Maybe we should go hiking *tomorrow*. Think it's going to rain." Jay opened the sliding glass door the rest of the way so that I could get out; we both stepped outside onto the concrete porch. Placing his hand over his eyebrows and staring up once again to study the sky he said, "The air is perfect! Now this is the perfect temperature!"

Our male cat, Ivan, leapt onto the patio fence. Front paws hung across the top of the moss-green picket fence, while his furry ears perked up tall and he widened his eyes; his tail flicked! Jay laughed at the curious expression on Ivan's face as he stayed perched on the fence and flicking his tail. The cat looked as if he were in the middle of an army maneuver, stealthily scoping out the enemy before making his decision. Cool gusts of wind blew up from the north, ruffling Ivan's fur. He raised his small wet cat nose and sniffed.

Scratching the underside of Ivan's soft chin Jay asked the cat, "Do you smell rain little puma?"

Walking across to join Jay and Ivan I said, "Yes, he does smell rain."

Jay cocked his head at Ivan then glanced over at me and smiled. "He's such a good cat."

"Yes he is. All our furry babies are precious."

Ivan perched at the top of the fence. Jay rubbed the inside of Ivan's ears and said to the cat, "You can be a stinker sometimes or get into things but we love you." More ear scratching. "Have you been out chasing mice?" Funnily, Ivan squinted his eyes at Jay, blinked, then let out an extended meow that ended with his small pink sand-paper tongue stretching out of his mouth in a wide-mouthed yawn.

"Oh! Is that right?" Jay asked Ivan. "Did you hear that 'mom'? Your furry son says he's been out chasing mice."

"I heard him. Think I smelled his kitty-mouth mouse-breath from here."

"Do you have mouse-breath Ivan?"

"Yep! He sure does Jay! Bend down and take a whiff. Our 'son' the miniature panther has mouse-breath for sure."

Jay bent over at the waist part way and kissed Ivan on the forehead. "He's the great puma. The hunter. Aren't you Ivan?"

"Say, Jay. How do you think that mouse faired that Ivan had brought for Aida?"

Cool wind blew through my hair, and as I asked my question our neighbor, James, came bouncing down both steps of the sidewalk. "Catch what mouse?"—gleamed James in a happy loud voice. James was fairly short in stature but he was lean and athletic with a shaved bald head; he was ex-military, looking younger than his years.

"Hey!"—Jay said happily greeting James with a smile and a nod of his chin.

"Hello James." I smiled at our neighbor. "We were just talking about Ivan and I had asked Jay about the mouse Ivan had brought to Aida; Jay had to put it in a jar." I chuckled. "Now, listen, and this is no joke; you won't believe it, it's the silliest thing." Pressings my fingers to my cheek and shaking my head, I laughed quietly at the thought of it. "We ran out of cat food, right? Only it's Aida's favorite cat food. She won't eat anything else and I don't blame her."

"It's the best stuff", Jay added in agreement. "It's called 'Unique'; have you heard of it?" (James smiled and shook his head 'no'.) "Well, it's whole fish."

"Doesn't have any ash added", I interjected.

"Yea, it looks like actual food."

"It sure does. Doesn't look like just a can of mush." I smiled at the cat.

"It has a lot more vitamins; healthier." Jay turned and said to Ivan who was now tip-toeing across the top of the fence toward James. "And you love it too, don't you fierce puma?"

Ivan looked over his shoulder at Jay then jumped off the fence and onto the sidewalk in one smooth stretch of his black sleek body. Ivan lifted his arm and turned his paw over to observe his claws. He studied his claws and they must have passed inspection because he gave them one short lick before setting his paw down again. He flicked his whiskers flat against his face; he sniffed at the raising wind. Everyone stood watching him as if with expectation. Several gold and orange leaves fell from the tree whose crumply-bark branches lifted up and out like an umbrella. The leaves swirled a spiral in the air then landed on the sidewalk. Ivan pounced down at them. Looking from leaf to leaf with huge circling eyes Ivan twitched his tail in excitement.

"So…anyway." I continued my story and put my bare feet on the bottom line of wood that arched across the fence; lifting myself up by grasping hold of its green picket top. "So it just so happens that the grocery store we always shop at has suddenly decided to stop stocking Aida's favorite canned food. And what happens? She gets depressed poor thing! Sulking. Not eating. Sad, so sad, that she won't even meow or purr when you pet her. Her nose stayed dry."

"It was terrible for her the poor baby", Jay threw into the story.

"What happened?" James smiled and raised his eyebrows with curiosity. His dark, tan colored, skin tightened around his ears from the smile and his barely there buzzed-cut hair pulled with the backward movement of his scalp.

"Well", I continued, "Ivan brought a mouse to Aida to cheer her up."

Jay rubbed his chin. "We did finally find her some 'Unique' cat food though. But we had to drive fifty miles just to find a place that carried it." Jay shook his head. "I'm going to say something to the store manager here. That's the best cat food they could have. Doesn't make sense for them to take it off the shelves."

James bounced on the heels of his clean white tennis shoes; the hair on his bare arms stood up on end as the breeze pushed through the air surrounding us all in a vibrant pace. The wind caused a ripple among the wisps of cloth and thread where the sleeves of James' black cotton shirt had been cut off at the shoulder. James folded both hands into fists and flexed all the well developed muscles of his arms as if to generate more body heat. "Well", nodded James, "I've got to get on to my jog."

Jay and I nodded and waved at James and then stood outside for a while discussing what we wanted to eat. After a while we decided to go to the grocery store and get some supplies to make Florentine pizza; we hopped in the car and rode with the windows down. Jay circled the parking lot of the store a bit more than necessary before settling on a parking spot he liked. We walked from the car purely enjoying the cooling wind. Sitting in front of the grocery store was a man in a folding chair with a box in front of him that had a sign on it saying, "Please help. Homeless. Vietnam veteran." The veteran was a skinny, hairy, man with a long-sleeved shirt buttoned up to his chin. The veteran was hugging himself by holding his arms and was visibly shaking from the chill in the air. It felt pleasantly cool to me but I do think a lot of other people would have considered it cold. While it was pleasingly cool to me, I knew it would get colder later in the day when the sun began to go down. "Can we go back to the house real quick Jay?"--I asked.

"What for?"—Jay wondered out loud. "We should get our groceries while we're here."

"I'm going to get that leather jacket that I've got. The big one; no one ever wears it. This guy looks like he could use it. It would fit him."

"Are you sure you want to give that away?"

"Do you want it Jay?"

"No. I can't wear it." Jay patted his belly. "Not with the weight I've gained." Jay had indeed gained weight, but he had also taken to wearing better clothes and keeping his hair nicely trimmed.

"So let's go back."

Jay shrugged. "Okay. Let's go back." Jay conceded, "I don't work today, so I guess I've got plenty of time."

We headed back to the car. Driving the short distance back to the apartment complex was quick enough. I pulled my leather jacket (really a man's jacket anyway) out of the closet where it had sat so long.

Then I made two cheese sandwiches and wrapped them in plastic. I put the sandwiches and the bag of the last half of the potato chips in a kept plastic grocery bag along with a fresh can of cold soda. Jay watched me put all this together with an expression of quiet amused perplexity.

"Let's go back to the grocery store!"—I said to Jay holding the leather jacket in one arm and the bag of food hanging on my other arm.

When we got back to the grocery store the Vietnam veteran was still looking cold as he sat in front of the box with his sign on it.

"Here", I said to the veteran, "take this coat and keep it; you look cold."

"It's freezing", said the shivering hairy homeless man. "Oh wow! This is a great coat! Thank you!" He immediately shrugged the black leather coat on and admired it; he seemed very happy with it.

"No problem." I handed him the bag of food. "Here's something to eat."

"Thanks!" The veteran reached in the bag and pulled out a cheese sandwich, unwrapped it, and began eating it hastily.

"And here", I reached into my purse and pulled out a couple of bucks and handed the money to him.

Jay also pulled a couple of bucks from his old blue wallet. It was the first wallet he ever bought when he was about eleven years old and he continued to use it out of some sort of old nostalgia. "Here man", Jay said handing the man the money.

The man took the money from both of us then looked up from another bite of his sandwich. "You've got a demon behind you", the homeless man said to me in a voice of complete and honest sincerity.

"What?!"—I exclaimed with an unsettling feeling of surprise and confusion.

"Behind you", the homeless man said. "You've got a demon following along behind you." The homeless man pointed; his arm out straight and his finger taut, to something just behind me.

Then the veteran took another bite of his sandwich and looked down at his cardboard box.

Shaken, I turned my head swiftly to look behind me out of sheer reaction. Jay also looked behind himself. Of course there was nothing that looked unusual behind us; I simply saw a typical grocery store parking lot. I wanted to scream from how ironic and uncomfortable the veterans words made me feel. At the same time I wanted to say with a smile and a quip, "What a coincidence that anyone should say that; sometimes I feel like there's a demon following me." But I was thrown too off-guard to say anything! Speechless and annoyed at the ridiculous mixture of emotions I was feeling I simply marched on in to the grocery store.

Jay followed behind me and caught up to step with me in the store. Jay leaned close to me and whispered in my ear, "That was strange."

"You have no idea!" I said with a little more anger in my voice than I'd intended.

"What?"

"Nothing Jay. Shall we shop?" I had to stop myself from walking so hard and so fast. I slowed down and took a breath and smiled.

*   *   *   *   *

Despite it all, what the homeless veteran said had left me itchy to run away again; to pack up and move again. Therefore it was with relief that I received the news from Jay that he had to drop on me. Much later in the day after the sun had set Jay confided to me that his father had made him a proposal. Jay's father said he wanted us to stay in his house (really a shack) way out in the boondocks and watch after his animals while he was out of the country. Plus he would help Jay to take the computer classes he'd been wanting. It seemed a good chance for Jay to continue his education. Although there would be no work for me way out in the middle of nowhere, I could nevertheless see it as a temporary opportunity for myself as well; I could finally work on condensing my seminar notes and scientific theorems.

Jay and I packed our bags, gathered up Aida and Ivan, and moved into the shack out in the boondocks. During our time at the shack Jay and I flew to Las Vegas to get married. (Finally! What was the man waiting for? I'd only dropped a hundred hints or more. I loved Jay! How long could we go on being room-mates?!) The whole experience turned out to be disappointing for many reasons. For one thing Jay had insisted on being the one to send out the wedding invitations. Thus I gave him my list of family members and their address's. Not a single person in my family showed up to the short, cold, wedding. Now considering that the wedding was in Las Vegas it would not be a surprise if I had family that could not make the travel. But no note? No phone call? It was only on the day of the wedding that Jay informed me he had forgotten to send the invitations to my family. I decided to try and be a trooper and not let this ruin my time in Las Vegas. Instantly I dropped the issue without comment. The 'milk being spilt' there was 'no point in crying over it.'

Yet! Picture this! No reception; we had dinner after the wedding at one of those Camelot castle places! Eek!! Scary!! One of those places where you sit pressed up against a gazillion people you don't know and watch live jousting. Now this might be a fun thing to do on any other night. But not for your wedding! Was Jay insane for bringing us here for our wedding?!

So if you can just picture me sitting at a crowded jousting, wearing my wedding dress, eating with my *hands*, and wearing a paper crown on my head! Oh!—And trying very, very hard to smile and be polite. *Ack!!* But it was nobody's fault; there had simply been a miscommunication.

*   *   *   *   *

When we came back to the Texas shack from our unhappy and bizarre wedding in Las Vegas, Jay and I had a hunger that evening for Mexican food. We had to drive half an hour into town to get provisions for a Mexican feast. We bought the makings for nachos, tacos, and burritos. We also bought a bottle of Mexican tequila that had two pickled worms in the bottom of it. Then I got an idea!

I turned to Jay excitedly—"Let's go to a store that sells toys!" We were sitting in the car at a red light with the groceries and tequila in the back seat.

"Toys?" Jay sounded perplexed. "What for? Suzanna?"

"I want to buy an 'Operation Game'."

"An Operation Game?"

"Yea. You remember those? Don't you? Those games with a cartoon like picture of a guy on an operating table and you have to take these tweezers to pull out the body parts, and if you miss and your tweezers touch the metal side…"

"Then the buzzer goes off and the nose…." Jay put his fingers over his nose with one hand while steering the car with the other hand. "The nose goes 'off' and the buzzer buzzes." Jay made a buzzing noise.

"The nose glows!" I put a finger on my own nose. "It glows and the buzzer goes off."

"Okay….and?"

"And…Jay… you know that urban legend about going to a foreign country somewhere and getting drugged into sleep and then when you wake up you've had an organ removed?"

"Uhh…", said Jay hesitantly, "yes?" He was trying to put the two ideas together.

"So we can pour a shot of tequila and then play the operation game, and whoever screws up and touches the edge with the tweezers and makes the nose glow and the buzzer goes off has to take the tequila shot. Since we're having Mexican food and tequila we can call it 'Mexican Hospital'! That's not very politically correct I don't think. 'Foreign Country Hospital'?!"—I tried out the name with excitement. Then I considered the amount of a tequila shot per 'buzzer'. "Okay, let's make it ¼ a shot in case we mess up a lot. And in the end, the loser has to eat the worm that's in the bottom of the tequila bottle. Only our bottle has two worms, so win or lose we can each have a worm."

Jay rubbed his chin. "I like it!"

"Woo-hoo!" I was very excited and in a completely silly mood. I had a feeling this would be a bit of silly fun, and I was right!

We laid out a picnic blanket. Plates of fresh cheddar infused with jalapeno slices melted into tortilla chips filled the room with a warm and tangy aroma. Plates of tacos with fresh lettuce, cheese, sour-cream, and tomatoes, graced the picnic blanket. One plate overflowed with four huge bean burritos. We took turns playing the Operation Game with a shot glass ¼ full of tequila as the penalty. We laughed heartily while we ate our Mexican feast and played the game. It turned out that I would lose the game. Yet there were two pickled worms for us to share! And I learned something very interesting:

a pickled worm both tastes and crunches exactly like a water chestnut!

*   *   *   *   *

One thing I did not learn from playing the tequila operation game was how alcohol can affect people differently. Somehow I had not noticed that Jay always drank a lot of alcohol every day. There wasn't any alcohol consumed in the household when I was a child so I had no point of reference. Something that I didn't understand is that some people have an "allergy" as it were to alcohol---meaning they can not have so much as even half a glass of wine without it causing a severe reaction in the person. Jay would drink; even just a little bit, and become a different person…someone who wasn't nice. I did not know he had an illness.

I had forgiven Jay's temporary cruelties because usually he was a very nice guy. I had not made the connection between his drinking and his temporary changes in personality; *not* changes for the good. The future that year in the shack out in the boondocks would involve a most unfortunate event, involving a very different type of hospital.

During the passing first year in the shack (the floor was horribly unlevel with the back half having sunk into the ground, with broken wood planks, busted out windows covered with plastic, and peeling yellow and white paint on the outside) I had developed the habit of never ever answering the phone. I was sick to death of the stalkers phone calls and my only defense was not to answer the telephone and let the call go to the answering machine. If it was someone I knew leaving a message, then I would either go ahead and pick up the receiver or call them back. During this time I noticed that Jay was drinking glass after glass of rum and cola when he got home from his school classes; he would drink until he passed out into sleep. I had never seen such behavior before. So I had still not made the connection between Jay's drinking and the steady ebb and flow of his temporary cruelties. Jay wasn't a bad person, he was ill. For Jay's defense, he had an illness that it turned out often led him to black-outs of the things he did or said. Jay was an alcoholic, but I didn't know it yet.

*   *   *   *   *

Come our second year living in the shack I had finally finished condensing my seminar notes and scientific theorems which I'd written in great depth in my childhood. (I am talking about the massive lengthy work that I created and taught in seminars so many times, and which I taught to the upper graduates at the summer Methodist conference.) I wanted to condense all of it down into just a few simple paragraphs and outlines. I wanted to share it with others, especially any *children* I might have some day, and I wanted for it to be short and condensed enough so that *hopefully* nearly *anybody* could read my laws and theorems and understand them.

There came at last the day that I was finally finished and through with taking the in depth information and had managed to condense it simply and completely. It had been a great deal of hard work to condense, shorten, and simplify my laws and theorems! I wanted them so simple practically anyone could understand them and after much labor I had achieved just that! (Again, I am talking about the work that I created and taught in seminars.) I was so excited over this strenuous accomplishment that I wanted to celebrate!

When Jay came home to the shack after finishing his day of school classes, I barely noticed his common habit of glass after glass of rum and cola. I was thrilled to the maximum at finally being finished with my work, so I bounced up to Jay while excitedly pressing the tips of my fingers together.

"Guess what! Guess what?!" I bounced up and down on my tip-toes. The pleasurable anticipation of a coming celebration beamed like white light shining in my eyes. "Guess what, Jay?"

Jay was stony and completely utterly silent. It was then that I noticed the harsh burning glare of pure hatred firing from his eyes. As if he *hated* me so deeply and so completely that it was a wonder we were even in the same room together; or that I didn't combust from the sheer glare.

Not knowing what to do about the situation, I continued. "My work! My work, Jay! I finished it! I got it so completely condensed you wouldn't believe it! Now I can pass it on to a child of mine someday, or to others as well hopefully, and not have to worry they didn't understand it!"

Jay remained cold and silent. He did not waver from his look of hatred. His lips were pressed together tightly into a bloodless, angry, line. *Hate for me burned out of his eyes*. It didn't make sense to me. I couldn't understand what was going on. I had seen that look before.

"My work Jay!" I was beginning to feel very afraid of him. "I finished condensing it! We need to celebrate! We can go out to a restaurant and call it a 'part-tay'!"—I swung my hips and elbows in a little dance.

Jays silence, and the pure hatred and malice he was pouring out upon me, wiped away any smile that I could muster.

"Jay?"—I spoke meekly. "We need to go out and celebrate", I said in hesitant fear, "my work is…finished."

Pushing forth from the malice in his eyes, down his nasal passages, and into his mouth, came a word that pressed past the pale, bloodless, thin line of his lips. One word that would be the straw that broke the camel's back.

Plopping from Jay's mouth in an eternally painful thud, Jay said with a voice of deliberate cruelty: **"So."**

I could not understand! I reeled from his malice! I did not know it wasn't Jay's fault and that he had an illness. My ears literally began to ring, with a high-pitched ringing that shrilled with the race of my blood-pressure. My blood-pressure rose much too quickly to unhealthy heights. Wasn't this the one person who was supposed to love me and care about me and in whom I was supposed to be able to trust?! His one cruel word flew into my brain and sprang back out again in a complete rejection of its implications.

My body felt instantly freezing cold and the room around me felt instantly hollow and distant. The air seemed thrust out of my lungs. I recognized the symptoms. *I was going into clinical shock.*

From a distance, as the room seemed to expand, I began to feel myself raising up as if coming out of my body. Hugging myself and feeling like I was stepping on uneven clouds as if floating, I walked slowly to the couch and sat down. My heart was beating uncomfortably fast. I stated softly and plainly that Jay needed to take me to a hospital because I could tell I was going into shock. I watched him as he walked out of the living room and he muttered, "Whatever."

I saw a flash of blinding white light. That was the last thing I remember until suddenly coming to consciousness again and finding myself curled up in the corner of the bathroom between the wall and the bathtub. I was shaking very hard and uncontrollably and my heart was racing to a point that felt lethal. I was terrified by my condition. "Jay!", I called, "Jay!"

Jay stepped into the bathroom with a grimace of unconcern on his face. "You've got to get me to a hospital, Jay. You've got to get me to a hospital or I swear I will call the police to come get me and take me to the hospital."

Jay turned to leave the bathroom and I saw another flash of blinding white light that completely overtook me. Flash! That was the last thing I remember until coming back to consciousness to discover I was standing in the kitchen drenched with sweat, yet I felt freezing cold. Shaking and trembling uncontrollably I felt afraid for myself. Looking up I saw two policemen standing just inside the kitchen door; Jay was standing next to them. "I've gone into shock", I said to the policemen, "You've got to get me to a hospital."

"Shock", one policeman repeated with obvious concern.

"She hasn't slept in five days", said Jay to the policeman next to him.

"Five days?!"—I shouted in utter disbelief, "It's been five days? You've got to be kidding me!" My body felt so cold. He was speaking the truth, it turns out it really had been five days passed and gone in a flash.

Flash! I was overtaken by another burst of white light. Flash! And the next thing I knew I was laying alone and on my side in the back seat of a police car. I sat up weakly and surveyed the squad car; there was only the one policeman driving and myself in the police car. I looked out the back window and saw another police car following behind us. FLASH!

FLASH! The all encompassing bright white light overwhelmed me. Flash! The next thing I remember is sitting at a table that was long and wide and oval. Men and women sat in chairs around me. A black woman, an oriental woman, brown and white men and women, all individuals of authority. The room seemed unusually dark to me. Another flash! I came to consciousness still sitting in this chair surrounded by authority and I took them all in and ascertained that I must finally be at a hospital! (*In fact I was at a court house; the police had driven me. Why wasn"t I at a hospital yet?! I don"t know if I or if Jay is the one that called the police. I had in fact gone into clinical shock.*)

I looked at the thick-set white man with the salt and pepper hair and the white doctor's coat and I tried to speak but my words came out in a frustrating mumble.

Then I noticed an angel with huge white wings standing in a beam of lovely glowing light. I was obviously still suffering from shock. The angel was standing just behind the right shoulder of the doctor I had tried to address. Lifting my heavy arm with great difficulty, I beckoned with my hand for the angel to come help me talk.

Nodding his head with ascent and understanding, the angel walked around the right side of the table and stood next to me. "I need to be able to speak", I attempted to say to the angel, but it came out of my mouth as a jumbled mumble.

The angel nodded his head in an affirmative motion, and then the angel put his hand palm-flat against the middle of my back. I was only able to communicate as if as a puppet. Suddenly I cleared my throat and although it was a struggle I was at last able to speak.

"Where is it?"—I asked the man across the table from me. For I was now quite certain that Jay's one plopped word-bomb had given me a heart attack and that I had died. Literally, died. Died of a heart attack.

"I know I'm dead", I spoke with difficulty; "But I'm obviously having a hard time crossing over."

"What?" The man across from me asked.

"Have you ever", I continued to speak, *"been so overwhelmed by the death of someone that you yourself feel dead inside?"* I took a labored breath. *"Have you ever"*, I continued, *"felt so pummeled by horrible events"*, I sucked in another breath, *"that you felt like you were walking around in the world and living your life as if you were the living dead?"*

The angel placed his other hand gently upon my shoulder. *"Or"*, I continued to speak, *"have you ever just felt so exhausted by life that every now and then you occasionally wished you were dead?"*

"Yes." Said the man across from me with an uncertain squint of his eyes and a nod of his chin.

"Well! Where is it?" I asked.

"Where is what?" Said the man with a deeper squint of his eyes.

"The Handbook For The Dead." I stated flatly.

*   *   *   *   *

As if pulling me away the intense white light sucked me into itself again and I saw a FLASH just before coming back to consciousness again, in time to look over my shoulder as I lay upon a hospital bed, to see a female nurse give me an injection shot in my hip. "This will make you sleep", the nurse said sweetly.

"Oh good", I heard myself murmur, "I need to sleep." Then I rolled over and saw nothing but the flash of white light again except this time the light seemed smoother, more flowing, gentler. FLASH! And I saw my white bed sheet covering my head begin to billow upward for a moment as I lifted it with my hand. The flowing white bed sheet wafted down across my face. And at last I fell asleep.

* * * After two days of pure sleep I at last woke up and was informed by a nurse that I had a visitor. It was Jay. He had brought me a soda and some fish and chips. He lifted the soda and the bag of food up to show me. "Is food still the way to your heart?", he asked.

I managed a smile and thanked him for the food. Just the smell of the fish and chips made me feel suddenly ravenous. What else was there to do? Sometimes when you feel things are not right, the best thing you can do is something very common and ordinary. So I ate. It tasted good. And later I would sleep some more. As I munched on my food I said to Jay with the smile of someone resigned yet finally rested, "You know, if I ever write a book and get it published, I'm going to name it: 'Handbook For The Dead, The Living Dead, and Those Who Occasionally Wished They Were Dead.' "

Jay just looked at the food and asked with a shy grin if it tasted good.

CHAPTER NINETEEN

KITH OF THE WHITE OWLS

Jay and I chose to work hard on our relationship and move forward with our lives. Yet unfortunately it had still not come to my awareness what Jay's alcoholism was, and that I couldn't help him with it; it was something he would have to do himself. I'd thought Jay's cruelties were his acting out some sort of old anger from his childhood. I listened to Jay when he said he would control his behavior and that he loved me; it appeared as if he sincerely meant it. It's perfectly fine that some people thrive on it, but I'm not the kind of person who can *stomach* 'drama' in my life. I happen to be a calm person; a quiet person; a happy person. So it was tearing to also be such a loyal person; I felt it was my duty to try and make the marriage work. There were times he tried so very hard that I felt sorry for him. He would cry and be so sincere; but he himself did not even realize he had an illness. Until I realized I could not change the situation I would keep thinking, 'could things be salvageable?' Letting go is hard.

I looked at my life and all it's events and the thought occurred to me that not answering the telephone anymore might have allowed me a false sense of relief and security. There were after all still an innumerable amount of hang ups received. Sometimes as many as twelve to fourteen hang ups in one day. There were simply too many unfortunate things to think about and all of them seemed absurd; ridiculous. Unnecessary. And yet no matter what has happened…you still have to live your life! Time flowed into the years like a river to the ocean, and seemed just as huge and overwhelming.

The blinds were open so that gentle silver shadows along bright beams of sunlight streamed into my bedroom, flooding across the wall and floor. Someone outside was mowing the lawn for what seemed to be all day long; it was Jay no doubt. The mower entering into the remnants of my lingering dreamy sleep. The purring whirr of the motor lulled me like a lullaby. I warmly reminisced that I had not felt so peaceful in the midst of lazy sunny day naps since I was a child at my Grandmother Oleta's house.

Not until late did I get up from sleep and flop my feet as I walked into the living room. Smiling, I rubbed my eye with a knuckle. Just yawning with a little sort of grumph-rumbllumph sound as I turned into the kitchen. Something yummy for my tummy. Thought of old Pooh bear foraging his cabinets for some honey. I opened up the fridge. Nothing looked particularly delicious to me except for the salty briny pimento stuffed green olives. Pulling the olive jar from it's cold spot in the refrigerator I poured a small bowl of the tasty pearly round treats. Plopping the olive jar back in its chilly spot I then proceeded to munch little bites one olive at a time. The cold tangy ocean water flavor filled the back of my mouth and the sides of my tongue. Shrugging with pleasure from the taste of the small green delights, I then went about making myself a cup of instant coffee with hot water from the tap—I wasn't specifically interested in the taste of the coffee however, I simply wanted the caffeine.

I noticed the sun was already shining brightly. Close to noon time. Pulling back the glass door I let in some fresh air and sunshine. Birds were singing their songs. Jay came out of the shower with his hair still wet but combed back and he joined me at the sliding glass door. Peering into the little bowl I held he reached in and grabbed a green olive and popped it in his mouth. "Mmm", he moaned before chewing it. I sat the bowl down on the coffee table.

Jay walked up to me and kissed my nose. I twirled behind him and hugged his back; he reached behind for me. Putting my hands on his shoulders I bounced up and down a couple of times. Then I jumped up and he caught my legs so that he was carrying me piggy-back. Gently he jogged around the kitchen and living room holding me piggy-back. I laughed so hard that I slid off. Jay and I plunked onto the couch and we leaned into each other laughing. With my teeth I play-bit at his arm and he pretended just the same by yowling "Ouch!"

Climbing onto his lap I wrapped my arms around him and smoothed back his hair. We hugged each other in silence for a moment. Then I leaned back comfortably and felt his hands supporting my spine. I pinched the skin on his leg with my toes. "Are you hungry?"—Jay asked.

"Kind of."

"Kind of? I hope your hungry, I went to the store and I've got everything ready to be cooked."

"Oh?" My curiosity peeked. "Did I by any chance request food again in my sleep?" I looked at him with one eye while the other eye stayed closed in a moment of jesting scrutiny. It seemed all a person had to do was talk to me while I was sleeping and I would invariably request very specific foods.

"Maybe." Jay grinned.

"In other words 'yes'. "

"Yes." He grinned again. "You asked for pancakes…."

"Pancakes!?"

"….and an omelet…you said you wanted it 'dripping' with cheese. And you told me that if you didn't get a donut with a ton of chocolate frosting on it you were going to 'fall over and hoodlepoot'."

"Oh, I did not."

"You did!"

"What? 'Hoodlepoot'? Oh that's ridiculous. Ohhhh, you should know by now I have a tendency to open my eyes in my sleep and request various food products." We both laughed.

"Well I got it all."

"Oh my goodness."

"You just sit there Suzanna and I'll cook it up."

Pulling Jay to me I gave him a big bear-hug. Then I covered his entire face from his forehead, nose, eyes and chin to his ears, with teensy-tiny kisses. He patted my shoulder and I slid back against the couch. He went to the kitchen and cooked very quickly. He set the table with a pile of fluffy buttermilk pancakes from a bottle you just add water, shake, and cook. Pats of butter melted and dripped from the cakes. Two glasses of cold milk sat wetly condensing the glass with little droplets of moisture. On two side plates were omelet's covered with large ripe black olives and juicy mushrooms and a large quantity of melted cheddar and mozzarella cheeses. A lone donut with chocolate frosting sat on a napkin. Sitting down at the table I chuckled at the sight of the spread and said, "Thank you. It's silly. But thank you."

After we ate Jay followed me outside; I was contemplating going for a walk. We both looked up at the lovely sky. I padded my bare feet onto the soft grass and clover beside the sidewalk. It had rained the night before and the clouds flowed and curved in the baby blue sky with hints of chalk-gray highlighted with an oddly gorgeous, creamy, pink-salmon as they plumped with unspent moisture. Viewing the field it looked as if it were spattered with a glorious dew. Sunlight streamed in long shafts here and there through soft round clouds. Delightfully I enjoyed the wet-cool feeling of the grass and clover underneath my bare feet. The day was so freshly perfect in beauty that it carried a near glowing surrealistic feel.

"They're everywhere; only you can't see them", Jay spoke aloud. "They're camouflaged." Blending perfectly into the scenery like those birds." He was still looking at the sky and acting very nonchalant.

"What?!", I exclaimed. "What are you talking about?" I realized by the glassiness in his eyes and the rum and cola in his hand that he'd been drinking. I felt afraid because when he'd been drinking he liked to play cruel mind games, but I still hadn't made the connection that it was the alcohol causing it. "What are you talking about?"

Jay shrugged his shoulders: "Oh… nothing."

"No. No"; I countermanded, "You said something about 'them' being everywhere; only camouflaged. That you couldn't see them." Nothing but the cool gentle breeze between us for a moment. He stared at the sky.

He looked at me smiling. Not so much as a flinch crossed his face. "That field of birds. You can't see them, but the field is full of a hundred birds or more."

Jay gestured upwards with his chin towards a hawk. "Maybe he'll show you."

Looking in the direction he gestured towards I squinted my eyes. "Who'll show me what?" Roving my glance over the field then turning my eyes up. In the center of the field stood a bare tree. Sitting in the tree was a red-tail hawk. I mentioned that I was impressed with the beauty of the bird; but Jay shushed me and nodded his head upwards again.

"There he goes", I heard Jay whisper. The red-tail hawk looked over at us, spread his wings, and leapt from the tree. Diving down the hawk swooped in a straight line towards the ground. Just as I thought it was going to land the red-tail hawk turned its body up, letting out a soft cry. At least one-hundred small brown birds flew up into the air from the field. Fluttering up their light-brown wings like dusted cinnamon. "Now watch"—said Jay as he pointed to the field again. "When they settle, it will be as if they disappeared."

The red-tail hawk circled close to the ground but didn't catch a meal. The large group of small brown birds floated downward, and absolutely disappeared in perfect camouflage within the field. No matter how hard I squinted, I couldn't see them. It was as if they weren't there.

There was a long, breeze filled silence that rested peacefully for several moments past the last chirping of the birds. "Ready to go back inside Suzanna?"

"How about we get in the car and take a ride through town?"

"Okay."

We hopped in the car and made the drive into the center of town. Cars crowded from bumper to bumper. Young people in a variety of clothes from laidback to imaginatively unusual walked or stood along the sidewalk. The antiques and used clothes store seemed full of activity. Across the street from the used clothes store had lain a makeshift trailer park surrounded by trees and stuffed in between two restaurants on either side. Several older couples and a few families sat munching their luncheon goodies on the outdoor patio of a restaurant next to a convenience store. Families wearing a usual costume for this date and time in history: jeans and button-up shirts on men; jeans and cotton tops on women with some women in skirts and clunky closed-top shoes. Pausing and watching all the activity from my rolled down window. Listening to the sounds. Birds and the noisy rumbling of cars mixed with the flushing of wind. People of all sizes and shapes and colors added the sounds of mumbling in various tones of conversation. A dog at the crosswalk barked towards his smiling master. Music lilted and flowed from patio restaurants and boomed from cars and pulsed from boom-boxes. The rustle of leaves on long tree-branches. My favorite background 'music' was the soothing breeze and birdsong.

Jay turned off the main street and into a neighborhood where the interesting houses were fun to look at. Green trees, their foliage thick with deep colored round and oval leaves. Smooth tailored yards. Bushes cornered off perfectly. Grass so trim it looked like soft lime carpet. I enjoyed the eye candy of a quaint cottage home to my right as Jay drove leisurely slow. On the side of the cottage was a small garden filled with rich, ripe, red tomatoes. Okra thickening; a line of sweet corn. Wearing a long flowered dress stood a woman staring down at the cabbage and black-eyed peas. A tiny tot all barefoot and curly white hair stood in the garden wearing only a diaper and pulling on one of the corn stalks.

My womb pulled in a twinge as I looked at that cute little child in diapers and I felt my deep longing for a child. I began the discussion with Jay of us getting on with our lives. There was not much time left to have a child; it wouldn't be to many years before my eggs would be considered old. Eggs? How weird and wonderful!

During that night beneath the Hale-Bop comet streaming through the starry sky a kith of owls came to sit on both sides of the gate at the end of the dirt driveway just in front of the boondocks shack. There were seven of the beautiful owls, and they were all pure white.

It was that same night just before we saw the kith of owls that a child was conceived outdoors beneath the star's and beneath the rushing, sparkling, flaming Hale-Bop comet. A child was conceived who would be named for the heavens and the music her presence brought to my heart.

"Look at the owls!" I wisped excitedly to Jay. My voice filled with a hushed pleasure and surprise at the magnificent sight.

"I know", whispered Jay, "I just saw them. I was about to point them out to you."

"They're pure white!"

"I know."

"I've never seen a white owl in real life before!" I still spoke with a hushed thrill. "I mean, I've seen them on TV…" Pure excited awe filled my heart.

"I know what you mean Suzanna." Jay reached over and held my hand sweetly. Together we inched closer to the gate and fence. The owls sat perched like calm royalty.

From that night on the kith of the white owls stayed with us. The kith were always on the gate and fence every time Jay and I looked; day after day, night after night. Even when we drove the car to and fro down the dirt driveway the snow white owls did not leave.

A little over eight weeks later the kith of the white owls were still there. When they left to feed they seemed to feed quickly and they always returned. It was at this time over eight weeks past the special night under the effloresce spray of blue, pink, white and orange comet and stars that I decided to go visit a friend of mine in Seattle; her name is Kindle and her features are as dark and beautiful as the true Cleopatra. She's a bit germ phobic, so bless her heart, wouldn't you know that I was sick from the moment that I arrived at her apartment. So sick was I that after vomiting into the toilet I found myself pressing the skin of my arms and legs against the cold linoleum floor of Kindle's bathroom and thinking: "Ooo, that cold floor feels good."

My friend Kindle was comical as she tried to keep herself from becoming sick too by spraying the whole house over and over again with disinfectant and wiping absolutely everything with rubbing alcohol. Kindle kindly brought a waste basket in case I needed to throw up again once I made it from the bathroom to the bed. On the side of the bed and overlooking the city from her high rise apartment was a huge wall-length window. Kindle called 800 'dial a nurse' and she also called poison control in an effort to find out what I had. Perhaps it was food poisoning, was the idea from the poison control. Yet then again perhaps it was the flu, came the offering from the nurse's 800 line. Fun flew out of the visit as I was unable to eat and wracked with vomiting for days. Then just as suddenly as it began my sickness flew away and vanished into leaving me feeling absolutely fine.

On the day when I blessedly felt better it so happened that Kindle's mother came to visit her. I had showered in cool water, washed my face with a scrubbing cream, brushed my teeth, and pulled my hair into a bun after drying it. Oddly I felt unfathomably alive as I stood freshly scrubbed in the living room to greet Kindle's mother. Kindle opened the door and her mother walked in. I smiled and said hello. Kindle's skin is a very dark creamy brown, and her curly hair looks as soft as down. Her gorgeous eyes are shaped like almonds with an exotic flare. Her mother glowed with a deeper darker coffee brown skin that shined from body cream and was scented with florals. I gave Kindle's mother a hug. Her mother pulled back after the hug and took one look at me, then as she walked across the room she said, "Girl! You are *pregnant!*"

Kindle and I looked at each other with a mutual gasp.

Kindle then made a 'humph' sound and squinted at me. Putting her hands on her hips with an exaggerated, frustrated gesture as she took it in. "Could this be true? Could you be *pregnant, Suzanna?*"

"Well, yes, I could be. Jay and I tried once to conceive; at night, outside; under the Hale-Bop comet."

"What?!" She slapped her forehead. "Oh!—I was so worried!"

I started laughing uncontrollably.

"It's not funny!"—Kindle retorted.

"Oh, but it *is*", I said deeply. Now I was laughing harder. "You sprayed that disinfectant and poured that rubbing alcohol all over everything, over and over. And you made those phone calls!" I wished she could see just how funny it really was. I accidentally snorted through my nasal cavity as I was laughing. The snort just made me laugh harder.

Kindle wrung her hands together and knitted her brow. Her almond eyes looked uncertain. "So. What exactly would you think about it if you *are* pregnant?" (Her mother smirked at her question and looked at her daughter with her arms folded across her chest.)

"Well I would love to be pregnant! I would be so happy I could hardly stand it! I've been wanting to be a mom since I was still just a kid myself!"

"Oh my gosh, girl! I should have known it!" Kindle sped across the floor and enveloped me in a tight embrace. Tears of excitement brimmed to my eyes as she hugged me so hard and rocked me from side to side. I sniffled as Kindle eased back from the gesture of affection and shared happiness. "Well come on! What are you waiting for? We need to get you a test!"

"A pregnancy test!" My arms tingled.

"Well *yea!*"

"I know, I'm just so excited!" Now my shoulders tingled too! "Do you want to come with me to the store Kindle?"

"You bet I do!"

"I'll just stay here", said Kindle's mother as she raised one hand with an expression of boredom.

Kindle and I walked the several blocks in the high rise city to the neighborhood store and I bought a pregnancy test. I enjoyed that walk more than I've ever enjoyed any stroll I've ever had in my entire life! When we were back at her apartment my heart seemed to stand still as the seconds ticked by so terribly sludge slow. Kindle and I were waiting with profound anticipation for the right time to look down at the pregnancy test stick.

When at last it was finally time and we looked down together at the stick it was a huge positive result! I was pregnant! I had never been so happy in my life! I immediately called Jay to let him know. And the following day I ended my visit with Kindle to go back home.

When I got back home the kith of the white owls were still sitting vigil on the long gate and fence. As if the world were suddenly new to me now that I knew I was pregnant, I took in the magnificent beauty of the pure white owls with deep affection and gratitude.

I went to my first doctor's visit that week; Jay and I had found a fantastic doctor named Dr. Maggie Land. We got our first ultra sound picture and confirmation that I was 9 ½ weeks pregnant! My life had never before been so full of joy! The kith of white owls stayed with us! The kith of white owls seemed to be there for the baby I was carrying.

During my pregnancy I craved fresh vegetables, tomato juice, and French fries. Yet the biggest surprise of all was my craving to watch scary movies! I had always hated watching scary movies and preferred to watch musicals. Especially musicals from the 1930's and 40's. "I think the soul I'm carrying must like a good scary movie", I told Jay with an amused smile. It was a delectable twist from what I expected to be surprised with in my pregnancy.

I put headphones on my stomach and played classical music and soft lullabies for the baby. I read aloud children's books and sang songs aloud to the baby in my womb. One night as I lay with my belly swollen huge and playing lullabies through the headphones on my stomach the baby began to actually *play* in my womb! Yes, play! I called Jay in to put his hands on my stomach and he was shocked and thrilled by what he felt. The baby would kick off with her feet from one side of my womb and slide-ping across to the other side of my womb where her head would hit. Then the baby would turn itself around and kick off with its feet to slide-ping back across my womb again where its head would again hit the side. Then the baby would turn around and do the whole thing over again! The baby played this way for a good ten minutes. It was amazing and wonderful.

When it was finally time for the baby to be born it was like a dream come true just to know that I was about to be a mother. I was in labor for eleven hours. Jay played the pleasant music I had picked out on the boom-box we brought. During the contractions I imagined myself filled with lilac colored light. And although the muscles in my body tensed and trembled horribly during the contractions, I stayed absolutely silent. I did not utter a groan or a sigh or a word.

At one moment the nurse at my side said during one of my worst silent trembling contractions, "I can't stand it! Why don't you scream, honey?! Why don't you scream, honey, scream out loud at the top of your lungs like the others do?!"

I managed to open one of my eyes and look at the concerned face of the nurse and say through tensed lips, "Because… the baby… the baby can hear me… and I don't want the child to come into the world hearing it's mother's screams." Just after I said this the contraction began to lessen.

Jay brought a ton of banana flavored popsicles for me to munch on in between contractions. I absolutely craved these popsicles at that time and a banana popsicle has never tasted as good since. At last Dr. Land informed us that my cervix was not dilating. Dr. Land announced that it would be an emergency c-section. I was so relieved actually. (I really did not want the child to come out of me the old-fashioned way. Eek!)

After Dr. Land quickly and expertly cut the child from my womb she declared it was a perfectly healthy 7 ½ pound baby girl! While I was on the operating table the baby was brought to me wrapped in a soft baby blanket. The baby girl was placed with her cheek against my own cheek. "Hello little Lilly Melody", I cooed, "Hello little baby, it's your mama. I loooove you." The child recognized my voice and turned into my lips and rubbed her nose in a sweet cuddle against my cheek! Happiness flooded through me in a sweet, warm, rush. Then as they took baby Lilly Melody away to be cleaned I was given an injection for an unfortunate reaction I was having to the medicine they'd given me; eventually I fell into an exhausted sleep.

Baby Lilly Melody stayed with me in the hospital room in my bed with me. As soon as I awoke from that initial snooze after my operation I began my motherhood by taking the baby in my arms and immediately beginning to breast-feed my daughter. Jay had tickled my funny bone by sneaking into my hospital room with a burger and fries; the food was so profoundly tasty just then.

* * * * Jay and I had the usual joys of parenthood. Yes of course it felt like we were the first people in the world to experience them. When Lilly was just crawling I would lay out a clean sheet on the floor and put little plates all over the sheet that were filled with different flavors, colors, and textures, of fruits and vegetables and crackers; she loved exploring the tastes and colors and feelings of the foods.

Lilly Melody's learning to walk and talk!—Wow! Little Lilly learning to count and read! Watching her teething on cold baby-dill pickles! (Watching her grin and throw the pickles!) Lilly's first birthday eating pizza (which she ate so much more of than I would have expected), and watching "Little Rascals" amid balloons and presents and cake. Every moment such a wonder to behold.

After Lilly's birthday we moved to Phoenix, Arizona where Jay had been offered a job. (I was still avoiding the stalkers calls and not answering the phone.) Jay and I took Lilly on many trips to the botanical gardens, theme parks, and the science museum.

As time trickled away Aida and Ivan would have both passed away from natural causes to leave us pet-less. It was extremely painful losing Aida and Ivan, I missed them deeply and have kept their ashes. Lilly personally picked out and kept several new pets from the pet store….two baby bunnies, and a baby ball python! Yet the fascinating surprise was that… guess what!—Lilly loved scary movies! When she was two years old she would always pick out the "Goose Bumps" movies in the children's section; and Lilly Melody would argue very well her desire to see the scary shows. I was afraid those shows would be too scary for someone of her tender age, yet she articulately argued: "I *want* the scary movie! If it gets too scary, I will tell you and you can turn it off!" So we at last agreed; she could watch it while I watched *her*. She loved the scary movies completely as it turned out. She sat watching them intently and eating popcorn with her little two year old hands, and loved every minute of it. (It wouldn't be until Lilly Melody turned nine years old that I would at last tell her about my odd craving to watch scary movies when I was pregnant with her.) My daughter taught me to enjoy a good scary movie while she was still in my womb!

At two years old Lilly made a friend her age with a little neighbor girl named Sadie in the apartment next door. Sadie and Lilly were inseparable. As best friends they played together every day. They took turns driving and riding in Lilly's red and life-like battery run jeep that we kept in the front portico. I brought Lilly and Sadie picnics with sandwiches and pickles and chips and milk; which they ate outside while sitting on a blanket. They ran through the apartment wearing dress up clothes. They played in the sprinkler all the time. Once they brought the water hose into the apartment and began watering the living room.

I calmly took the water hose back outside and turned it off . I gently and sweetly said to the girls, "No water hose in the house. It makes a mess. Okay?" They smiled and giggled and chimed 'Okay' back to me and they never did it again.

* * * * By the time Lilly Melody was three years old I knew things could not go on the way they were with Jay. Jay was hardly ever home as he drifted farther away into his own head. When he was home he drank alcohol until he passed out. Jay would throw every bit of trash he had straight onto the floor. If he drank a soda he would throw the can, empty or not, straight onto the floor; if he ate a bag of chips he threw the bag onto the floor, and so on with any other trash. On and on it went. When he came home from work he would start stripping off his clothes from the moment he walked in through the door and throw each piece of clothing onto the floor as he walked through the apartment. He had piled dirty underwear into a mound all across the bathroom floor. Although I don't personally like to cook, I nevertheless happily cooked all of our meals and bought and paid for all of our groceries for my beloved family. I packed lunches with food and snacks and chilled water bottles for Jay to take to work.

I tried to ignore Jay's overwhelming mess and just do the best I could. Turning on the boom box one morning, I put in a CD of Andreas Vollenweider and pressing repeat play, I danced lightly in the kitchen while turning on the water to wash the dishes in the sink. Of course I secretly wished we had a dishwasher. Sunlight through the glass door shimmered against a sprinkling of dust hanging in the air. The wet warm bowl was smooth in my hands as I washed it. The smell of minty-lime soap filled my nose. Small popping soap bubbles burst against the dishes. Rhythms of music sounding like sweet floating suspended notes of harp, flute, and drums, flowed through the air. Finishing the dishes I stopped to watch the sunlight pouring into the room from a clear blue sky. I took in a breath of air and held it. Blowing air from my nostrils when I felt the first need to breath again gave me a calm feeling. Walking across the kitchen; the music playing, the inner quiet, the calm peaceful nothing; keeping my breathing slow and even. I decided I would make some biscuits to eat. Thinking of Oleta's biscuits I began to enjoy the process of stirring the milk with the biscuit mix; fluffing it together with a fork and adding a tad more biscuit mix so that the bread felt silky beneath my hands. Rolling it into a soft powdery-moist ball and placing it onto the floured woodblock. Cutting small bite-sized biscuits that Oleta always called 'baby biscuits'. Melting the butter into the pan so that each bite-size biscuit could be dipped until glistening with the salty sweet cream before baking. The house felt warm and cozy because of the smell of the baking bread brimming through the air.

Lighting an incense of myrrh and amber I took the blue line of scented smoke into the bedroom where Jay was sleeping. Noticing the morning sun shaded in the room with the passing of a cloud. Leaning over I kissed Jay on the cheek. "Wake up sweetheart", I softly said.

Looking up at me, he squinted one eye and made a moan that sounded like a question. Closing his eyes but leaving his mouth parted he moaned again. As he breathed a low toned snort rumbled from the back of his throat. Kissing lightly on his ear and rubbing his arm I said softly, "Jay honey, why don't you go ahead and wake up? It's a pretty day." Opening his eyes and blinking Jay looked around the room. Then he sat up on one elbow to plump the pillow with his other hand and rest back against it. "You can go back to sleep if you want Jay. You still tired?"

"Awww hmmnn, oh—no. Mmn-mmn, something smells good."

"It could be the myrrh and amber incense. Or the baby biscuits in the oven." I still held the incense with its thin blue-purple swirl of smoke. "Lilly is still asleep on the bed in the living room."

"Ohhh… myrrh."

"Myrrrrrrrh", I repeated as if humming a tune.

Sitting down next to Jay in the bed I rubbed his knee. Then I slipped my hand underneath the white cotton sheet and tickled the bottom of his foot. He smiled and shook his foot; then he laughed as I pulled the sheet off of him and patted his belly.

"You", he said in a teasing tone, "Now I'm gonna be cold. So are you gonna keep holding that incense or are you going to put it someplace? Oh wait a minute… put it on top of the TV."

Having already stood up I shifted my direction from the window where I was going to set the wood incense holder to the television set on top of the dresser drawer. Placing down the ancient-oil, sweet-musty, scent to burn curls of purplish blue smoke from above the TV. Turning around I bent my knees for one great big hop onto the bed. Bouncing up and down on my knees four or five times I then lopped on top of Jay and pressed my lips against his bare tummy and blew on it. The blowing on his skin made a sound our daughter called 'frog-farts'.

Enjoying Jay, patting my shoulder, I told him the baby biscuits should be ready soon. "As a matter of fact they're probably ready to come out of the oven now. Makes the whole house smell like fresh baked butter-bread, doesn't it? Would you like some baby biscuits Jay?"

Sitting up with his feet over the side of the bed he ruffled his short hair with the ball of his fingers. With a stretch of every muscle in his back he groaned out a long yawn. Jay looked at me with sleepy eyes and spoke with a short crisp song-note in his voice: "No."

"No?"

"Nooooo not hungry."

"No…? My goodness, oh my oh my oh my… mmn-mnn not even with melted creamery butter smothered all over it. And honey? Oh yes, honey dripping off the edges?" Leaning in his direction I shook my eyebrows up and down invitingly. "And as a matter of fact you know", I said teasingly, "it's actually a law in some states that you have to have a tall glass of cold milk with hot buttered baby-biscuits and honey. Hmm?"

Jay looked at the clock and jumped to his feet. "Damn and I'm supposed to be there early today!"—he yelped. He put his shoes on his feet then pulled them back off again immediately, throwing them to the floor. He ran into the hallway to look through the closet. Tugging his pants on quickly he stood in the spot for a moment. "Great!"—he hollered at the closet of clothes. "Great!! JUS-ssst grrrRREAT!!! AAAHHH!!!"

"Jay, calm down, what is it?"

He flew in a fluster back into the bedroom. "Where are my socks?! I can't find any clean socks!!" He looked from side to side of the room. "All my socks are filthy dirty!" He fumbled through the basket of dirty laundry, throwing clothes everywhere. He pulled out two socks from the basket that totally did not match and held them up in disgust: "Look! They're crusty!!" He sniffed the socks with a sour expression crumpling his face. "And they smell!" He thrust the socks in my direction. "Here! Smell this!!"

A half giggle escaped my throat as I tried to suppress a laugh at the silly request. Did he really expect me to walk up and smell them? Holding my hand over my face I said, "No thank you. I trust you on that one."

"I'll never make it to work now!!" He threw the socks on the floor and sat down on the bed for a second before hopping up and snatching the socks off the floor again. He turned and screamed at the clock: "ACK!"

Jay then looked at me and asked, "Do you think you can get it done?"

"Get what done?"

He walked to the bathroom with his whole body drooping as if he'd simply resigned himself and given up. He snapped up a sock from the bathroom floor that matched one of the socks in his hand. I ran to the kitchen and pulled the biscuits out of the oven and sat them on the stove to cool. They were a lovely golden brown. Then I ran back to the bedroom and peered into the bathroom where Jay stood slumped. "Get what done honey?" Walking over to him I gently rubbed his back. "What sweetie?"

"I'm tired."

"Ohhh. I thought you loved your job."

"I do."

"Well do you have any sick time built up? So you could call in and get more rest?" I felt compelled to offer a solution since he seemed so frustrated.

"No, no. I can't do that. I don't want to do that. I wanted to get there early!" He turned on the faucet at the sink and began washing out his socks. Sarcastically he grumbled, "It would save a lot of time if you would do this."

"Oh! That's what you want done!" I reached for the wet socks. "Here love, let me do it." He acquiesced the socks into my hands and I began to scrub them together under the water. I paused. What was I doing? "Actually, you know what? I've got clean socks for you in the clean-laundry basket that's in the living room. I just hadn't put the clean clothes away yet. Let me go check." Prancing into the living room I bent over the basket of clean clothes and didn't have to dig at all before I found a pair of clean socks. Scrambling back to Jay with the clean socks in my fist I stopped short as I saw him holding the wet dirty socks in one hand and in the other hand he sported the hair-dryer which rumbled at a noisy low speed.

"They're dirty." He raised the dripping socks upward.

"I know." I offered my fist full of clean socks to him. "*Here*. These are clean." We exchanged packages and I threw the dripping socks to lay over the side of the tub. "Can I get you some breakfast Jay?" He shook his head to the negative.

He quickly finished dressing. (Lilly had continued sleeping through the entire event.) Grabbing his wallet and car keys he suddenly had a completely unfettered demeanor. Jay appeared calm and cool and collected with a big grin on his face: "Alright. See you." It was strange.

Running up to him I handed him his packed lunch and snacks and cold water and then gave him a kiss on the lips and said: "Okay. Love you. Have a good day." With a nod of his chin he turned and left.

* * * * Several hours after his work schedule had already ended Jay came home and left his clothes everywhere on the floor as he stripped them off and threw them down at his feet as he was walking. It was night time already. He was four hours late. He made a bee-line directly for the kitchen as he stripped off his clothes and he only stopped a moment to pull two cans of soda from the fridge and grasp his bottle of rum off the counter-top. He downed three glass's full of rum and cola quickly before striding towards the bathroom to take a bath. I could hear the water running into the tub. I could hear him turn off the water and slosh in.

"BINGO!!"—Jay shouted very loudly from the bathroom. I had just begun reading Lilly a book in the living room.

"What?!"—I hollered at Jay with confusion.

Jay shouted at full volume: "BINGO!! YOU GOT IT!!"

"What are you shouting about Jay?"

"Come here!"

"What?"

"COME HERE!!"

Kissing Lilly Melody on the top of her head I told her I would be right back. Trotting to the bathroom I opened the door and then closed the lid on the toilet so that I could sit down on it. "What do you want?"

"I said BINGO!"

"Huh?"

"You got it!" Jay raised his arm in a wide gesture. "Taaah-Daaaa!" He sloshed around the bath water; splashing it with his fingers. "What's this song?"--(He began humming.)—"HHmmm Hmnn Hmnnnmn mnn mnn mmm hmmhmn."

"I don't know Jay, I can't figure out a song by hmn-hmm."

"You already know it; you got it! HMMhmmm hmmm hmn hmn… it's a Billy Joel tune. Isn't it?"

"I don't know Jay… your just hmm-hmming!" Jay was still humming that tune as I left the bathroom. Going to our music selection I picked out the Billy Joel CD and put it in the boom-box to play. "Jay! I'm putting on the Billy Joel CD. Maybe you'll hear that tune your trying to remember." I pressed random selection and then pressed play.

"You don't need the music for the song, you already know it, you've already got it! *You* tell me what it is!"

"You're not making sense Jay."

The CD began playing and the very first song it selected seemed very familiar when I realized it was the same tune Jay kept humming. I hummed along with it. "Oh!", I shouted to him from beside the boom-box, "I know what tune you were trying to remember! That's it; it's the one that's playing. Right?"

"You tell me what it is!"

Picking up the plastic compact disc case I looked at the back to check the title of the song number playing. "It's 'She has a way of knowing'." Feeling frustrated I had a silent momentary sarcastic thought: What? Do I get a prize for figuring it out?

"That's right!" Jay shouted from still in the tub. "You win the prize!"

It was synchronistic; and his behavior was creepy. "Jay, you're acting strange." I walked back into the bathroom and Jay was drying off by rubbing a towel against his back. Jay grinned closed-mouthed and wide. I smiled back at him and then turned to the mirror to freshen my make up. Pulling my mascara and blush out of the little wood basket on the sink I gave my face a quick touch-up.

Jay threw the towel on the bathroom floor and broke into rolls of laughter. He put his hand on my shoulder and laughed like a madman until he was red in the face. Then he clutched his stomach and laughed so hard tears fell down his cheeks. Jay looked at me and said, "I hate blonde hair on women. I even look at a picture of a woman with blonde hair and I think, 'that looks so ugly'."

I stood stunned and fragile but not broken. I looked at Jay with so much hurt in my heart and then turned and looked in the mirror at my natural ash-blonde hair; and then my gaze fell again on Jay's grinning face. *I have blonde hair.* I looked in the mirror one last time. It was another one of his increasing cruelties.

"Yes!"—he exclaimed. "I've always hated blonde hair! I think it's so ugly it's sickening!" Jay laughed. "I've always been attracted to *red* hair!" Jay took a breath between laughs. He leaped forward so that his face was right up to my nose and said, "Paranoia is just another word for heightened awareness!!" He buckled over laughing.

I felt fear. "Jay, your scaring me…" I backed out of the bathroom. Taking a breath and consciously slowing down my breathing I concentrated on focusing and clearing my mind of all thoughts. To still my mind; to find inner silence. Walking over to the bed I leaned down and put my head on the pillow while trying to keep my heart from beating too fast.

"Hey!" Jay walked into the bedroom and pulled on his shorts. Bending his knees slightly and placing his hands on his thighs he said, "You know that song?"

"Ohhhh no, Jay, what song now?"

"It's by that guy, you know, from that band called 'Nirvana', it's sooo funny!! That song?— Where he sings: 'Just because you're paranoid don't mean their NOT after you!" Laughing as if he'd just heard the greatest joke he stood up straight and slapped his hands together. "Isn't that hilarious!! HA! I just get such a kick out of that! That's a great line!"

Jay sauntered out of the bedroom and into the kitchen (which was attached to the living room) and I got up and followed him. I felt sick to my stomach. It was then that I realized Lilly had left from playing with her stuffed toys to follow both Jay and I into the kitchen. Lilly Melody's scrunched expression showed she had become aware that something very wrong was going on and she was listening to us intently. I was uncertain of what to do.

Jay poured himself another rum and cola and drank half of it down in one gulp. I grabbed the bottle of rum and began pouring it out into the sink. "Oh, no."—said Jay with growing anger in his voice. I was suddenly afraid of what he might do or say so I stopped pouring it out and sat the large bottle down on the counter.

I said as calmly as possible, "Well something's making you *mean* Jay. If it isn't the alcohol then what is it? Something is making you *mean*."

Jay's face reddened in anger and his lips pressed into that blood-less thin line. He picked up a candy bar from off the counter and tore off the wrapper. He wadded the wrapper up into a ball in his fist. Then he raised his balled fist in the air as if about to throw it on the floor.

"No! Don't", I interjected, and his fist with the wrapper froze in the air. "Jay, I have asked you very politely many, many times to not throw trash on the floor." I tried to speak in as calm and quiet and yet as firm a voice as I could muster. "You can't keep throwing clothes and trash all over the floor Jay. I've asked you time and time again not to do that. I swear to heaven Jay that if you throw that candy wrapper onto the floor I am taking Lilly and I am leaving you."

Jay grinned a terrible grin and lifted his balled fist higher into the air and with complete deliberateness he threw the candy wrapper down hard onto the floor.

Lilly Melody gasped and began crying hard. Lilly never cried!—She was such a happy child! So I knew this was a terrible and serious event for Lilly. Hot tears rolled down her face. She had been listening to us, my little three year old.

"How could you do that?!"—Lilly screamed through her tears. "How could you do that Daddy?!" She gasped for breath. "You threw the wrapper down! You don't want us! Now we have to leave you!" (Gasping and choking on her tears.) "Now we have to leave you! Daddy! You don't want us!" Tears streamed hot down Lilly Melody's red face. "I hate you! I hate you! I hate you!"

Jay bent down hard and fast and thrust his face directly up into Lilly's face; just barely an inch between their noses. He drew in a deep ugly breath and shouted at Lilly in the loudest, hardest, most horrible voice, while flexing his arm muscles as if he might hit her, and he shouted and *growled* out: "*YOU*! SHUT UP!!"

It was too awful to watch. I saw Lilly's soul just melt down into the floor. Melt down into terrible pain; her body shaking and her shoulders convulsing as she closed her eyes and cried in great huge sobs and streaming flowing tears. The cry of the broken-hearted. It wasn't Jay's fault due to the illness, but I *was making it my fault* if I kept fighting with Jay in front of Lilly and if I kept Lilly in this environment.

Immediately I grabbed Jay's shoulders and pulled him away from Lilly. I didn't say a word at this point during this event. Picking up the bottle of liquor and the bottle of cola I shoved them both into Jay's arms so fast that he instinctively grabbed hold of them. Then I took hold of his shoulders again quite quickly and I pushed him into the bedroom alone by himself and closed the door. To my relief he wouldn't come back out of the bedroom for the rest of the entire night.

Gently lifting Lilly into my arms I hugged her tight and laid down onto the bed in the living room. "I love you baby", I said and kissed her forehead. "I'm so sorry you had to hear all that. Hey…" With the tips of my fingers I tickled lightly under her chin. Her breathing became more regular. "Hey, do you know what animal is really *smelly* when you say it's name twice?"

"No." Lilly spoke with her bottom lip still puffed out and her tears still dripping from her gorgeous blue eyes. I gave her a kiss on her cheek then said, "Tigger Tigger. Roo Roo. Eyore Eyore. *Pooh Pooh*."

A huge puff of air inflated her cheeks and flapped past her lips; a grin crept up one side of her mouth.

Her last tears fell as her eyes closed tightly for a moment and then she began laughing. "Ahhh!", she hooted as she threw her head back and looked up at the ceiling and laughed again. Then Lilly Melody fell onto her side on the bed and wriggled while she laughed.

Next she sat up with a smile on her damp pink cheeks as she repeated it saying in her little voice: "Tigger Tigger. Roo Roo. Eyore Eyore. *Pooh Pooh*!!" She threw her head back. "Ahh-ha!", she burst into a laugh and then fell onto her side again in giggles. Apparently it was very funny to her indeed, because she repeated it once more and then said over and over again afterwards, "Pooh POOH! Pooh Pooh! Like *poo-poo*!! Smelly animal! Ah-ha!"

Picking up Lilly's book about one of the puppies born to the Lady and the Tramp dog characters, which had been resting against the bed, I smiled and fluffed some pillows for Lilly and I to lean back upon. "Come on", I said to Lilly, "I'll read you this book." Lilly Melody snuggled up against me and I put one arm around her. With my free hand I held the book and gave different voices for the different characters to make it more interesting for Lilly. A Texas drawl for one character. A New York accent for another character. A Mae West impression for one of the old fluffy girl dogs. Soon Lilly relaxed and fell asleep.

Easing myself out from under my daughter, I managed to get up from the bed without waking her. Padding carefully and quietly over to the phone I picked up the receiver and called my mother.

"Mother", I said beginning to choke up, "Mother I'm taking Lilly and I'm leaving Jay." Pressure welled up in my eyes and nostrils and I knew I was losing my struggle not to cry. "But...", I stuttered, "But I'm going to need your help to make the move"; I sniffled, "And I'm going to need your help to find a place for Lilly and I to stay." My mother said she would help. I was grateful. I could hardly sleep after hanging up the phone and ending the conversation with my mother. With this I put my fingers to my forehead, and I wept.

Walking over to Lilly I kissed my sleeping daughter on her forehead. Then I walked outside past the sliding glass door and onto the tiny patio. Looking up into the night sky I stared at the shining white moon. And all at once I felt a sudden and inexplicable longing to once again see the Kith of the White Owls.

CHAPTER TWENTY

POLICE CATCH THE STALKER

Sunlight beamed in slanted shades of pale through the blinds of the sliding glass door. Lilly and I lay sleeping on the bed in the living room. I awoke first just to the sounds of my three year old daughter laughing. Laying with my eyes closed I felt pleased at the sound of my daughters laughter. Laughter was the sound of my daughters happiness. Lilly Melody's happiness always filled me with a shining light that beamed with Love. Lilly Melody laughed in her sleep quite a lot. Gradually I became aware that Lilly was not laughing in her sleep. Lilly was awake and calling for me as peals of laughter rolled from deep down in her belly.

"Mom! Mom! Ha! Ha! HA!"—Lilly Melody called. "Mom! You've got your face in my stinky armpit!"

"What?!"—I asked; uncertain that I had heard her correctly.

"You, ha! You've got your nose stuck right up in my stinky armpit! Ha, ha ha …. Wake up! Ha, ha ha…"

"What?" Opening my eyes I realized that all I could see was pink skin. Pulling my nose back a little and blinking some I became aware of the fact that I had been sleeping with my face pressed into Lilly's underarm!

"Oh my goodness! I *do* have my face in your stinky armpit!" It was so absurd that I had been sleeping with my nose pressed into her armpit that I too began to laugh.

We both sat up, the covers tangled across the bed, and the two of us fell into uncontrollable laughter. In pealing rolls of sound we ebbed and flowed between laughter and giggles until our tickled ribs were sore. It was the day I was to pack up the moving van and leave Jay to go back to Texas and we had woke up laughing with my nose ground into her armpit.

I had expressed to Jay that I wished he could make the trip and help drive the truck with bunnies, python, child, and boxes, back to Texas. It was imperative to me that Jay and I remain friends, specifically because we had a child together. Jay agreed and volunteered to drive the moving van. I was grateful for his driving as I felt it would be an act of goodwill on both our parts for the sake of our child. Although Jay would not make it easy over the next few years for us to maintain our friendship, I kept at it with a great pull of will and patience and love.

The trip did not seem to take as long as I expected it to and it wasn't long before Lilly and I were settled into our new home and living just the two of us. I made my ends meet by baby-sitting from my home. I would wait a long while before making my divorce from Jay final; hoping to salvage the marriage. With my insistence Jay came to visit around a year after Lilly and I moved in. Jay brought a bottle of red wine. We all sat on a picnic blanket on the living room floor to eat sushi. Lilly Melody was doing very well picking up her sushi with chopsticks. Fifteen minutes after Jay had drank only one half glass of the wine his demeanor and personality changed. He barked at Lilly for dropping one of her bites of sushi from her chopsticks onto the picnic blanket. He lifted himself onto the couch and folded his arms across his chest and stared straight ahead at the wall with that look of stony anger plastered on his face. This made Lilly cry.

So I ushered Lilly to her room and told her I'd be with her in a minute and we'd play; I shut Lilly's bedroom door behind me.

Walking into the living room and standing there I said, "You've like an allergy to alcohol Jay; you can not even so much as have half a glass of wine. Isn't there any part of you that recognizes you are not the same person you were twenty minutes ago? Can't you tell that you feel different?"

Jay stared at the wall, unmoving, with that glare of hate on his face for a very long 35 seconds or more before he lifted an eyebrow and looked up at me. "I do feel different!"—he said with earnest surprise.

I asked him to leave at that moment, and without much ado he did leave. Yet it is important to note that he quit 'cold turkey' some time after that and has not drank a drop of alcohol to date. He has behaved normally since he has not been drinking alcohol, which makes it so much easier to maintain our friendship. Later down the road I would invite him to have Saint Patrick's dinner with Lilly and I; I did the cooking and the table was covered in a luscious feast of corned beef roast, new potato's roasted in a sprinkling of sage and paprika, cabbage that had been boiled down and smothered in butter and lemon-pepper. We drank the sparkling water Perrier.

* * * * Moving my car off of the driveway and onto the street, I taught Lilly to ride her bicycle by starting her off by going in circles on the driveway. Her golden hair down to her waist, her short-sleeved pink and tan shirt under coverall denim shorts, and her clear blue eyes shining, I walked along beside Lilly and watched her ride her bicycle for the first time ever without help and without training wheels! Lilly Melody was getting older. She was a little over four years old now. We celebrated her bicycling achievement with a banana-split ice cream that was a huge mountain of three different kinds of ice cream in chocolate, vanilla, and strawberry, topped with chocolate and strawberry and caramel sauces over banana's and whipped cream. "I'm so proud of you", I beamed over at Lilly and gave her hug after hug, "You learned to ride a bicycle! You rode all by yourself!"

Lilly and I still took walks around the block, often holding hands and singing songs. Lilly's favorite songs for our evening walks were "Ojibwa Love Song", "Little Indian Maid", and "Edelweiss". As we walked we oo'ed over the twilight colors of auburn and purple, pink and orange, covering the sweet sky. Yet now we also had bicycling that we could do together. Lilly could usually pedal faster than I. We'd ride our bikes down to the fenced pasture to the south of our house and feed the hungry looking horses from our flat palms with carrots and sugar-cubes we had stuffed in our pockets.

Lilly and I played 'catch' in the back yard with a soft ball. "Keep your eyes on the ball", I would tell her with a smile and a calm tone, and without worry as to whether she did it right or not. To my surprise and pleasure it turned out that Lilly had really great eye-hand coordination and learned quickly. I would take Lilly to the park to take turns shooting basketball hoops. I slid down the slides and swung on the swings along with Lilly. With more than a huff and puff on my part I turned the merry-go-round for Lilly while she lay in her 'skorts' and cotton shirts with her long gold hair flowing as she whirled on the merry-go-round looking up at the baby-blue sky with her aqua-blue eyes.

Lilly Melody would become considered the lucky child with the nicest mom by all the other kids her age on our block, and in preschool, because Lilly never got "in trouble". Which meant I never yelled at Lilly; I do not believe in spanking unless you have to stop the child immediately from hurting themselves or hurting someone else. And I parented with lots of love and positive reinforcement such as lots of "I love you(s)" and tons of hugs, and shiploads of patience. I had read innumerable parenting and child-development books including "Parenting for Peace and Justice", and I had taken "Living Love" parenting classes, and I stuck to what I learned in the classes even if it took longer to teach the child because of using love and positive reinforcement as the tools. My daughter and I were both happy people; because I personally chose to be happy. I treated my child with respect.

Each night I read a book of my daughters choice to my precious Lilly Melody at bed time and I sang songs to her after reading. I sang such songs as "Eskimo Baby", "La La Loo", and "My Own Home." Every night I made it a point to kiss my daughters forehead and tell her "I love you Lilly".

Four days a week I would sit down with my child and we did Hooked On Phonics, Hooked On Math, and together worked on her Jump Start preschool games on the little computer we shared. It was fun for Lilly, but I was teaching my daughter to read and write and do math.

The first day of preschool would turn out to be a day of rank turtle pee. Yes, turtle pee!

"Mom! Suzanna!" Lilly Melody ran into the kitchen where I was putting dishes into the dishwasher. (Thank heaven for dishwasher's!) "You've got to pull my hair into pony-tails! I want my bunny pony-tail holders! Suzanna! You can *do* dishes *later*!" Lilly had worked herself into a worried tither. She had put on her anklet socks with the pink lace on them and her very best black shiny Sunday shoes. She'd put on her olive shirt with the rhinestones on the front in the shape of a heart and her prettiest green plaid 'skort'.

"Hey! You look nice Lilly! Great clothes. You look pretty."

"Do you think my outfit matches?"—Asked Lilly as she turned in a circle and modeled her clothes with her arms out to her sides and her palms facing up.

"Yes. You did a great job of getting dressed."

Lilly lifted her feet one at a time and gestured at them with her hands. "And my shoes?"

"Yes, I like them."

"But do they match!?" Lilly exclaimed anxiously.

"Yes! They match perfectly. The black shoes are great. Black goes with everything."

"Whew!" Lilly let out a breath of relief. Then she put her hands on her hips and tapped her foot at me. "Oh, Suzanna! You can do dishes later." Lilly blinked her four year old ocean-blue eyes at me and tapped her foot with a bit more impatience. "Mom!"

"What, Lilly?"

"Do you want me to be late?! I can't be late! I just can't be!" She paused and crossed her arms across her chest. "Today's my first day of preschool!"

"I know honey; we still have twenty minutes."

"But I don't want to be late!"

"Okay, I've got the dishes in now. Just let me put in some soap." I poured some powdered dish detergent into the receptacle, closed the door, and turned the knob to normal wash. "All done. You want to leave now and stop by the store and pick out a snack for you to have after preschool?"

"We don't have time!" Lilly was still feeling worried. Then she looked me up and down and said,

"Is *that* what your wearing?"

I looked down at myself. "What."

"That's *not* what your wearing to take me to preschool is it?"

Looking down at my blue sundress I realized it was somewhat wet on the front from rinsing out the dirty dishes to prepare them for the washer. "Oh. I guess I did kind of get it wet."

"*Kind* of?"

"Okay, I'll go put on my purple dress." Walking into my room with my little one following me, I took off my sundress and put it in the laundry basket I kept in my closet. Picking my purple dress with the tiny flowers on it from off of a hanger and then slipping it on over my head. Going over to the wood dresser with the faux marble top and large gold-rimmed mirror I picked up my hairbrush and brushed through my pony-tail which I then twirled into a bun on my head and held in place with bobby pins. Lilly was sitting and watching me from the mattress of my white metal four poster bed. She was fluffing the pale green bed-curtain up and down with her hand.

"How's this?"—I asked and turned around to let Lilly view my dress and hair-bun. "Aren't I a beautiful Mama?"

"Let's go!"

"Okay; let's go." Reaching out my arms and wriggling my fingers, Lilly grasped hold of my hand, and we walked holding hands down the hall and through the living-room to the front door. Locking the door behind me I then pushed the button to unlock my car and opened the passenger door to let Lilly Melody climb in. "Put your seat belt on My Love."

"I know."

Blinking at the extremely bright sunshine in the baby-blue cloudless sky and taking note of the soothing sound of the wind rustling the emerald-green leaves of the large oak tree in our front yard.

Climbing in the car and starting the motor, I clicked on my seat belt and double checked to make sure Lilly was buckled in.

First I traveled down the empty small town streets in my little car and then turned into the convenience store parking lot with one singular beat-up blue truck already parked in front of it.

"What are we doing here?" Lilly lifted her face and peered through the window with wide worried eyes and squinted at the convenience store.

"I thought you could pick out a snack for after preschool."

"No, no. We can do that later! I just want to get to preschool on time."

"Okay, we'll get snacks later. We won't be late, we'll be a bit early. Don't worry. Your preschool is right across the street at that church there." I pointed and Lilly followed the direction of my finger to look at the church. Pulling the car out of the store parking lot I turned right at the corner stop sign and then pulled up in front of the church on my left and parked on the street. Lilly unbuckled herself while I walked around the car to open the passenger door.

"I've been here before Mom!" We walked hand-in-hand on the sidewalk towards the church door.

"Yes you have."

"I came here for Bible school!"

"Yep." I opened the church door and followed my daughter into the room. Introducing myself and my daughter to the teacher, I noticed that several other children were there early. Lilly now looked very concerned about my leaving her. She tapped her hands together and furrowed her brow. Bending down on one knee I gave Lilly a kiss on her forehead and hugged her. "You'll be fine Lilly. It's only for one hour."

"One hour is a long time, isn't it?" Lilly bit down on her bottom lip. "Isn't an hour thirty minutes two times?"

"Yes, you smart girl; it is thirty minutes two times." I petted her soft gold hair. "But it is not very long. I'll be back soon." The teacher took Lilly's hand and led her over to the other children. I waved at her and she waved back. Then I smiled at Lilly Melody before turning to walk out the door.

Sniffing the fresh clean outside air and the pungent marigolds waving in the breeze, and feeling the warmth of the bright sunny day on my arms. I thought that this would be a great day for Lilly and I and the little girl I was to baby-sit today to go to the park. Sliding into the car I drove home thinking that I would check the kids station on TV and see if there were any good movies for Lilly and I and the child I baby-sat (who would come over at noon) to watch together after dinner.

So I got home and sat on the couch looking at the digest of shows coming up on the kids channel during the evening. "Pete's Dragon" the musical was coming on at seven p.m. and I set a reminder for it. Next I sat out the hour Lilly was at preschool just thinking about things and searching for the Montel Williams Show or the Oprah Show.

I thought about my decision to home-school Lilly. I wanted her to do kindergarten first in a school where she could develop friends. Yet I wanted to switch to home-schooling once she met some friends because she would be so much safer and would learn one-on-one. Lost in these thoughts it was a surprise to me when I looked up at the clock and saw that I only had fifteen minutes left before I had to go pick up Lilly Melody from preschool. To my disappointment I never did find an airing of the show by the strong Montel Williams or the magnanimous and fabulous Oprah Winfrey.

Figuring I'd go ahead and leave now and pick up that snack before getting Lilly, I grabbed my keys and hopped in the car, put on my seat belt, and proceeded to rove down the small town streets. I rolled down the car window and peered out of it and honked the horn. "Move along little baby!"— I shouted out the open window at the creature in the road. "Come on Now!" Honking the horn some more I studied the creature blocking my way. "Move, move, move!" Leaning farther out the window I realized the creature was in no mind to move at all. Honking my horn I said, "Move, pleeeese." It was no use. The creature was feeling too stubborn and sedentary.

So I backed up the car and parked on the side of the road. Stepping out of the car I walked up to the creature sitting stubbornly in the street. I leaned over it and said, "What on earth are you doing?" It looked up at me with it's big eyes. It was a very big turtle with just his eyes and nose sticking out while all his limbs were tucked into his large shell.

"Poor thing", I said to it; "Don't you know you could get hurt? Stay out of the street for peats sake you silly thing." Bending down I picked up the turtle by the sides of it's shell. Immediately the turtle popped it's head *out* at full length and popped out *all* four of it's limbs! Mr. Turtle began swimming all it's legs round and round in the air. "Come on", I said, and began carrying the turtle across the street. It was then that this shelled creature decided to prove its ultra super powers! The turtle began to pee *like a horse*! It peed all the way across the street; it peed all the way into the meadow beside the local nursing home. It kept peeing! It peed, and peed, and peed some more! How on earth could there have been any room in that shell for anything else? This turtle was *all bladder*! Just a great big huge bladder inside that shell! It was a great gushing ridiculous amount of pee! And guess what? Turtle pee smells just like the sweaty wild turtle *itself* smells! Wild or not, turtle pee is *rank*!

Now I felt I must fairly waft from a mile away of stinky sweaty turtle pee. I was wet with the nasty stuff on my dress, calves, and feet. There was no way I could pick up my daughter like this. I left the turtle to quite safely chew on some grass and leaves in the meadow and got back in my car and drove home.

Once inside the house I pulled off my purple cotton dress with the tiny flowers and threw it into the washing machine with extra soap. The washer and dryer sat in the garage which we used as a play room. I threw my sandals in the washer as well. Then I went to the bathtub in the small hallway bathroom. Pulling back the burgundy with green and gold print shower curtain, I sat at the edge of the tub and set the water to steamy hot. Picking up the body-brush and pouring rose soap all over my feet and legs, I scrubbed hard and quick before rinsing with the hot water. Drying off with the burgundy towel that hung from the silver sunflower hook.

I padded into my bedroom to look at the clock that sat on the faux black marble top of the dresser drawers. Only three minutes left until I had to be at the church to pick up Lilly. Lifting the slim spray bottle with the light purple liquid in it off of my dresser, I sprit my feet and legs with lavender spray. Opening the door to my little closet I looked through the clothes and chose a sleeveless cotton sun-yellow dress and pulled it on over my head. Slipping my feet into my tan loafers, I grabbed my keys and left for the church. Being three minutes late when I arrived bothered me but I noticed that there were still quite a few other children there whose parents hadn't even arrived yet. Lilly was not too impressed with preschool. It was not near as fun an experience as Lilly and I had both hoped it would be. The child I baby-sat would be showing up soon so my daughter and I just went on home.

* * * * The little girl, Makayla, showed up with her shorts and tee-shirt on her bony body, with her brown hair tangling around her neck. I escorted Lilly and Makayla into the fenced back yard to swing and slide and climb on the play-set. Leaving the backdoor open where I could keep a watch on the children, I prepared a picnic for the girls. Bread with mayonnaise and thin deli sliced ham with sliced pickles and lettuce and a slice of cheese. Milk into two spill-proof sippy-cups would be their drink. Potato chips. On the patio out back I sat the picnic yummy's on the little kid sized green plastic table and pulled up the kid sized chairs to either side of it. Kids get such a big kick out of picnics. Their happiness over it is so cute.

"Come on children, your picnic is ready!"

"Yeah!"—They both shouted together and came running to sit at the little green table on the patio. A few fluffy and cotton looking puffs of clouds floated in the blue sky. Birds were singing. The gold colored metal tubes of the chimes wagged lazily in the wind and pinged their gentle bell-like musical tones.

"After you girls finish your picnic we'll make some cookies; okay?"

"Yeah!" The two girls sang out in unison and wiggled little dances of excitement in their chairs.

So the girls would feel they had some privacy to enjoy their picnic I sat just inside the kitchen near the open back door where I could keep a clandestine eye on them and also read some of a book I'd been on for the last month. When the girls had finished their picnic lunch they came running into the house shouting, "Cookies! Cookies! Cookies!" The two girls ran laughing and running in circles all around the dining room and kitchen. Opening the chocolate chip cookie box I put one big silver bowl on the kitchen table and poured half of the cookie mix package equally into two smaller plastic bowls. Into two cups I poured equal halves of the water that was to go into the mix. Placing a cookie sheet on to the table and grabbing two large spoons and four small spoons, a can of cooking spray, and we were ready to make cookies!

"Alrighty girls, your going to each share making the cookies together."

"Okay", both girls agreed and stood up against the table biting their lips in excitement. Their eyes sparkled in anticipation as they looked over all the items on the table. Each child got to pour some of the cookie mix into the large silver bowl; and each child got to crack an egg and pour part of the water and oil. It was completely equal for them to both stir the mixture and spray down the aluminum covered cookie sheet. Of course the best part for the kids was spooning out dobs of dough onto the greased sheets, and best of all licking the spoons!

They enjoyed the warm, aromatic, soft chocolate chip cookies with cold creamy milk. For dinner later we all had spaghetti and then played the Ladders and Rainbows board game until "Pete's Dragon" came on TV. I pulled out the hide-a-bed from the couch, gave the children pillows and blankets and a big bowl of popcorn to munch on while they watched the televised musical. As always Makayla fell asleep during the show and woke up sleepy with her walnut-brown hair tousled and sticking to her cheeks as I transferred her to her mother's arms at ten o'clock that night.

*   *   *   *   *

I had allowed my choice to let the answering machine catch the constant hang-ups and breather calls and the creepy calls that barraged me wherever I moved to become a bad habit of hardly ever answering the phone at all no matter what the circumstance! Yet my dear sweet Lilly was so young to the world that she wanted to answer the phone every time it rang! I refused to tell Lilly anything much about the past and certainly nothing ever about the stalker. I didn't want to scare her.

All on her own Lilly became extremely creative with the silent breather calls when she answered the phone. "No, no, My Love", I would say, "don't answer the phone, let the answering machine get it!"

"No, I got it! I got it!" Lilly would shout with energy and run for the telephone. "What if it's one of my friends!"

"Well wait until you hear your friends voice on the answering machine first before you pick it up."

"No! What if they don't leave a message?"

Lilly hated the never ending onslaught of the stalkers calls; of which she was unbeknownst as to it even being a 'stalker'. She thought everyone got phone calls like that. Thus Lilly was full of giggles and tickled silly at her own personal responses to those eternal calls of nuisance. Lilly started off with "Hello? Hello! Say something you dweeb!!" Then Lilly Melody would make rude noises into the phone, most of which sounded like farts. "Hello? Hello! Poo-poo head dweeb! Phhhht-blaht flat-lat-phhht!" And occasionally a burp sound…"Brrrraaach!"

Lilly became astonishingly superfluous in her abandon and adeptness at fart and burp noises. We went through a ton of cheap plastic whoopee-cushions as well.

I would stand worried and wringing my hands and ready to grab the phone away, while Lilly was busy saying into the telephone receiver "You're a fart-knocker! You know what that is? Your butt's so big you put your buns to the door and your fart makes your buns knock on the door! Stop calling!! You…fart-knocker! Phhht-blatflat-tat-lat-phhht!" Then Lilly would hang up the phone feeling vindicated for all the (stalkers) crank and creepy calls and she would fall onto her back on the floor and laugh and hee-haw hysterically while rolling from side to side and holding her ribs.

My reading to Lilly with the characters having different voices with varying accents had rubbed off on Lilly's ability to create accents as well. Although for whatever reason Lilly was able to drive home a New Delhi, India accent far better than I could ever hope to simulate. Lilly Melody's quality of jokester excellence had also lent itself to taunting the occasional telemarketer that called. One day a telemarketer called about maintaining a warranty on my car and Lilly did her most impressive accent from India that I've ever heard. Lilly answered the telephone after the machine had answered (to my relief); so the machine continued recording and I could hear the whole thing.

Telemarketer: "This may be your last chance to extend the warranty on your car. To speak with a live representative, press 'one'."

Lilly presses 'one' on the phone and giggles wickedly.

I can't help but smile and giggle a bit myself as I just watch and wait to hear what she says. The representative comes on line and says, "Hello, I'm Becca, and I can save you money while getting you the best warranty for your car!"

Lilly: "But I do not even own a car, please."

Telemarketer: "Excuse me?"

Lilly: "Yes, yeeees, I must to have hitch-hike with dee mailman everyday, Punjabi."

Telemarketer: "Mam, I have here that the warranty on your vehicle has run out."

Lilly: "My, my, yes. My vehicle…I almost soon forgot about dat…but all I own is a little bitty pink scooter. But I eat tons of chocclate every day so I am very fat.

I rode my little bitty pink scooter to da corner and I smashed it because I eat so much chocolate."

Telemarketer: "What?!"

Lilly: "Do you have a warranty for itty bitty pink scooters?

Because dat would vurk berry berry good for me."

The telemarketer says, "Okay, I'm hanging up now." The telemarketer hung up.

Lilly also hung up and then she paced the floor laughing and giggling and talking excitedly. "Did you hear that?"—Lilly asks. "I asked if she could insure my itty bitty pink scooter! Ahhh ha ha ha! She called me '*Mam*'! Ahhhh ha ha "

"Okay."—I said with a mixture of amusement and trepidation as I watched her. "Yea, okay, that was funny Lilly. Actually, I'm impressed too; that was a great accent from India. You sounded very much like my friend Sushila."

"Who?" Lilly sat down at the kitchen table next to me, still chortling.

"My friend, Sushila. I've shown you her picture before. I'll have to show you again. She's from India. I met her when she was living with her son and daughter-in-law in the same apartment complex I was living at."

"In India?"

"No. That was in Austin. Austin, Texas. I miss her though. She was beautiful. Long white hair she wore in a single braid."

"How come I never met her?"

"She's living in India now. Or last I heard. We stayed pen-pals but I lost contact with her. Her family would send her to live with one relative after another, and I lost her address."

"Why was her hair white?"

"Because she was old."

"Ohhhhh." Lilly hopped up from her chair and continued hopping as she hollered while the excitement stirred the fire in her blood. "I want to call Jay and tell him about asking the telemarketer to insure my itty bitty pink scooter! I want to tell him she called me 'Mam'!" She was still hopping like a bunny.

"Alright. You can call him. But I'll bet you'll have to tell it to your Dad's answering machine. He sleeps in the day."

"Okay!" Lilly's long gold hair fell around her hips and her clear blue eyes shined. So Lilly called her dad, Jay, and indeed received his answering machine. Yet I think she experienced nearly as big a kick leaving the message. Lilly's eyes sparkled with her own delicious anticipation at repeating the story again when she finally spoke to Jay in person on the mass communication wonder called the telephone. Can you insure my itty bitty pink scooter please?

*   *   *   *   *

Come the end of the year well into mid-summer Lilly would leave to visit her father for the first time ever in two years. Lilly would soon be in kindergarten. She would stay with Jay for nearly two months and it was agony for me. She and I had never been separated before. Calling her every day, I sang to her and talked with her on the phone. I had sat down the day she left to visit Jay and I had written a dozen letters for her. I kept it up to make sure she would receive a letter from me every day, and each letter contained a gift, a toy or a treat. On the day Jay had come to pick her up I said to him, "Whatever you do Jay, make sure Lilly is never ever left alone with your real father. Not even for a minute. If she's going to visit him make sure you're right there with her the whole time. You know how mean your father is. I don't want her to be around him and see the way he treats women. I don't want her to think it's alright to be mentally and emotionally abusive to women."

"Alright", Jay had agreed.

I reiterated to Jay when speaking to him on the phone that Lilly should never be around his real father for long, and certainly not alone. Sometimes I would like Jay's father, as he would be witty and interesting. Yet it was sadly apparent that Jay's father couldn't keep up the ability of treating a female with love and kindness. Jay's father had his own problems that caused this I'm sure, but you can not condone the behavior either.

"Absolutely", Jay had said, "you don't have to worry. You worry too much."

Thankfully Jay was raised by his mother and stepfather. Jay's real father was a monster to at least three of the wives I'd known him to marry. He'd been married many times. He could be so interesting and humorous sometimes. Yet then he could also be a cruel man and a cheater and a liar.

He would bring young girls from foreign countries home to America to stay with his wife and himself and lo and behold at least one of those girls wound up pregnant. It was a worry.

Guess what? Jay took Lilly to his real father's shack house and left her alone with him.

When Lilly came home to me, we had a celebration at a family games and pizza place. She wanted a piñata. So she received a piñata. Every year of Lilly's childhood we would always have a birthday party at a family friendly games establishment so it seemed a good place to have a reunion party. She had a great time. We invited her young friends and had a cake and Lilly Melody said it felt as if it were her birthday!

Yet something had changed in Lilly. She dearly needed to sleep with me to keep from having insomnia and bad dreams. She was angry a lot.

One fine day with cloudy coverage to block the brunt of the far too bright sun, there was a lovely lavender gray sky to be enjoyed. Streams of baby blue and aqua here and there flowed across the horizon. Lilly's friend J.C. had come over once again to play. Outside the temperature was a pleasing 72 degrees. Blowing from the lavender sky and tickling the leaves in the three big trees in the backyard was a breeze so delicate and feathered as to make a smooth tinkling of the two wind-chime trinkums hanging from the metal roof that covered the patio.

J.C. and Lilly ran atwitter into the garage/game-room with the walls painted with flowers and rainbows. Skittery with the exhilarant passion of childhood imagination the two girls scanned their eyes over the costumes and dress-ups that hung on nails on the wall of the garage. Pondering and choosing as they took in the array of adornment the girls eyes lighted. J.C. was taller and rounder with oak-brown hair that had grown out from a layered cut to fall across her cheeks and chin. Choosing a bright pink feather boa which J.C. wrapped around her neck, the finely plump girl picked out a light-pink sequin dress and pulled it up onto herself by stepping into it first.

Lilly grabbed the lion costume with the tail in back and the mane fluffing sand-brown around the face and ears of it's hood. Lilly scattered her gold hair that wisped to her waist so that it was partly inside and out of the costume as she pulled it over her head. "Aaaarrrgh!"—Lilly growled at J.C. and the two girls waddled into a chase that took them into circles around the garage. Then they both bounded into a screaming, growling, hurricane of sounds as they sprinted from the garage back inside. The growling and screaming and laughing and giggling took the full course of the entire house. Around and around they went and then flew in a goofy blur out of the open back door.

Smiling, I peeked out the doorway to take a pleasing drink with my eyes of the happy children. The girls rounded one oak tree then landed onto their stomachs over the swings next to the fruitful pecan tree. The game gave way to their swinging on the swing-set back and forth on their stomachs. J.C. and Lilly began hollering for me: "Can you make us a treasure hunt? We want a treasure hunt!"

Stepping outside onto the patio I breathed in the cooled gentle breeze swirling from the lavender sky and answered them, "Okay, I'll make you a treasure hunt, but you'll have to give me some time. Okay? It takes some time to put together." This was followed by the joyous belts of "Yay!" from J.C. and Lilly. The children flipped themselves off of their stomachs to sitting down on the swings. They proceeded to twirl in circles until the chains of the swings tightened, then they lifted up their feet and spun wildly as the chains unwound.

Walking back inside I sat down at the hexagon shaped wood table that I had turned the top of into a convincing black faux marble. Reaching for my stationary basket I pulled out eight blank pieces of typing paper and a pen. I wrote rhymes on seven of the pages that would lead a clue from one page that would tell the girls where to look for the next page, and so on. On the eighth piece of paper I wrote, "Congratulations! You have found the treasure!" And I put a big black 'X' in the middle of the page with thick permanent marker.

Barefoot and wearing my satiny blue shirt with the beads on the front and my faint-blue gypsy skirt with the beads and sequins at the bottom, I lifted myself from the table and went to the garage to scrounge through the flat-top rectangle freezer. At the bottom of the freezer was the brown paper bag half full of last years Halloween candy. Our new dog named Nanook had eaten more of the candy from the Halloween haul than Lilly had eaten so I'd put the rest of the unwanted candy in the freezer to snack on at some later time. (We had acquired a half husky and half malamute one year old female dog that had been saved from 'the pound'.) Nanook turned out to be naturally adept at holding a lollipop between her paws and eating it like some perspicacious little lady. To the great amusement of my daughter and I it so happened that if the lollipop had gum in the middle of it then the dog would chew the gum until she was tired of it and then spit the gum out onto the floor.

Wrapping a handful of the chilly candy in some old Christmas wrapping paper and taping it, I then taped the eighth and final 'you found the treasure' note on top of the package of candy. At last I asked the girls to come inside from the fenced back yard and stay playing in the house until I had finished hiding the treasure and all the rhyming clues. I hid one rhyming clue in a tree. I hid another clue on the ladder of the slide. One clue went inside Lilly's fort, another in her play-house, and so on. It took the girls nearly an hour before they finally found the treasure. They were thrilled!— Good! Immediately the girls turned around and asked me to make them another treasure hunt. I informed them one treasure hunt would have to be enough for now as it would probably take a week just for me to think up new rhymes and new hiding places.

So I set the girls up with paints and brushes and large sheets of paper. I sat on the couch reading and it wasn't long before the girls came padding into the living room and asked if they could paint on the walls! "There is one wall in the garage that you can paint on", I told them, "but only on that one wall and no where else in the house." The two young girls looked stunned. I think the girls were a bit stupefied that I had actually said 'yes'. Next J.C. and Lilly jumped up and down cheering 'yay'. I made them promise to stick to the wall I pointed out to them and not paint elsewhere. Leading them into the game-room/garage I took them to the left wall where I had painted a huge rainbow. "You can paint all you want in the space beneath the rainbow." The children kept their promise. My favorite part of their wall art was their wonderful hand-prints!

After Lilly and J.C. had cleaned up from their wall art we all baked a cake. The girls got a bit of joy at doing all the work. I simply halved everything and guided them on what to do. By the time I pulled the cake out of the oven J.C.'s grandmother came by to pick her up and take her home. Poor J.C. didn't get to help frost the cake but I cut a huge piece of cake out and swabbed some frosting on it and then sent it home with J.C. on a paper plate. Dusk was falling by this time and a warm orange and magenta color was flowing over the moist earth from the burgeoning sky.

"Mama I have something to tell you", Lilly said to me after J.C. was gone.

"Okay honey. Go ahead and tell me. You can tell me while we frost the cake!" I pulled up the plastic white stool and helped Lilly climb on top of it. Passing out a butter knife for each of us I set the cake between us and put the canister of frosting on Lilly's side. Bits and pieces of cake teetered in and around the parts we were frosting but it didn't matter. "Go on Love"; I said, "What did you want to tell me?"

"No, no", Lilly Melody sputtered in consternation. "Not now. I want to frost the cake."

"Ah! Let me guess! You want to tell me that you want grilled cheese sandwiches and tomato soup for supper tonight."

"Noooo."

"Spaghetti?"

"No."

"You want to tell me that you want to eat popcorn and watch a movie after dinner?"

"No!"

"Hey Lilly?"

"What?"

"Guess what."

"You love me?"

"I love you! You guessed it!"

"That's because you always say that Mom."

"You want to tell me later?"

"Yes."

"Okay honey-bunny." I smiled and leaning over to her gave Lilly a kiss on the forehead.

We each grasped hold of a fork after frosting the cake and took a couple of bites; too sweet. (Lilly and I would slowly nibble on the cake the following day but then it would end up just sitting untouched until it began to show signs of going bad and we would feed some of it to the dog and throw the rest away.) Yet at that particular moment I complimented Lilly on making a good cake and began to do the dishes.

Darkest Deepest ocean-blue, and bruised onyx, had injured the lavender sky into the vilification of nights inky ashes. Not a moon for the sky and the only saving grace was the hope of the shining diamonds up above as the stars began to twinkle and grow stronger in their sweet illumination. From the kitchen window I could see the pitchy night falling down its nocuous soot color upon the sky. I began singing out loud an Ojibwa love song as I rinsed the dishes in preparation to put them in the dishwasher.

"Mama I have something to tell you." Lilly looked anxious.

"Okay honey." One at a time I began putting the rinsed dishes into the dishwasher. "Go ahead." I put two cups onto the top rack of the dishwasher. Lilly's silence caused me to stop dead and look at her. She was blinking at me with her brow furrowed in an expression of worry. With my palms placed on my thighs I bent to look at her closer and I said, "Go ahead." Pausing. Silence. "I'm listening My Love."

"Not here." Lilly's face was twisted in a gloomy fret.

"What? What is it Baby? You can tell me anything."

"You know when I was at Daddy's?"

"Yes."

"Daddy took me to Grandpa Jared's."

"Jay took you to his Dad's place? He didn't leave you there alone, did he?"

"Yes."

"Oh Baby."

"I was sleeping in bed and I woke up and I saw a demon."

The disturbing shock of what she said caused me to straighten up flat as if a pole had just been shoved up my spine. A quick wave of dizziness slashed through me for an instant. Suddenly as I summoned a response I suffered an acceleration of picking up the dishes from the sink. Unbearably unsure of how to respond I found my hands and arms stuffed with nearly more dishes than I could hold. Tumbling and then straightening them back up again I put the gorge of dishes into the dishwasher.

I took in a deep breath and let it out. Finally I said, "Sweet Love, did it look like a costume of a demon, or a mask, or something?"

"A mask." Lilly answered with such certainty that I felt as if my breath had been taken away. Lilly's facial expression was a mixture of being upset and feeling confusion.

Snatching the last two cups in the silver colored sink, I quickly placed them in the dishwasher to hear myself saying with expediency, "Maybe you dreamed it?" Had I really said that?! *Why* did I say that? I had never told Lilly Melody anything about the stalker; never. Nor had I ever told her anything about my past that wasn't pleasant. I never would tell her anything about it if I could help it. This thought flew through my mind at breakneck speed. Turning quickly to look at my daughter I saw her face darken and glower as she spoke.

"That's what I thought…but…"

Bending down I gave her a hug. "Oh honey, I'm sorry. I'm so sorry…I don't know why I said that…I…I don't know what to say." Giving Lilly another hug I rocked her slightly before pulling back and looking at her face. "But I do want you to know that I believe you." I was about to say that she should go ahead and describe everything she saw.

Lilly spider-pumped her fingers up and down against each other in consternation as she frowned. "I wasn't finished!"

"What?"

"I wasn't finished talking Mama! You interrupted me!"

"Oh, honey, I'm sorry. I'm listening My Love. Go ahead and tell me." I was still bent down on my knee to meet her eye level. "My Love, I'm listening."

"Not here Mama!"

Sputtering, I somehow managed to consider the situation, "You…you want to tell me some place else?"

"Yes!" Lilly's eyes grew moist, making them even more blue.

"Well…." Raising up I took hold of Lilly's hand. My blood pressure was raising. My heart was accelerating. Yet I behaved calmly as a parent should. "Let's go into my bedroom. You can tell me there."

"Okay, I guess." Lilly looked down at the floor with a look of uncertainty regarding the choice of my room. Her face was twisted with a mixture of worry and fear. Leading her into the bedroom we both walked in and sat down on my bed. Keeping my hand on her hand I could see the deepening anguish on my daughter's face. "Hold on." Lilly leapt off the bed and closed the door. Coming back towards me she suddenly stopped dead in her tracks and looked around the room with fear. "Not here."

"You don't want to tell me here?"

"That's right."

"Well….how about the bathroom? We can close the door."

"Okay", Lilly said miserably.

Taking her hand again I led her into the bathroom. Feeling so much concern for her I felt my heart would burst. Closing the bathroom door behind us I used my own hand to give her a gentle squeeze of reassurance.

"No, no….not here!"

"Lilly, what's wrong? Why not here?"

"Because I don't want anyone to hear me. Grandpa Jared said I was to keep it a secret."

Unfortunately I was unable to contain from crossing my face the fear and extra red-flags that I felt going up as I uncontrollably gasped. "What happened Lilly?"

"I saw the demon; the mask over his head. He didn't have a shirt on. And I closed my eyes to go back to sleep. But I was scared so I looked again, but it was Grandpa Jared with no shirt on." Lilly bit her lip and shook her head while looking at the floor with apprehension. "I know…", Lilly blurted out, "the car!" Lilly grabbed my hand and opened the bathroom door.

"What are you doing Lilly?"

"I'll tell you in the car."

"There's more?" My breath caught down deep and heavy in my lungs. Allowing Lilly to lead me to the car I felt barely able to think at all as I snatched the keys up off the couch on our way outside. We climbed in the car and Lilly demanded the half-open windows rolled up. Then she required I lock the doors; then for me to double check that I had locked them. Every red-flag imaginable started going on in my head. Something was very wrong here. Very wrong. Even worse than what she had already just told me. I felt an oncoming horror and fear for my child that was worse than I could have imagined.

"You know how you say I can tell you anything Suzanna?"

"Yes; absolutely, you can tell me anything, no matter what."

"Grandpa Jared…." Lilly beckoned me closer and cupped her hand over her face and her lips and then leaned so that her cupped hand pressed against my ear. What she whispered in my ear curdled and chilled my blood. I'd been there and some myself, so I knew what she was feeling. I'd been there; 'a *long, long* time ago.' My heart ached with sorrow because when I had kissed my baby-girl on the day she was born I had promised her that I would never let anybody hurt her. Where I had already been horrified at what had happened to her the horrific wrenching in my soul climbed to unbearable levels. Lilly Melody's whispers of the event ended with the cessation of her soft warm breath against my ear. She pulled back to look me in the eye. Immediately I wrapped my arms around her and hugged her tightly.

What I had already known intellectually thus began to meld into my brain on an emotional level. She had seen the demon mask on a man with no shirt on, closed her eyes, and when she looked again she saw her Grandpa Jared standing there without his shirt. In fact, he was not wearing any clothes at all. The rest that she told me I will not repeat out of benefit to her privacy. All this time the perpetrator, the stalker….was Jay's real father….or at least that's how it looked to me. Although sometimes things aren't always what they seem to be. But what were the chances of the coincidence of the mask?!

I kissed Lilly's head and rocked her as I hugged her. I thought about that day when Jay moved in to the same house-apartment on the same day, the same hour, right down to the same minute…. how Jay didn't even know where the rental's office was…. how I thought it was such an amazing coincidence. Suddenly Jay's moving in at the exact same time as I did no longer seemed like such a coincidence anymore.

"What happened wasn't your fault in any way, Lilly. It wasn't your fault."

I continued: "Usually when a grown-up tells you to keep an unpleasant secret, if it's a fist in the face or something else, it is because they have committed a crime. And this was a crime, Lilly. What Grandpa Jared did was a crime."

"Why didn't you come and stop it Mama?" Lilly looked up at me with her wet eyes shining a brilliant blue.

"You mean, why didn't I know it was going to happen and come save you from having to go through that experience?"

"Yes."

Her question took me aback because I truly wished I could have done that and saved her from the terrible experience. "Oh Lilly, I'm so sorry for what you've been through. You should never have had to go through that. I really, really wish I could have come and saved you from ever having it happen; I didn't know Lilly… I really and truly did not know that was going to happen. If I had of known, believe me I would have come and got you right away before anything could even take place. I am so sorry for what happened. What Grandpa Jared did to you was wrong." I took her hands in mine. "What Grandpa Jared did is a crime; and he is going to go to jail for a long, long time."

I petted her hair and said, "I love you Baby, and I'm going to get you help, and I am going to help heal you."

Lilly and I left the car and went back into the house. It didn't matter that it was already night-time, I called the police. This time the police took the situation seriously. I called the police; I called child protective services. I called and left messages with all of the information and with the request for an appointment with a therapist and also a counselor and also with a doctor.

Later, Lilly would have to go into a room by herself with counselors, doctors, and policemen, and tell them her entire story. I got her counseling, and she also had *active* therapy in addition to counseling, also work derived from the book "Trances People Live" by Stephen Wolinsky, Ph.D., and the Native American technique of Soul Retrieval. The detective assigned to the case, Detective Parson, asked if Jay or I would look at photographs they had obtained in Grandpa Jared's possession to see if either of us recognized any of the children in the photographs.

On this particular night of revelation, however, I finished my report to the police and protective services; and finished making my initial appointment requests with a therapist, a counselor, and a doctor, which I would follow up with later. I turned to Lilly and told her how proud of her I was for telling me everything that happened; and how brave she is.

Lilly asked me that night as I cooked us some pizza, "Why does God let evil people live on earth?" Leading my daughter by the hand we both sat down at the kitchen table after she asked this. "And Mama, does God have to be called 'God'? What about like the Egyptians and they called the dog animal part of God Osiris? *Is there a God?*"

Smiling at my daughter, I answered her. "Well, God is Unconditional Love." I nodded my head. "God is the intelligence of the universe." I patted her shoulder. "And 'God' by any other name would *still be* 'God' anyway like it or not."

"*But why is there evil?*"

"Well, honey, it's easy to understand. Just a second; let me get some water and I'll be right back and I'll tell you." Rising up from the table I padded over to the adjoined kitchen and grabbed two glass's from the basket in the cabinet. Filling them with purified drinking water I then went back to the table and handed Lilly one of the glass's full of the good and healthy stuff. She and I both drank our water down completely as we sat silently at the table.

"So"; I said, "Get a piece of paper."

Lilly retrieved a sheet of paper from my stationary basket sitting on the table. I continued—"And a pen, My Love, get a pen."

Lilly dug through the stationary basket and pulled out an ink pen. She pushed the items across the table in my direction. "It might help you to envision it like this." Taking the sheet of paper and placing it between us, I also took hold of the pen.

I drew a line down the middle of the page. I drew a circle on the far left of the line and another circle on the far right of the line. I also drew a circle in the middle. "*Now. It is a scientific fact that nature works towards its own perfection.*"

I smiled at her. "A flower, for example, keeps working towards it's most perfect state. Like…being more colorful or having a longer trumpet… so that it's nectar will be chosen by a hummingbird, and thus the flower thrives. For example, you see?"

Lilly nodded. I knew she would not hesitate to ask me anything she did not understand. "So, now you see, it is a *scientific fact* that nature works towards it's own *perfected end result.*"

I paused. "You know how you and I have talked about that if an astronaut goes in a rocket up in space, that he could come back in fifty years and all his friends on earth would look old but he would still look young, because the laws of time and space change as you get far away from gravity…we saw that show on the science channel about it. Remember."

Lilly nodded; of course she remembered. "Well there are as many universes as you could possibly imagine. Our universe being like a round bubble and other universes like round bubbles… like the bubbles we blow with a wand and soap?" Lilly smiled. "Each 'bubble' is like a 'kingdom'… there are many 'kingdoms'."

"Right now people think there are only many galaxies. But a long time from now. Probably a long time after you and I are *both* dead…. the scientific community will discover there are many universes." I took a breath.

"Well anyway, the intelligence of the universe didn't create evil just to spit on it and smash it about. The … let's say God… or the intelligence of the universe, is *Unconditionally* Loving. And each human being must Know Who They Are, and, how to be themselves."

Lilly's face squinted up at me and she said, "How does someone not know who they are!? That's ridiculous!"

"Oh", I said, "you'd be surprised."

"Now", I continued, "someone who is evil could do all sorts of good jobs that would be very hard for a good person to do… but the evil person must not commit evil against others… because not everybody on this earth is the same. What evil needs to know is that Good really does exist! And how much easier to know what you are if you come across what you are not! Some people though, might not be evil but may be possessed with an illness. Since we do not always know who people are or if they are ill, the thing for you to do Lilly is to have as much respect as you can for others. But if an evil person commits a crime against another then they must face the justice of the law and go to jail. Understand?"

"Yes."

"Now, *like* souls or persons come from the same perfected end result universe. An evil person *might* have great fun with their friends of like-mind in their perfected end result universe and tear each other up with swords and all manner of things and have their body parts grow back right away just like a lizard..you know, like how a lizard can grow it's tail back… and they would all find it pleasurable…it would not hurt…it would be fun and pleasurable for them."

"I want to play swords and have my limbs grow back!" Lilly's eyes sparkled.

"Now Lilly, where you're from they have… I guess the best way to describe it is to say holographic games, where you can play all sorts of things but nobody gets actually hurt."

"You know what", said Lilly, "I knew that."

I pointed to one of the circles on the far side of the paper and said, "Now this circle is a planet. Now this planet. Let's say we're talking about you and I and other people like us who are very, very good souls…good, good people, but people who are actually like *us*…and by that I mean of like spirit. Now here on this Home Planet, or Heaven, if that's what you'd rather call it…"

Pausing, I looked my daughter in the eyes. "By 'Home Planet' *I do not* mean that we are aliens or something! You and I are human. We're in human bodies… we are all just human here after all."

"I know what you meant *Mom*." Lilly wrinkled up her nose.

"Okay. Just want to make sure." I pointed again to one of the circles on the far side of the paper and repeated, "Now this circle is a planet. Like I said, let's say we're talking about you and I and other people like us who are very good souls…good people, but also people who are actually like *us*…and by that I mean of like spirit, or *like consciousness*, you know. Now here on this Home Planet, or Heaven, like I said if that's what you'd rather call it… I will call it a Perfected End Result of Nature just because it is easier." (I explained what such a natural end result for such a planet could be like.) "That circle is our Home Planet…or Heaven…or Natures Perfected End Result, if you'd rather call it that. It's all the same. That is *our* Home Planet."

After this explanation I continued: "Now Lilly, if a person thinks that life on earth is the only life that exists in all this vast, vast space, then they're nuts!

So here, on this other circle on the very far other side of the sheet of paper here….that would be one of natures perfected end results for evil. For people just opposite of you and I. Maybe they share one mind together, and maybe they could shoot off each other's arms and legs and it would feel good to them and those arms and legs would grow back, and that would be *fun* for evil. The point is that for them, for evil, what they do and experience is for *them* fun and enjoyable, it is pleasurable for them. It's their pleasure; their Heaven if you like. But if a good person were to look at evil's perfected end result, then a good person would look at that and think it was hell. Because for a good person it *would* be hell."

Lilly said, "And a good person's heaven would be hell for an evil person."

"Yes." I nodded my head. "And a good person can't go to the perfected end result for evil…. And evil can not go to the perfected end result for good people.

So….and I'll just color in this circle in the middle of the line, in the middle of the sheet here. This will be earth, and on earth there is both good *and* evil. So, here in the middle you will see earth, which is one of the very few places that evil can come and check out good. And good can come and check out evil.

There are all kinds of different people here on earth. And here…" I dotted little bitty spots and circles all over the page. "Here is an example of all the many worlds that exist.

Including the many where nature has perfected itself, and only souls or people or creatures *understand*, of like *kind*, can live there...where nature has perfected itself."

"Because it's already perfect!" Lilly grinned as she said this.

"Yes! Because nature has already perfected itself there, for each draw of spirit…or conscious being.

And you can not separate consciousness from Nature!!"

I went to the study and Lilly followed me. "You can not separate consciousness from nature!…Consciousness also works towards its own perfected end result." I pulled from the dresser drawer my laws and scientific theorems which I had worked so hard to condense.

This was it. The moment had come. I had written my laws and scientific theorems, and worked so hard to condense them to be as easy to understand as possible, so that I could share it with a child of mine someday. The day was here already.

I walked back into the kitchen with Lilly next to my side and we both sat back down at the kitchen table. I read Lilly all my laws and theorems carefully. And I took great care to make sure she understood them. I had always wondered when this day would come.

Then I went back to explaining evil to my daughter. "Evil exists. It does. Evil has a right to exist; it really does…. The Intelligence of the universe and nature's intelligence, or God, say, is loving on a truly *unconditional* level. But good and evil don't belong together. Good and evil should not be together. *You"ve got to keep them separated*!!"

Hugging Lilly tightly and kissing her cheek, I then patted her back and rose from the table. Walking to the oven I peered in at the pizza. "Hungry?"

"I don't want pizza." Lilly said this with a roll of her eyes and a lift of her chin.

"Well that's alright. I'll eat the pizza. You can have something else." I opened the refrigerator's top freezer and glanced at the cold chamber's piles of packaged microwave meals. "Want a children's cuisine meal? You could have nuggets or corndogs…."

"No."

"No? I've got some cans of sausage gravy and several packets of biscuits and…"

"No." Lilly Melody looked from the floor to the ceiling and then over at me. "What's the best thing to do on earth about evil people?"

"Well Lilly, the only way for a person to know their crime is unacceptable, something a soul will remember… is prison….so that evil people know that good people *really do exist* and that is why you can not do those bad things." I paused in midsentence to pull the pizza out of the oven and set it on top of the stove. I took a deep breath and regained my thoughts. "But good people will automatically do what they can to help, based on their economic , that means money, situation, to give to charity, to help the world, to do good things. But to stay satisfied with their lives and still do what they can, good people often have to *turn their heads and look away from evil*. Understand? Unless they're in the business of catching the bad guy."

Walking to the cabinets I opened the lower cabinet door and pulled out a medium-sized sauce pan. "Want spaghetti?"

"Yes! Yes! Yes!"—Lilly chimed with excitement. "I'm so hungry! How long will it take?"

"Well if I use angel-hair pasta I'd say the whole thing would take about seven minutes."

"Woo-Hoo!!"

"I agree. I'm hungry too. Only I think I'm going to have some of the pizza." Bending down to the lower cabinets I retrieved the olive oil and then put some of the olive oil in the pan. Lifting on to my tip-toes I pulled open the top cabinet and extracted a pasta drainer and two caramel colored plates. It did not take long to boil the water and then the delicate pasta. I put the pasta with some red sauce on one plate and put a few slices of pizza on another plate. I poured Lilly and I each a glass of cold milk. As I always do for our dinner I lit up the candles on the table; I turned on the TV to play music from the 1930's and 1940's. (My favorite years for music or movies!) Both the candles and the music with our dinner was such a habit that it had become routine. We sipped on our milk and heartily savored our meal. The food and music and candles seemed to make us both feel so much better.

"Guess what Lilly?"—I said while we were eating.

"You love me?"

"I love you with all my heart and soul. I love you up to the moon, around all the planets, and back again." Lilly gave me a smile. I reached over and touched her hand. "I love you *unconditionally*. I'll help you look that word up in the dictionary. You might as well learn it because you're gonna hear it a bunch of times from me."

"I love you around the moon and back again and back *again*!" Lilly grinned widely and made a little wiggle with her shoulders.

"Wow! Lilly! That *is* a lot!" I was pleased to hear Lilly Melody giggle.

Satiated happily from our meal, Lilly and I played a couple of board games. Then we played 'Go Fish' with Lilly's playing cards. After the card game Lilly and I played pat-a-cake games with our hands and Lilly showed me the secret handshake which involved bumping elbows that she and J.C. had created. Then Lilly and I finger-painted for a while until she at last became tired.

Our late night ended not with my usual reading of one book to Lilly but with my reading five books to her. We lay down after the books were read and at last I rocked Lilly in my arms and sang out loud her favorite night time songs. Heavy even breathing from Lilly Melody signaled her resting within deep sleep. Flipping on the night-light and turning off the overhead light I then crept in bed and covered up to my ears with the sheet and blanket and fell asleep next to my daughter.

My sleep was a mother's panged and aching heart of fretfulness and worry. I woke up to find myself drenched in sweat and huge tears rolling down my cheeks as I cried silently. Staring at the ceiling I allowed my tears for my child to fall. Wrapping my arms around Lilly I at last fell asleep again. In my slumber I dreamed for a second time a dream I had previously experienced already. I was standing at a door surrounded by sparkling white light. Just as I had dreamed it before I opened the door and walked into a well kept and well loved cabin type of home. Oleta, my grandmother, was at an old stove cooking baby biscuits and I knew it was *her* even though she wore a big round black skinned body with dark brown molasses eyes and ebony hair pulled up on her head. I said to her, "I like the body your wearing." And my sweet smiling Oleta said in the dream that it was from one of her favorite life times. She ushered me to a table to feed me baby biscuits. Once again as I had dreamed it before I did not want to leave; I wanted to stay by Oleta's side. And once again Oleta said I couldn't stay there with her, I had to go back and live my life. --"You still have to live your life." When I awoke that morning I opened my eyes to see my daughter still slumbering. Wrapping my arms around Lilly I simply lay and watched the sunlight creeping purple and pink through the window blinds and listened to the sleeping breath of my child.

*   *   *   *   *

Out in the country at an old run-down shack of a house a SWAT team pulls its van up in readiness. They are at the home of 'Grandpa Jared'—Jay R. Jared. The SWAT team with the black woolen masks covering their heads and faces so that only the eyes show, and wearing their strong solid black boots, prepares for the worst. Their bullet proof gear covers their shoulders and chest. Long black rifles, and SIG Saner P220 handguns are poised. Helmets and knee pads have been donned. Black gloves with the fingers cut out are on the hands of the SWAT team as they rush out of their van. The Special Weapons and Tactics special paramilitary unit flow in a well-trained flourish towards the house.

Helmets with a face protection shield, and a large thick shield with a see-through rectangle at the top are carried by the front man. "Alpha!"—The man with the shield shouts as the entry team approach the front door.

"Bravo!"—Shouts another SWAT team member and he with his men take the left side of the house.

"Delta!"—Shouts another brave man as his team take the right side of the house.

The Delta and Bravo teams breach the home by breaking the windows with a large ram and steadying their rifles.

"Hard Cover!"—Shout the men with rifles at the Delta and Bravo sides.

"Charlie! Charlie! Go! Go! Go!"—Shouts the lead man as he and his group cover the back door and rear of the house.

The Alpha team rushes the house. "Go! Go! Go!"—they yell. They ram open the front door. The first man to enter calls "Point", as the next man to enter calls "Wing".

"Cover!" –You hear from more SWAT members as they provide cover for the members sliding inside in pursuit of the suspect.

Down on one knee to the left; and down on one knee to the right, the team members in the house cover for the Point Man as they pass the hall into the den where the sliding glass door shows the man pulling Charlie. They cover the bathroom and two bedrooms but the old wrinkly perpetrator they are looking for is not there. Jay R. Jared is not at home. The police, however, gather a wealth of evidence against him as they scour the house; including confiscating the rotten old perpetrator's computer.

*   *   *   *   *

Autumn came in with wispy colors of yellow and gold, burgundy, and burnt red touching leaves and bushes. Flowing like tears to a precipitous descent upon trees shading from green to an incandescent ruby. Children everywhere had their mercurial elation stirring atwitter for the simple community tradition of dressing up in costumes and getting candy from the neighbors. Bearing upon the beautiful changes of season were the vaporous delicate ethers of colder breezes. Spirits raise with the excitement of seasonal metamorphosis. Lilly and I had bought *several* pumpkins so that we could frolic in the creative amusement of carving and decorating some pumpkins several weeks apart.

Here, on our first two pumpkins our fun recreation involved marking pictures on the pumpkins with markers. With a knife in my hand and a safety-carver in Lilly's hand, we opened our pumpkins over the spread of newspapers on the floor. We both laughed in amusement at the gooey stringy insides full of seeds that we plunged our fingers into. Pulling out the slick mucky seeds and pulp we toss the stuff into a huge silver bowl. Classical music played with notes flowing from the stereo. Fluid notes of Overture to Suite No. 2 by Bach cascaded into its final blossoming current. I hummed along happily enjoying my time with Lilly Melody. Streaming flowing notes of royal resonance filled the room following Bach and the Flower Duet from Delibes Lakme began to play.

"I just love the Flower Duet", I said to Lilly as we both relished the music. The phone began to ring.

"AH! Answer it! Answer it!"—Lilly whooped. "It might be one of my friends!"

"Oh my." Rubbing my hands over the newspaper I knocked off pulp and seed.

"Hurry Mama! *Suzanna*!" Lilly inadvertently abraded her pink shorts and pink short-sleeved shirt with her hands; spreading pumpkin muck on her clothes.

"Okay, Baby." Lifting myself from the floor I ran into the kitchen. Holding my hands out in front of me with my fingers splayed I quickened towards the telephone. Snapping the kitchen towel off of the counter I rapidly wiped my right hand through the towel. Then absently patted my left hand which was holding the towel against my blue house-dress that I wore anytime Lilly and I did something messy. Plummeting my right hand towards the telephone, I plucked up the receiver and spoke, "Hello?"

"Hello. Is this Suzanna?"

"Yes." I recognized the voice of the caller. My lungs leapt in a low-gasping heave that I thought was going to give me the hiccups. I took in the Texan slow, warm, embers of the voice. My pulse went qualm.

"Hey, girl!" It was Detective Parson's deep auburn, warmed-caramel, tone of voice.

"Hi."

"This is Detective Parson. How is Lilly doing?"

"Oh she's great. She's doing therapy, and retrieval work, and counseling. And she's taking lessons too—she's learning to ride a horse!"

"Good job!"

"Yeah, the horse she rides is named 'Pepsi'."

"That's just great!"

"She's really doing so much better. The anger has gone, the nightmares are gone. She's getting back to her happy self."

"I'm proud of you. You're doing the right thing. Lilly's a real sweet girl."

"Thank you Detective Parson."

"I've got some great news. *We got him*!"

"Grandpa Jared? I mean… Terrell senior?"

"Yes! We got him!" Detective Parson pulled in a deep audible breath. "He actually turned himself in! He's a bad guy. We've got so much evidence. We're also pressing charges for child pornography and human trafficking."

"Oh my gosh!" Tingling spikes of disgust and horror flew across the hairs on my arms, neck, and scalp.

"This is a bad, bad, man. Very bad. I dedicate my life to finding this type of criminal. My wife and I adopted; and it's this very type of criminal that has led us to try and bring a home of love and safety to children. Believe me…this guy is going away for a long, long, time. I doubt he'll ever see life outside of prison ever again."

"Well I want to thank you. Thank you so much Detective Parson. I appreciate your calling, and I appreciate everything you've done. You're a good man. Thank you so very much. This is the news I've been waiting for. I'd…I'd appreciate it if you could keep me updated and let me know how things go."

"I'll keep in touch , Mam. I'll call you and keep you up to date with everything regarding this case. You just take good care of that girl of yours."

"Oh yes."

"Call me anytime you need too. And I'll keep you up to date."

"Thank you Detective Parson."

"You're very welcome. He's going away for a long time. Take care, ya hear?"

"Thank you; goodbye."

"Goodbye."

Hanging up the phone I took in a giddy breath and smiled. A thrill of hope and relief coursed like a sweet, soothing, warm spiced-wine, through my heart and soul. Blessings flowed like soft warm sunlight, singing a delicate ticklish euphonic tune in my mind.

"Hey!" I inflected with a modulating musical tone to my voice. "Guess what Lilly?!"

"You love me?!" Lilly hollered to me from the pumpkin-carving activity on the floor of the living room.

"Well…yes, I *do* love you, but…" I hollered back with a giggle of surprise. "But that is not what I was going to say!"

Running from the kitchen then stopping abruptly and skipping up to Lilly in the living room; I grinned broadly. My face felt flushed with pink warmth as I looked down at my daughter sitting on the newspaper on the floor. She was already beginning to carve out a happy face on her pumpkin. Lilly looked up at me with her cool-blue aqua eyes glimmering, and she responded, "You love me up to the moon and back again?"

"Oh!" I giggled. "Yes!" I bent down onto my knees beside Lilly Melody. "Yes, I *do* love you! Around the moon and back again Baby… but that's still not what I was going to say." I giggled again.

"What?!" Lilly looked at me with wonder.

"That was Detective Parson on the phone."

"Ah! I want to talk to him!"

"Oh honey, I didn't think about that. But next time you can talk with him, I promise."

"Okay." Lilly shrugged her shoulders. Then she raised an eyebrow and looked at me with curiosity. Lilly smiled with the beauty of an angel.

"Detective Perry says they've caught Grandpa Jared. They've arrested him. He's going to prison, sweetheart. He's going to prison for a long, long time. Detective Parson says he'll spend the rest of his life in prison. Detective Parson says Grandpa Jared is a bad, bad man." Wrapping my arms around Lilly I gave her a congratulatory hug and a huge smile.

"I can feel safe now I know they got him."—Lilly said honestly and somberly.

"Yes, sweetheart. We should celebrate!"

"Oh boy!" Lilly stood up onto her little feet and pranced in a little dance up on her tip toes. "Yeah! Can I get a toy?"

"Yes you can get a toy! And how about we get that carrot cake we saw at the store that you liked so much!"

"Yes! Yes! Carrot cake! Carrot cake! Can we stick regular carrots like candles in it?"

"We still have a bunch of baby carrots in the fridge, and we can stick them all over the cake if you like."

Looking at my daughter I thought how proud I was that she had such a healthy appetite. I loved that she liked all sorts of fruits and vegetables. She was getting bigger; no longer a little baby. My mind floated back to when she was a little baby still crawling. When I would put the clean sheet on the floor and place on it different colors and flavors of food: carrots, banana's, apple and orange slices, baby dill pickles, celery, cheeses, corn, sliced beets, sesame seed crackers. She would crawl around and taste them all. Love gushed up as an overflowing fountain of love and joy as I looked upon my daughter's face while she hopped up and down with the fortuitous joy of celebrating with carrot cake! I hugged her and hopped up and down in rhythm with her.

Giving her an extra squeeze and a hop I then lifted up and walked over to the stereo. Pressing my finger on the stereo button to replay the Flower Duet again, I told Lilly to get her purple Velcro shoes that I had glued dozens of shiny purple stones onto and slip them on her feet. Listening to the music I gathered up her sweater and my jacket. Yet as it turned out the autumn burning sun gleamed away the days earlier gentle cool breeze.

Lilly and I did indeed celebrate with carrot cake. We made a homemade black-olive pizza together. We played twister. Then we played hide-n-seek over and over so very many times. Lastly she rode on my back while I sang, "This is how the horses go…", on my hands and knees and toddling all over the house. Finally I told Lilly I was too exhausted to play some more and that I just wanted to sit and watch some TV for a while. So Lilly begged me to turn my large make-up mirror on in the playroom/garage, and to turn on the fog machine, so she could play 'rock star' while I watched TV.

I turned on the mirror light to a pale green and sat it on the garage/playroom floor. Plugging in the fog machine I placed it on top of a box and filled its chamber up to the top with some more fog juice. Lilly asked me to put on some rock and roll music in the boom box and place it in the garage for her. Picking a CD of the best of the 1980's songs from the wood and iron treasure chest in the living room, I placed the music and the music box in the garage and turned it on. Then I closed the door as per her request, and I sunk with a tired and relieved sigh into the couch to watch some television.

Time passed as I watched television and I felt the coffers of my soul replenish. I could hear it as "Girls Just Wanna Have Fun" sung by Cyndi Lauper poured from the garage. I got up to check on Lilly. Opening the garage door a gigantesque wave of billowing fog flooded out of the door! I laughed! Wafting clouds of fog flowed and swirled so thickly that I couldn't even see Lilly Melody. Waving aside the hazy flowing whirls of fog gushing and swooshing about I laughed even harder. Looking in at my child as I waved my palms through the whorl of purple-blue fog, I saw that she had her pink wig on and her pink sequin costume dress on. She had her guitar resting against her stomach as it's shoulder-strap kept it in place. She was strumming the guitar and dancing and singing, "girls just wanna have fu-*un*…."

Giggling and grinning, I said to Lilly, "Are you being a rock star, honey?"

"YES!"

"Well it looks like you're doing a great job of it! I'm going to get the video camera and film you, my rock star."

"Okay! Close the door!"

"Okay!" Closing the door, I went to my bedroom and pulled the old video camera out of my closet. Very nearly tip-toeing back to the garage, I gently pulled open the door and taped a few minutes of film as my daughter rocked out. The whole scene was so funny and so adorable!

*   *   *   *   *

So Grandpa Jared turned himself in to the police. I don't know if Grandpa Jared was "THE" stalker. For all I know each harassing phone call, offensive person, or very strange stranger, was a completely different person to themselves, and it all simply added up to one coincidence after another.

But all that mattered to me was that after Grandpa Jared turned himself in to the police the demeaning phone calls stopped completely! I have had no bizarre strangers show up at my door. So it may all be coincidence. Yet coincidence or not, I have not had a harassing call since then. Coincidence it may be, yet this is all that matters to me: the phone is quiet now; there is at last some peace. My daughter is healing. I still have the old habit of usually just letting the answering machine catch a call. Wounds are finally healing, however slowly. Let go of the shame. Let go of the fear. Time progress's from the sweet cool of Autumn's colorful spray. Cold chills blow into winter's fragile frothy breath. Crystals of spun ice frost the windows delicately. Summer will come again all too melty hot and glaring. But what matters?--*It was over*.

*   *   *   *   *

One day I was laying on my bed with my eyes closed so that it would look like I was asleep to anyone who saw me; specifically Lilly. Inside I was wide awake while having a pity-party of fear and worry over how I would make ends meet, worried about my daughters mental and physical health after all she'd been through, and how my daughter would hold up to the ordeal of having to testify against Grandpa Jared on the stand in court at such a young age.. I remember closing my eyes and thinking, that if our thoughts and emotions affect our overall well-being, then what if through the morphogenetic energy field my thoughts and emotions could effect others?—So I pressed my palms together, laying there with eyes closed, and while breathing deliberately slow I *prayed* and visualized pure Love… that's it… just a pure unconditional Love within myself that I could feel and imagine. My daughter came into my room and sat down beside me on the bed. She said, "Mom…" I opened my eyes to look at her and tried not to look like I was frowning any. Lilly looked as if she were bathed in light; she simply glowed. It caused me to sit up on one elbow and blink my eyes. "Mom", said Lilly, "you should take your work and write a book. *You should write your book!*" She said this with such calm sweetness in her voice; an intonation that sounded like an adult's, not that of a small child, so much so that it caused me to sit up completely. I must have had a look of surprised awe on my face. I felt humbled completely. "You're right", I said, for it sounded in her voice as if she had not made a suggestion but had given me a directive. I wiped my eyes and face to remove any tears that she might see. Then I thought to myself: 'Your right Lilly. For there have been so many times where I have had No Hope… so much 'No Hope' that *Hope was all I had* …and Hope Floats. It can keep you above water long enough to realize… it's gonna be okay. And this is REAL.' Sometimes answers can be so very simple that it is just like not seeing the forest for the trees. I gave my child a hug. Lilly then calmly walked out of my room. I followed her. She went back to playing with her dolls in her room. Without saying a word I went to get the computer that we shared. Turning the computer on and opening a blank page I began to write for some reason without any concern as to spelling or grammar or what exactly I would write. I simply started writing with the first memory that popped into my mind… I began to write:

"**A** *long long* time ago the Indians would make themselves brothers and sisters to their best friends by mixing their blood together." ---Suzanna.

"How do they mix their blood together?" ---Holli.

I, Suzanna, answered with a tingling joy in the words. "They cut their fingers open. Then press their fingers together at the wound until their heart pumps each others blood into the other person."

How was I to know that tonight my world would change forever? That I'd become like a person haunted.

Holli leaned her head against the side of the open window. Far out in the flowing galaxy stars beamed their light down into her already twinkling eyes. Tonight as every night the alluring and mysteriously provocative howls of coyotes echoed from the deep countryside. Sizzling, the air was like the sweet dreamy songs of bewitching sirens. Each howl teased with the ravishment of strange shivers washing from the toes to the elbows and down the arms. What other creature of the night can wail and moan so hauntingly?

The fresh clean scent of rain enticingly began to engorge the air. Moisture deepened on the windchimes down below on the outside porch. Celestial music blissfully jingled from the long gold cylinders as the wind brushed against the chimes. Lunar light sparkled glamorously upon the metallic musical chimes as if they were jewels. ---------------------------

BREAKING THE SEALS:

SUZANNA TERRELL'S

FIVE

LAWS OF

EXISTENCE

THE LAWS

1/ <u>SUZANNA TERRELL'S LAW OF</u>

<u>THE PRESENT # 1</u>

The past, factually, scientifically is not happening… is not taking place here right now in this present moment… it may exist in books, films, or in your head; but the past is not actually happening right here right now, where your conscious-awareness is at this precise moment. (Year 1700 AD is not happening right here and now at this precise moment.)

Now, in your human universe you can through physics view a point in space where past, present, and future would look like one string of energy, rather like a suspended animation… Bur down to earth; here on earth right here and now where you are in your life, consciously aware, the past is *not* taking place right here and now: This is an actual *Scientific Fact*.

SCIENTIFICALLY, FACTUALLY, RIGHT AT THIS MOMENT, THE PAST DOES *NOT EXIST*.

It only 'exists' in books, film, or in your mind, but it is not actually taking place right here and now.   Neither is the future. It is a Scientific Fact that the future is not happening right here and now at this exact moment where you are consciously aware.

SCIENTIFICALLY, AS ACTUAL FACT: THE FUTURE *DOES NOT* EXIST.

The only thing that exists right here, right now, where you are consciously-aware, IS

the Present Moment… this is just scientific fact.   THE PRESENT IS THE ONLY

THING THAT SCIENTIFICALLY, FACTUALLY, EXISTS, AND IT IS *ALWAYS*

THAT WAY.

2/ <u>SUZANNA TERRELL'S LAW OF</u>

<u>CONSCIOUSNESS #2</u>

YOU CAN NOT SEPARATE YOUR CONSCIOUSNESS FROM THE UNIVERSE THAT YOU ARE A PART OF.

CONSCIOUSNESS IS NOT A SUPER-NATURAL PHENOMENA, IT IS NOT ABOVE AND BEYOND THIS PHYSICAL UNIVERSE. YOU ARE CONSCIOUS. AND YOU ARE A PART OF THIS UNIVERSE, SO THE UNIVERSE IS CONSCIOUS.

Therefore: HUMANKIND ARE CONSCIOUS.

HUMANKIND ARE PART OF THE UNIVERSE.

SO THE UNIVERSE IS CONSCIOUS.

3/ <u>SUZANNA TERRELL'S LAW OF</u>

<u>AWARENESS #3</u>

CONSCIOUSNESS IS NOT ABOVE AND BEYOND THE UNIVERSE THAT IT IS A PART OF. YOU ARE CONSCIOUS. YOU ARE NOT ABOVE AND BEYOND THE UNIVERSE THAT YOU ARE A PART OF.

YOU ARE CONSCIOUS. AND YOU ARE PART OF THE UNIVERSE. YOU ARE AWARE OF THE UNIVERSE. SO THE UNIVERSE IS AWARE OF YOU. (I.E. YOU ARE AWARE OF YOURSELF.)

4/   SUZANNA TERRELL'S LAW OF

TRANSFORMATION #4

CONSCIOUSNESS IS NOT A SUPER-NATURAL PHENOMENA, IT IS NOT ABOVE AND BEYOND THE VERY ATOMS/VIBRATING-ENERGY THAT YOU ARE MADE OUT OF.

YOU ARE CONSCIOUS. AND CONSCIOUSNESS IS A PART OF THE ATOMS/ENERGY THAT YOU ARE MADE OUT OF.

AND IT IS A LAW OF SCIENCE, THAT ENERGY ONCE CREATED CAN NOT DIE, IT CAN ONLY TRANSFORM.

SO IN ACCORDANCE WITH THE LAWS OF SCIENCE IT IS COMPLETELY IMPOSSIBLE FOR YOUR CONSCIOUSNESS TO DIE. IT CAN ONLY TRANSFORM.

5/ SUZANNA TERRELL'S LAW OF NATURES

PERFECTED END RESULT #5

IT IS A SCIENTIFIC FACT THAT NATURE WORKS TOWARDS ITS OWN

PERFECTION.

NATURE WORKS TOWARDS ITS OWN PERFECTED END RESULT.

CONSCIOUSNESS ALSO WORKS TOWARDS ITS OWN PERFECTED END

RESULT.

CONSCIOUSNESS IS NOT ABOVE AND BEYOND THE NATURE THAT IT IS A

PART OF; YOU CAN NOT SEPARATE CONSCIOUSENESS FROM NATURE.

(Just as we see the light that has traveled through time and space of star's that are already dead; so too are our Perfected End Results already created and alive.)
In layman's terms: We Have Heaven.

THEORY

SUZANNA TERRELL'S THEORY

OF ANTIMATTER AND MATTER

WITHIN THE SAME TIME-SPACE

CONTINUUM.

THEORY OF ONE.

SUZANNA TERRELL'S THEORY OF ONE:

ANTIMATTER AND MATTER WITHIN THE

SAME TIME-SPACE CONTINUUM.

C^2 ----The speed of light, times itself.

(The speed of light is 3×10 to the 10th power. Which is 300 million. 300 million times 300 million totals 9×10^{16})

First let me state:

All things material; including the human body, are called *Matter*. All Matter; including the human body, are made up out of atoms. Atoms, at their most basic level, are vibrating energy.

Also:

Ex: When a rocket is sent into space: that rocket does not blast off and enter nothing.

Space Is something !
SPACE = ANTIMATTER   !
ENERGY = MATTER

SPACE EQUALS ANTIMATTER:
9×10^{16} divided by 9×10^{16} Equals 1 .... or $C^2/C^2 = 1$
$9 \times 10^{16} \div 9 \times 10^{16} = 1$
Space + Energy = Antimatter + Matter

Antimatter And Matter Within The Same Universal Continuum:

$$S = A\, C^2/C^2 + E = M\,C^2$$

S E = A M 1

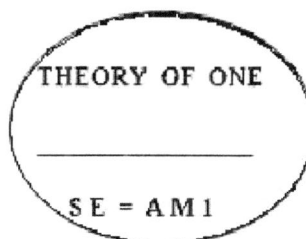

THEORY OF ONE

S E = A M 1

285

HOW SUZANNA TERRELL'S LAWS

AND

SUZANNA TERRELL'S THEORY OF ONE

CAN AFFECT YOU PERSONALLY

HOW SUZANNA TERRELL'S LAWS AND SUZANNA TERRELL'S THEORY OF ONE CAN AFFECT YOU PERSONALLY:

[TERMS OF SCIENCE :]   [TERMS FOR PERSONAL USE :]

------------------------------------   --

THEORY OF ONE
$S = A\,C^2/C^2 \;+\; E = M\,C^2$

EQUALS : $\underline{S\,E \;=\; A\,M\,1}$

PEACEFUL-NOTHING

ONE

PIVOTAL POINT OF *BALANCE* WITHIN *PERSONAL* HUMAN EXPERIENCE(S) OF THEORY: *EMOTIONAL QUALITY*—A CALM PEACEFUL-NOTHING.

CONSCIOUSNESS IS PART AND PARCEL OF THE ATOMS/ENERGY THAT I AM MADE UP OF. IT IS IMPOSSIBLE FOR CONSCIOUSNESS TO BE SEPARATE OR ABOVE AND BEYOND THE ATOMS (ENERGY) THAT I AM MADE OUT OF.

SPIRIT

ATOMS AT THEIR MOST BASIC LEVEL ARE ENERGY, AND ENERGY AT IT'S MOST BASIC LEVEL IS LIGHT.

ENERGY ONCE CREATED CAN NOT DIE, IT CAN ONLY TRANSFORM.

ETERNAL

I AM CONSCIOUS AND I EXIST, AND IT'S SCIENTIFIC FACT THAT ALL THINGS INCLUDING MYSELF ARE FORMED COMPLETELY OUT OF ATOMS. (ENERGY)

AM I

PHOTOS

As per *request*, by family members, some names and a character role have been changed in this book, to protect the privacy of those involved.

This book is dedicated to my daughter.

I would like to thank my sweet daughter, my friend Kristi, and my friend Frank, for encouraging me, and for being proud of me. Thank You!

"Lilly Melody"

Suzanna Terrell

Happy Grandparents
(baby-biscuits)

Young Suzanna Terrell